LAWLESS CAPITALISM

Lawless Capitalism

The Subprime Crisis and the Case for an Economic Rule of Law

Steven A. Ramirez

NEW YORK UNIVERSITY PRESS
New York and London

NEW YORK UNIVERSITY PRESS
New York and London
www.nyupress.org

References to Internet websites (URLs) were accurate at the time of writing.
Neither the author nor New York University Press is responsible for URLs
that may have expired or changed since the manuscript was prepared.

LIBRARY OF CONGRESS CATALOGING-IN-PUBLICATION DATA
Ramirez, Steven A.
Lawless capitalism : the subprime crisis and the case for an economic rule of law / Steven A.
Ramirez.
p. cm.
Includes bibliographical references and index.
ISBN 978-0-8147-7649-0 (cl : alk. paper)
ISBN 978-0-8147-7650-6 (ebook)
ISBN 978-0-8147-7729-9 (ebook)
1. Global Financial Crisis, 2008-2009—Moral and ethical aspects. 2. Financial crises—
Moral and ethical aspects—United States. 3. Capitalism—Moral and ethical aspects—
United States. 4. Corporate governance—Moral and ethical aspects—United States.
5. Business and politics—United States. 6. Financial institutions—Law and legislation—
United States. 7. Law and economics. 8. Liability (Law) I. Title.
HB37172008 .R36 2012
174—dc23
2012024880

New York University Press books are printed on acid-free paper,
and their binding materials are chosen for strength and durability.
We strive to use environmentally responsible suppliers and materials
to the greatest extent possible in publishing our books.

Manufactured in the United States of America
10 9 8 7 6 5 4 3 2 1

To the entire Ramirez Family, who stand as testament to the benefits of broadly distributed economic empowerment

CONTENTS

ACKNOWLEDGMENTS

I am greatly indebted to the following individuals for reviewing all or part of this book and improving it: Laura Caldwell, andré cummings, Joe Grant, Chunlin Leonhard, Katrina Ramirez, Mary Ramirez, Barry Sullivan, Alexander Tsesis, and Spencer Waller. The book also benefited from helpful discussions with Timothy Canova, Richard Delgado, Christian Johnson, Tayyub Mahmud, Bud Murdock, John Nowak, Christopher Peterson, Jean Stefancic, and Cheryl Wade. I also received excellent suggestions from a number of anonymous reviewers. Loyola University Chicago generously provided financial support of this project. NYU Press, and Deborah Gershenowitz in particular, provided perfect editorial support at all phases of the project. Professor Regina Burch of Capital University, Professor Linda Crane of the John Marshall School of Law, and Professor Steven Bender of the University of Seattle helped arrange presentations of this book at their respective institutions. Professor Neil Williams arranged for the book to be presented at the Midwestern People of Color Legal Scholarship Conference held at Marquette University in April 2012. The Wayne Morse Center for Law and Politics at the University of Oregon also hosted a presentation of this book. Of course, all errors and omissions remain solely my responsibility.

It is to be regretted that the rich and powerful too often bend the
acts of government to their own ends.
President Andrew Jackson (1832)[1]

On September 13, 2008, CEO Jamie Dimon told his senior management
team at JP Morgan Chase: "You are about to experience the most unbeliev-
able week in America ever."[2] Dimon summed up the outcome for the Chase
bankers of extended late night meetings with government officials and fellow
banking executives: The government would not bail out Lehman Brothers,
and he envisioned a systemic failure of many other Wall Street banks, leading
to a near-total financial collapse. On September 15, 2008, Lehman Brothers,
one of America's oldest investment banks, declared bankruptcy. On Tuesday,
September 16, 2008, the Reserve Primary Fund, the nation's oldest money
market mutual fund, "broke the buck" when its shares fell to 97 cents, after
accounting for losses on short-term debt obligations issued by Lehman. This
caused a massive and historic run on money markets and short-term debt
markets around the world. Holders of such obligations reacted to risks of
loss that previously seemed remote—that the government would permit a
major financial institution to fail—and this deep risk aversion spread rapidly

throughout global capital markets. The flight from risk restricted credit supplies to all borrowers regardless of credit-worthiness.

That evening, the Federal Reserve System (the Fed) of the U.S. announced an unprecedented bailout of the largest insurance company in the world, AIG, and extended an $85 billion government-backed line of credit to keep AIG afloat. The next day, September 17, 2008, the Dow Jones Industrial Average fell 440 points. The Fed's bailout had failed to quell investor fears. More panic spread throughout financial markets around the world as all investors desperately fled from all risky assets, not knowing which teetering megabank would topple next.[3] A historic meltdown of global capitalism loomed, threatening a second Great Depression.[4] The core problem boiled down to trust. Lenders and investors around the world failed to trust any creditor other than the U.S. government, and they accumulated massive amounts of Treasury obligations instead of any risky assets. All other assets—from stocks to commercial paper—plunged in value in the wake of the financial panic.

On September 18, 2008, the Chair of the Fed, Ben Bernanke, and the Secretary of the Treasury, Henry Paulson, convened a meeting with senior congressional leaders. The two represented the pinnacle of government power over the economy. They informed Congress that the nation's largest banks needed a massive federal bailout or "we may not have an economy on Monday."[5] Three days later the Treasury Department submitted a three-page bill providing for $700 billion in emergency funding for the big banks with only the thinnest oversight. Popular outrage stalled the bill in the House of Representatives. The Senate, however, passed alternative legislation and loaded it up with additional pork for House members. On October 3, 2008, the Emergency Economic Stabilization Act of 2008[6] became law, and hundreds of billions in government funds flowed into the largest financial firms shortly thereafter. The Act, however, marked only one of many government bailouts for the banks.[7]

On November 23, 2008, the Fed, the Federal Deposit Insurance Corporation (FDIC), and the Treasury injected $20 billion more in capital into Citigroup and guaranteed the value of $306 billion of its assets. On January 16, 2009, the government similarly injected $20 billion into Bank of America and guaranteed the value of $118 billion of its assets. By the end of 2008, the Fed had lent $1.2 trillion in emergency loans to prop up global financial institutions—often based upon questionable collateral.[8] Throughout 2009, the government guaranteed another $304 billion in bank debt so that the banks could raise capital at a lower cost. The Fed purchased $1.45 trillion in mortgage-backed securities through the spring of 2010, so that banks could sell their mortgage assets and so that the real estate market would not collapse from a lack of capital for loans. It further purchased hundreds of billions of dollars in commercial paper to ensure that the business sector would not collapse from a sudden loss of short-term credit. The government guaranteed the value of trillions of dollars in outstanding mortgages through its costly takeover of government-sponsored entities (Fannie Mae and Freddie Mac) that operated at the core of the mortgage financing business.[9] Finally, in the spring of 2009, the government passed a $787 billion stimulus bill in an attempt to revive a credit-starved economy.[10] These actions constitute only the most high-profile bailouts.

At the height of the crisis, President George W. Bush asked Treasury Secretary Paulson, "How did we get here?"[11] How did American capitalism find itself in a position where such massive and extraordinary rescue efforts became necessary? In a word: recklessness. The nation's largest financial institutions gorged on levels of risk—particularly in the subprime (even predatory) mortgage business—unparalleled in U.S. financial history.[12] Reckless mortgage lending triggered a global meltdown of capitalism. Very often, mortgage lenders did not even bother, for example, to verify borrower income, instead simply telling borrowers the income they should state on their applications in order to qualify for a given loan. Down payments nearly vanished.[13] Amazingly, they even failed to secure the right to foreclose through the execution and recording of valid mortgages.[14] Worse yet, they lost original promissory notes—negotiable instruments under law.[15] Most recklessly, some banks even destroyed original notes.[16]

In an era of more computing power than ever, and with hordes of mathematicians modeling risk on Wall Street, the most sophisticated financiers in history botched mortgage lending, a business that seems as old as business. Worse, the financial institutions took this risk on board through very high levels of debt—or leverage—on their own balance sheets, meaning that even small losses could wipe out the Wall Street firms' equity, rendering them insolvent. Leverage ratios on Wall Street reached as high as $60 of debt per $1 of equity. The managers of these firms knew (or at least should have known) that these excessive risks would sink their firms.[17] Incredibly, CEO Jamie Dimon testified to the Financial Crisis Inquiry Commission, "In mortgage underwriting, somehow we just missed, you know, that home prices don't go up forever and that it's not sufficient to have stated income" from the borrower.[18] As early as mid-2007, the Citigroup CEO stated that if liquidity dried up in the financial sector "things will get complicated" but that Citi would keep "dancing" despite the dangers, along with the entire deregulated financial sector.[19]

Unfortunately, even more risks emerged. The banks also made sour business and commercial real estate loans. Moreover, through a variety of nontransparent transactions known as credit default swaps, the firms placed enormous bets, through financial institutions like AIG, on the viability of other firms or the securities they issued or held, often just for pure speculation. AIG placed $500 billion of such bets, securing $300 billion of capital at other banks and financial institutions.[20] The entire Wall Street financial sector apparently rested upon a house of cards built on speculative excess. The house of cards collapsed in the fall of 2008, taking the economy down with it, under the weight of massive financial losses.

The story seems improbable at best, except for the raw profitability the risk gorging generated (over the short term, at least), and the distribution of the risk-generated profits to the most economically and politically powerful within our society, at the expense of the most disempowered. Only by following the money from the risky lending to illusory profits to compensation paid to senior managers and from campaign and lobbying expenditures to the massive reimposition of discredited laissez-faire policies in law and regulation does the crisis make sense.[21] Most Americans do not enjoy ready access to information regarding the sums of money involved in these flows. Indeed, Project Censored (a media watchdog group) named the influence of Wall Street on Congress as the top censored story of 2010. According to the group, financial companies spent $5.1 billion in campaign contributions and lobbying expenditures to influence lawmakers in the decade preceding the crisis.[22]

The government rescue effort of the economy stands without historic precedent. Never before has the government of the U.S. expended more resources to maintain the economy while protecting those whose misconduct caused so much harm (in this case crashing global capitalism) from their own mistakes.[23] Yet, tellingly, the great weight of government expenditures to save the economy made their way into the pockets of the most powerful elements of the U.S. For example, the government guaranteed trillions of dollars in outstanding mortgages without really directly assisting any particular preexisting mortgage borrower. Lenders received the windfall of the government guarantee, but borrowers still paid rates that did not reflect the explicit guarantee. Similarly, the government injected capital into the banking system on terms far more generous than otherwise available, without any significant conditions or reforms and without replacing the reckless (and very wealthy) bankers who crashed the system. Indeed, many of these reckless bankers continued to collect massive bonus payments even in the wake of the huge government bailouts. AIG's senior officers in the very division that generated the lethal credit default swaps collected $165 million in bonuses immediately after the government extended the company a $185 billion lifeline.[24]

The bailouts triggered outrage from across the political spectrum. The noted financial journalist William Greider called the bailouts a "historic swindle" and fundamentally unfair because the bailouts saved the "villains" of the crisis but inflicted more pain on the "victims."[25] The former president of the Federal Reserve Bank of St. Louis termed the bailouts an "affront to the market" and an "affront to democracy" because the executives of the failed firms hauled in millions while saddling the taxpayers with trillions in financial obligations.[26] The speed and scale of the bailouts suggest a fundamental problem with American democracy: The problems of the corporate class command the government's attention regardless of economic merit, even while far more needy and less blameworthy citizens languish on the margins of the system regardless of economic potential. The economic system of the U.S. bears more semblance to crony capitalism, corporatism, or corporatocracy than to competitive capitalism. Those in control of multinational corporations seemingly enjoy windfall government largesse while ordinary citizens suffer increasing deprivation of economic opportunity.

Because the inept financial elites remained at the apex of the American financial system, loan loss recognition lagged reality. Regulatory forbearance permitted the bankers to retain the toxic assets that nearly sank the system. The government never insisted that the insolvent banks recognize all losses and repair their balance sheets. As such, the bailed-out bankers still feared insolvency, which caused them to hoard massive capital. The initial withdrawal of credit thereby led to a historic contraction in bank loans that continued for years after the crisis.[27] The American economy thus suffers from a "zombie" banking sector that consumes massive capital but does not lend.

By the end of 2010, more misconduct emerged. When the bankers foreclosed they systematically submitted fraudulent affidavits—perjured testimony—in support of efforts to seize homes as cheaply and as quickly as possible.[28] To save a few dollars in recording fees, the banks listed false nominees as mortgagees, even though others claimed to own the underlying mortgage notes.[29] Often banks destroyed notes en masse rather than expend funds to track and preserve documents that bear upon real property rights.[30] This misconduct means that banks threw property rights in America into a state of chaos that could well take years to repair.[31] Secure and certain property rights form the foundation of every sound capitalistic economy.[32] This misconduct raised the question of whether any rule of law applied to our economic system.[33]

All of this imposed untold costs on the global economy and the U.S. tax-payer. The global economy suffered a loss of $4 trillion in forgone output in 2009 alone.[34] That translates into more unemployment, more home fore-closures, and more cutbacks in government services or tax increases world-wide. Indeed, as the Nobel Prize–winning economist Joseph Stiglitz notes, the crisis led to 50 million job losses and an additional 100 million people in poverty.[35] Although the final tally of the total cost of all the bank subsi-dies and bailouts remains years down the road, it surely exceeds trillions in the U.S. alone.[36] Unemployment doubled and projected government debt increased by 67 percent (or $8.5 trillion).[37] Simply put, this is a multi-trillion-dollar debacle by any measure. The subprime crisis (or financial crisis) of 2007–9 imposed economic costs not matched since the Great Depression. Those costs continued to mount through 2013 and beyond, as foreclosures and loan defaults continue at a historic pace, lending remains frozen, the financial sector still holds billions in toxic assets, unemployment threatens a new round of loan defaults, consumption continues to stagnate, and govern-ments around the world face fiscal crises. Today, the economy barely grows at all, and the crisis still threatens to create further disruptions. A depression, or a prolonged era of economic stagnation, appears certain.[38] Some, such as the economist Nouriel Roubini of New York University, even call into ques-tion the viability of global capitalism itself.[39]

Despite all of this economic carnage, top managers at the financial firms at the center of the crisis emerged unscathed. One study found that 92 percent of all senior financial managers remained in power one year after the crisis peaked.[40] Another study found that top managers at key financial institutions enjoyed "decidedly positive" monetary returns from their reckless steward-ship.[41] In 2009, financial firms paid record compensation, even as sharehold-ers suffered catastrophic losses. Compensation set another record in 2010.[42] The federal government actually lobbied to shield the bankers from civil and criminal sanctions.[43] Capitalist norms of accountability for failure vanished during this crisis.

Since the economic tsunami that engulfed the global financial sys-tem struck in the fall of 2008, many voices offered many explanations for the causes of the crisis. This book offers a unique diagnosis and prescrip-tion: The crisis arose from a massive breakdown in the rule of law, and the American economy will suffer a parade of economic crises until it repairs its legal system and reverts to a system that successfully limits the power of concentrated economic interests to profit from the subversion of the general economy. In fact, a systematic breakdown in accountability under law marks the crisis.[44] In a modern capitalist economy, an economic rule of law must

prevent those controlling great wealth from using that wealth to stifle competition and rig the economy in their favor. The subprime mortgage crisis of
2007–9 should be viewed as a harbinger of things to come if corporate and
financial elites continue to dominate the U.S. economy with a view toward
entrenching themselves at the cost of everyone else.[45] This book catalogues
the use of concentrated economic power to maintain the incumbency of
corporate and financial elites at the apex of the American economy and the
devolution of American law to "a system of incumbents, by incumbents, and
for incumbents."[46]

Instead of resources flowing to their most productive uses, corporate
elites subverted government to ensure that resources flow to them regardless
of productivity. Instead of law and regulation based upon sound policy and
evidence, America gets distorted law and policy dictated by the interests of
those in control of the largest corporations in the nation and the world. Legal
or regulatory evolution based merely upon sound policy analysis yields to a
devolution serving the needs of those in control of transnational corporations and banks. This reality necessarily means a chronically broken financial system and compromised macroeconomic performance, as the costs of
economic privilege take their toll. Essentially, this book lays responsibility
for our dysfunctional economic system squarely at the feet of those holding
the greatest power over the legal structure underlying that system—a relative handful of financial and corporate elites in league with their government
cronies. Following the money leads to those few in control of vast wealth.

Capitalism ceased to exist in the U.S. in the wake of the failure of Lehman
Brothers on September 15, 2008, on profound levels.[47] Political power displaced the virtues of competition at the very heart of the American economy
as elites used political power to elude the costs of their misconduct. Taxpayers, the great majority of whom had zero responsibility for the fiasco, ultimately paid massive costs as a result of the chicanery of those in charge of
other peoples' money—the financiers and the corporate titans—and will
continue to pay for decades to come. Professor Joseph Stiglitz has termed
this system "Ersatz Capitalism."[48] Government strove mightily to save the
economy in the aftermath of the crisis, with all of the tools at its disposal—
except fundamental and deep reform of our economic system. Indeed, as discussed in detail throughout this book, the Dodd-Frank Wall Street Reform
and Consumer Protection Act,[49] signed by President Barack Obama on July
21, 2010, implements marginal reform at best and reaffirms the power and
misconduct of the financial elites at the center of the crisis at worst.[50]

Yet only deep reform can prevent further costly macroeconomic crises. Competition must be restored and must displace entrenchment and

economic privilege through an economic rule of law. Traditional notions of accountability must be restored so that ineptitude and deception do not pay. The wealthy must face the same kind of criminal penalties for their antisocial misconduct that the poor face—and penalties should reflect social costs. Regulatory and legal infrastructure must operate securely from the influence of those controlling concentrated economic resources. Regulation should be based upon an objective accounting of all costs and benefits (including macroeconomic costs and benefits) rather than on ideology that too often leaves those with power unbound. An economically rational playing field means that marginalized and disempowered groups must enjoy basic economic opportunity in order to disrupt the efforts of economic elites to entrench themselves and their progeny.

The commanding heights of the U.S. economy today resemble a baseball game from before 1947 (the year Jackie Robinson broke the color barrier): Too much talent is missing and some players may not reach current levels of success if they really competed against a broadly empowered population. In fact, traditionally oppressed racial groups in the U.S. suffered disproportionate economic losses as massive wealth flowed from victimized communities of color to privileged white corporate elites, highlighting the role of imbalances in economic power in the crisis.[51] Other nations successfully tap female human resources better than the U.S.[52] The massive disempowerment pervading the U.S. economy today renders the notion of an American meritocracy suspect at best.

In short, in a modern capitalist state, an economic rule of law is necessary to prevent the subversion of capitalism arising from excessive concentrations of wealth. This reconstructed form of capitalism—marked by maximum competitive opportunity for all and minimal economic privilege for elites—would vastly outperform the current system plaguing the American economy today. Capitalism can reach its full macroeconomic potential only through the operation of a sound economic rule of law that can resist the political influence of elites and evolve toward a more perfect competition that serves to unleash human productive capacity to the maximum extent possible. Law must impose appropriate economic incentives for all. Lawless capitalism will lead to an economy that suffers ever greater distortions in favor of enriching small bands of growth-retarding elites at the expense of all others.

The consequences for human welfare involved in questions like
[growth] are simply staggering: Once one starts to think about
them it is hard to think about anything else.
Robert E. Lucas Jr. (1988)[1]

Law plays a pivotal role in economic growth and stability. This book highlights the role of corrupted law and regulation in the financial crisis of 2007–9
(and its ongoing macroeconomic consequences) and articulates a legal
framework that comprehends the links between law and macroeconomic
stability and growth. The subprime mortgage crisis illustrates the costs of
subverted legal and regulatory frameworks. Pervasive legal failure to control
economic power and align the interests of corporate and financial elites with
the interests of economic growth and stability caused the crisis. The U.S. cast
aside sound regulation in favor of unconstrained elites. It allowed the most
powerful corporate and financial managers to prey upon the most powerless
within our society. The American legal system permitted those controlling
great wealth (individually and within financial corporations) to short-circuit
competition.[2] Such elite privilege necessarily means excessive economic disempowerment. High inequality reached a boiling point in 2007 and continues to threaten the economy today.

Corrupted legal and regulatory frameworks distort capitalism and impede its ability to deliver mass prosperity, growth, and stability. Optimized legal and regulatory infrastructure hold the key to capitalism's promise of greater prosperity, poverty alleviation, and stability. As the economist Joseph Stiglitz observes, "[t]here has been no successful economy that has not relied heavily on markets."[3] A more robust economic rule of law endows capitalism with the ability to reach its full potential rather than undermine it. In short, law should secure an optimal competitive environment founded upon rational incentives and disincentives for all to excel to their full economic potential.

The ultimate question this book addresses concerns the content underlying this vision of an optimal economic rule of law or optimal economic constitution. Unregulated capitalism can and will devolve into a system of elite privilege wherein insulation from competition displaces a capitalistic meritocracy and deep economic disempowerment belies capitalistic opportunity to excel. Law should operate to ensure a level playing field for all, whether hailing from the heights of power and privilege or from the depths of poverty. Law at least must curb privilege and ensure basic opportunity. The subprime crisis shows that modern capitalist societies cannot afford poverty of basic opportunity or economic entrenchment of elite privilege. Law must similarly secure accountability and responsibility of all regardless of economic power. Law must further operate to ensure regulation based upon sound policy instead of on elite self-interest. The subprime crisis demonstrates that the costs of legal failure may quickly mount into trillions of dollars in losses— and that translates into constricted opportunity for all.

No one answer fits all nations. Culture and social values necessarily influence the structure and operation of every economy. Yet many nations take the wrong approach, by any standard. Most notably, the American experiment with mindless deregulation in the late 20th century failed. Conservative ideology trumpeting less government failed. Agnosticism toward distributional concerns failed. These failures in American capitalism led to trillions in losses worldwide. Even prior to the financial crisis of 2007–9, American capitalism suffered from clear flaws. For example, it failed to deliver reasonable living standards to significant portions of its population as evidenced in its modest ranking in the inequality-adjusted United Nations Human Development Index, behind twenty-two other nations.[4] In the wake of the crisis, the ranking of the U.S. in terms of controlling corruption fell to as low as sixty-eighth, on a par with Gambia.[5] Worse, poverty exploded to nearly 50 million, and the poverty rate reached a seventeen-year high.[6]

Arguments regarding American economic exceptionalism crumbled in the wake of the financial crisis, which emanated from the U.S. and its deeply suboptimal legal infrastructure. The global economy, built upon an American vision of capitalism, propagated the financial crisis throughout the world, spreading economic misery to the four corners of the globe. American capitalism took several wrong turns, and understanding these mistakes informs the quest for a more perfect capitalism, one that admittedly is at odds with the current laissez-faire dogma permeating our culture.[7] Reconstructing capitalism requires a renewed cultural bias against excessive economic power like the bias against excessive power that emerged after the Great Depression and ushered in mass prosperity along with a robust middle class. America's potential to offer exceptional economic opportunity rests upon the ability of its legal system to curb excessive power.

The Problem of Excessive Concentration of Economic Power

Concentrated economic power poses serious threats to macroeconomic performance. First, those possessing excessive economic resources will rationally seek to subvert the rule of law in order to entrench their privileged position and insulate themselves from competition, at the expense of an optimal legal infrastructure to support macroeconomic growth. Second, the concentration of economic resources in the hands of a small number of powerful elites means that others—especially historically oppressed classes or minority groups—face restricted economic opportunities. Yet superior economic growth requires a society to unleash the full economic potential of its people. The combination of growth-retarding elites and large segments of disempowered citizens may threaten to destabilize the economy—especially inherently unstable financial markets—in ways that will lead to financial crises and potentially severe macroeconomic contractions. Large disparities in power among discrete groups encourage predation and exploitation in the name of profit—even unsustainable profit.[8] The subprime crisis demonstrates these threats.

A rationalized economic rule of law will operate to reduce concentrated economic power, to ensure basic economic opportunity for everyone, and to create sufficient regulatory and legal infrastructure to stabilize financial markets regardless of elite resistance to sound regulation. The economic rule of law must optimize incentives so that all economic actors face incentives for maximum productivity, and it must impose disincentives to discourage predation, exploitation, and disempowerment. History and economic science prove that capitalist societies require an economic rule of law (or constitution) to maximize macroeconomic growth. Unfortunately, reality differs radically from this vision of legally fragmented power, as vividly proven in the context of the subprime crisis commencing in 2007. The concentration of economic power in the hands of concentrated elites, arising from a recent and dramatic increase in economic inequality in the U.S. and concentration of power within the corporate and financial sectors, led to concerted efforts to subvert legal infrastructure, eliminate competition, and facilitate predation and exploitation.

This concentration of economic power comes in the immediate aftermath of a revolution in economics that increasingly unlocked the secrets of macroeconomic growth. That learning shows that economic opportunity must be widely distributed in order to unleash the economic potential of the population to the maximum extent possible. The society that maximizes the ability of its people to produce will be the most productive society. Innovation requires empowered citizens. Innovation also benefits from more extensive markets, meaning that maximizing effective buying power maximizes opportunities for innovation. Nevertheless, elites too often ignore these basic truths. Recent empirical studies demonstrate that elites become more interested in entrenching their relative positions of power and insulating themselves from competition rather than general economic growth. According to the World Bank, "high levels of economic and political inequality tend to lead to economic and social arrangements that systematically favor the interests of those with more influence."[9] The power of growth-retarding elites must be constrained through law in order to secure maximum macroeconomic growth.

Elites will rationally exercise their influence to engage in rent-seeking behavior, including government subsidies and bailouts. Mancur Olson long ago warned that concentrated interests will prevail over diffused interests because diffused interests will face the problem of free-riders: "There are vast numbers who have a common interest in preventing inflation or depression, but they have no lobbying group to express their interest."[10] Individuals with only a small perceived stake in an issue will rationally assume that others will bear the expense of organizing to defend their interests. The subprime fiasco validates these economic insights in full. Small bands of powerful corporate and financial elites subverted law in their favor on a systemic basis. The U.S. economy fell prey to the logical implications of excessive economic inequality and suffered catastrophic losses.

Legal infrastructure consists of law and regulations that support a market-based economy by generating economic benefits that exceed any associated costs, such as compliance costs or transaction costs arising from higher taxation. Economists and other financial scholars now identify certain elements of economic and financial regulation that enhance the functioning of financial markets to spur economic growth. For example, the federal securities laws facilitate the flow of information and lower agency costs, thereby encouraging the productive deployment of passive capital to fund risky investments. Legal infrastructure addresses inherent market flaws from asymmetric information to agency costs to manias and panics that periodically plague markets.[11] Basic legal infrastructure, present in virtually every advanced economy, enjoys proof that it supports maximum macroeconomic performance.

Human infrastructure in particular requires legal support to ensure that businesses can exploit a nation's human resources to the maximum extent possible. Human infrastructure generally suffers from insufficient funding across much of the world. Funding of all levels of education generally pays for itself and facilitates every employer's ability to generate profits through a more skilled human infrastructure. Governing elites too often underfund public education in favor of privileging their own children. This dubious tendency manifested itself in the subprime crisis through distorted global economic development and consumption patterns and an ill-educated, disempowered underclass in the U.S. The law should operate to secure the funding of human capital.

In the subprime crisis, the law also failed to limit the ability of financial elites to undermine the financial regulatory system to their benefit. CEOs led their firms to originate, distribute, and invest in the riskiest subprime mortgage loans in history. Ultimately, these loans sank the global financial system, even while CEOs raked in millions. Because CEOs lobbied to reduce their accountability for negligence and securities fraud and to untether themselves from financial regulatory infrastructure, they destroyed their firms and the economy with impunity. Regulatory infrastructure must be "hardened" to resist elite subversion.

At some point, powerful incumbents may rig the system so much in their favor that severe macroeconomic costs and crises result.[12] The subprime crisis proves that the U.S. is now at that point. In sum, deficiencies in America's legal infrastructure caused the subprime fiasco and its bloom into a worldwide economic catastrophe. Elite influence supplanted the rule of law and secured irrational indulgences. Our society is now paying for this lawlessness. Law and regulation reflected power imbalances instead of sound policy. Today this lawlessness continues.

The Potential for an Economic Rule of Law

Constitutions traditionally exist to impose the rule of law even upon the most powerful and to limit the influence of concentrated political power. In general, constitutions enjoy a successful (if less than perfect) history around the world.[13] An economic constitution can limit the influence of economic power and secure macroeconomically sound economic rights and account-ability, as a supplement to the current constitution. Constitutions may take the form of an integrated writing, but that is not a necessity. Great constitu-tional democracies, such as Great Britain, may use multiple and fragmentary documents and unwritten principles as the source of constitutional prin-ciples. The idea of controlling the exercise of concentrated power exceeds the importance of the format. The concept of limiting the exercise of power means limiting the role of purely political outcomes. Certain core values enjoy enhanced insulation from often transitory political outcomes. A new emphasis in economics on the elements of growth demonstrates that cer-tain core economic values must enjoy enhanced political insulation. Modern industrial states must embrace this new reality to achieve maximum macro-economic growth and stability.

Even beyond the obvious need for tax policy which ensures that the wealthy pay in accordance with their disproportionate benefits, or reason-able campaign finance regulation, the law may quell excessive economic power. For example, the judiciary may impose traditional notions of com-mon law accountability without political interference. Until recently, in the U.S., all persons within the economic sphere could be held to account for tra-ditional notions of fraud and negligence. Administrative agencies may enjoy a depoliticized structure through such regulatory innovations such as a self-funding mechanism or long terms for regulatory chiefs that operate to free an agency from the immediate influence of the more political branches. The Federal Reserve Board exemplifies this point. Actual written constitutional provisions may secure positive economic rights that form a foundation for individual economic opportunity. Entitlement regimes can secure funding for positive economic rights such as Social Security, medical care, or higher education. Professional regulatory schemes may serve to impose higher pro-fessional standards of competence and ethics free of political tampering. Attorneys, physicians, and stockbrokers all must adhere to such professional regulation. No perfect mechanism for controlling the exercise of power exists, but these instruments benefit from a long track record of success in the U.S. to some degree. Under any reasonable definition of the rule of law, such mechanisms secure the accountability of all—regardless of wealth. Irra-tional indulgences for those holding concentrated economic power corrode the rule of law.[14]

Constitutions also serve to allocate power to institutionally well-suited government organs. Congress does not act as commander-in-chief in time of war, and the judiciary does not inspect meat. An economic constitution can serve a similar function. To some extent the present U.S. Constitution already functions to ensure that proper institutional expertise controls certain issues. Congress does not debate monetary policy. The allocation of economic policy making should ensure that issues not appropriate for political negotiation meet up with institutional expertise and structures to match the complexity and importance of the issues. Certainly, an administrative body of professional economists can achieve superior monetary policy outcomes relative to Congress, which must attend to a wide array of legislative needs and which lacks any particular professional competence.

History, economic and financial science, and other social science learning from around the world instead of closed-door political bargaining or partisan ideology should drive important economic policies. The current reality suggests that much political negotiation on important economic issues can hardly qualify as democratic outcomes; instead, too often political and economic insiders negotiate indulgences outside of public view. Democratic values suffer sacrifice on the altar of stealthy special interest influence and corruption. On the other hand, a depoliticized agency structure may well operate in accord with democratic expectations. For example, even the Chair of the Federal Reserve Board must reckon with congressional power to restructure the Fed and presidential power to appoint a replacement every four years. In this sense, monetary policy is not politically negotiable, but the administrative means of implementing monetary policy exists as the result of constant democratic oversight and negotiation, as successive Congresses and Presidents supervise those charged with the awesome economic power of administering independent monetary policy. An economic constitution therefore offers the possibility of superior economic outcomes without the sacrifice of true democratic negotiation.

Ultimately, an economic constitution (as with all constitutions) works only when backed by cultural support. People get the rule of law they demand. So it is with an economic rule of law or constitution. Maximum economic growth requires cultural support for shifting issues toward more appropriate institutional frameworks and for resisting the power of those with concentrated economic resources. The body politic and its leaders must appreciate that certain issues are better removed from the arena of political power and toward expert policymaking organs to the extent the issue is determined not by democratic processes but by special interest influence. They must similarly recognize the economic growth potential of empowering their fellow citizens. The point is to insulate key issues from the influence of concentrated economic power. This will happen only if a given culture demands it. Law can reflect this cultural demand and perhaps memorialize it for future generations, but law cannot autonomously impose elite accountability. Ultimately a sound economic rule of law arises from a well-educated populace with a deep cultural appreciation for the imperative of maintaining capitalist competition under law and controlling excessive imbalances in economic power.

The Crisis in Context

The crisis started with a rash of defaults on subprime mortgages in the U.S. Suddenly riskier loans than ever before infected the entire global financial system. Global financial liberalization permitted the migration of toxic subprime mortgages to banks around the world. Global credit markets ultimately collapsed under the weight of this excessive risk. The failure of U.S. law to curb the exercise of concentrated economic power caused this debacle.

Executives garnered windfall compensation based upon illusory profits while their firms and the system as a whole faced catastrophic risks. Disempowered racial groups suffered deep economic exploitation, leading to massive social wealth losses. Globally, governments expended trillions to rescue the global financial system in response. Even as of 2012, the costs of this economic catastrophe mount, and the system remains in the same state of disrepair that caused the crisis. As of this writing, the world is still saddled with a dysfunctional global economic system built upon laissez-faire rhetoric that serves as only a thin veil for legitimizing a fundamentally pernicious distribution of economic and political power. Moreover, traditional mechanisms of accountability, such as civil and criminal sanctions, remain frozen.

Predatory lending lies at the root of the crisis.[15] This lending was concentrated in communities of color.[16] Executives at mortgage originators and securitizers pocketed large profits from predatory loans and society absorbed huge risks.[17] For instance, Wells Fargo paid $85 million in fines to the Federal Reserve to settle allegations that it steered prime borrowers into more costly subprime loans and that it falsified income information in mortgage applications.[18] According to the Fed, Wells Fargo compensated its agents for generating more costly loans, and this practice extended for more than two and one-half years, affecting potentially tens of thousands of mortgage loans.[19] The unregulated global financial system distributed these kinds of toxic loans to investors worldwide through inordinately complex financial derivatives that rendered adequate risk assessment impossible. Corporate governance in the U.S. allowed financial titans and other corporate elites to garner obscene bonuses and compensation for essentially destroying the long-term viability of their own firms as well as the system as a whole. Financial deregulation starting in the 1980s lifted restrictions on the ability of the financial sector to originate, distribute, and invest in more risky assets than ever before. Elites convinced governments to allow their firms to become "too big to fail." This lowered the cost of capital for such firms and encouraged more risky conduct. The focus became maximizing short-term profitability (and thus bonuses to senior executives) even while saddling our financial sector with huge risks of staggering losses.

Ultimately government did in fact bail out the firms, effectively extending government guarantees to executive compensation agreements and other unsecured creditors. Bank executives won big.[20] Most shareholders suffered huge losses. This extension of government welfare to the most powerful and reckless in our society belied free market rhetoric that operated to deny government assistance to the most needy. It also made a mockery of the great mythological American meritocracy. Instead of rewards and responsibility flowing to the most able, government acted to rescue the most irresponsible, inept, and reckless. One wonders exactly how such executives and managers achieved their positions in the first instance. Ability and character seem irrelevant to advancement in the American economic system. Instead, crony capitalism infects the apex of the American economy.

The flood of financial losses that followed in the wake of this debacle caused a historic contraction in credit in the context of a historically over-leveraged U.S. economy. Indeed, the economic and political interests who effectively control the process of globalization rigged it to rely upon massive debt for its survival because that alone temporarily spurred consumption in the face of lower wages (and higher short-term profits) for transnational corporations. Corporate elites co-opted the legal structure of globalization to generate more profits built on cheap labor for transnational firms. As jobs moved overseas to cheap labor locales, durable buying power vanished. Low-wage jobs displaced high-wage jobs. Capital could move freely under this so-called neoliberal regime, but labor remained trapped in low-wage locales.

The profits generated by this low-wage model of globalization enriched executives at transnational firms, but, in order to prop up demand for their products, Americans, as consumers of last resort, needed ever higher levels of debt to maintain consumption. This model of globalization left much of the world's population disempowered and economically marginalized. Globalization made little provision for economic development to support wider-based consumption. Thus, the low-wage model of globalization relied on cheap production abroad and consumption centered in America where debt supported growing consumption even in the wake of lower wages. This proved unsustainable.

When the house of debt collapsed under the weight of subprime lending in the U.S., elites panicked. In the U.S., the government spent $700 billion to bail out reckless bankers and to fortify the power of the very institutions and managers that triggered the crisis. The Federal Reserve (and other agencies) injected trillions more in an effort to save the banking system. As a result of these bailouts banks survived, but too often in zombie form; they refused to lend because of the prospect of insolvency from ever-increasing loan losses. By the end of 2008, risk-averse financiers primarily lent money to the federal government so that the federal government could bail out the banks. This ran up massive public debt but added minimal stimulus to the economy. Meanwhile, businesses and consumers faced ever more restricted credit conditions. The government literally spent trillions to bail out the reckless lenders that caused the crisis, with little assistance for their victims. The U.S. consumer today remains mired in unsustainable debt, and the government owes more than ever. The bailout efforts to date thus simply postponed the underlying debt crisis.[21]

A Squandered Opportunity for Reform

Certain conditions suggest the possibility of real reform, in terms of diminishing the power of elites and enhancing opportunities for the disempowered (and hence for all citizens). Unfortunately, it appears that reform occurs only in response to severe social, economic, and geopolitical crises. Even in the face of such crises, the political context is important, and the reform moment produced by a crisis can possibly be exploited to further entrench the power of elites. Only fear convinces elites to part with their full complement of privileges in order to maintain most of their relative positions. The body politic must demand reform. History demonstrates that legal structure matters, and reforms may be entrenched through a variety of institutional arrangements, as evidenced in the administration of monetary policy. Moreover, legal reforms may prove culturally transformative in ways that permanently alter expectations and behavior, as is the case with constitutionally fragmented political power in the U.S. Law can operate to secure reform.

Global competition may also spark reforms. If other nations outperform the U.S. continually while pursuing a more egalitarian distribution of economic opportunity, then the American body politic will demand reform. The alternative is an inequality trap. Some societies have allowed persistent differences among socioeconomic groups to retard macroeconomic growth over long periods of time because of the elite domination of law and other institutions. The subprime mortgage crisis reveals such deeply corrupted legal infrastructure that the possibility that America is mired in an inequality trap cannot be dismissed. Disrupting an inequality trap is difficult. Nevertheless, there is some cause for optimism, because the U.S. has a unique historical appreciation for curbing unlimited power through the rule of law, and the greatest experience with making capitalism work.

Unfortunately, the first American effort for reform, the Dodd-Frank Wall Street Reform and Consumer Protection Act,[22] failed to produce fundamental reform. While Dodd-Frank empowers regulators to break up large financial firms, there is no mandate for regulators to exercise this power, and in the past regulators facilitated the aggregation of economic power on Wall Street. The law makes only a cursory effort, if that, to address power imbalances within America. No regulatory agency will enjoy any further structural protections from special interest influence under the Act. Certainly, Dodd-Frank ends the deregulation march of the past thirty years, but much of the regulation effort remains in the hands of the very regulators who led that march. Thus, the law appears too timid and modest, unless regulatory authorities and the Obama administration use their newly minted powers with a level of urgency and aggressiveness that heretofore has seemed missing.

This book highlights the macroeconomic toll of allowing the economic and political power of elites to operate with insufficient legal restraint and of allowing oppression to fester. A corollary to this reality is explored in the Epilogue. Specifically, the Epilogue addresses the economic potential of an optimal legal infrastructure, an optimal distribution of economic opportunity under law, and the imposition of optimal legal constraint on the most powerful elements of society. Such an economic constitution would greatly enhance social justice and move society toward Rawlsian notions of social justice, in a pragmatic sense. By definition, empowering the most disempowered would unleash the greatest benefit to macroeconomic growth.[23] Consequently, enhanced social justice in the current global economic context will lead to massive macroeconomic benefits. This reality is possible under a reconstructed capitalism that distributes economic power in accordance with competitive norms rather than raw political power and crony capitalism.

Chapter 1 articulates a new Law and Economics framework to supplement the current neoclassical paradigm that dominates the field and proved inadequate in the context of the subprime crisis. It builds upon the recent revolution in macroeconomics that entails the scientific study of growth dynamics and institutions that facilitate growth. This represents a challenge to law: how best to identify and structure interventions that can operate to enhance economic growth. Human capital development and market development prove crucial to facilitating innovation and therefore to stable growth. The chapter highlights evidence demonstrating economic losses attributable to excessive concentrations of power as well as excessively disempowered elements of a society. The law must secure institutions and legal infrastructure to address financial manias, business cycles, and institutional support for maximizing human innovation. The chapter closes with a vision of perfect competition that transcends the use of markets to allocate resources and places individual innovation at the center of capitalist ideals.

Chapter 2 highlights the dynamic of excessive elite influence in the specific context of corporate governance law applicable to public corporations. CEOs and other corporate elites constitute a cohesive and concentrated group backed by unfettered control of concentrated economic resources. Beginning in the 1980s, this concentrated group of individuals freed themselves from, among other constraints, traditional notions of accountability for negligence and securities fraud. Combined with their ability to stack their nominal supervisors, the board of directors, with their cultural clones through the process of homosocial reproduction, they were able to exploit affinity bias to operate with maximum latitude. In fact, the system of corporate governance underwent a "pathological mutation" from shareholder primacy to CEO primacy.[24] The crisis resulted from CEOs' garnering huge compensation payments for conduct that destroyed their firms. Distorted incentives led to excessive risks, and these incentives arise from a CEO-centric system of corporate governance. The chapter closes with remedies for CEO primacy.

The theme of excessive deregulation in defiance of economic history also drives chapter 3, which addresses the problem of financial regulation. The government facilitated the concentration of economic power when it repealed the Glass-Steagall Act. This raised the specter of too-big-to-fail firms that the government would bail out rather than permit them to fail; it also fundamentally encouraged excessive risk. The government also declined to regulate derivatives. This allowed further risk to masquerade as financial innovation. The Federal Reserve and other federal agencies ignored the burgeoning subprime loan market as well as evidence of predatory lending. This permitted riskier loans than ever before. Regulators (and misguided courts) permitted rating agencies to pursue profits at the expense of independent professional risk assessment. Regulators also permitted financial institutions to gorge on risky debt in order to leverage profits. This deregulation destabilized the capital structure of the entire global financial system. The system yielded superior bonuses and compensation to financial elites, at the expense of excessive risk systemwide. The chapter concludes that comprehensive and depoliticized financial regulation is needed to correct the inherent instability of financial markets.

CEO power figures prominently in the distorted legal framework governing globalization, as examined in full detail in chapter 4. As Joseph Stiglitz highlights, the legal structure of globalization can be understood as "thinly veiling special interests" that, in fact, dominated the evolution of globalization.[25] If free market ideology dictated the course of globalization, then it would make provision for the free movement of labor as well as the free movement of capital. If economic growth dictated the course of globalization, then legal infrastructure and human capital formation would be legally secured. Instead, the construction of globalization emphasizes capital liberalization and ever cheaper labor, without any means of mitigating inherent economic instability arising from these values. This leads to the massive destruction of buying power, and the destabilization of capital markets. The accumulation of dollar reserves (among other currencies) stoked an enormous credit bubble in the U.S. (and ultimately Europe) that overwhelmed regulators. The subprime crisis proved the unsustainability of this system of globalization.

Chapter 5 addresses traditionally oppressed groups. Generally such status inherently results in the massive destruction of human capital and limits the extent of the market. This analysis starts with the recognition of the irrational basis of such oppression and the operation of malicious social constructs to always and everywhere support the wanton and pervasive destruction of human capital. Any society that continues to tolerate such mechanisms of disempowerment (including but not limited to race and gender) suffers stunted macroeconomic performance. On the other hand, a nation that seeks to overcome disempowerment and embrace the diversity of experiences and perspectives of traditionally oppressed groups will achieve superior cognitive insights as well as the breakdown of groupthink and homosocial reproduction. In the U.S. today, race continues to operate to disempower large segments of the population and to create artificial social distance that empowers elites. The reality of race in America contributed to the full array of legal infrastructure infirmities that led to the subprime crisis—and following the massive flow of wealth from the most disempowered in the U.S. to the most powerful inexorably indicts the continued sway of race in America as a key driver of the crisis.

Law and regulation alone will never fully prevent economic crises; capitalism always remains vulnerable to swings in human psychology that cause inherent financial instability. Globalization and financial innovation amplify this infirmity. This means that legal frameworks must be in place to deal with economic crises, a topic addressed in chapter 6. Optimal monetary policy should be perfected by authorizing the Fed to address asset bubbles, as well as unemployment and inflation. Fiscal policy must be optimized to operate in the face of monetary impotence. Ideally, a depoliticized fiscal authority would be empowered to orchestrate government investment in harmony with economic conditions: Such investment would be increased in the face of severe economic weakness and decreased in boom times. Otherwise the norm should be a balanced budget. Bailouts would be highly restricted and punitive to management in recognition of the distorted incentives that arise from subsidizing failure. Elites subverted each of these elements of crisis management, to varying extents. Bubble management is non-existent, despite overwhelming evidence of the existence and costs of bubbles as an inherent feature of capitalism. Fiscal policy is hopelessly compromised by politics and seems permanently inclined toward structural deficits and tax cuts for the wealthiest citizens. Bailouts are doled out to the most elite interests and tend to cause the diversion of massive societal wealth with little reflection of economic considerations. This has compromised future economic vitality and the government's ability to manage the crisis with minimal cost.

Chapter 7 addresses the means by which the rule of law can be restored and expanded in the economic sphere. First, severe power imbalances must be remedied. This suggests a combination of steps to reduce the excessive accumulation of economic power and a durable floor upon economic disempowerment. Positive rights to education, social welfare, and basic economic opportunity must be secured. This implies a level of protection beyond simple statutory grant. Second, important elements of economic regulation must be secured from elite subversion similar to the means by which monetary policy operates free of political influence. Elite overreaching damages the rule of law, on a vast array of legal issues. A new economic wisdom must displace laissez-faire dogma so that the entire body politic comprehends the costs of excessive economic power concentration. Judges and lawyers generally need to comprehend the importance of preserving the rule of law and fragmenting economic power. In short, a new paradigm of cultural suspicion needs to emerge with respect to concentrated economic power as it did with respect to concentrated political power. The failure to impose essentially an economic rule of law in the U.S. will simply hobble our nation economically relative to other nations that more successfully limit undue concentrations of economic power.

There is perhaps a principled argument in favor of smaller government and a greater role for markets unsupported by legal infrastructure, beyond basic contract and property law. That argument holds that a large state inherently threatens individual autonomy and liberty. A larger government may become corrupted and transmogrify into an instrument of oppression. This laissez-faire political philosophy is not addressed in this book. Rather, this book simply shows that such an austere vision of government intervention ignores the macroeconomic damage caused by excessive elite power.

Further, laissez-faire philosophy ignores the gains in individual autonomy and liberty caused by state disruption of concentrated economic power. Poverty in particular is anathema to any reasonable definition of liberty, and an optimized macroeconomic environment supported by law empowers everyone. As the Nobel laureate Amartya Sen highlights: "Development requires the removal of major sources of unfreedom: poverty as well as tyranny, poor economic opportunities as well as systematic social deprivation, neglect of public facilities as well as intolerance or overactivity of repressive states."[26] Thus, legal infrastructure in support of human capital development and maximal economic performance operates as a great net liberating force. Regulatory infrastructure by definition leads to frameworks that cost less than the economic benefits produced. The focus of this book is to spotlight and detail legal frameworks supported by evidence showing that benefits exceed costs and to articulate a means of durably securing such beneficial regulation through law while maximizing economic opportunity for everyone.

Capitalism delivers powerful economic and social benefits to societies that pursue its logical ends. Adam Smith, however, long ago recognized: "People of the same trade seldom meet together, even for merriment and diversion, but the conversation ends in a conspiracy against the public or in some contrivance to raise prices."[27] More pointedly, he stated that "whenever the legislature attempts to regulate the differences between the masters and the workman, its counselors are always the masters." Therefore, "when the regulation is in favor of the workmen . . . it is always just and equitable; but it is sometimes otherwise, when in favor of the masters."[28] He also stated that the government role in a market economy includes "maintaining those public institutions and public works, which, though they may be in the highest degree advantageous to a great society, are of such a nature, that the profit could never repay the expense to any individual or small group of individuals."[29] Finally, he argued, "The expense for institutions of education . . . is likewise, no doubt, beneficial to the whole society, and may, therefore, without injustice, be defrayed by the general contribution of whole society."[30] Smith's vision of capitalism thus comprehends the need to curb those with economic power, to secure infrastructure, and to encourage human capital formation.

Rationalization of these elements, within the framework of sound legal infrastructure to support capitalism, forms the foundation of this book. It seeks to demonstrate the power of legal infrastructure to perfect capitalism and to articulate principles underlying such legal and regulatory frameworks. The devolution of capitalism in the U.S., as evidenced in the crisis of 2007 to the present, proves the need to stem economic lawlessness. A massive breakdown in the economic rule of law fueled the crisis. Durable legal infrastructure can stabilize capitalism and provide a foundation for sustainable growth. In the recent past, law has so operated; reconstructing capitalism requires only taking these lessons on board and extending them to modern global and economic realities.

1

A Revolution in Economics (but Not in Law)

As it is the power of exchanging that gives occasion to the division of labour, so the extent of this division must always be limited by the extent of that power, or, in other words, by the extent of the market.

Adam Smith (1776)

Adam Smith long ago recognized that the extent of the marketplace drove ever-increasing specialization. Larger and deeper markets support a more developed division of labor, which enhances economic growth.[1] He further recognized the importance of financial regulation, to contain panics and system risk.[2] Smith evinced skepticism that governing elites would impose "just and equitable" laws upon themselves and expressed empathy for the plight of ordinary workers.[3] Indeed, he doubted that any society could prosper if it permitted too much poverty: "No society can surely be flourishing and happy of which the greater part of the numbers are poor and miserable."[4] These ideas encapsulate the legal deficiencies leading to the subprime fiasco. In other words, traditional economic ideas and principles, principles more recently abandoned in favor of politically convenient elite interests, light the way for reconstructing capitalism.

Today these ideas form the basis of modern growth theory and modern trade theory. Growth theory holds that new ideas give rise to increasing returns to scale rather than diminishing marginal returns spurring rapid macroeconomic growth. The initial fixed cost of creating ideas or knowledge can support mass production at ever lower average unit costs.[5] Trade theory now holds that opening greater markets expands increasing returns to scale and accounts for an increased volume of trade, beyond trade driven by traditional notions of comparative advantage.[6] In other words, under both New Trade Theory and Endogenous Growth Theory, ideas drive average costs lower, leading to higher productivity and consequently greater economic growth. Ideas benefit from nonrivalry, meaning that an unlimited number of people can use an idea at no additional cost. Increasing returns from nonrivalrous ideas constitute a boon to economic growth, and larger markets multiply these benefits. Maximum economic growth therefore requires maximizing the generation of valuable ideas and permitting their application within broader and deeper markets.

This innovation-led growth requires appropriate institutions under law to fully empower human resources.[7] "Institutions are the rules of the game in a society or, more formally, are the humanly devised constraints that shape human interaction."[8] Thus, economic scholars increasingly focus on law and institutions as key to macroeconomic growth.[9] According to these economists, institutions and law will not always arise to secure growth because of a divergence between the interests of rulers versus the interest of all citizens in growth.[10] Law must operate to secure property rights for everyone (including investor protection), constrain elite political power, and broadly empower citizens to participate in economically productive activities. Law must preclude elites from exercising excessive power to rig markets and create uneven playing fields. History shows that these legal institutions—property rights, human rights, and an economic rule of law—powerfully form the root causes of growth.[11] Failure to secure such laws and institutions explains the persistence of poverty in many societies.[12]

Law and institutions create appropriate incentives to encourage appropriate economic behavior. The genesis of the recent financial crisis lies in a bipartisan consensus to dismantle important elements of the New Deal and to deregulate business and the financial sector. These regulations delivered stability and prosperity in the U.S. for more than seven decades following the Great Depression. During this period, major financial disruptions and crashes vanished.[13] "Once deregulation had taken hold it was only a matter of time before these horrors of the past would return."[14] Financial systems must appropriately allocate capital to the most promising investments. Economic activity can be hobbled if financial stability is not secured. Massive misallocations of capital (into Internet stocks, subprime mortgages, or even tulip bulbs) will occur in the absence of sound financial regulation. Regulatory infrastructure must address these challenges through means that raise the return to capital or lower the cost of capital, just as a superhighway may permit trucks to last longer and deliver more goods in shorter time. Elites will not naturally seek optimal market infrastructure if they can profitably rig unregulated financial markets in their favor.

Law must secure rationalized human capital formation, market development, and regulatory infrastructure in order to maximize macroeconomic performance. Stunted human capital formation, market development, and legal infrastructure form the root causes of the financial crisis of 2007–9. Global growth rested excessively upon American consumption because governing elites put little effort into market development elsewhere. American consumption rested upon an infirm foundation of debt, as corporate elites relentlessly moved jobs from the U.S. to low-wage locales, eroding middle-class buying power. Ultimately capital flows from developing nations to the U.S. funded highly exploitative debt—predatory and subprime loans to the most disempowered elements of society. Excessive American debt exploded and crashed the global economy. Law facilitated this exploitative pattern of global finance. Corporate elites profited mightily from these flows because corporate governance permitted compensation arrangements that created incentives for senior managers to take reckless risks. Elites distorted law to achieve irrational indulgences from traditional notions of accountability for fraud and due care. Although the system collapsed, financially, in the fall of 2008, the basic structure persists and seems destined to produce further economic pain.

Law could disrupt this reality. Unfortunately, Law and Economics (as taught in American law schools) retains a moribund focus on market efficiency, narrowly interpreted to mean laissez-faire principles, with no emphasis on macroeconomic growth. Indeed, the work of economists regarding the endogenous factors associated with growth does not even warrant a mention in two primary Law and Economics texts. Essentially, law schools taught generations of legal policymakers that growth does not matter to law and that law does not matter to growth, despite the learning from economics. This empowered elites to hide behind laissez-faire dogma to justify the elimination of legal and regulatory constraints. Thus, an economic revolution went by unnoticed by law. The Law and Economics canon rested upon shaky economics and even shakier history. This would lead to devastating consequences in the context of the subprime debacle. Law must comprehend the full breadth of economic learning—including macroeconomics.[15]

Traditionally, economics said little about growth. Traditional economic models deemed the dynamics of growth exogenous—growth fell from the sky in the form of technological change. In 1957, the Nobel laureate Robert Solow calculated that economic models of growth focusing only on capital and labor accumulation could not account for the great weight of growth. The Solow residual—the amount of growth unaccounted for—represented technological change that drove growth above and beyond capital and labor expansion.[16] Soon thereafter, economists focused on the enhanced capabilities of human capital to drive economic growth and innovation. As the Nobel laureate Robert Lucas stated, "The main source of growth is the accumulation of human capital—of knowledge—and the main source of differences in living standards among nations is differences in human capital."[17] The nation that empowers its people to achieve maximum productivity will outproduce those nations that do not.

Maximum economic growth requires meta-ideas—meta-ideas that serve as platforms for the generation of more ideas.[18] Legal frameworks support institutions that secure the propagation of ideas. Economists now study the relationship between law, institutions, and growth. "[P]eople's innovative activities are conditioned by the laws, institutions, customs, and regulations that affect their incentive and their ability to appropriate rents from newly created knowledge."[19] This chapter explores the link between macroeconomic growth and law from the perspective of economic science (and other social science evidence).

This chapter first reviews the importance of growth to social well-being and the central role of free market capitalism in fostering growth. Then, the chapter reviews evidence regarding sources of macroeconomic growth. A theory of legal infrastructure follows. Thereafter, the chapter reviews evidence regarding the economic threats posed by inequality. Next, the chapter highlights the key shortcomings of the current mainstream Law and Economics approach—laissez-faire ideology—and articulates a theory of perfect competition that focuses on maximizing human potential. The conclusion of the chapter summarizes the legal infrastructure flaws creating the subprime debacle. Economics will serve to illustrate the key elements of this chapter, even though economists concur unanimously on very little, and they often condition their models and studies on many (often profligate) assumptions.

The Virtues of Growth and Capitalism

Macroeconomic growth should not monopolize the attention of policymakers. First, growth must be sustainable in the sense that any environmental costs should give rise to resources that can repair the environment so that each generation inherits roughly the same environmental resources. Growth founded upon environmental degradation simply shifts costs to future generations. Such growth is illusory at best and can impose staggering long-term macroeconomic costs in the form of diminished human capabilities at worst. Growth nevertheless appears more sustainable than many imagine. The right kind of policies can enhance economic growth and environmental sustainability simultaneously.[20] More than 200 years ago, Thomas Malthus predicted that population growth would outstrip earth's resources.[21] History shows that Malthus simply underestimated human ingenuity.[22] Human ingenuity is perhaps the exclusive means of dealing with environmental challenges.

Second, not all economic activity benefits society. Most notably, in the U.S. massive resources support the criminal justice system, yet the U.S. incarcerates more of its citizens than any nation on earth. This certainly signals a social malignancy inconsistent with social well-being. Excessive prison expenditures may enhance short-term growth, but only at the cost of any reasonable measure of aggregate social happiness—a society that imprisons many of its citizens suffers from either an abnormally high concentration of dangerously violent people (unlikely) or an out-of-whack criminal justice system.[23] Mass incarceration (along with accompanying stigmatization) fails to maximize human productivity, notwithstanding the short-term impact on macroeconomic output that prison-related expenditures may generate.[24]

Third, other measures of social well-being beyond per capita GDP may prove more insightful. For example, the United Nations annually assesses national development through its Human Development Index. The index includes life expectancy, educational attainment, inequality, and GDP per capita as four dimensions of development. As of 2011, twenty-two nations scored higher than the U.S.[25] In general, however, economic growth is an important consideration and one measure of the well-being and quality of life within a given society. Sustainable macroeconomic growth gives society the resources necessary to address longevity, education, and other elements of well-being.

Countries with higher GDP enjoy longer life expectancy, better health, more leisure, and higher educational attainment. Modern capitalist societies deliver astonishing social outcomes without historic precedent. In Great Britain, over the past 200 years average height has increased by 3.6 inches. In the U.S., the average work week plunged since 1870 and the prospect of retirement soared, even as previously unaffordable amenities became widespread. Meanwhile, real GDP per capita increased sevenfold. "A Japanese baby born in 1880 had a life expectancy of 35 years; today life expectancy in Japan is 82 years."[26] The spread of capitalism served to lift 200 million Chinese citizens out of poverty over 20 years, from 1981 to 2002. The number of people worldwide living on less than one dollar per day declined by half during the same period.[27] This is the promise of modern capitalism.

The political consequences of growth also matter. Economic stagnation harms community values and encourages intolerance. For example, Nazi Germany arose from the extended economic chaos facing Germany in the 1920s and early 1930s. Japan and Italy also took an extremist path. World War II illustrates that wars frequently follow economic disruptions. Nations experiencing economic turmoil may well be drawn to extremist government, even if the U.S. followed a more moderate path out of the Great Depression. Prosperity encourages support for the less privileged elements within a society.[28]

Maximizing economic growth represents an urgent need today, as nearly 1 billion people still survive on less than one dollar per day and 2.6 billion live on less than two dollars per day. In poor nations, 10,000 children per day die from contaminated water. The 573 million world citizens who live in less-developed nations face a life expectancy of 46 years, while the 1.3 billion living in rich nations can expect to live 78 years. Educational attainment in the poorest nations averages less than two years; in the richest nations it reaches as high as 13 years. Getting economics and law right enhances longevity as well as the quality of life within a nation.

The record of market-based economies regarding growth suggests that capitalism remains humanity's best economic hope for organizing economic activity. Every major episode of explosive growth occurred in market-based economies (whether in China, eastern Asia, or Japan). Worldwide growth amounted to essentially zero for centuries prior to the advent of modern capitalism.[29] Capitalist systems benefit from a strong historic record in terms of producing wealth relative to centrally planned economies. Thus, West Germany outperformed East Germany economically, just as South Korea outperformed North Korea.[30] In the absence of any real alternative, and in view of its decentralized decision-making structure, which supports individual autonomy, capitalism merely requires law to vindicate its essential value of competitive meritocracy rather than any radical change.[31] This book therefore suggests that law facilitate the evolution of capitalism in the direction of greater and more broadly distributed human empowerment as a means of yielding greater macroeconomic growth and stability.

The many benefits highlighted above—from longevity and health to educational attainment—suggest huge leaps in living standards even if environmental degradation and resource depletion diminished GDP growth. Moreover, these increases in living standards defy longstanding pockets of pessimism which suggest that economic collapse and environmental disaster loom. Capitalism, properly reconstructed, constitutes the most powerful means yet discovered of unleashing human ingenuity. "There is no reason to expect slackening in the rate of output through exhaustion of technological possibilities."[32]

Indeed, shortages of resources seem unlikely to stifle growth as high prices automatically encourage searches for substitutes.[33] There is no reason why alternative energy platforms (such as solar energy) cannot form a nonrivalrous source of growth (as the Internet functioned) to stir innovation through lower cost and cleaner energy.[34] Once such a network is in place, the costs of additional use are very small compared with the network's ability to spur innovation by increasing the returns to capital. In other words, new ideas can save the environment and support more innovation rather than leave humanity in permanent economic downturn.[35] Environmental damage simply does not wash away past growth gains, and mitigating the cost of damage to the environment could well spur positive growth, much like massive public works projects or the government's investment in the creation of the Internet. This book is premised on the notion that further environmentally sustainable growth is possible, even highly probable. In fact, such growth may well provide the exclusive path out of environmental degradation.

The central point of this book concerns the potential for legal frameworks to create a more robust capitalism, a capitalism that minimizes the power of elites to subvert competition and maximizes the power of all to enter competitive markets in accordance with their highest economic potential. Capitalism operates to support longer, healthier, more enlightened lives than ever before in human history. Consequently, the prescriptions herein seek to optimize capitalism through law, not its abandonment or radical redesign. The reconstruction of capitalism merely means pursuing the lessons from economic history to their logical ends in the context of a modern knowledge-based economy to support maximum human empowerment.

The Revolution in Economics

A revolution occurred in the world of economics during the past few decades.[36] Specifically, the study of economic growth exploded in the field of economics.[37] It started with Solow's residual in 1957 and accelerated after Professor Paul Romer's two landmark papers *Increasing Returns and Economic Growth*[38] and *Endogenous Technological Change*.[39] Economists sought to endogenize the key factors driving economic growth—technological change—into economic models. They concluded that technological advances drive growth, ideas drive technological advances, human capital development drives ideas, and the current global economy chronically underfunds human capital investment.[40] The focus on underlying growth dynamics meant that rather than treating technical change as exogenous (falling from the sky, like "manna from heaven"[41]), economic science sought to explain the genesis of economic growth.

Knowledge, ideas, and innovation assumed central roles in growth because these nonrivalrous goods generate increasing returns to scale (because the expense of the idea can be spread across more units of a given product). Further, because of the difficulty of excluding others from the use of many ideas and knowledge (particularly those not protected by intellectual property regimes), ideas tend to generate significant positive spillovers to the economy. Finally, network ideas can lead to additional positive spillovers when a product is used by others—such as Microsoft Word—in a way that makes the product's use by each individual consumer more valuable. These network effects can create more economic growth. Ideas, know-how, and innovation thereby generate rapid economic growth.[42]

Economists also recognize that private markets likely will underfund the creation of ideas. Spillovers suggest that public returns to the generation of ideas exceed private returns—blunting the incentive for private actors to invest in research and development of innovations.[43] While patents and intellectual property protection may restore the balance to incentives to innovate to an extent, competitors will seek to invent around such protections.[44] Firms will also pause before investing directly in the human capital of individuals because the law will not require workers to serve an employer against their will. These realities create opportunities for policies to encourage innovation beyond intellectual property protections.

Government can assist business through education subsidies and other human capital development policies. Naturally, the more individuals the government empowers to engage in innovative activities, the more innovative an economy can become. Thus, human capital policies should encourage both enhanced aggregate human capital and widely dispersed human capital accumulation.[45] Indeed, the democratization of intellectual property law in the U.S. spurred innovation relative to more exclusive European intellectual property regimes because it empowered more people to innovate.[46] Creativity and innovation defies measurement and predictability. "Technological possibilities are an uncharted sea."[47] This highlights a critical role for government to distribute widely the power to innovate.

A more highly educated population will lower the cost of innovation and increase the number of those able to innovate, at no expense to companies seeking to innovate through research and development. A more educated workforce will adapt to new technologies with greater facility.[48] Empirical evidence shows that enhanced cognitive skills among workers will enhance macroeconomic performance, particularly when economists screen out unproductive human capital investments undertaken in corrupt nations where economic prospects dim.[49] Recently, economists have shown that skills development (as opposed to years in potentially unproductive schools) constitutes the "key" issue facing developing nations, where skills are generally "truly dismal."[50]

Powerful empirical evidence demonstrates positive macroeconomic spillovers from a more educated workforce.[51] Wages for all levels of education seemingly rise as more college-educated workers enter the labor force.[52] Social returns further include lower crime and incarceration rates.[53] Higher levels of education also lead to superior health outcomes.[54] All of this means that the social returns to education exceed just the private returns, which raises the prospect of underfunding for educational attainment in the absence of government action.[55] The college wage premium, however, increased across the globe in recent decades, meaning that the demand for college graduates exceeds the supply of college graduates.[56] Therefore, government funding fails to meet the economic thirst for educated workers.

Additional financing challenges threaten educational investments. Imperfect financial markets seek to lend based upon social connections and collateral (i.e., wealth) instead of academic promise, which can be difficult to observe and verify. Without access to wealth or finance, many poorer children must forgo education.[57] Even in developed nations, such as the U.S., credit constraints seemingly play a major role in the inability of many students to complete college.[58] These credit constraints combined with the excess public returns to education mean that without vigorous government action, educational funding—and by extension innovation and economic growth—languishes, particularly for disempowered groups. Thus, a major longitudinal study over a period of twenty years shows that eighth-graders in the U.S. with high scores on standardized tests but from low-income families attend college at less than half the rate as high scorers from high-income backgrounds. Further, rich students with low scores attend college at ten times the rate as low-scoring students from poor backgrounds.[59]

These impediments to financing education carry real consequences. In the U.S., the most influential factor determining an individual's socioeconomic status is the socioeconomic status of that individual's parents; family wealth holds far more sway than even so-called IQ tests, which themselves suffer infection from socioeconomic circumstances, as discussed in chapter 5.[60] Similarly, economic mobility—the ability of an individual to achieve upward (or downward) class movement—in the U.S. has fallen in recent decades.[61] Indeed, the income gains of women mask decreasing mobility for men, and minorities have gained little in recent decades.[62] Economic mobility in the U.S. now lags behind that of virtually all other modern industrialized nations.[63] This suggests that funding challenges for education impede a fully competitive market for human resources, creating economic drags on growth, as a consequence of too much privilege and disempowerment.

The U.S. chronically under-invests in higher education, as shown by the rising wage premium college graduates enjoy. In the early part of the 20th century, the U.S. led the world in public funding for education. The wage premium earned by college graduates fell between 1915 and 1950, meaning the American educational system met the needs of the American economy. Inequality declined and America enjoyed unprecedented prosperity. Over the past thirty years, by contrast, the U.S. developed the most unequal distribution of income and wages of any high-income country. Beginning in the 1970s, the nation lost its commitment to education, leading to a highly unequal nation with little mobility. Today, the income differential between high school graduates and college graduates exceeds 80 percent compared with 45 percent in 1970. Empirical studies confirm this shortage of highly educated workers, finding higher productivity gains for increases in college graduates within a given workforce but little impact for increasing secondary educational attainment.[64] Our economy thirsts for more highly educated workers. Meanwhile, the U.S. fell from second to fifteenth among developed nations in university graduation rates between 1995 and 2009.[65]

Insufficient educational expenditures suffer further from distorted policies and a lack of innovation. Even with respect to higher education, a source of traditional strength in the U.S., elite universities base the allocation of opportunity upon wealth, fame, or legacy status rather than on any notion of pure merit.[66] The continued use of the SAT as a basis of college admission borders on a national scandal, given its patent bias toward power and privilege.[67] Many effective innovations, such as charter schools, remain the subject of debate rather than widespread practice.[68] In sum, education in the U.S. appears mired in a political morass wherein power trumps merit.

While economists today can identify the key drivers of growth, theoretically their policy prescriptions often lack focus. For example, while the expansion of intellectual property rights might create more powerful incentives to innovate, it also may impede the free flow of knowledge.[69] The excessive enforcement of intellectual property rights may well serve to stifle creativity.[70] Moreover, the use of intellectual property protections can serve to entrench monopoly power and hurt consumer welfare.[71] Economists face similar challenges assessing the appropriate level of antitrust law enforcement, where simultaneity issues render efforts to endogenize antitrust enforcement problematic.[72] Expanded funding for education can facilitate the creation of useful ideas without the drawbacks of changing either competition law or intellectual property law.

Professor Romer extended the power of ideas further when he recognized that some ideas serve as platforms for the generation or transmission of more ideas; he terms these ideas meta-ideas. Thus, patent law, the Internet, and the modern research university all exemplify the power of meta-ideas.[73] Notably, meta-ideas usually require legal frameworks, as meta-ideas generally enjoy public funding. For example, the U.S. government founded the Internet.[74] Romer's work helped to create an entirely new field of macroeconomics termed Endogenous Growth Theory or the New Growth Theory. Endogenous Growth Theory provides a key lesson that animates this book: Ideas support growth through increasing returns to scale. Simply put, ideas about new ways of doing things, once formulated, cost nothing and thereby drive economic returns ever higher when deployed in larger and deeper (i.e., more prosperous) markets. Meta-ideas hold the potential for achieving increasing returns across the entire economy.

Education creates the possibility of new ideas and insights and thus constitutes the ultimate meta-idea. Yet productivity in the educational sector in the U.S. lags. According to the Organisation for Economic Co-operation and Development (OECD), the U.S. spends as much as any major industrialized nation. Nevertheless, the high school graduation rate in the U.S. (at 77 percent) falls far below the OECD average.[75] In 2009, the U.S. ranked twenty-first in secondary school graduation rates.[76] Educational outcomes in the U.S. seem destined to worsen: The OECD's current assessment shows the nation's fifteen-year-olds scoring lower than those in thirty-one of thirty-two developed nations in math and faring well below average overall; and a recent ranking of the best universities in the world showed that those in the U.S. typically cost tens of thousands of dollars per year more than comparably ranked foreign universities.[77] These stark facts support only one conclusion: The U.S. under-invests in education and fails to use its resources effectively. Given the centrality of ideas to economic growth, the U.S. abdicated economic leadership over the past twelve to fifteen years.

Recently economics suffered criticism for its failure to predict the depths of the financial crisis of 2007–9. Economists generally failed to provide guidance on the macroeconomic dangers of excessive debt, uncontrolled predation, leveraged asset bubbles, the dangers of perverse incentives, and the problems posed by undercapitalized banks.[78] Nevertheless, certain lessons from economics simply failed to garner much support among governing elites despite a strong consensus that growth hangs in the balance. Human capital development enjoys powerful support from economics. Yet the U.S. ignored this lesson and its own history and attempted to build a knowledge-based economy with insufficient mechanisms to secure human capital development. This necessarily created a chronic underclass in America and exacerbated inequality.

The Importance of Effective Buying Power

Nonrival ideas generate increasing returns to scale, giving rise to profit without further cost, thus boosting productivity. Another contributing factor to growth is market size. A large market permits greater specialization. Additionally, a larger market allows business to allocate its cost over greater scale; viewed differently, a larger market allows each consumer to bear fewer fixed costs of production. This necessarily supports a bedrock principle of globalization: Opening markets as broadly as possible to all businesses benefits every economy because it unleashes maximum profitability for a given idea. In 2007, the Princeton economist Paul Krugman won the Nobel Prize in Economics based upon this essential insight.[79]

Krugman explained that comparative advantage, the traditional intellectual basis for international trade, needed to be supplemented to account for trade between nations with similar factor endowments. Krugman's model put increasing returns at the center of much of the increased trade seen in the world. Increasing returns meant that nations with unique products could generate enhanced profits with enhanced market access. Additional market access could support new ideas for product differentiation. Product differentiation within larger markets extends increasing returns and encourages new ideas to cater to more varied consumer tastes. Krugman subsequently transcended international trade and applied these same concepts to explain economic geography generally. Krugman concluded that core urban areas offered entrepreneurs larger markets in which they could apply new ideas for product differentiation and enjoy increasing returns. Thus, opportunities for further application of increasing returns in the form of product differentiation critically depended upon the extent of the market, again.[80]

Adam Smith recognized that the extent of the market turned upon two factors: wealth and population. According to Smith, a larger market drives greater specialization, which in turn leads to greater productivity and wages. Krugman's analysis mirrors this bedrock insight. Everywhere and always a broader and deeper market supports more effective buying power, permitting greater specialization or product differentiation and creating more room for growth. The value of ideas is not really a function of market size so much as effective demand. Market depth logically operates to drive profitability as much as market size.[81] The insight that a broader middle class creates demand for more innovation commands broad empirical support.[82]

The upshot of the importance of market size combined with the fact that labor productivity is dependent upon market prosperity suggests government responsibility for market maintenance. Government should see to it that the foundation of consumption is maintained. The starting point for these efforts must focus on human capital formation because that alone forms the basis for durable buying power in a globalized economy. The GI Bill, which President Franklin D. Roosevelt signed in 1944, more than doubled the number of college graduates in the U.S. between the beginning of World War II and 1950. Congressional estimates suggest a payback ratio of up to $12 for every dollar the government expended for the GI Bill, based solely upon the enhanced income of recipients.[83] Similarly, the Guaranteed Student Loan Program and other financial aid programs from the 1970s operated to deliver $4.30 for each dollar invested because of enhanced income.[84] Nevertheless, the trend in the U.S. suggests that college education costs are outpacing government financial aid and that college affordability has declined in the U.S. in recent years.[85] The problem of affordability of higher education explains the fading U.S. advantage in higher education. It also evinces a short-sighted governing elite as human capital development spurs both innovation (supplying innovators) and market development (demand for innovation).

During the Great Depression, the U.S. demonstrated the efficacy of supporting steady and robust consumption. The National Labor Relations Act facilitated unionization, which in turn facilitated a robust middle class with secure employment. Social Security freed consumers from the worries of sustaining themselves through retirement and unleashed further consumption. The New Deal also empowered consumers to purchase homes like never before; indeed, the New Deal ushered in the thirty-year mortgage, which became the bedrock of the American middle class.[86] Beyond the New Deal, the Civil Rights Act of 1964 moved a significant portion of the population from the economic margins of society to the threshold of the middle class. Every one of these government initiatives subsidized growth: They created consumers committed to high levels of expenditure and continuing employment; they expanded both the consumer base and the pool of skilled, committed employees for every business; and they expanded the ability of every American business to allocate its fixed expenditures across a wider consumption base. The New Deal tripled America's middle class.[87]

These efforts mirror the recommendations of economists as a means of spurring innovation; "government policies relating to health, education, etc., that help increase the size of the middle class are important for future growth."[88] Thus, government support of health care provides business with healthy workers who can innovate. Healthier workers are more productive workers. Enhanced life expectancy encourages human capital formation and investment. Healthy children can learn better.[89] The gains from these types of social investments prove macroeconomically significant.[90] A higher income share for the middle class correlates to higher income and higher growth, as well as better education, health care, and infrastructure.[91]

Consumption raises a tragedy of the commons. Robust consumption supports the profitability of all businesses. Yet each business faces incentives to undercut consumption through low wages and to prevent government from propping up consumption through programs that increase taxes. Thus the paradox: Every business wants prosperous and secure consumers, but no business wants to bear the costs of maintaining such stable consumption.[92] In fact, the role of consumption in creating a demand for innovation suggests that permitting consumption to erode not only destroys effective demand today but also harms growth tomorrow through diminished demand for innovation. This need to protect the commons of consumption falls to government because of the distorted incentives of each business to maximize only their individual profits rather than general macroeconomic growth.

Neoliberal globalization under the so-called Washington Consensus (which emphasizes globalization based upon laissez-faire principles) ignores the commons of consumption. To the contrary, the neoliberal agenda sought to lower wages and allow corporations to shirk the need to consider demand for their products. Of course, the New Deal secured consumption for decades following the Great Depression; the U.S. therefore maintained sufficient consumption to feed the growth of the global economy for years. In the face of declining wages for most workers, however, debt replaced a robust middle class as a key driver of consumption.[93] This proved unsustainable. Debt ultimately killed the New Deal's golden goose. That killer debt flowed directly from the legal structure of our globalized economy, as will be discussed in chapter 4. In sum, internationally as well as within the U.S., government paid little attention to the need for market development in the years leading up to the subprime crisis.

A Theory of Legal and Regulatory Infrastructure

Legal and regulatory infrastructure can secure human capital formation and superior market development, each of which spurs growth. Further, a sound system of government regulation serves as a foundation of macroeconomic growth and stability. Basically, legal and regulatory infrastructure should seek to lower the cost of capital or raise the return to capital, throughout the economy. If law can achieve such an end, then the economic benefits of government intervention likely will greatly exceed the costs of intervention, in terms of compliance or transaction costs. All government action implies transaction costs or compliance costs, even if only in the form of taxation or the cost of legal counsel. Yet lowering the cost of capital or raising the returns to capital across the economy certainly spurs innovation and entrepreneurial activity on a wide scale. Thus, interventions can support macroeconomic growth.

Of course, identifying and structuring such interventions may prove challenging. Economic science can help. Usually, economic science analyzes interventions in general terms only rather than testing specific legal or regulatory approaches or language. Further, a model is only as powerful as its assumptions. Similarly, because correlation is not causation, economics must reckon with issues relating to the direction of causation, possible exogenous factors to a given study, as well as data quality. Insights from economics nonetheless may form powerful mosaics that serve to guide the structure of law and regulation.

Other social sciences also may serve to support and illuminate successful government interventions in favor of economic growth. History, in particular, can serve to support lessons from economics or to dispel economic myths. Law changes over history, and understanding the historic impact of legal changes can provide insights on how law should structure interventions into the economy. Bringing all social science evidence to bear on the question of how precisely government can best support the economy may well achieve the best possible outcome given the inherent limitations of economic science. Notably, this interdisciplinary approach also supports a superior platform than the current approach of Law and Economics, which too often relies heavily on theory and even speculation over a balanced view of economic science as tested in the cauldron of history and other social sciences.[94]

I relied on history as well as modern economic science in 2003 to assess the efficacy of the New Deal seventy years after President Franklin Roosevelt assumed office. While some elements of the New Deal failed, other elements provided a solid foundation for future growth. The New Deal created legal and regulatory infrastructure to support the operation of free markets (particularly financial markets) and to lower the cost of capital or raise the return to capital. These elements supported macroeconomic growth for seven decades, uninterrupted by major financial disturbances. From securities regulation to deposit insurance to the creation of the modern Fed, the New Deal essentially forged the modern American economy. Certainly the Roosevelt administration erred, particularly when it acted to suppress markets (through interference with market prices, for example) rather than to facilitate market action. Overall, however, the New Deal succeeded in placing the American economy upon a firmer legal foundation.[95]

The U.S. benefits from a long history of imposing powerful regulatory infrastructure. For example, the federal securities laws, with their traditional enhanced enforcement mechanisms and mandatory-disclosure regime, enhanced public firm financial performance. In a particularly well-designed study, exploiting the change in law in 1964 that expanded the applicability of the federal securities laws to a wider universe of companies, Professors Greenestone, Oyer, and Vissing-Jorgensen found that mandatory disclosure causes managers to focus more intently upon shareholder wealth maximization. The enactment of the 1964 amendments to the federal securities laws allowed the authors of the study to compare financial performance of firms newly subjected to securities regulation with those subject to such regulation all along. After controlling for industry, firm size, and book-to-market value, the expansion of the coverage of the federal securities law triggered substantial gains in firm value and financial performance.[96] Even longstanding advocates of laissez-faire now recognize the importance of mandatory-disclosure regimes such as the federal securities laws.[97]

Other forms of regulatory infrastructure also hail from the financial sector. For example, according to Professor Gary Gorton, the financial crisis started in August 2007, when the global financial system disintegrated under the weight of a wholesale bank run. Bank runs occurred regularly in the U.S. prior to 1934 (when the New Deal provided deposit insurance for every bank customer) with devastating economic effects from the accompanying constriction in credit. Since 1934, bank runs have disappeared. Unfortunately, the global financial system evolved in the shadow of laissez-faire deregulation, and an entire wholesale banking system cropped up entirely free of any real banking regulation, including deposit insurance. This wholesale banking system is widely termed the shadow banking system. This global shadow banking system ultimately funded the activities of traditional banks through the purchase of securitized debt generated by banks. Uninsured banks, however, remain vulnerable to panic whether at the retail or wholesale level. Thus the panic of 2007 involved an electronic run on the shadow banking system, which in turn locked up the funding available for the purchase of securitized debt. Large institutional investors—including traditional banks—demanded funds en masse and rendered the global financial system insolvent. A credit crunch hit the global economy. The lesson Gorton draws: New regulation is needed to facilitate the operation of the shadow banking system, making it less vulnerable to runs.[98]

The dismantling of much regulatory infrastructure played a central role in the crisis of 2007–9. Chapter 3 reviews the main elements of financial deregulation that led to the crisis. Here, the key point is simply that government intervention in the market can spur growth. The securities laws lower the cost of capital by inspiring investor confidence and raise the return to capital through more diligent management. Deposit insurance lowers the cost of capital by eliminating the risk of bank runs from the retail banking system, greatly stabilizing the economy and allowing bankers to loan money to business at more generous terms. Unfortunately, governing elites, in thrall to laissez-faire, ignored history—that finance requires regulatory infrastructure if it is to thrive—and risked an avoidable financial meltdown. That risk persists unabated today.

Legal infrastructure may also secure appropriate human capital development. Recently economists discovered that refined data sets lead to more robust links between human capital development and economic growth.[99] Those studying China's remarkable growth record over the past thirty years attribute much of its economic performance to its "quite rapid" development of its human resources.[100] It expanded literacy by 7 percent in one seven-year period and quadrupled educational expenditures over seventeen years. With respect to the so-called East Asian Miracle of growth during the 1980s and 1990s, human capital development again figured prominently.[101] The nation that best secures human capital development under law will no doubt enjoy the greatest economic success in the globalized economy, which handsomely rewards innovation. I address the most promising legal frameworks for securing human capital development in chapter 7.

Legal infrastructure must also cabin excessive economic power. Here the subprime crisis of 2007–9 speaks loudly. The subprime crisis arose from the "money-driven American political system." Campaign contributions and lobbying influenced the repeal of the Glass-Steagall Act, the decision to deregulate the derivatives market, the ability of financial firms to use leverage to enhance current profitability at the expense of longer-term risk, and the use of balance sheet vehicles to hide risk and create illusory profits—profits that failed to appear when risks manifested themselves in real losses, among other regulatory deficiencies.[102] The bailouts associated with the crisis also reflect the influence of money over sound policy. The rule of law requires that legal frameworks supporting economic growth be secured from the often pernicious influence of governing elites.

The Problem of High Inequality and Growth-Retarding Elites

Inequality may support economic growth or harm economic growth. Certainly, a society exhibiting perfect economic equality regardless of effort fails to create appropriate incentives for human innovation and excellence. On the other hand, a society burdened by high levels of elite privilege fails to unleash the full economic potential of its entire population. Privilege destroys competitive opportunity. The question of the optimal level of inequality within a society is also doubtlessly influenced by cultural mores, norms, traditions, ideology, and social cohesion. Transnational regressions of growth and various measures of inequality therefore may provide misleading conclusions to the extent they fail to consider that some societies may be able to positively manage more inequality than others.[103] When elites fail, however, to appropriately fund human capital and market development, or when elites accumulate so much power they act to subvert legal and regulatory infrastructure, then inequality harms growth.[104] This danger can be most acute in the context of a knowledge-based economy where human capital formation plays a critical role.[105]

Professors Castello and Domenech computed measures of inequality based upon educational attainment measured in years of schooling. They found that nations with higher levels of human capital inequality suffered impaired macroeconomic growth relative to nations with lower levels of human capital inequality. "Policies, therefore, conducted to promote growth should not only take into account the level but also the distribution of education, generalizing the access to formal education at different stages to a wider section of the population."[106] Others find that nations with high levels of initial inequality failed to fund broad-based human capital formation or to create institutions to facilitate growth.[107] Thus, those concerned with macroeconomic growth must address unequal access to human capital development.

Inequality also threatens the rule of law. In *The Injustice of Inequality* Professors Glaeser, Scheinkman, and Shleifer "argue that inequality is detrimental to growth, because it enables the rich to subvert the political, regulatory and legal institutions of society to their own benefit." Inequality empowers the established to impede the efforts of innovators with initially inferior resources. The excess wealth of the established determines the extent to which they may subvert law. Ultimately the "initially well situated . . . pursue socially harmful acts recognizing that the legal, political and regulatory systems will not hold them accountable." Glaeser, Scheinkman, and Shleifer test their argument against historic evidence from the Gilded Age in the U.S. and the transition economies of eastern Europe during the 1990s. They find abundant historical evidence that in both instances powerful elites subverted law and harmed macroeconomic performance. The authors next test the proposition through a constructed index of the rule of law to determine if nations with weak legal systems suffer impaired growth. They find that inequality is "bad for growth" in countries with a weak rule of law.[108] Thus, the law must account for the subversion of legal regimes arising from high levels of inequality.

In 2004, on the occasion of the fiftieth anniversary of the Supreme Court's landmark decision in *Brown v. Board of Education* that American apartheid must end (with "all deliberate speed"),[109] I surveyed evidence related to inequality and growth and concluded that inequality arising from the oppression of minorities continues to harm economic growth through the destruction of human capital. I argued in favor of mitigating racial inequality within the U.S. through enhanced funding for human capital formation. Because racial hierarchies draw zero support from science, their existence necessarily evidences economic oppression.[110] The modern U.S. is hardly exempt from the threat that economic inequality may reflect the operation of illegitimate economic hierarchies that lead to impaired human capital formation.

Far from finding any kind of immunity, economists recently demonstrated that in the past, high inequality compromised human capital formation in the U.S.[111] Other researchers find high excess returns (of 11 to 15 percent) to state educational outlays, particularly in high-inequality locales.[112] The U.S. therefore appears prone to the same dynamic that economists identify in other nations: Governing elites will not fund appropriate human capital formation for the children of others under conditions of high inequality.[113] Historically, land inequality operated to impede human capital formation in the U.S. and abroad while land reforms and egalitarian land ownership gave rise to enhanced educational outlays.[114]

Mancur Olson articulated *The Theory of Collective Action* to explain the mechanism underlying elite subversion of law. Large, diffused groups face the temptation to free-ride, based upon the assumption that others will press government to vindicate their interests. Small groups with concentrated interests and resources do not fall prey to the same temptation and may coordinate their efforts without the dilution of their interests as implied in free-riding problems.[115] Naturally, high inequality means more resources in fewer hands and leads to smaller groups with more concentrated interests. Olson's theory has been extended to explain the behavior of legislators in seeking out issues that attract the interests of concentrated groups so that lawmakers may exploit their lower costs of organization and attain higher levels of campaign contributions, or other largesse, such as future employment. Although this complex negotiation between lawmakers and supplicants for legal indulgences can be "well hidden," law must evolve in view of these powerful theoretical insights, backed with strong empirical evidence.[116]

This theory of collective action dovetails with evidence showing that inequality within the U.S. reached a historic peak immediately prior to the subprime debacle in 2007. Economic inequality operated to concentrate more income than ever before in a very small number of hands. The accompanying graph shows the concentration of income held by the top 0.01 percent (1 in 10,000) of the population. The amount of income controlled by this small number of Americans is at an historic high, a high that has not been rivaled since just before the Great Depression.

The economists Thomas Piketty and Emmanuel Saez assiduously combed through U.S. tax return data from 1913 to 1998 to focus on top share of income.[117] Recently, Saez updated his and Piketty's landmark work and found that in 2007 the top 0.01 percent of the income distribution in the U.S. (consisting of 14,988 families making at least $11.5 million) controlled more than 6 percent of the nation's output, more than in the prior peak year of 1928. Concentration of income in the U.S. peaked in 1928 (prior to the Great Depression) before being eclipsed in 2005 and reaching an all-time peak of

Figure 1.1 Top 0.01% income share (Source: Saez, 2009)

2007 (prior to another historic financial catastrophe). According to Saez, this increased concentration of income arises from "an explosion of top wages and salaries" particularly among top corporate executives.[118] These facts mean that more of our nation's resources are more concentrated in fewer hands than ever before.

Such a high level of income concentration encourages "investment" in rent-seeking subversion of law. More concentrated wealth reduces collective action costs. It also allows concentrated elites access to more resources. At some point, the increase in access to resources leads to increased access to political leaders, with all the consequent implications regarding cognitive and cultural capture. Ultimately, economic and political elites homogenize, as revolving doors in government and business lead to a high velocity of exchange between government and business leaders. As the real economy atrophies (when elites attend more to the indulgences of cronies than to facilitating growth), investment opportunities dwindle and rent-seeking opportunities from governmental subsidies and legal indulgences attract further investment. In the U.S., the damage to the rule of law is evident in its current ranking of fiftieth in the world in trust in politicians and the ability of the government to deal with the private sector at arm's length.[119]

Professor Simon Johnson and James Kwak document precisely these mechanisms in the context of the subversion of financial regulation in the run-up to the subprime fiasco. First, the concentration of economic resources of the six largest commercial and investment banks within the financial sector surged from under 20 percent of GDP in 1995 to over 60 percent in 2009. Second, from 1990 to 2006 campaign contributions soared from $61 million to $260 million, while lobbying expenditures reached $3.4 billion. Third, the leaders of the Wall Street firms and the policymakers in Washington, D.C., shuttled between the two power centers seamlessly until the mindset of the two melded into the same antiregulation, pro–financial sector mantra. Finally, the compensation paid in the financial sector soared. From 1980 through 2007 the financial sector successfully freed itself from a wide array of regulations and consolidated to the point where a handful of mega-banks exerted inordinate control over the economy.[120] Chapter 3 reviews the parade of regulatory indulgences in the financial sector, but this pattern of elite subversion of regulation pervades this book and transcends the financial sector.

Control of corporate wealth—within the financial sector or otherwise—unlocks concentrated power. CEOs now dominate the public firm in the U.S.[121] CEOs use the prodigious wealth within their corporations to sway law and regulation in a direction that serves CEO interests. In recent years, senior managers have amassed massive annual compensation and used their political muscle to restructure the American economy. Now, they have offloaded massive risks onto to the taxpayer, saddled the American economy with unsustainable debt, relieved themselves of trillions in tax liabilities, and shredded the middle class. Indeed, corporate and financial elites now constitute about half of the top 0.01 percent of the income distribution, and virtually all of the growth in the American economy over the past few decades fueled huge salary gains for this group even as most Americans endured extended economic stagnation.[122] American governing elites, the majority of whom are financial and corporate senior managers, used their political power to rig markets and entrench themselves at the cost of general economic growth, as detailed in coming chapters. Thus, the U.S. faced a perfect storm of concentrated wealth on the eve of the crisis: gaping income inequality, a cancerous growth in finance concentrated among a handful of firms, and the consolidation of power at the apex of the American public firm, in the hands of CEOs.

Elites may retard growth even beyond subversion of law. If retaining their privileged status rationally supersedes any concern with general macroeconomic growth, there is no reason to limit their influence to politics. Growth means change, and change threatens the status quo. Sustained economic growth results from new ideas and involves continual transformation. Often these new ideas require wrenching changes, as the status quo proves itself inept or unable to adjust. "Economies that cease to transform themselves are destined to fall off the path of economic growth."[123] Only the nations that engage in the never-ending process of economic development will enjoy ever-increasing prosperity. A wealth of historic evidence shows that elites can and will block threatening economic development and technology if they have the political power to insulate themselves from the potential turbulence accompanying economic change.[124] "It is not the owner of stage-coaches who builds railways."[125]

Similarly, high inequality leads to media capture, whereby elites expend funds to influence public opinion (and hence law) in their favor.[126] Compromised property rights followed the concentration of wealth in the hands of an oligarchy in post-communist Russia.[127] In a comparison between high-growth Asian countries and low-growth Latin American nations, another study found that Asian states benefit from political insulation from elite subversion while Latin America suffers from pork barrel politics.[128] High inequality also leads to excess debt accumulation among working classes, sowing the seeds for financial crises such as the Great Depression.[129] Much evidence indirectly validates the key point of this book: Concentrated elites (such as those in control of transnational firms and banks) can and will use their position to undermine growth if they deem it profitable to do so.

Economic evidence cannot definitively establish that economic inequality always leads to deficient legal institutions and impaired growth.[130] In addition to the usual problems of endogeneity, simultaneity, and possible omitted variables, more data would be required to establish when inequality becomes threatening.[131] This book adds clarity to this important issue by tracing the use of elite influence on law and following the elite profits as well as damage to the general economy in the specific context of the financial crisis of 2007–9 and its ongoing economic impact. In the end, the *potential* that high inequality may exact a macroeconomic toll suggests that the law should mitigate the means by which this toll is paid by society at large. Empowering the disempowered will naturally mitigate that potential, as will rational market development. Similarly, sound regulatory infrastructure will operate to curb the exercise of economic power. These elements each benefit from an independent economic justification, as discussed previously. In any event, the underlying causes of the subprime mortgage crisis furnish compelling evidence on the pernicious economic influence of excessive elite power, through the failure of governing elites to ensure rational human capital and market development as well as their subversion of law.

Human capital formation is a central issue of excessive elite domination. One may easily imagine that a highly educated population would enjoy sufficient capabilities that the democratic negotiation of market development and regulatory infrastructure would yield optimal macroeconomic outcomes. Further, a reallocation of economic opportunities toward the disempowered would necessarily mitigate inequality. Empowering the most disempowered axiomatically yields the greatest economic benefits. Thus, human capital formation may rightly constitute the prime goal of legal and regulatory infrastructure. In chapter 4, I discuss economic human rights in depth as an example of an ineffective international legal framework for securing human capital formation, and in chapter 7, I discuss historic episodes in the U.S. that triggered elite commitment to human capital development.

The Failings of Neoclassical Law and Economics

Neoclassical Law and Economics (synonymous with neoliberalism and market fundamentalism, because of its emphasis on market efficiency) postulates that all regulation interferes with the market's ability to allocate resources efficiently, and the more austere the role government plays in the economy, the better.[132] As Professor George Priest highlights, the Law and Economics movement originated as a political philosophy rather than as the application of economic science to legal problems and issues.[133] This approach dominated the path of globalization and formed the foundation of mainstream Law and Economics.[134] It also proved politically potent for the past several decades.

Under this view, law need do little more than enforce contracts and establish clear property rights.[135] Only a demonstration of strong proof of market failure in presumptively efficient markets justifies government intervention.[136] Yet despite its influence, the neoclassical paradigm is a macroeconomic dead end. Market fundamentalism suffers from serious flaws.

One fundamental flaw stems from the nature of so-called market failures. Conceptually, all markets fail at multiple levels. Market theory demonstrates that markets are excellent constructs for moving social wealth to its highest and best use. That theory, however, is limited by its underlying assumptions, including the assumption of perfect information and zero transaction costs.[137] Markets never operate in accordance with these assumptions. Specifically, as the economist Joseph Stiglitz states, "[W]henever there is imperfect information or markets (that is always), there are in principle interventions by the government—even a government that suffers from the same imperfections of information—which can increase the markets' efficiency."[138] This hardly means that all markets should be abandoned or regulated by the government. Regulation may or may not generate net benefits. Rather than presume that markets do or do not require enhanced regulation, policymakers should approach the issue of regulation with a clean slate. "Free market ideology should be replaced with analyses based upon economic science, with a more balanced view of both market and government failures."[139] History and other social science may shed further light on appropriate government action in support of market economies and growth. Laissez-faire economics holds unwarranted faith in the power of markets.

There are other problems with neoclassical Law and Economics. For example, a well-functioning market economy should create some level of inequality as a natural result of the operation of market incentives and disincentives. Some individuals may value leisure more than additional income or wealth accumulation. Others may enjoy natural skill advantages or entrepreneurial instincts. Markets may not value the full spectrum of human talents. On the other hand, economic inequality may arise from economic oppression. Jim Crow laws in the American South definitely created economic inequality. Persistent discrimination thereafter certainly prevented the full actualization of human potential within the American economy. Law and Economics ignores issues of privilege and disempowerment.

The neoclassical paradigm also ignores growth. It ignores consumption maintenance. It ignores human capital development. It ignores the incentives facing elites to shift expenditures from investment to subverting the rule of law to entrench their relative position. It ignores the need to search for appropriate regulatory and legal infrastructure. In short, it ignores every key element of dynamic macroeconomic growth.

For example, the primary Law and Economics text on the eve of the crisis, *The Economic Analysis of Law*, by Judge Richard Posner, simply assumed that market efficiency will also maximize economic growth regardless of distributional considerations. The text failed to address the necessity of regulation in the financial sector and instead simply suggested that all regulation is inefficient.[140] Earlier editions termed employment, inflation, and output "mysterious macroeconomic phenomena."[141] Posner opined that legislation and regulation should be presumed economically inefficient.[142] He incorrectly stated that economists "widely accepted" that the securities laws do not help investors, claiming that "securities regulation may be a waste of time."[143] Even those texts taking a broader approach to Law and Economics fail to substantively address distributional considerations and fail to address the law's role in securing institutions necessary for economic growth.[144] Law and Economics as taught in law schools across the U.S. holds that market efficiency constitutes the primary focus of law insofar as economics is concerned, and this essentially operates as a throwback to laissez-faire.

Very recently, Judge Posner, to his credit, modified many of his views. Rather than dismiss macroeconomics as "mysterious," he now recognizes that law and regulation centrally influence macroeconomic performance. Judge Posner identifies the "withering" of financial regulation as an underlying cause of the subprime debacle and what he terms the descent into depression. He now recognizes that an "intelligent" government must keep the economy "from running off the rails." To be fair, Judge Posner by his own admission is not a macroeconomist. Moreover, high-profile macroeconomists such as the Nobel laureate Robert Lucas thought that modern monetary policy had slain severe economic downturns. Therefore, perhaps the conventional Law and Economics movement could be forgiven for its sanguine attitude toward risky deregulation and its agnosticism toward distributional issues.[145] Still, a revolution must occur in Law and Economics so that legal policymakers can exert sway over the evolution of the legal system with the full perspective of economics and growth—and Judge Posner's most recent edition of the *Economic Analysis of Law* (2011) fails to significantly change course from his prior volumes notwithstanding the financial crisis of 2007–9.[146]

Generations of legal minds and policymakers have been inculcated in this dogma. Law and Economics served to imbue lawyers with misguided ideology parading as sound economic policy. Posner's epiphany may prove important even if belated. As the author of a key Law and Economics text, he can uniquely influence future lawyers to think more deeply about the relationship between law and macroeconomics. Posner's new-found skepticism regarding the hazards of laissez-faire law and regulation, although clearly a positive step, will prove too little, too late when the next crisis driven by elite overreaching and subversion of law strikes.[147]

Even under its own terms, the neoclassical paradigm fails to secure the foundation for growth. The paradigm relies upon markets to move resources to their highest and best use. Consequently, a key assumption is the free movement of resources, with a minimum of transaction costs. Indeed, the entire Law and Economics edifice is founded on the concept of perfect competition, as only that model ensures that resources are allocated efficiently. That model demonstrates the theoretical power of markets to allocate resources so long as perfect information (i.e., all facts, past, present, and future) is available to all actors, all resources are perfectly mobile, products are homogenous, and each actor cannot influence prices. If this model of perfect competition holds throughout an economy, then general equilibrium is achieved and the economy achieves efficiency in the allocation of resources—meaning no reallocation of resources may occur that would enhance utility or wealth.[148]

Economists have long recognized that this theoretical construct never holds in any real markets. Moreover, the model neither addresses nor even includes any allowance for technological progress. It is a static model.[149] The model can accommodate even the most oppressive distribution of resources and fails to address the capabilities of a population to achieve economic excellence.[150] In short, it ignores the three elements identified previously as critical to empowering citizens to achieve maximum economic productivity: human capital development, market development, and legal and regulatory infrastructure. The market mechanism enjoys both theoretical and empirical proof that it may ideally allocate resources assuming some preexisting distribution of wealth—but that does not maximize growth. Law schools should teach market theory as market theory, not as a general theory of Law and Economics, and certainly not as a growth theory.

Rethinking Perfect Competition

The market mechanism does not operate to address maximum productivity of human resources, precisely because of its agnosticism regarding distributional issues. An efficient market can leave vast swaths of humanity impoverished and disempowered. Capital will not flow to impoverished humans no matter their potential. In order to construct a capitalism that secures maximum human productivity, a different set of assumptions must take hold, different from those that secure market operation. The concept of maximum human productivity requires optimal incentives and disincentives under law, and opportunities allocated in accordance with economic merit. Finally, the macroeconomy in general must support maximum economic opportunity. Idealized markets fail to attend to these basic needs for maximum economic opportunity.

The idealized conditions for maximum growth instead require the total elimination of competitive privilege and competitive disempowerment. Each and every element of economic privilege leads, axiomatically, to an element of disempowerment suffered by some victim of the unfair privilege—a victim deprived of the ability to compete on the basis of merit. Privilege also breeds arrogance and hubris within the recipient, which invariably undermines effort to compete. Economic disempowerment leads to hopelessness and discouragement, which similarly undermines efforts to compete. Privilege as well as disempowerment corrodes human productivity, and the perfect elimination of both privilege and disempowerment essentially forms the foundation of a vision of perfect competition that maximizes productivity and thus macroeconomic growth.

The elimination of privilege necessarily means that elites lack power to subvert law and regulation—that they are essentially rule takers as opposed to rule makers. If law can evolve free of elite subversion, then the law ought to impose ever more refined economic institutions to secure growth. In the absence of elite ability to subvert law and regulation, legal frameworks should inspire maximum confidence among elites as well as non-elites in such a way as to maximize incentives to invest. Therefore, if all economic actors face the law as equals, with no ability to prospectively or retroactively change law in their favor, or to undermine accountability, then all actors can achieve maximum productivity in a legal environment as conducive to growth as possible.

The current vision of perfect competition holds that resources must enjoy perfect mobility—that is, that there are zero transaction costs. But suppose transaction costs yield more in economic benefits than the cost. For example, given the power of the federal securities laws to enhance investor confidence and encourage more diligent management, the lower cost of capital and higher returns to capital associated with the federal securities laws apparently yield much higher benefits than the costs imposed. The maximization of human productivity assumes government support of the macroeconomy, and that means that all cost-justified government interventions occur and that all non–cost-justified interventions do not occur. In other words, government action must yield a present value that exceeds the present value of all associated costs. Thus, a mandate of rational transaction costs displaces the traditional requirement of zero transaction costs.

This new vision of perfect competition (zero privilege, zero disempowerment, all actors are rule takers, and rational transaction costs) should operate to create the best possible incentives and disincentives for unleashing human economic potential. Like traditional notions of perfect competition, as used to illustrate the power of markets, this theoretical construct may be unattainable. The new vision of perfect competition nevertheless supplements that traditional model of perfect competition by highlighting the benefits of truly subjecting all within society to competitive pressure and opportunity. This places human excellence rather than mere markets at the center of the model. As such, the construct furnishes aspirational insights into creating a more powerful macroeconomy under law. The key concept revolves around maximizing the productivity of all citizens.

Other scholars articulate similar approaches in related contexts. The philosopher John Rawls promulgated a theory of justice which holds that all inequalities should operate to the benefit of the most disadvantaged but that otherwise deep equality of opportunity is the signal of a just society.[151] The Nobel Prize–winning economist Amartya Sen posits that economic freedom requires economic capabilities and that development of such capabilities (such as health care and education) plays a crucial role generally in economic development.[152] While the articulation of a new version of perfect competition here is rooted in macroeconomics (with a view toward legal policy), it is noteworthy that this view of a human-centered capitalism focused on the broadest possible economic empowerment is fully consonant with social justice and economic freedom.

The neoclassical paradigm has now been proven to be macroeconomically bankrupt. The issue becomes articulating a framework that may displace laissez-faire economics. Microeconomic analysis of law remains critically important to those involved in legal policymaking, including practicing lawyers. I simply posit a long-overdue expansion of Law and Economics, with a new emphasis on the role of law to secure macroeconomic performance. My analysis pivots upon macroeconomic growth and stability as well as deep suspicion of too much economic power concentrated in too few hands.

I argue that legal infrastructure arises from certain fundamental principles of economics and law. Legal infrastructure consists of those laws, regulations, and institutions that spur economic growth, stabilize an otherwise unstable capitalist system, curb dangerous concentrations of economic power, and unleash maximum human potential to support economic growth.

Viewed in this manner, legal infrastructure is no different from other types of infrastructure. Legal infrastructure should operate to raise the return to capital or lower the cost of capital.

The Subprime Crisis

All of these failings in mainstream economic thinking came together to create an economic tsunami in 2007–9 (and beyond) that revealed in vivid detail the flaws in the neoclassical paradigm. Elites freed themselves from basic economic regulation, particularly financial regulation. The corruption reached depths that at one point in our history would have been unthinkable: The law provided insulation to securities fraudfeasors instead of legal penalties; the law operated to insulate directors from any duty of care; policymakers eliminated basic consumer protection at the behest of lobbyists representing the most powerful interests in society; historically oppressed groups were laid disempowered at the economy's fringes, begetting a vicious episode of economic exploitation that proved costly economically as well as morally; globalization spawned massive debt for elite profit; and taxpayers faced an extortion of epic proportions under the guise of the doctrine of "too big to fail." These distortions created tremendous economic costs that remain incalculable even years after the start of the crisis. Indeed, the crisis spawned even more massive misallocations of resources than existed before the crisis commenced. A perverse socialism for the rich and powerful seized the commanding heights of the American economy.

We live in an economic Dark Ages relative to our potential, and law provides the key meta-ideas to facilitate our transition out of this morass. The world teems with unexploited human potential and unharnessed ideas. The fact that 2.6 billion (almost one-half) of the world's population subsists on less than two dollars per day proves this central point.[153] Such a reality leaves too much potential brilliance untapped, too many ideas locked into poverty. Moreover, it understates the issue to focus only on deep poverty; in the U.S., there are private high schools that expend almost $65,000 per pupil, compared with an average expenditure of about $9,000 at public high schools.[154] If economic logic supports educating the children of the wealthy so exorbitantly, it also supports similar efforts to educate the children of the disempowered. No such effort exists in the U.S., where educational attainment has stagnated (at best) from 1980 to the present.[155] Even in developed economies, human potential languishes at the margins of the economy. The problem with such a deep chasm in human capital formation is that it encourages predation—as social distance increases, power disparities lead to precisely the type of exploitation that fueled the subprime mortgage debacle. These realities remain undisturbed today.

The subprime mortgage crisis illustrates the problems associated with too much inequality. All three legal and institutional props to maximum economic growth eroded significantly in the years and decades leading up to the financial meltdown. In financial regulation, corporate governance, globalization, and human capital policies, the seeds for the crisis lay in subverted legal and regulatory infrastructure. At each turn, the fingerprints of the elites' overreaching can be found. The next few chapters will explore the subversion of law in detail, with a specific purpose of spotlighting excessive elite power—where elites untethered themselves from sensible accountability or social responsibility at great loss to the global economy and much economic pain in the U.S. Ultimately, this book is a legal case study in the macroeconomic consequences of unbridled inequality and concomitant elite overreaching, with a specific focus on the optimal legal means of controlling such overreaching. In short, it chronicles the erosion of legal and regulatory infrastructure and stunted human capital formation that economic theorists predict under conditions of high inequality, culminating in a historic crisis of capitalism that will persist until inequality retreats into historic balance or otherwise submits to law.

2

The Corrupted Corporation

[W]hat went wrong in corporate America . . . was a pathological
mutation in capitalism—from traditional owners' capitalism, where
the rewards of investing went primarily to those who put up the
capital and took the risks—to a new and virulent managers' capitalism, where an excessive share of the rewards of capital investment
went to corporate managers and financial intermediaries.
John C. Bogle (2006)[1]

Legal infrastructure created the corporation, and it qualifies as one of the
most economically powerful legal innovations in history. Yet governance
issues plague the modern publicly held corporation, and sophisticated investors like John Bogle (founder of one of the largest mutual fund families—the
Vanguard family of mutual funds) see the dementia.[2] Increasingly, corporations exist to serve the interests of managers instead of shareholders. One
study found, for example, that between 1993 and 2003 the compensation paid
to senior executives doubled as a percentage of profits.[3] The publicly held
corporation in America today fails to operate in accordance with its economic policy basis. In the course of the subprime debacle, firm managers
took in billions in compensation payments based upon illusory profits generated through excessive risk while their firms crashed.[4] This reality imposes
massive costs upon society, and the subprime debacle constitutes the latest and greatest multi-trillion-dollar catastrophe attributed to deeply suboptimal corporate governance. This time CEOs manipulated risk for more

compensation—and taxpayers picked up the tab when the excessive risks blew up the financial sector.

Powerful corporate elites (concentrated in number with access to concentrated resources) corrupted the legal infrastructure underlying the public corporation beginning in the mid-1980s and transformed its strengths into liabilities that turned the corporation upside down; public corporations in the U.S. now operate to enrich CEOs and other senior managers at the expense of society and shareholders.[5] This model of CEO primacy costs untold trillions and leads to serial financial disruptions.[6] The failure of law to secure the underlying policy basis of the corporation created perverse incentives at the apex of the American financial system.[7] Numerous economists identify corporate governance law as a key cause of the subprime debacle.[8]

Thus, Paul Krugman argued, "the subprime crisis and the credit crunch are, in an important sense, the result of our failure to effectively reform corporate governance after the last set of scandals."[9] Joseph Stiglitz asserted that CEOs run corporations as their "personal feifdom, not for the shareholders, but for their own benefit."[10] CEOs manipulated risk to generate high profits for a short time, leading to high bonuses; when the risk came to fruition, the firms plunged into insolvency, leading to golden parachute payments.[11] Either way, senior executives made large sums of money.

Financial firms often funded their operations with as much as $60 of debt for every dollar of equity.[12] Much of the debt flowed from massive overnight borrowing, exacerbating the riskiness of this leverage. The firms used these funds to invest in opaque derivatives instruments. For example, on the eve of its insolvency, Lehman Brothers held 900,000 derivatives contracts, rendering an accurate risk assessment of the firm impossible. When credit conditions inevitably tightened, creditors shut down the supply of debt to Lehman, forcing it into bankruptcy in September 2008. Senior corporate managers sabotaged the entire financial sector with risky investments founded on risky debt. As stated by the Financial Crisis Commission, created by Congress to investigate the causes of the crises, "dramatic failures of corporate governance and risk management" drove the crisis.[13]

This chapter first reviews the potential of the corporation to fuel growth. Next, it demonstrates the role of corporate governance in fomenting the subprime crisis. It then spotlights the parade of legal indulgences leading to CEO primacy, and the displacement of shareholder primacy, with a focus on the political power of CEOs to subvert longstanding principles of accountability. The chapter concludes with a review of the most promising proposals for reform.

The Promise of the Modern Public Corporation

Corporations function to facilitate the flow of passive capital to productive investment and entrepreneurial uses. Small pockets of capital that otherwise would require expensive intermediation through financial institutions may instead directly fund economic growth through the purchase of shares of stock issued by publicly traded firms. Facilitating this flow of capital fuels investment, entrepreneurship, and innovation.[14] If public share markets are well developed, then investors can enjoy the benefits of risk diversification, which further lowers the cost of capital.[15] Nations with more developed financial markets naturally enjoy more growth in capital-intensive industries.[16] Today, a broad economic consensus holds that well-developed capital markets with widely dispersed share ownership consistently appear in successful modern economies and enjoy a close association with superior economic growth.[17] The modern public corporation appears essential to macroeconomic growth because it holds the promise of lowering the cost of capital.

Five key legal elements undergird this function. First, limited liability protects passive investors from any liability for corporate obligations, shielding them from unnecessary risks. Second, shareholder claims on the corporation, including its assets, are transferred to freely trading shares, meaning that the firm need not concern itself with the possibility that its owners (or their creditors) could disrupt operations by calling back capital.[18] Third, centralized management means that shareholders are legally stripped of all control over the firm (save electing directors) and cannot bind the corporation improvidently; instead, managers control the firm through their expert business judgment.[19] Fourth, shareholder primacy (which at least rhetorically means that the corporation should be operated with the primary goal of expanding shareholder wealth) gives shareholders confidence that they will benefit from the fruits of their investment.[20] Fifth, perpetual existence gives the corporation a very long investment horizon, making it the ideal means of holding long-lived assets.[21] Each of these elements gives the corporation a capital-raising advantage, by eliminating risks or creating potential economic benefits. Shareholder primacy lies at the core of the corporation because the point is to attract capital at a lower cost, and any move away from shareholder primacy likely would defeat this purpose. All of this allows the corporation to operate as the perfect capital aggregator under law.[22]

None of these elements imposes costs upon society because shareholders do not have power over the firm, and the duty to manage the firm rests with a board of directors that, at least theoretically, owes a duty of care to the corporation. If a shareholder cannot control a corporation—which the law mandates—then there is no basis for holding the shareholder liable for any torts committed by the corporation. With respect to contracts, limited liability functions as a default rule only. Perpetual existence encourages investment in long-lived assets and does not impose any cost. Free transferability of shares extends stability to the capital base of the corporation. Against these nonexistent costs, the macroeconomic benefits of corporations are compelling. "[T]oday limited liability has become a nearly universal feature of the corporate form. This evolution indicates strongly the value of limited liability as a contracting tool and financing device."[23]

Despite its benefits, the corporation bears more than its fair share of allegations of mischief, and even worse. Professor Lawrence Mitchell argues persuasively that corporations focus too much on short-term considerations. He terms the modern corporation "the perfect externalizing machine."[24] Short-term outlook flows from CEO primacy, not the essential characteristics of the corporate form; to the contrary, the corporation's perpetual existence renders it the perfect business form for holding long-lived assets, which boosts economic growth relative to the costs implicit in less extended investment horizons.

Every business and every individual will rationally seek to externalize costs. The corporate structure includes nothing sinister that operates to encourage externalization of costs relative to any other limited liability business form. Indeed, if directors manage the business of the corporation subject to a vigorous duty of care, then the prospect of their personal liability rebalances any incentive toward excessive risk arising from limited liability. Large-scale businesses may seek to externalize more costs than small-scale businesses if the distance between the individual actor and the victim of externalization expands in proportion to scale. If so, the problem is large-scale enterprises, not the corporation itself.[25]

Excessive short-term focus as well as excessive externalization should be controlled through legal infrastructure. A robust duty of care can operate to diminish these problems. Corporate governance should try to align the corporation's perpetual investment horizon with the interests of its managers, and the general legal system should strive to strip out the profitability of inappropriate externalization by all economic actors whether acting through a corporation or any other business form. Corporations will naturally seek to maximize profits through adherence to community norms. Therefore, broad disclosure obligations reduce the temptation to externalize costs.[26] In fact, corporations existed for centuries prior to the subprime debacle but previously inflicted no similar economic catastrophe on any society, aside from flawed governance law and regulation.

The corporation stands as a powerful example of legal infrastructure. The legal innovations associated with the corporation lower the cost of capital throughout the economy. These innovations create an institution every modern capitalistic society needs: an entity that can soak up the passive savings generated by individuals with neither the interest in managing nor the expertise to manage a business venture. The creation of a centrally managed firm with the ability to hold long-lived assets proves critical to macroeconomic performance. Virtually every successful economy relies upon these innovations to mobilize passive capital and fund innovation and entrepreneurship. Extending limited liability to passive investors and assuring them that the entity will focus upon their enrichment serve to eliminate risks to investors and lower the cost of capital. If the corporation did not exist, it would need to be invented.

Lowering the cost of capital empowers entrepreneurs and spurs innovation. As such, the corporation functions as what the economist Paul Romer terms a meta-idea—an idea that serves as a platform for the economic actualization of other ideas.[27] This explains why commentators term the corporation the "greatest single discovery in modern times."[28] Other commentators go further. They state that the corporation is the "most important organization in the world" and "the best hope for the future of the rest of the world."[29] The power of the corporation to facilitate investment, innovation, and entrepreneurship boosts macroeconomic growth. In an ideal world, the corporation would operate as a capital aggregator for the best, most economically powerful ideas. The corporation would do this without regard to race, gender, or class. A powerful capital aggregator would meet powerful ideas. This vision challenges the law to optimize the corporation. Getting governance right would be a step in the right direction. The problem with the corporation lies not with its essential elements but with deeply suboptimal corporate governance law.[30]

The Costs of CEO Primacy

Without appropriate mechanisms to contain agency costs at either the federal or state level, corporations degenerate into weapons of mass economic destruction. Agency costs arise inherently from any agency relationship wherein one person commits to act on behalf of another. Such costs can arise from theft, shirking, dishonesty, negligence, or miscommunication. "[I]t is generally impossible for the principal or the agent at zero cost to ensure that the agent will make optimal decisions from the principal's viewpoint."[31] The problem of agency costs plagues the corporation, which separates ownership and control. Shareholders capitalize the corporation only with the expectation that its operations aim at maximizing shareholder wealth. Controlling agency costs is the key to the economic basis of the public corporation. If CEOs deploy shareholder wealth only to enrich management, then the cost of capital will soar rather than decline and society will suffer massive misallocations of capital. The policy basis for the corporation vanishes.[32] Moreover, if CEO primacy exists as a matter of law—or systemically—then shareholders will lack power to impose market discipline through investment allocation to other firms or to diversify away the risk of excessive agency costs.

Corporate governance deficiencies erupted dramatically in 2001–2, when a series of giant firms, including Enron, vaporized overnight with little warning to shareholders, and despite the mandatory-disclosure regime imposed under the federal securities laws. Although Congress responded to this debacle with the Sarbanes-Oxley Act of 2002,[33] that Act did nothing to disrupt CEO primacy.[34] As the former Harvard Business School Professor D. Quinn Mills stated in 2003, "CEOs have found a way to enormously increase their own wealth by a variety of means in a period in which shareholders have been losing their shirts."[35] Audit experts found that "highly placed executives used their power . . . to achieve financial targets fraudulently, boost the stock price, and further enrich themselves via compensation schemes that rewarded those achievements."[36] The loss of investor confidence associated with these corporate governance failures devastated shareholder wealth.

Even after these huge losses, CEO primacy persisted and reared its ugly head again in the context of the options-backdating scandals of 2003–6. Here, executives simply backdated their options grants to reflect dates in the past when their company's shares traded at low prices, in order to turn "incentive" compensation into a rigged game. Former SEC Chair Arthur Levitt stated: "It is stealing, in effect. It is ripping off shareholders in an unconscionable way."[37] Such misconduct upsets the investment-backed expectations of shareholders and is not a zero sum game. In fact, financial economists found that backdated options at forty-eight sampled companies resulted in approximately $500,000 in extra compensation for executives while costing shareholders at each company $389 million in market capitalization.[38] Thus, even before the financial crisis of 2007–9, the system of corporate governance applicable to publicly traded corporations in the U.S. suffered from manifest flaws.

Economists assessed the costs of weak corporate governance before the crisis of 2007–9. In 2003, one study found that weak corporate governance diminished long-term firm valuations and that the economic benefits of creating superior corporate governance law and regulation would be "enormous."[39] Another study found that mechanisms that entrench managers—such as poison pill provisions, staggered boards, limits on share-holder bylaw amendments, and golden parachute arrangements—contributed powerfully to diminished returns.[40] Strengthening investor protection laws would lead to more dispersed ownership because of incentives to diversify. Lower investor protection encourages concentrated ownership, as investors forgo diversification benefits to control agency costs. Superior investor protection regimes support a lower cost of capital, including the benefits of more dispersed ownership. Ownership of equity securities seems far too concentrated worldwide, suggesting that investors forgo the benefits of diversification in favor of the power to control agency costs.[41] Investors provide more capital at a lower cost if they face lower risk of loss from agency costs and may enjoy the benefits of diversification. That fundamental insight enjoys broad if not unanimous empirical support.[42]

The subprime mortgage crisis demonstrates the losses that CEO primacy can inflict upon society under financial stress. The U.S. system of corporate governance did not perform well as the real estate bubble emerged and then burst. The global financial meltdown showed that "checks and balances at each level of the corporate hierarchy broke down."[43] Strong evidence demonstrates that CEOs at such firms knowingly exposed their firms to very high risk of failure even while collecting hundreds of millions of dollars in compensation. Agency costs spun out of control within the key public firms at the center of the crisis during 2007–9. The entire global economy absorbed huge losses, but the CEOs at these firms enjoyed huge windfall paydays.[44]

For example, the nation's largest mortgage lender, Countrywide Financial, entered into the largest predatory lending settlement in history in 2008, agreeing to over $8 billion in loan modifications to resolve lawsuits brought by eleven states. The states alleged that Countrywide misled borrowers regarding fees, costs, and risky loan features. Former employees corroborated many of the allegations, including the fact that Countrywide steered borrowers into subprime loans even though they qualified for prime loans. The firm's CEO, Angelo Mozilo, earned total compensation (much from the exercise of stock options) of $102 million in 2006 and $229 million in 2007. This includes $127 million that Mozilo took in from the exercise of options in 2007, the same year that Countrywide announced massive mortgage losses. Shareholders lost 80 percent of their share value before Bank of America acquired the firm. Ultimately, Bank of America recognized $33 billion in loan losses arising from its acquisition of Countrywide.[45] The Financial Crisis Inquiry Commission (FCIC), a congressionally authorized commission charged with investigating the financial crisis, found that as early as 2006

Mozilo termed Countrywide's subprime loans "poison" and "toxic," and likely to lead to bankruptcy.[46]

The nation's largest bank, Citigroup, also lost billions in subprime lending. Citigroup's CEO infamously stated in 2007 that if liquidity dried up, "things will be complicated" but that "as long as the music is playing you have to get up and dance."[47] Citigroup actually worked to keep the music playing; when demand for its subprime loan packages declined, Citigroup started to provide investors with so-called liquidity puts that allowed purchasers to put subprime mortgages back onto Citigroup's balance sheet in the event of a market breakdown. In late 2007, Citigroup disclosed for the first time that its subprime mortgage exposure amounted to $55 billion after the market breakdown for subprime loans. The Chair of Citigroup's Executive Commit-tee, former U.S. Treasury Secretary Robert Rubin, claimed he knew nothing about the risks of the liquidity puts. Ultimately, the U.S. taxpayer paid bil-lions to bail out Citigroup. CEO Charles Prince, on the other hand, earned more than $66 million in the three years prior to his resignation in 2007, as well as $40 million in severance benefits.[48] The FCIC found that when a veteran banker repeatedly warned Citigroup's top managers and Rubin that the bank faced billions in mortgage losses, the banker suffered a pay cut and demotion.[49]

The world's largest insurer, AIG, lost more than any other firm—ever. On March 2, 2009, AIG announced the largest loss in corporate history, totaling $61.7 billion. According to Fed Chair Bernanke, AIG "made huge numbers of irresponsible bets."[50] AIG guaranteed the payment of billions in subprime mortgage products through a financial instrument known as credit default swaps (CDS). Credit default swaps did not trigger any regulatory require-ment that the issuer create reserves against the risk of payment—as is the case with any regulated insurance product. Therefore the fees paid to AIG in exchange for credit default swaps generated unencumbered income that in turn generated huge bonus payments for executives. AIG issued $440 billion in credit default swaps, more than double its total market value. Shareholders and the U.S. taxpayer paid for this gambling. The price of AIG fell from $70 per share in 2007 to as low as $2 per share.[51] The CEO's severance package upon resignation provided a $47 million exit payment. The senior manager overseeing the credit default swaps at AIG pocketed $300 million between 1987 and 2008. AIG told investors that the risks from the CDS transactions approached "zero" even after AIG paid more than $2 billion to counterpar-ties. AIG's accounting firm warned senior management of a material internal control weakness because the firm did not track its exposure to the credit default swaps. Management did not respond.[52]

The basic pattern transcends the details of each company. CEOs and senior managers rang up short-term profits at the cost of undisclosed and excessive risks. Shareholders lost vast wealth. Global financial markets crashed and taxpayers bailed out CEOs and other managers (as well as unsecured creditors). The regulators across the financial system—banking, insurance, mortgage lending—failed to use their powers to stem the recklessness. Merrill Lynch (the largest securities firm) and Washington Mutual (the largest savings and loan or thrift) evince the same basic pattern of vast losses for all but senior managers.[53] In fact, the *New York Times* commissioned a study of compensation at the seven firms at the epicenter of the crisis (all of the above-mentioned as well as Bear Stearns and Lehman Brothers). Their findings echo the above.

"Executives at seven major financial institutions that have collapsed, were sold at distressed prices or are in deep to the taxpayer received $464 million in performance pay since 2005."[54] Yet, these same firms lost $107 billion and shed $740 billion in shareholder value between 2007 and 2009.[55] The CEOs of these firms received compensation for profits that quickly transmogrified into cascading losses. Nevertheless, the executives faced little or no prospect of liability and owed no obligation to repay their "performance pay" when the profits turned to losses that sunk their firms.[56] The deputy director of the Council of Institutional Investors, Amy Borrus, stated, "Poorly structured pay packages encouraged the get-rich-quick mentality and overly risky behavior that helped bring financial markets to their knees and wiped out profits at so many companies . . . yet many of these C.E.O.'s have pocketed enormous compensation."[57] CEOs and other managers enjoyed sufficient autonomy to inflict massive agency costs upon shareholders, trigger a global financial crisis, and still achieve huge pay for themselves. As one bank CEO, Jamie Dimon, candidly stated, "In mortgage underwriting, somehow we just missed, you know, that home prices don't go up forever and that it's not sufficient to have stated income."[58] According to Dimon, the entire fiasco arose from reckless management: "I blame the management teams 100% and . . . no one else."[59]

Scholars studied the degree of loss senior executives suffered as a result of lost share value. Most executives do in fact hold significant shares in their own company. The study of compensation for the top five senior executives at Bear Stearns and Lehman Brothers found that while the executives made billions from the sale of stock (as well as in salary) from 2000 to 2008, shareholders faced massive losses. The managers pocketed large amounts of incentive compensation, both from bonuses and stock sales, during the years immediately preceding the failure of the firms. "As a result, the bottom line payoffs for these executives during 2000–2008 were not negative but rather decidedly positive."[60] Far from suffering financial devastation, management of the firms during 2000–8 made huge profits from their risky stewardship, even while shareholders were ultimately wiped out, or nearly wiped out.

The March to CEO Primacy

The only free lunch available to investors is the pursuit of a diversified portfolio that lowers risk and raises returns. This fact naturally fragments ownership. Diffused ownership also fragments incentives to monitor managers—as smaller investors face free-rider temptations. Scholars recognized decades ago that fragmented share ownership would operate to increase agency costs and expand managerial slack.[61] The exploitation of diffused ownership loomed ominously over the corporation. Simply put, without appropriate governance controls the corporation's power to attract capital represented an economic danger.

For decades, corporate law scholars debated corporate federalism as a source of legal laxity.[62] Some argued that Delaware was leading a race to the bottom by exchanging subpar corporate governance for enhanced tax revenues from corporate franchise tax payments and that federal law should disrupt this dynamic.[63] Others argued that Delaware law must be optimal as capital market pressure would lead a race to the top.[64] In fact, corporate elites acted to subvert both state and federal law for at least the past twenty-five years.[65] Blaming state law for the problems of corporate governance ignores federal laws that operated to insulate corporate management.[66] In lieu of a focus on state law versus federal law, scholars must focus on a theory of corporate governance law that accounts for elite subversion of both federal and state notions of accountability.

Politically, corporate CEOs and other senior managers benefit from their concentrated number and their high stakes, in terms of political organizing, lobbying, and campaigning. Mancur Olson's focus on free-rider problems inherent in the pursuit of any collective political action would predict a highly pro-CEO outcome in corporate governance law and regulation, given the concentrated number of CEOs and the barriers to organization that diffused shareholders face. "In the now standard view of politics . . . small groups with high stakes arise independently, motivated by common interests[,] and are able to solve the 'free rider' problem of collective action on account of their small size."[67] More recent work suggests that Congress seeks out such actors to exploit their concentrated numbers and high stakes to political advantage.[68] Economists predict that growing inequality would lead naturally to a legal system that favors the rich and powerful.[69] The highly pro-CEO law of corporate governance fits these theories of special interest power better than any race-to-the-top or race-to-the-bottom thesis. CEOs enjoy economic and political resources superior to those available to the investing public.[70] Economists recently created testable models showing how such interests outweigh interests with a stake in more optimal corporate governance standards.[71] That reality manifests itself across corporate governance law and regulation.

Joel Seligman warned in 1990 that legal constraints upon CEOs and other corporate managers evinced excessive laxity. He stated, "The most distinctive aspect of the last decade in corporate law was the celerity with which traditional constraints on corporate managers weakened."[72] Dean Seligman's analysis turns on three facts. First, the restriction on shareholder suffrage rights arising from an SEC rule change permitting dual class voting for listed shares threatened to allow management to dilute shareholder voting power. Second, limitations on shareholder derivative litigation diluted managerial accountability in court for breach of fiduciary duty. Third, the decline of hostile takeovers as a result of constitutionally permissible antitakeover statutes removed a major threat to management's control. Each of these mechanisms for managerial entrenchment developed over a relatively short period of time before 1990.[73] Since 1990, further laxity has emerged.

Federal Law Failures to Control Agency Costs

Prior to the Great Depression, corporate governance law and regulation operated free of federal intervention and provided scanty shareholder protection. For example, public corporations owed no continuing obligation to disclose anything to their shareholders absent an affirmative request that could be defeated in litigation. This system allowed agency costs to fester and ultimately proved unstable. Federal law intervened to remedy the most egregious shortcomings.[74] As part of the New Deal, Congress enacted the Securities Act of 1933[75] and the Securities Exchange Act of 1934,[76] on the basic premise of the power of disclosure.[77] "Sunlight is said to be the best of disinfectants; electric light the most efficient policeman."[78] These federal laws required for the first time that public firms periodically disclose all material facts as well as audited financial statements to their shareholders.[79] Unfortunately, Congress betrayed these basic and time-tested laws in the 1990s.

The Acts extended robust remedies to deceived investors over preexisting state law. Indeed, for several decades after the enactment of the securities laws the courts broadly interpreted remedies available under the federal securities laws to vindicate their "broad remedial purposes."[80] Private rights of action created privatized enforcement incentives that did not depend upon government funding and that operated free of political clout. It also inspired investor confidence by putting money in the pockets of victims. Robust remedies meant that investors would more freely invest, and therefore granting such recovery rights lowered the cost of capital.[81] Substantial empirical evidence lends support to the extension of private rights of action in favor of investors in public firms.[82] Moreover, managers required to disclose material facts regarding the firm's operations attend to shareholder wealth maximization more than if they are not subject to disclosure, which improves financial performance.[83] Thus, the courts' broad interpretation of private rights of action rested on a strong economic and historic foundation.[84] For at least six decades the combination of broad disclosure obligations and broad private remedies worked, in that corporate governance functioned appropriately to channel capital and spur macroeconomic growth with no major financial disruptions.

The death of private securities litigation followed shortly thereafter. In 1995, Congress enacted the Private Securities Litigation Reform Act (PSLRA)[85] in response to a flurry of campaign contributions and lobbying efforts from business interests.[86] Corporate interests backed the PSLRA with $30 million in corporate lobbying efforts. Indeed, *Money* magazine named the PSLRA as the top example of the pernicious influence of moneyed interests upon sound policy in 1996.[87] Another commentator asserted that money fueled the effort to enact the "draconian" PSLRA, especially money from the accounting industry.[88]

The PSLRA requires, among other things, that plaintiffs prove defendants' fraudulent state of mind (or at least allege facts giving rise to a strong inference of fraud) at the initial pleading stage without the benefit of any discovery mechanisms.[89] Because of the difficulty of finding evidence regarding state of mind (i.e., intent to defraud) without the benefit of discovery, federal law long permitted state of mind to be averred generally at the pleading stage, leaving to the jury the final determination on fraudulent state of mind.[90] The PSLRA materially changed the prospect of proving securities fraud and arbitrarily rendered many viable claims impossible to prove.[91] This provision lacks any policy foundation.

In addition, the PSLRA includes an explicit safe harbor for fraud. A fraudulent "forward looking statement" will not support liability for securities fraud if it is accompanied by "meaningful cautionary statements."[92] The exemption from liability for fraud includes issuers of publicly traded securities, underwriters, and others reviewing materials supplied by issuers such as accountants. It is the first time that actual securities fraudfeasors benefit from any type of safe harbor. This is the reason one commentator termed this provision a "license to lie."[93] It is difficult to imagine a more reactionary revision of the New Deal than these provisions.

Yet a bipartisan coalition enjoying overwhelming support in Congress followed up in 1998 with the Securities Litigation Uniform Standards Act (SLUSA),[94] which preempted state law liability for securities fraud involving public corporations when relief is sought for shareholders generally in the form of a class action.[95] Traditionally, the federal remedies that investors enjoyed under the federal securities laws operated cumulatively with state law remedies. This meant that federal law could only strengthen the rights of investors. After SLUSA, federal law now operates to give perpetrators of securities fraud special protections not available under state law. Given that widespread securities fraud can potentially wreak havoc on the economy, this special protection for securities fraudfeasors represents an irrational departure from traditional norms of accountability. Unfortunately, the odd protections of federal law for corporate managers do not stop there.

The federal proxy rules, promulgated under the Securities Exchange Act of 1934, impose a system of corporate democracy reminiscent of "democracy" in Stalinist Russia. Under state law, shareholders elect directors. Dispersed ownership, however, typically means that a public firm must solicit shareholder authorization to vote via proxies (rather than in person at the annual shareholder meeting), and those proxy votes determine the election. Current management will solicit proxy votes routinely, and the director-candidates in practice are therefore nominated by management. Management's slate will run essentially unopposed, unless a shareholder also solicits proxy votes on behalf of shareholder nominees. This process involves much expense and generally requires legal counsel. These costs must be borne by the shareholder. Management's proxy solicitation will be funded from the corporation's coffers, meaning that shareholder wealth essentially funds both sides of a proxy contest.[96] Management's proxy solicitation could act as a vehicle for contested elections if shareholders had access to it for shareholder nominees for the board.[97] The SEC, however, has long blocked shareholder access to management's proxy solicitation for the purpose of director elections.[98]

Disrupting management's control of the proxy machinery could mitigate the negative effects of CEO primacy. Empirical evidence shows that firms which nominate directors without CEO involvement outperform other firms with CEO involvement.[99] Although the SEC frequently discusses the possibility of proxy reform, it never approves broader proxy access. Occasionally the SEC floats a proposal to reform so-called corporate democracy, but the proposal usually attracts massive lobbying efforts by corporate elites and ultimately languishes.[100] Big business simply wants to control the proxy process.[101] After the Dodd-Frank Act, the SEC sought to give some shareholders proxy access, only to suffer a defeat in the federal courts at the hands of well-heeled corporate lobby groups.[102] Consequently, corporate democracy resembles elections in the former Soviet Union—there is only one candidate on the ballot, nominated by management. Insurgencies are rare.[103]

Management's domination of the proxy process encourages homosocial reproduction and affinity bias.[104] Boards retain the last vestiges of white male supremacy because CEOs will naturally pick white males like themselves for board positions—most frequently other CEOs with a vested interest in pumping up CEO pay norms.[105] Other commentators refer to the same dynamic as affinity bias; affinity bias enjoys solid empirical support for the basic proposition that a person who shares affinity with another person (even trivial affinity) will treat that person more favorably.[106] White male CEOs will rationally exploit affinity bias and indulge in homosocial reproduction to maximize their potential payouts from board-approved compensation. Today homosocial reproduction and affinity bias dominate the corporate boardroom as white males constitute nearly 75 percent of all board positions and 95 percent of board chairs for Fortune 500 companies, and this self-perpetuating domination has actually increased since 2004.[107]

Allowing greater diversity in the boardroom as a means of combating homosocial reproduction and affinity bias enjoys sound theoretical and empirical support. Boards that are more diverse reduce CEO autonomy. In fact, mortgage lenders with more diverse boards engaged in less subprime lending and experienced lower mortgage losses than lenders with less diversity.[108] On balance, the evidence suggests that diversity among managers can disrupt affinity bias, enhance a board's monitoring functions, and lower agency costs.[109] Recently, the SEC imposed disclosure requirements regarding the role that diversity plays in board selection.[110] Nevertheless, so long as management selects management, board diversity will not increase. As of today, the SEC, Congress, and the federal courts continually decline to disrupt the control of senior management over the board selection process.

Federal law also failed to control agency costs within the banking industry—thanks to a dubious Supreme Court decision. In 1989, President George H.W. Bush signed the Financial Institution Reform, Recovery, and Enforcement Act (FIRREA).[111] The Act specifically sought to heighten accountability for errant bank managers after the savings and loan crisis. Before FIRREA, federal courts long imposed more demanding liability on bank managers under the duty of care, for simple negligence.[112] Perversely, the Supreme

Court found that FIRREA diminished accountability for federal bank managers under federal law, to gross negligence only.[113] After FIRREA, federal law operated to relieve directors of longstanding and traditional notions of accountability for negligence. At the time of the Supreme Court's decision, a government study identified director laxity as a prime cause of the crisis. The total cost of the crisis approached $1 trillion. Thus, in 1996 I predicted that excessive laxity in the standard of care owed by bank managers would lead to more costly bank crises.[114]

On very simple issues, federal law operates to entrench management. It makes no sense to allow managers to select directors. It makes no sense to eliminate traditional notions of accountability for fraud. Federal law entered the field of securities regulation in order to enhance the rights of investors and in order to restore "ancient" norms of accountability for those managing other people's money; therefore, it is senseless for federal law to betray its traditional purposes and preempt state law notions of accountability.[115] Federal law shifted during the 1990s from a source of enhanced accountability for corporate elites to a source of enhanced indulgences. These indulgences represent extreme deviations from traditional norms of accountability. Although special interest influence may be "well hidden," the fingerprints of massive lobbying expenses appear pervasively throughout the dilution of federal standards of accountability.[116] Consequently, these indulgences appear to suffer from such deep irrationality that they subvert the rule of law—they reflect elite power to evade traditional principles of accountability generally applicable to all other economic actors.

State Law Failures to Control Agency Costs

The political structure applicable to corporate governance law at the state level further erodes basic accountability within the public corporation. Corporate federalism denotes the unique power allocation between federal and state law with respect to corporate governance for publicly held corporations. Traditionally, federal law operated (primarily through the federal securities laws) to fill in manifest gaps in state law. These federal initiatives apply to all publicly traded corporations. State law provides general corporation laws and charters corporations.

The internal affairs doctrine requires that the state which incorporated the firm also supplies the substantive law governing the internal operation of the firm, including corporate governance law and standards. Most public firms incorporate in Delaware and thereby become subject to Delaware corporate governance law. Firms incorporate in Delaware because (among other reasons) it offers a well-developed body of case law and provides for a conservative legal evolution. Over the years, Delaware has also earned a reputation for responsiveness to the needs of management. For example, the Delaware Constitution provides that the Delaware General Corporation Law can be amended only by an affirmative vote of two-thirds of both of its legislative chambers. This implies a stable corporation law and empowers management interests to foreclose any radical change. This responsiveness to the needs of management is important to Delaware because it obtains 22 percent of its revenues from the franchise tax payments made by firms it charters, far more than any other state.[117]

Virtually all of Delaware's corporate law changes originate in the Governing Council of the Corporate Law Section of the state bar association. An elite group of law firms form the Governing Council of this subsection of the Delaware bar. That council consists of twenty-one lawyers who meet in secret with no record of their deliberations, primarily drawn from firms that represent the interests of management. Of the twenty-one council members, fourteen are nominated by large law firms in Wilmington, Delaware. According to one insider, the council aims to be conservative, not seeking to upset the current balance of power between managers and shareholders. The council seeks to maintain flexibility for self-ordering within corporations. Amazingly, the core values driving Delaware's corporation law include no reference at all to the control of agency costs.[118] Agency cost control rests with the federal government. Delaware's law of fiduciary duties applicable to its corporations evinces its laxity in accountability.

The directors of a corporation traditionally owed the corporation a duty of care, and the senior officers as agents of the firm owed more stringent agency duties of care. In practice, courts invoked the business judgment rule to insulate directors from expansive duty of care liability, and liability resulted only in egregious cases. A noted scholar lamented the paucity of reported cases (four) that imposed liability upon the directors of nonfinancial corporations and concluded that the movement toward "protecting corporate executives" had gone far enough "and perhaps a little farther."[119] To the extent the business judgment rule focuses on the decision-making process instead of on outcomes, the rule seems appropriate in a context that requires risk. Still, to the degree managers act untethered to any obligation to care, the business judgment rule encourages recklessness at the heart of the economy. Courts have long wrestled with the appropriate formulation of the business judgment rule, and over the years a judicial rule of deference to managers has taken root with a relatively narrow zone of liability.

This narrow zone of liability functioned effectively (along with robust securities fraud remedies) to rein in corporate elites and limit agency costs to minimally acceptable levels. No major macroeconomic disruption linked to corporate governance occurred for seven decades. Today, it is fair to say that corporate elites face zero exposure to liability for the breach of the duty of care. Instead, those occupying the commanding heights of our economy may be infinitely careless and face no monetary sanction. One study found only one confirmed case resulting in payment of monetary damages since 1980.[120] The story of the death of the duty of care in the public corporation boardroom is the story of how political power can be wielded to obtain legal indulgences not generally available to all.

The Delaware Supreme Court's 1985 decision in *Smith v. Van Gorkom* marks the starting point for the shift to CEO primacy.[121] The Delaware Supreme Court found that the director-defendants in that case breached their duty of care notwithstanding the business judgment rule by acting in a grossly negligent manner. The *Smith* decision supposedly shocked directors. The insurance industry also feigned shock, as if they had no idea directors could be found liable for breach of the duty of care, even though the insurance companies took in premium income for assuming that very risk. In any event, insurance industry interests, combined with management interests, lobbied for the end of the duty of care.[122] The Delaware legislature (or, more precisely, the representatives of the large law firms of Wilmington, as discussed above) responded with section 102(b)(7), which for the first time authorized a Delaware corporation to eliminate the duty of care for directors pursuant to a provision in the articles of incorporation.[123] Under our federal proxy system, management can easily amend the articles of incorporation; thus, this change in Delaware law meant the "evisceration of the duty of care."[124] Within two years, more than forty jurisdictions followed suit. The duty of care for the American public corporation died. In fact, no reported decision since *Smith* holds a director of a public firm liable for breach of the duty of care.[125]

The CEO, however, Jerome Van Gorkom, certainly acted with gross negligence. Van Gorkom initiated negotiations to sell the firm without conferring with the board. He set the price for the sale without any expert analysis of the firm's value. The board met to approve the merger but attached an important condition: They insisted that other firms could bid for the company to create an auction.[126] Unfortunately, CEO Van Gorkom, an attorney and a CPA, signed the merger agreement (drafted by the purchaser) without reading it and without sharing it with the board or other senior officers. Instead of facilitating an auction for the company, the agreement (and a subsequent amendment) failed to secure the conditions for an auction. Still, the other directors pursued a unified defense with Van Gorkom, telling the Delaware Supreme Court that if it found Van Gorkom liable it should find all the directors liable.[127] The Court therefore found all the directors liable along with Van Gorkom.[128] Van Gorkom's conduct amounted to gross negligence, and the other directors erred in pursuing a joint defense with Van Gorkom. Nothing in this outcome warrants eliminating the duty of care.

Since *Smith*, opportunities for imposition of duty of care liability have certainly presented themselves. For example, the Supreme Court of Delaware found no liability arising from Disney Corporation's employment agreement with Michael Ovitz. After a short stint of fourteen months with the company, Ovitz was fired and collected $130 million in severance pay. The court found no breach of the duty of care because only intentional and deliberate misconduct is actionable under section 102(b)(7).[129] More recently, the Delaware courts turned back shareholder claims of negligence against the board of Citigroup for mismanaging the risk of subprime-related derivatives it sold. Citigroup was forced to take back billions in subprime-related instruments and absorbed huge losses as a result. Not even the Vice Chair of the Board, former Treasury Secretary Robert Rubin, understood the risk of the so-called liquidity puts. Simply put, Citigroup took risks that the board neither understood nor controlled. Nevertheless, Delaware dismissed the suit against the board based upon section 102(b)(7).[130] The upshot of Delaware law on this point is that directors may be infinitely careless without incurring liability. Moreover, because of the influence of Delaware within state corporate law across the nation, the same result must hold true in other jurisdictions or these other jurisdictions would face a risk that franchise tax revenue would migrate toward Delaware.

Promiscuous corporate governance standards also apply with regard to compensation agreements with managers. Typically public firms may grant any compensation the board sees fit, subject to very narrow circumstances that constitute waste. Moreover, although Congress enacted compensation reforms as part of the Sarbanes-Oxley Act, SEC enforcement of these new reforms failed to materially alter compensation practices.[131] Essentially, state law permits the board, which is beholden to executive management, to shower managers with compensation without real limitation.[132] Unlimited board discretion regarding compensation agreements played a central role in the subprime crisis. Compensation arrangements spawned distorted incentives.

The system of corporate governance in place from 1934 through 1985 functioned well enough to avert major macroeconomic disruptions. Isolated scandals did not trigger any financial meltdown. The public corporation generated steady increases in shareholder wealth. Unfortunately, as memories of the Great Depression faded, so did elite commitment to maintaining appropriate legal infrastructure within public firms. Ultimately, easy profits trumped the attractiveness of sound corporate governance. From 1985 through 1998 corporate and financial elites used political power to free themselves from traditional constraints and thereafter plundered public corporations, again and again.

Corporate executives of large public firms constitute a small group with large stakes in corporate governance of public firms. Shareholders face temptations for free-riding on the lobbying efforts of others, owing to their vastly greater numbers and their reduced stakes relative to those of managers, whose livelihood is on the line. Further, managers control shareholder wealth held within corporations and may access that wealth to lobby against shareholder interests while shareholders must expend their own funds. The theory of collective action would not predict much success in curbing CEO autonomy under these circumstances. Indeed, at both the state and federal level CEOs have fared better than shareholders over the past few decades, until CEOs enjoyed so much power that the system now puts the interests of the CEO above that of the shareholders. This expansion of CEO power under law coincided with soaring CEO compensation.

In 1980 the ratio of CEO pay to that of the average blue collar employee was 42:1, and in 2000 it was 475:1.[133] By the cusp of the crisis, the enhanced power of CEOs over their firms led to compensation that far outpaced not only wages of ordinary workers but corporate profits as well.[134] Similarly, as of 2008, CEO pay in the U.S. exceeded CEO pay in Japan by a factor of ten, and a factor of two in Europe.[135] American corporate governance law simply leaves too much power in the hands of the CEO, and that power leads directly to excessive compensation relative to historic CEO pay or CEO pay under other legal systems.

Agency Costs in Historic Perspective

Courts strived to contain agency costs generally for centuries outside of corporate law prior to the subprime debacle. The culmination of these efforts forms the basis of the *Restatement (Third) of Agency*, which was drafted by a variety of legal experts (judges, law professors, and practicing lawyers) to reflect and summarize controlling common law principles for agency–principal relationships. An agent must exercise ordinary care on behalf of a principal. An agent owes broad disclosure duties of material information. The agent must follow the principal's instructions. The agent must avoid acting adversely, or in competition with the principal, and must act in accordance with the duty of good faith and fair dealing when negotiating with the principal.[136] All of this exudes sensibility as a means of diminishing agency costs through the imposition of fiduciary duties.

In contrast, the managers of publicly held corporations generally owe no duty of care because of the business judgment rule as well as insulating statutes such as Delaware section 102(b)(7). They bear little disclosure obligation, separate and apart from the obligation of the firm which itself has been diminished under the PSLRA and the SLUSA (at least with respect to enforceable disclosure obligations).[137] With respect to compensation, they may grant themselves employment agreements that impose huge risks upon their firms but guarantee windfall payments for them. They owe no obligation to seat board nominees proffered by shareholders and may instead use shareholder wealth to lobby policymakers and impede the ability of shareholders to nominate directors. This upsets the reasonable expectations of shareholders. Today the executives that made so much money in pursuit of reckless short-term profits retain their ill-gotten gains with both civil and criminal impunity.[138] Compared with the culmination of judicial effort to tame agency costs, corporate governance for public firms in the U.S. today defies rationality.

Prior to the turn of the 21st century, corporate governance functioned in accordance with reasonable expectations in terms of containing agency costs. I date CEO primacy to the abolition of the duty of care in the late 1980s. Congress joined the battle in favor of management interests in 1995 and again in 1998, to grant special protection to securities fraudfeasors for the first time in history. I argue that these indulgences threw the system of corporate governance out of balance. The parade of scandals proving excessive CEO autonomy followed: the accounting scandals (including Enron) (2001–2), the options-backdating scandals (2005–6), and now the subprime scandals at the center of the financial sector.[139] Other scholars point to other legal indulgences that developed in the 1980s and 1990s as a source of declining accountability for corporate managers.[140] These indulgences no doubt reinforced those I identify. Corporate governance law applicable to American public firms simply permits CEO autonomy to run amok.[141]

Alternatives to CEO Primacy

The law could revert to the configuration of shareholder rights and private causes of action that endured between 1934 and 1985, when the combination of potential duty of care liability and exposure to securities fraud sanctions secured the basic economic mission of the modern public corporation. A number of scholars argue in favor of such proposals.[142] Despite the corporate scandals of 2001–2, the options-backdating scandal, and the subprime fiasco, however, no significant political effort to roll back the legal indulgences granted to corporate elites has materialized. Nevertheless, other proposals may ultimately prove more politically sustainable, given the trillions that investors plow into corporate America annually. CEO primacy takes an intolerable economic toll within the investor class. The latest episode of CEO autonomy run amok crashed the entire global financial system. Further overreaching holds the possibility of well-designed reform.[143]

For example, the New Deal professionalized the securities brokerage industry, including competency exams, sanctions, and self-regulatory oversight.[144] Given the power of corporate managers and their ability to inflict trillions in costs upon society, it is odd that they are not subject to any similar regimen of accountability. Holding corporate elites to professional norms of ethics and competence makes economic sense. Corporate managers should be forced to take competency and ethical examinations in order to retain their positions of power. If they violate professional norms and standards, they should face disbarment, fines, or similar sanction. This would effectively mandate professional management of the great wealth held in public corporations. Meritocracy would displace cronyism.

Substantial support already exists for the concept of professionalizing corporate governance. Ira Milstein, a prominent and respected New York corporate practitioner, proposed enhanced professional standards for the board of directors in 1995. Milstein concluded that the continued acceptance of the corporation as the locus of economic activity necessitates "increasing professionalism of directors" complete with ethical standards and a gradual displacement of amateurs.[145] Since 1995, other voices have joined Milstein's call for increased professionalization of corporate governance.

A group of concerned MBA students (working under the supervision of Professor Rakesh Khurana) from the Harvard Business School wrote a *Public Policy Proposal for the Corporate Governance College* in April 2009. They argue that corporate governance lags behind the "intensely complicated" business environment. They propose the creation of a nonprofit and private directors' college that could serve as a clearinghouse for high-quality directors prepared to serve on boards. The students call on regulators or Congress to mandate that certain "at-risk" companies seat three such directors on their boards. Other firms could participate voluntarily with the hope that market pressure would create demand for directors certified by the corporate governance college. The college would enjoy a depoliticized structure, including self-funding mechanisms. The students' proposal presents a detailed and dramatic path for change. As future business leaders, they have demonstrated with their proposal the depths of concern regarding the structure of the current system.[146] Their proposal adds detail and content to the general proposal of Harvard Business School Professors Khurana and Nohria.[147] Empirical evidence suggests that professional competence standards could operate to reduce excessively risky conduct such as subprime lending.[148]

Another means of achieving superior corporate governance involves optional federal incorporation.[149] Corporate governance could be committed to an expert and depoliticized administrative agency. Using the Fed as a model, such an agency could levy fees against public firms and thereby cost taxpayers nothing while also freeing itself from congressional appropriations. The field of corporate governance evolved over the past fifteen years into more of a science and should no longer rely upon a common law guess or the product of legislative bargaining as its basis. An expert administrative agency seems more likely to impose reasonable norms of accountability than either the courts or legislatures. The agency's corporate governance standards would face a market test through empowering shareholders to "opt in" to the agency's corporate governance regulatory scheme. Such an agency could operate to move corporate governance standards to ever more optimal levels.[150]

A federal corporate governance authority endowed with a depoliticized structure should severely limit the influence of corporate managers. The experience of the SEC suggests that an ordinary independent commission suffers from insufficient structural protection to support sound corporate governance law and regulation. Indeed, former SEC Chair Arthur Levitt wrote in 2002 that the "business lobby" and "CEOs" thwarted his efforts to impose corporate governance reforms.[151] Recent events illustrate the inability of the SEC to function appropriately as the primary federal regulator of the securities industry and public firms. From the early 1990s until late 2008, Bernie Madoff pulled off the largest Ponzi scheme in history from his perch on the board of directors of the NASDAQ and amidst a bevy of Madoff family connections with regulatory bodies in the securities industry, including a position on an SEC advisory commission.[152] Madoff also generously supported key members of Congress.[153] The SEC's inspector general found that Madoff used his connections to short-circuit SEC inquiries.[154] Certainly, the SEC lacks sufficient structural insulation to withstand the influence of the well-heeled and well-connected.

Any corporate governance authority must be carefully structured to resist political influence. Perhaps the solution would require term limits and a limit on the total percentage of corporate manager representation on the governing board. Other board seats, say 75 percent, should be reserved to shareholder representation, institutional investors, and academics from economics, finance, and law. Post-employment restrictions, long terms, and generous compensation (all part of the Fed's structure) must form a part of the depoliticized structure of the corporate governance agency. Most important, the agency must enjoy a self-funding mechanism to free it from congressional appropriations and influence.[155]

The goal requires the curtailment of CEO autonomy and the use of the best available science to set corporate governance standards. Standards would be based upon learning and experience from across the world rather than upon the interests of managers holding political power. Institutionally, the Delaware legislature appears hopelessly captured and unwilling to attend to controlling agency costs. Congress fares little better, granting special legal indulgences even to securities fraudfeasors. Similarly, the federal court system as presently structured operates to entrench privilege rather than to curb the exercise of economic power, a point I address further in coming chapters.

An expert agency could enforce standards with refined precision. For example, typically corporate managers do not pay money out of their pockets for their wrongdoing. The business judgment rule cut off almost all liability for negligence. In *Smith v. Van Gorkom*, after the Court actually assessed liability, the Delaware legislature essentially abolished the duty of care. This result obtained even though no director or officer in *Van Gorkom* paid a penny in liability.[156] Only in exceptional cases did corporate directors or officers ever pay money out of pocket for any liability.[157] This system secures neither deterrence nor compensation.

An administrative agency, on the other hand, could impose fines calibrated to the degree of culpability of the individuals responsible for, or participating in, securities fraud or other misconduct. Calibration eliminates the need to reduce substantive legal standards of accountability in order to avoid a disproportionate assessment of damages that may amount to billions in losses. Calibration also involves a careful assessment of professional misconduct under the watchful eye of professional peers, or alternatively an expert administrative agency. This approach closely mimics current professional regulation regimens.[158]

Service as a senior executive or director of a public firm brings status and wealth. The most powerful members of society serve as directors. Former cabinet members, ambassadors, and senior federal officials serve as directors of public firms. Therefore, there is little prospect that restoring accountability of corporate elites would cause a diminution in the number of those willing to serve.[159] More instances of accountability for lower amounts of personal payouts should serve to attract quality board members as well as elevate standards of conduct within the boardroom.

Even if elevated accountability narrows the pool of those willing to serve, perhaps the very point of elevated standards of conduct ensures that only those willing to meet such standards serve in the boardroom. Screening out the most docile directors benefits corporate governance. Empirical evidence suggests that enhanced accountability does not diminish the pool of those willing to serve.[160] Anecdotal evidence to the contrary seems counter to logic. No director can reasonably believe that holding the levers of economic power in America involves no responsibility. Current legal frameworks imposing near-zero accountability operate to defy reasonable expectations and history. The deterioration of boardroom accountability preceded historic crises in corporate functioning. Separate and apart from any windfalls to corporate management from the zero accountability legal environment, eliminating legally imposed responsibility proved macroeconomically catastrophic.

The possibility of organic evolution for corporate governance structures could provide a means of reducing agency costs. The Sarbanes-Oxley Act of 2002 (SOX)[161] approach to the audit committee supplies the model for redesigning corporate governance to reduce CEO autonomy. The SOX reform reflects the fact that the CEO suffers from institutional infirmities with respect to managing the audit function. CEOs should not possess autonomy over audit reports because the audited financial statements are the basic report card to shareholders to inform them of the firm's financial performance. There is no mandate that the CEO possess the expertise of a certified public accountant. Thus, the CEO should keep out of the audit process and function. Basically, SOX left CEO autonomy with respect to business operations intact. Yet, the question of appropriate CEO autonomy animates the basic reforms embodied in SOX.[162]

SOX mandated that the CEO relinquish control over the audit function. SOX focused primarily on limiting the ability of the CEO to subvert or manipulate the audit function by moving control of the audit function to an independent committee of the board.[163] SOX included a modest but specific definition of "independent."[164] Congress endowed this audit committee with specific powers to hire, fire, and supervise the auditor.[165] Each public firm must seat one audit committee member with specific accounting expertise (or an explanation regarding the lack of financial expertise).[166] SOX undertook this historic intrusion upon state law autonomy over corporate governance in response to the historic string of corporate corruption scandals beginning with the bankruptcy of Enron in 2001. Those scandals arose from the flawed framework governing the public corporation's supervision of the audit function. Consequently, audit reform assumed a center stage in the SOX reforms. All of this effectively stripped the CEO of autonomy over the audit function.

The SOX reforms of the audit function appear successful. Independent audit committees are associated with a lower cost of capital.[167] Business scholars suggest the SOX approach (as refined by SEC regulations) is "optimal" because it allows firms flexibility in defining the precise contours of the audit committee. Independent audit committees appear to facilitate higher-quality audits. The SOX reforms therefore operate to enhance the quality of audits and reduce improper earnings management.[168] Moreover, it is noteworthy that in the context of the subprime mortgage crisis, audit failure has not materially contributed to the subprime crisis.[169] The problem revolved around the manipulation of risk, not the accounting system. SOX audit reforms, therefore, appear to enhance the operation of corporate governance.

Using the SOX audit reforms as a model, I recently argued that further organic changes to the legal structure of corporate governance would constitute one appropriate response to the subprime fiasco. Specifically, I proposed an independent committee of the board to manage enterprise-wide risk-management policies. I also suggested a mandate that firms create an independent Qualified Legal Compliance Committee, to oversee the legal risk and compliance risk of public firms. Finally, I suggested an expansion of recent efforts to remove the CEO from the process of selecting board members. This suggestion would require not only an independent nominating committee that would nominate director candidates without CEO input but also shareholder nominees, selected by the independent nominating committee, to run in contested elections. All of these suggestions focused on eliminating excessive CEO autonomy over non-operational activities. CEOs would remain free to pursue strategic visions and implement appropriate tactical operations. The board would simply exercise enhanced oversight.[170]

These reform proposals responded to the vacuum Delaware creates in its command over the evolution of corporate governance law. Delaware dominates the business of chartering publicly traded firms; indeed, Delaware behaves like a monopolist in this field. As such, Delaware can afford to ignore the issue of controlling agency costs, which could alienate management interests holding control of incorporation decisions. The need to maintain its revenue stream from franchise taxes paid by firms incorporated in Delaware acts a prime motivating factor of Delaware policymakers. Thus, Delaware harbors little interest in allowing corporate law to evolve in response to events or new empirical findings regarding corporate governance law. Only pro-management evolution can occur in Delaware.[171]

The U.S. Supreme Court in *Citizens United v. Federal Election Commission* ruled that the Constitution prohibits limits on independent corporate expenditures to influence the political process.[172] This ruling will amplify managerial power. Given the control of CEOs atop the largest corporations in the country, the case seems destined to operate for the benefit of CEOs, who now may exercise control over the largest capital aggregations the world has ever seen to sway the political system to their greater benefit. Perhaps this case demands a response from the more political branches to separate CEO autonomy from the political expenditures of the corporation. A truly independent and professional committee of the board could at least channel such expenditures in a way that serves shareholders rather than the power of entrenched CEOs. Instead, the Supreme Court removed a significant barrier facing CEOs seeking to expend shareholder wealth for the purpose of pro-CEO legal and regulatory outcomes. The Supreme Court must be oblivious (or worse) to the power CEOs currently hold and the central role of CEO autonomy in the subprime meltdown.

Dodd-Frank: Corporate Governance Reform Deferred?

The Dodd-Frank Wall Street Reform and Consumer Protection Act includes provisions that could potentially spur revolutionary reform in the system of American corporate governance law and regulation. For example, the Act includes a provision that authorizes the SEC to reform the proxy system by giving shareholders access to management's proxy materials to nominate directors. It also mandates an independent (as defined through SEC regulations) compensation committee for all public firms. Further, the Act eliminates broker voting of shares held by brokers in street name (but beneficially owned by the brokerage firm's customers); this will operate to weaken management control because brokerage firms traditionally voted overwhelmingly with management. Finally, the Act requires SEC rules to enhance compensation disclosures and gives shareholders some say on executive pay. This could all end management's control of the proxy machinery and impose real corporate democracy in America.[173]

That appears highly unlikely, however, given the political realities at work. For example, the Dodd-Frank Act imposes so many regulatory actions that the Act threatens to overwhelm the regulators charged with administering the great majority of substantive provisions.[174] Meanwhile, the financial industry and other corporate interests seem poised to unleash a lobbying blitz on financial regulators complete with an army of recently hired ex–financial regulators.[175] These interests viewed the 2010 midterm elections as an opportunity to correct the harshest reform measures within the Act and spent millions in campaign contributions to influence lawmakers.[176] Indeed, business interests quickly stymied SEC efforts to give shareholders access to management's proxy to nominate directors in the courts.[177] The Dodd-Frank Act likely simply offers yet another chance for financial and corporate elites to subvert legal and regulatory infrastructure and leave America with under-developed corporate governance standards.

The stunted development of corporate governance law in America leads to massive misalignment of incentives for corporate elites. Instead of focusing on shareholder wealth maximization, they focus on short-term compensation payouts. The direct economic costs of CEO primacy amount to trillions, as shown by the impact of the Enron and subprime crises on shareholder wealth. That marks only the beginning of the costs of dysfunctional corporate governance law. In the following chapters, I show that the unbridled power of CEOs operated to compromise legal and regulatory infrastructure regarding financial regulation, globalization, and other legal and regulatory infrastructure. CEO primacy creates unacceptable costs across a range of issues. Finally, given the recent U.S. Supreme Court decision in *Citizens United*, CEO primacy left undisturbed likely will spawn more problems. If concentrated economic power spawns distorted legal and regulatory infrastructure as well as stunted human capital development, then the largely unencumbered power of a small number of CEOs and senior managers at the apex of the greatest aggregations of capital in history (U.S. public corporations) constitutes a potentially lethal economic threat to the continued viability of capitalism.

3

Animal Spirits and Financial Regulation

There is the instability due to the characteristic of human nature
that a large proportion of our positive activities depend on . . . animal spirits.
John Maynard Keynes (1936)[1]

So long as free capital markets permit all holders of assets to sell at once, a
risk of panic looms. For example, an exogenous shock such as the terror-
ist attacks of 9/11 can deter all buyers and cause financial markets to crash.
Human psychology (or "animal spirits") influences investment decisions and
as such injects inherent instability into the financial system. Financial markets consequently suffer from cycles of boom and bust. Booms encourage
corporate and financial elite complacency, regulatory laxity, and public dor-
mancy.[2] Further, with respect to financial regulation, corporate elites seemingly always oppose regulation without regard to its macroeconomic benefits. Elites even opposed the federal securities laws, claiming that "the grass
will grow on Wall Street."[3] Apparently elites would rather operate free of legal
and regulatory constraint than create a regulatory environment conducive to
growth, and therefore they bitterly oppose any regulation.[4] The financial crisis of 2007–9 shows the macroeconomic costs of regulatory failure, particularly regulatory failure to account for the influence of concentrated financial
and corporate elites with control of concentrated economic resources.[5] This

means that regulatory infrastructure must be structured pursuant to legal frameworks designed to meet these challenges.

According to the economists Thomas Ferguson and Robert Johnson, the "money driven American political system" drove "every phase of the crisis."[6] A steady drumbeat of deregulation, nonregulation, and misregulation paced the entire causal chain of the financial crisis. Financial elites stood behind the apparently inept regulators and the laissez-faire lawmakers, garnering windfall profits even while saddling the global financial system with enormous losses. From campaign contributions to lucrative job offers, financial elites held sway over lawmakers in ways that vividly illustrate the costs of runaway inequality.

For example, Clinton Treasury Secretary Robert Rubin headed Goldman Sachs and led President Clinton's efforts to raise money from Wall Street interests. He subsequently spearheaded the effort to repeal the Glass-Steagall Act and ended up as the Vice-Chair of Citigroup, the greatest beneficiary of the repeal, raising ethical questions.[7] Although some hoped otherwise, nothing much changed with the Obama administration, as Peter Orszag went from member of the Obama cabinet to Vice-Chair at Citigroup, the largest federal bailout recipient.[8] On the GOP side, Senator Phil Gramm of Texas pushed for derivatives deregulation and the repeal of the Glass-Steagall Act. He ended up as Vice Chair of UBS. While a senator, Gramm received more support from the financial industry than any other.[9] His wife, Commodity Futures Trading Commission (CFTC) Chair Wendy Gramm, also worked to ensure the nonregulation of derivatives, which permitted Enron to engage in dubious transactions. She found herself on the Enron board of directors.[10] Financial elites hedge their political investments to ensure bipartisan access and influence. They win regardless of election outcomes.

This chapter first shows the nexus of political influence, elite self-interest, and the subversion of legal and regulatory infrastructure in finance. By 2007, these connections led to an unprecedented concentration of wealth within the financial sector with all the adverse implications for law and regulation.[11] Next, the chapter seeks solutions in the form of durable legal and regulatory frameworks. Unfortunately, the political prospect for financial regulatory reform dims in the face of increased concentration of wealth within the financial sector, increased CEO power over the public corporation, and general increased concentration of personal wealth held primarily by corporate and financial elites.[12] On the other hand, further foreseeable, deep, and painful macroeconomic disruptions could induce the American voting public to repudiate unbridled wealth and lawless concentrated economic power once and for all.

The Erosion of Regulatory Infrastructure in the Financial Sector

Tracing every major regulatory change that contributed to the current financial crisis may prove impossible. For example, the Garn–St. Germain Depository Institutions Act of 1982[13] and the Depository Institutions Deregulation
and Monetary Control Act of 1980[14] paved the way for subprime lending by
relaxing interest rate limitations, preempting state usury laws, easing loan-
to-value ratios, and expanding the powers of banks.[15] Other acts opened the
door for wider mortgage securitizations in the early 1980s.[16] Yet the home
mortgage market functioned well for years after these acts, suggesting these
laws may not inherently destabilize finance. This chapter focuses on more
proximate causes arising from more patent elite overreaching than mere
marginal deregulation. I argue that deeper elite subversion of accountability and other limitations on power (i.e., the economic rule of law) drove the
financial crisis.

Subprime Mortgage Deregulation

Throughout the 1990s, bank regulators steadily expanded the range of permitted activities. Among the activities that regulators left open to banks was
subprime (even predatory) lending—meaning loans to riskier home buyers
with lower down payments than traditional real estate loans.[17] One regulator,
Sheila Bair, at the time an Assistant Secretary of the Treasury, endeavored
in vain to impose reasonable regulations on subprime lending just prior to
the period during which subprime lending became a dominant form of real
estate lending. In 2001, she urged development of national and uniform best
practices for subprime loans that would apply to all industry players. Bair
noted that although subprime lending operated to expand home ownership,
it also posed risks of predatory lending. She called on the federal banking
regulators to impose standards and for nonregulated entities to pledge compliance with those standards.[18] The industry refused this sensible regulatory
effort to address excesses.[19]

The regulators could have forced the adoption of industry best practices.
The Federal Reserve Board (Fed) in particular obtained a broad regulatory
charter from Congress in 1994. Under the Homeowner's Equity Protection Act (HOEPA)[20] the Fed had the power to prohibit unfair and deceptive loans.[21] Unfortunately, the Fed failed to fully implement any reasonable
regulation of subprime lending under HOEPA until the summer of 2008—
long after the reckless subprime lending and attendant risks infested the
global financial system.[22] Even beyond HOEPA, the Fed also enjoyed broad

regulatory powers over many subprime lenders. Nevertheless, between 2003 and 2007, at the height of the subprime storm, the Fed brought just a single enforcement action related to subprime lending, levying a $70 million fine against Citigroup. The Office of the Comptroller of the Currency (OCC), as primary regulator of all national banks, and the Office of Thrift Supervision (OTS), as primary regulator of all federal thrifts, similarly ignored problems at national banks and thrifts. Regulators opted for lax enforcement of lending standards rather than risk losing "client" financial institutions to more permissive regulatory schemes. The OCC and the OTS each depend upon fees levied against constituent banks. In fact, Countrywide's banking subsidiary switched to a thrift charter in 2007 to take advantage of more lax regulation.[23] Thus, Bair's call for regulation fell on deaf ears.

In the backwater of this regulatory neglect, subprime lending exploded, increasing fivefold between 2001 and 2005. By 2006, 40 percent of all mortgage-backed securities (MBS) included at least some subprime loans.[24] Inevitably, problems emerged. The problems, according to Bair, involved the financial literacy of subprime borrowers (many of whom were subject to America's subprime educational system for disempowered classes), adequate disclosure of the true costs and risks of subprime loans, and the dispersal of risks through securitization of loans to investors across the global financial system.[25] Bair claims that the profits available to all from subprime lending created a political vacuum in Washington in support of any regulation and that regulatory frameworks allowed compensation incentives to be focused too much on the short term. The profits in subprime lending delayed any reasonable regulation until long after the crisis advanced to a critical stage.[26] In the meantime, the most economically powerful within our society continued to exploit the most disempowered at considerable profit.[27]

Ability to repay indebtedness and abusive costs generally defines the line between subprime lending and predatory lending. If generating fees and high-interest payments displaces the object of loan repayment, then the loan evinces predation. Asset-based lending, wherein the lender looks to underlying collateral for repayment rather than borrower income, similarly indicates a predatory intent. Steering prime borrowers into subprime loans, with higher costs, also suggests predation. Fraud marks many predatory loans.[28] Predatory lending lies at the core of the current financial crisis. Securitization facilitates predatory lending because the original loan may shift the risk of default to the end-investor. Subprime loans flowed via securitization to investors across the world so the originators lacked incentives to underwrite the loans in terms of credit risk. This exacerbated the predatory nature of the lending.

Many subprime loans appear intended to lead to default. The Financial Crisis Inquiry Commission (FCIC) found that a common industry practice among hedge funds involved sponsoring pools of loans and simultaneously purchasing credit default swaps that would pay huge profits if the loans defaulted. Investors in the mortgage pools did not know of the credit default swap positions or that the sponsor participated in the selection of loans for the pools. By 2006, half of all collateralized debt obligations issued included loans selected by (among others) hedge funds that held credit default swaps that would lead to profits for the hedge fund if loans defaulted.[29] Default rates on these deals reached as high as 96 percent, far higher than deals without this patent conflict of interest at the core of their structure.[30] One Wall Street trader termed the loan portfolio underlying one of these deals: "the best short ever" and "dogsh!t."[31] As of early 2012, Wall Street banks (including Goldman Sachs, Citigroup, and JP Morgan Chase) paid $1 billion to settle charges brought by the SEC concerning these fraudulent practices, with more to come.[32] The borrowers on such loans truly acted as prey for Wall Street's massive predatory lending machine.

Early on, the regulators knew that many subprime borrowers actually qualified for prime loans.[33] At the height of the lending frenzy, 61 percent of subprime borrowers qualified for prime loans, according to a *Wall Street Journal* study.[34] Numerous studies show that many subprime borrowers qualified for lower-cost prime loans.[35] One study found that high-cost subprime loans defaulted at a rate as high as eight times the default rate on prime loans, even after controlling for credit characteristics[36]; another found that borrowers with poor mathematical and cognitive skills defaulted at a much greater rate than otherwise.[37] Thus, the "mortgage foreclosure crisis was driven not by lending to poor people, but by lending to poor people with terms designed to extract short term profits through abusive fees."[38]

Predatory lending and exploitation, as opposed to subprime lending, led to very high mortgage delinquencies and foreclosures. Countrywide (the nation's largest mortgage lender) settled claims of predatory lending affecting 400,000 loans nationwide for payments totaling $8.7 billion. The Federal Reserve fined Wells Fargo $85 million for similar misconduct involving thousands of mortgage loans. These actions constitute only the most recent settlements.[39] Little doubt remains today that billions and billions in predatory loans form the foundation of the subprime debacle. Deregulated mortgage lending and securitization facilitated this lending.

The story of securitization of home mortgages begins with two government-sponsored entities (GSEs) called Fannie Mae and Freddie Mac. The GSEs started to purchase loans and bundle them for sale to investors as mortgage-backed securities (MBS) in the 1970s. This added liquidity to the home mortgage market and expanded capital available to fund home mortgages. The GSEs maintained sound underwriting standards and experienced the lowest default rates in the mortgage business. In the 1990s, Clinton administration officials determined that Fannie and Freddie should invest in subprime mortgages to expand home ownership. The GSEs ultimately facilitated the creation of an entirely new MBS market for subprime loans.[40] In 2004, the Bush administration ordered Fannie and Freddie to adhere to expanded affordable housing mandates.[41] They invested $434 billion in subprime mortgages (through MBS originated in the private sector) between 2004 and 2006. Thereafter, the GSEs cut back their subprime investments. By 2007 their total subprime investment constituted only about 15 percent of the total subprime MBS outstanding.[42] Competition from private banks rendered Fannie and Freddie increasingly irrelevant in the subprime mortgage market.[43] The GSEs did not invest in the riskiest subprime loans, as evidenced by the modest $3 billion loss suffered on such investments from 2008 through 2011.[44] One scholar stated the role played by Fannie and Freddie (as investors) well: "[T]hey were suckers."[45] Yet the bipartisan decisions to push the GSEs into subprime mortgages fueled subprime lending's initial profitability, opening the door to abuse.[46]

As the subprime market developed, the banking industry enlisted the federal financial regulators in a campaign to free themselves from the strictures of state law. In 2004, the Office of the Comptroller of the Currency, the primary regulator of national banks, preempted state efforts to regulate predatory lending. This followed the earlier effort at the Office of Thrift Supervision to do the same, with respect to all federally charted thrifts such as savings banks and savings and loans.[47] The U.S. Supreme Court joined this effort (under heavy lobbying in the form of *amicus* briefs) and upheld the ruling of the federal regulators that preempted state predatory lending restrictions applicable to subsidiaries of banks and thrifts.[48] Federal law therefore operated not only to permit predatory lending but also to denude state efforts to crack down on predatory loans. Subprime lending festered in this deregulatory environment.

The states proved more interested in imposing legal sanctions than any federal regulator. Countrywide Financial, for example, settled the largest predatory loan in history, agreeing to more than $8 billion in loan modifications, in a suit pressed by eleven states.[49] The states charged that Countrywide paid its agents to steer borrowers into riskier, high-cost loans and inflated borrowers' incomes (without borrower involvement) so that they could qualify for larger, more profitable loans. Countrywide also misled borrowers regarding closing costs and other hidden fees. Countrywide's sub-prime loans carried a delinquency rate of 33 percent in 2007. In one two-year period, Countrywide securitized more than $100 billion of the loans it originated.[50] Countrywide cared little about the repayment of its loans, and the law permitted this predatory lending to occur. Unfortunately, state action simply proved too little, too late to fill the regulatory vacuum at the federal level.

Investors similarly lacked incentives to ensure repayment of the subprime and predatory loans. The securitized pools of mortgages frequently featured various forms of credit insurance or credit default protection. For example, AIG issued hundreds of billions of dollars in credit default swaps (a type of credit derivative whereby AIG agreed to pay if mortgage loans defaulted) in exchange for fees that inflated AIG's present income (and compensation for executives) while ignoring long-term risks. Further, companies like Citigroup conveyed securitized assets with the proviso that under certain circumstances they would repurchase the securities. Many subprime MBS included differing tranches or interests, and disclosures to investors indicated lenders or packagers retained risky tranches. Many of these retained interests met with quick sale or otherwise proved illusory. All of this encouraged lax underwriting because investors thought originators or securitizers would not retain interests in excessively risky loans, or that loan losses would be covered by someone else. Finally, the predatory loans benefited from the sterling images enjoyed by the most prolific securitizers, including Lehman Brothers, Merrill Lynch, Bank of America, and Bear Stearns. In the end, the lack of legal and regulatory infrastructure to channel the securitization process ensured that no appropriate risk assessments occurred anywhere along the securitization chain.[51]

Along those lines, the Private Securities Litigation Reform Act (PSLRA) distorted incentives for all players in the securitization process. As noted in chapter 2, the PSLRA bars securities fraud claims if plaintiffs do not possess sufficient facts to plead a strong inference of defendants' intent to defraud before any discovery, and this chills the ability of shareholders to hold managers to account. The PSLRA also operated to bar shareholder claims of securities fraud against a subprime lender[52] as well as against a subprime loan securitizer.[53] Countrywide used the PSLRA pleading standards to defeat claims brought by an investor in MBS that it issued.[54] Even in cases involving egregious nondisclosures, the PSLRA operates to narrow securities fraud claims significantly.[55] Thus, the PSLRA directly facilitated the massive fraud underlying subprime lending by diminishing the legal sanctions for fraud.[56]

The unfortunate consequence of all this led directly to the origination of massive subprime mortgages. Those mortgages, resting on a foundation of fraud and predation, infected the entire global financial system through derivatives.

Derivatives Nonregulation

Banks created a variety of instruments that derived their value from pools of subprime mortgages. These derivatives played a key role in the subprime debacle of 2007–9 and continue to haunt the global economy today. Derivatives are simply contracts that derive their value from reference to some other asset. Only the imagination of financial experts and the capacity of computer programs limit the complexity of derivatives. The financial engineers on Wall Street created ever more convoluted versions of derivatives that ultimately depended upon subprime mortgages for their value—ranging from credit default swaps to collateralized debt obligations. Whatever the label, the underlying value of many of these derivatives depended upon the performance of subprime mortgages.[57] The total lack of regulation of these derivatives burdened our financial system with excessive risks, to the breaking point.

The story of Brooksley Born, former Chairwoman of the Commodity Futures Trading Commission (CFTC), tellingly illustrates the ability of those with concentrated economic power to evade important regulatory infrastructure necessary to support financial markets. From her position as the first female president of the *Stanford Law Review*, Born rose to become an internationally reputed attorney, specializing in derivatives law. Many derivatives contracts, like stock index futures, are traded in open exchanges such as the Chicago Board of Options; over-the-counter derivatives contracts trade privately, meaning only the parties to the contract know of the existence or terms of the contract. Financial institutions generate income from derivatives in the form of transaction fees as well as trading profits. To the extent that the value of derivatives springs from a complex mathematical model requiring complex computer programs, an investment firm may enjoy enhanced pricing capability relative to a plain vanilla instrument, as more complex instruments create unique pricing opacity.[58] Such complex derivatives typically trade in opaque over-the-counter markets.

These unique market advantages created accompanying risks. Even firms as sophisticated and well resourced as Procter & Gamble found themselves unable to control the risks of trading in derivatives. P&G sued Bankers Trust for $100 million in losses resulting from derivatives trading in the 1990s.[59]

Similarly, Merrill Lynch paid $400 million to settle claims arising from the bankruptcy of Orange County, California, which was triggered by risky derivatives trading, later in the 1990s.[60] Born understood that over-the-counter derivatives contracts implied unknown risks that too often went undisclosed and unregulated when she ascended to the top of the CFTC.

Born quickly identified fundamental risks within the burgeoning over-the-counter derivatives market, which had grown to such an extent that our largest financial institutions and banks had unknown trillions in exposure. Born termed the market a "completely dark market" because the government did not have even basic information regarding bank derivatives activities. In 1998, Born and the CFTC released a concept for prudential regulation of the over-the-counter derivatives market. In response, a buzz-saw of opposition attacked Born and her regulatory initiative. Banking executives literally stood in the office of Deputy Secretary of the Treasury Lawrence Summers as he berated Born for launching the entire regulatory effort. Fed Chair Alan Greenspan, Secretary of the Treasury Robert Rubin, and SEC Chair Arthur Levitt joined the effort to shut down derivatives regulation. Ultimately, Congress convened hearings on the CFTC's regulatory initiative. Even the failure of Long Term Capital Management in 1998, which threatened global financial stability and needed a government-coordinated bailout after losing billions in opaque derivatives transactions, failed to stem the opposition to Born's regulatory initiative. In fact, Congress thereafter threatened to freeze the CFTC's regulatory authority. All of this opposition caused the CFTC to abort its regulatory initiative. Born resigned.[61]

Later, Congress formalized its laissez-faire approach to the derivatives market in the Commodity Futures Modernization Act of 2000 (CFMA).[62] This Act allowed large financial institutions and other firms to trade over-the-counter derivatives with no regulatory oversight at all. The CFMA eschewed basic disclosure mandates regarding loss exposures to derivatives contracts. Congress did not see fit even to regulate fraud or manipulation in the derivatives market. In the wake of these failures, firms took spectacular risks, often failing when the risks came to fruition. Scholars link the failure of firms such as Enron, Global Crossing, Qwest, and Barings Bank to risks inherent in undisclosed derivatives trading. Enron used derivatives to mask losses and create the appearance of a successful energy-trading operation. Global Crossing and Qwest swapped access to broadband networks to create the appearance of greater economic value. The opportunity to book profits, even illusory profits, fueled the efforts of corporate and financial elites to undertake a "dizzying lobbyist barrage" in support of the CFMA.[63]

The market for over-the-counter derivatives soared to $595 trillion by 2007. When the credit crisis fully bloomed in late 2008, financial markets had no means of knowing which firms had what exposure to the failure of other firms, or the deterioration in value of which securities (or which subprime MBS). Raw panic shut down credit markets. Born's nightmare became reality. The risks of massive and unknown exposures pursuant to over-the-counter derivatives rendered every major financial institution suspect in global financial markets. Eventually the U.S. government stepped in and committed trillions to prop up the entire financial sector. According to Joseph Stiglitz, "[I]t is absolutely clear to me that if we had restricted the derivatives, some of the major problems would have been avoided." Stiglitz states that unfortunately voices within the Clinton administration felt the need "to make the world safe for Goldman to sell derivatives in Korea."[64] In late 2009, Born warned that the failure to close the regulatory gap relating to over-the-counter derivatives will lead to further financial cataclysms.

Warren Buffet, perhaps the most successful investor in the world, called derivatives "financial weapons of mass destruction."[65] Derivatives played a major role in the subprime crisis, the Long Term Capital Management crisis, and the Enron debacle. Yet, they persist, and they persist without any real regulatory infrastructure at all. Today, the notional amount of derivatives outstanding approaches $1 quadrillion.[66] This represents giant wagers on sovereign debt, interest rate movements, the financial vulnerability of a wide array of firms, commodities, currencies, and a host of other computer-generated elements.[67] Today, an even more painful financial disruption looms, arising from European sovereign debt and bank deleveraging, sending creditors scurrying for the protection of U.S. Treasury obligations and other safe havens.[68] Derivatives and the uncertainty they breed will exacerbate this crisis and further damage the real economy.[69] As John Maynard Keynes said in 1936, "When the capital development of a country becomes a by-product of the activities of a casino, the job is likely to be ill-done."[70]

This bizarre reality exists only as a testament to the political power of financial elites. Derivatives produce profits, and profits produce compensation payments. Further, the dizzying array of derivatives of dizzying complexity permits financial executives greater latitude to manipulate earnings, hide losses, and create illusions of profitability. Thus, Enron infamously traded derivatives to generate profits but hid losses from such trading in off-balance sheet entities. Derivatives trading formed the core of Enron's business. Combined with more than 3,000 special purpose entities, Enron used derivatives to hide large losses, to hide debts, and to inflate the value of firm assets. Essentially, derivatives allowed Enron to use sophisticated financial engineering "as a kind of plastic surgery, to make itself look better than it really was."[71] After the Enron debacle, experts once again called for federal regulation of the derivatives market; once again, the call for regulation fell on deaf ears.[72]

The unregulated derivatives market permitted AIG and others to guarantee subprime MBS in the event of default, through credit default swaps, a type of derivative. AIG thereby facilitated the flow of subprime MBS to investors around the world. Ultimately, AIG set new records in corporate losses. This "stunning" incompetence led to a massive federal bailout that saved banks around the world.[73] The combination of easy guarantees from AIG and excessively high ratings from credit rating agencies created a toxic brew of subprime mortgages that infected global financial markets and investor portfolios around the world. This strange alchemy (whereby subprime mortgages transform into safe securities) could occur only if ratings agencies enjoyed the latitude to overrate bonds.

Ratings Agencies Misregulation

All of this derivatives trading could not have occurred if the interests traded lacked sufficient ratings to be held in the portfolios of insurance companies, banks, pension funds, and other regulated entities, or to otherwise meet the needs of cautious investors. As debt securities, subprime MBS generally triggered ratings based upon risk from credit rating agencies such as Standard & Poor's or Moody's. The ratings agencies essentially license securities for financial institution investment. The ratings agencies enjoy this quasi-governmental power pursuant to a wide variety of regulations in the financial industry, such as the SEC's net capital rule, which generally governs the calculation of capital required to operate in the securities brokerage business.[74] The rating agencies thereby assumed a central role in the flow of subprime mortgages to investors worldwide.

"Their role in the current crisis is . . . characterized as active complicity, as they helped create residential mortgage–backed securities and related derivatives products."[75] In fact, industry experts term July 10, 2007, "Pearl Harbor Day" in tribute to the importance of the ratings agencies, as that day marks the simultaneous downgrades by the two primary ratings agencies of $20 billion worth of subprime mortgage–backed bonds.[76] In 2008, the ratings agencies downgraded more than 220,000 classes of asset-backed securities, highlighting the central role of the ratings agencies in perhaps the most massive mispricing of risk in the history of financial markets.[77] The lack of regulatory infrastructure explains how the ratings agencies got it so wrong.

Theoretically, they faced incentives to assess accurately the credit quality of subprime MBS. Higher-quality credit rating agencies could, for example, seek to build a reputation for integrity that could inspire greater investor confidence in their ratings, leading to competition based upon quality. In reality, however, the investment banks (the issuers of subprime MBS) selected and paid the ratings agency for rating a particular subprime investment. Internal conversations among employees of rating agencies confirm that the prospect of losing business from the investment banks for unfavorable ratings treatment drove the agencies to dilute their risk assessments.[78] Former analysts testified before Congress that the investment banks would shop the MBS from agency to agency until the rating conformed to the demands of the issuer. In response to an internal survey, one ratings agency executive stated, "These errors make us look either incompetent at credit analysis or like we sold our soul to the devil for revenue, or a little bit of both." Another former ratings agency employee stated that senior managers "intimidated" analysts and wanted employees who were "docile" and "afraid to upset the investment banks."[79] Rating analysts often achieved higher bonus compensation based upon the performance of the ratings firm. Even as late as 2008, the SEC found that ratings analysts at rating agencies seek to maintain their firms' market share and are actively involved in fee negotiations. Thus, the SEC concluded that firms failed to mitigate the inherent conflicts in the issuer-pays model for rating agencies.[80]

Investors face uphill struggles to hold the ratings agencies accountable. In fact, some courts rule that the ratings agencies may not be held liable under the First Amendment of the U.S. Constitution in the absence of actual malice.[81] Under the PSLRA, only claimants who can show a strong inference of intent to defraud before any discovery may prevail.[82] Professor Frank Partnoy sums up the legal landscape regarding efforts to hold the ratings agencies accountable: "The only common element . . . is that the ratings agencies win."[83] Consequently, the economic incentives for the rating agencies amounted to seeking revenue by diluting any due diligence regarding the risks of a given subprime deal.

Efforts to regulate the ratings agencies generally met with resistance not just from the agencies themselves but from their clients that paid for their services—the investment banking and securities industry. A 2006 effort to enhance regulatory power over the ratings agencies failed in Congress. Senator Charles Schumer of New York led this effort. Schumer raised millions (more than any other senator save one) from the very Wall Street firms that benefited so much from their cozy relationship with the ratings agencies.[84] As a result of these efforts, the Credit Rating Agency Reform Act of 2006

(CRARA) required the SEC to issue rules preventing unfair and abusive conduct by the rating agencies but mandated that the SEC not regulate the substance or methods of credit ratings.[85] The Act further mandated that the SEC promulgate only "narrowly tailored" rules.[86] Hence, commentators conclude that "CRARA is a pointedly free-market piece of legislation."[87]

The conduct of the ratings agencies in connection with the subprime debacle does not flatter the industry. One analyst admitted that she used models that did not capture "half the risk" of mortgage-backed securities. Another analyst claimed that staffing could not keep up with the workload. Yet another hoped that the analysts would all be retired and wealthy when "the house of cards collapsed." The ratings agencies did not verify information received from issuers and failed to insist that the issuers undertake any due diligence.[88] Facing no effective regulation and no real prospect of civil liability, the credit ratings agencies sought to generate maximum profits at the expense of the economy in general.

"Too Big to Fail" and the Repeal of Glass-Steagall

The too-big-to-fail issue dovetails with the ability of financial titans to hide losses, pump up profits through excessive risks, and hide risks through complex derivatives transactions and investments like subprime mortgages. Too-big-to-fail firms are those businesses, especially in the banking and financial sector, that are so intertwined with the general economy that their entry into bankruptcy or other receivership proceedings would supposedly threaten general economic peril or financial disorder. Derivatives link the fortunes of firms in ways that are not transparent, even though the amount of exposure can exceed many billions in capital; and the failure of one firm therefore can pose a credible threat to the entire financial system. Politicians and policymakers are not likely to allow large, interconnected firms to fail and risk blame for a general macroeconomic collapse. The financial resources and political power of financial titans give them easy access to policymakers in times of trouble and cognitive sway over the relevant policymakers. Lawmakers respond to financial disturbances with massive state resources to ensure the viability of large, dangerously interconnected financial firms.[89] In such times, the line between government and private financial institutions blurs.

Capital markets understand this blurring and will extend more credit on cheaper terms to too-big-to-fail banks. Paradoxically, this fact itself will encourage excessive risk taking as such firms gorge on cheap capital and financial elites assume that government resources will backstop their failure.

Too-big-to-fail means massive market distortions and excessive risk at the very heart of the economy. Thus, the too-big-to-fail firms will gorge on risk in an otherwise inexplicably inept way—particularly if such risks lead to short-term profits and thereby enhance compensation. Soon competitors seek too-big-to-fail status and the market distortions spread. [90] Once implicit government subsidies take hold, reckless derivatives trading and dangerous investments in subprime mortgages become more tempting.

Ultimately, management enjoyed complete insulation from risk. The government committed hundreds of billions of dollars to save megabanks like Citigroup from failure. The winners achieved unbargained-for government guarantees of their claims against Citigroup—including compensation claims held by Citigroup managers. CEO Charles Prince gained at least $50 million in additional compensation after the government bailout.[91] In FDIC liquidation, such claims would normally be paid only pennies on the dollar, at best. The government similarly allowed management to continue in power. This created pressure for management to conceal losses and hoard capital in the hope that they could continue to run the bank in its "zombie" (not quite dead, but on government life support) form. New managers, on the other hand, always have incentives to recognize all losses immediately so that legacy problems do not reduce future earnings; in fact, when excessive losses are recognized immediately, future income is enhanced. New managers are also unlikely to hoard capital and instead would make loans to generate profits.[92]

Government guarantees for speculative activities (such as investing in high-risk subprime loans and related derivatives) will create too much risk in an economy. Too-big-to-fail policies create grotesque incentives, particularly if top management is incentivized to achieve high profits. Government guarantees encourage anything that creates profits today at the expense of risk tomorrow. Indeed, the government will even bail out the executives who saddled their firms with too much risk if they hold political sway. Executives seek too-big-to-fail status because they can then seek maximum profits regardless of risk and then rely upon government to socialize the risk. Managers emerge unscathed financially after the collapse of 2008.[93] This exacerbates the problems in corporate governance law, highlighted in the previous chapter.

Too-big-to-fail policies combined with lax regulation of derivatives and other risky investment instruments create a particularly dangerous outcome. If capitalists do not know the precise contours of derivatives risks, then in an uncertain market environment capital will flee all firms suspected of derivatives exposure and a credit crunch will ensue. Without basic financial transparency,

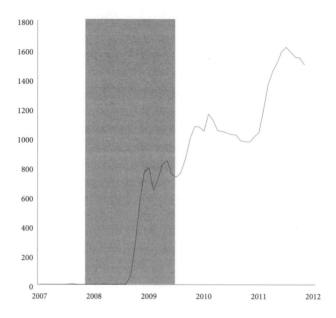

Figure 3.1 Excess Reserves of Depository Institutions in billions (EXCRESNS) (Source: Federal Reserve Bank of St. Louis)

systemic financial collapses become inherent to the financial system because rapid shifts in risk perception lead to panics. This in turn creates more pressure to deem more firms too-big-to-fail. Government too-big-to-fail policies then become necessary to avert a complete and total financial collapse. Pervasive and costly bailouts follow. The aftermath of such policies may operate to poison the entire economy. Economists often cite Japan as an example of the economic malaise that can set in when banks allow nonperforming loans to fester and instead become "zombie" banks that fail to appropriately provide the credit needed to fuel economic growth. Banks that enjoy government backing therefore threaten a "doomsday cycle of booms, busts and bailouts."[94]

Without incentives to cleanse balance sheets of toxic assets and new managers, banks will hoard capital, knowing that their balance sheets remain loaded with questionable assets. Too-big-to-fail policies create a zombie financial sector unlikely to lend, as depicted in the acccompanying graph showing the accumulation of excess reserves within the banking system in the aftermath of the financial crisis and the government's bailouts.

This $1.6 trillion in excess reserves represents dormant capital resources that impede economic recovery. Nevertheless, the Fed paid interest on these reserves and thereby encouraged this hoarding. Economic experts term this interest benefit a "big gift" to the banks.[95]

Economists and financial scientists study economies of scale in the financial sector. Their findings suggest that financial performance of large banks peaks at about the size of $10 billion in assets.[96] Nevertheless, the law permits and even facilitates vastly larger financial conglomerates. In 1999, for example, the Financial Services Modernization Act[97] repealed the Glass-Steagall Act.[98] Glass-Steagall limited the size of financial institutions by prohibiting the combination of commercial banks and investment banks. This effectively limited the concentration of economic power, and as Joseph Stiglitz highlights, New Deal regulations like Glass-Steagall ushered in a remarkable era of rapid economic growth, financial stability, and enhanced economic equality.[99] Strong financial regulations did not stifle economic growth; they secured it. Critics of the repeal of Glass-Steagall specifically warned that its elimination would lead to financial catastrophe and huge government bailouts of the financial sector, and their predictions proved accurate.[100]

In fact, one of the most notorious banks at the eye of the financial maelstrom, Citigroup, specifically needed the Financial Services Modernization Act to give legal legitimacy to its previously unlawful merger with Travelers in 1998. "Armed with boatloads of cash," Citigroup undertook a lavish lobbying effort to secure the repeal of Glass-Steagall. Yet the promised benefits of consolidation and so-called financial supermarkets never materialized. Instead Citigroup became too-big-to-manage as serial setbacks infected each of its many operating divisions. One commentator notes that the market value of Citigroup fell from $274 billion to $16 billion in the decade after its union with Travelers. Economically, allowing these megabanks to emerge proved an "utter disaster," and even Citigroup's former CEO and chairman state that they regret the repeal of Glass-Steagall and that the bank is now "too big to manage."[101]

After the repeal of Glass-Steagall, a key barrier to financial concentration fell. Regulators—with the Fed leading the charge—long facilitated massive financial sector consolidation even prior to the formal repeal of Glass-Steagall.[102] Early on, critics predicted that this consolidation would lead exactly to the financial crisis we just experienced.[103] This legal indulgence of consolidation run amok mirrored a generally docile approach to competition law policy and consolidation of firms generally, which included unregulated financial firms such as mortgage originators.[104] According to Robert Scheer, the repeal of Glass-Steagall resulted from the most massive lobbying effort in congressional history, amounting to $300 million. Treasury Secretary Rubin strongly supported the repeal, and he made $33 million at Citigroup the year after he left the Clinton administration.[105] The fingerprints of concentrated power permeate the effort of financial elites to free financial firms from any regulatory constraint upon their size.

Leverage Deregulation

Excessive leverage became the final ingredient to the deregulatory brew that led to the financial mania at the root of the subprime crisis. Leverage involves the use of debt to amplify profitable trading or other investment activities. Leverage will increase profits to the extent profits exceed the cost of debt. If losses instead of profits result, then leverage will amplify losses. To the extent a firm overleverages itself through the use of much more debt than equity to finance its business, then losses can rapidly deplete the firm's equity capital and render it insolvent. Financial firms dramatically overleveraged themselves in the years prior to the crisis, as the ratio of financial company debt to GDP soared from 16 percent to 116 percent. This created serious instability, for any sudden asset losses would quickly threaten individual firm insolvency, and systemic insolvency to the extent firms became more interconnected through the unregulated derivatives markets.[106]

The most notorious deregulation of leverage limits occurred when the SEC in 2004 succumbed to the nation's largest investment banks and permitted the firms to regulate their capital levels themselves. Essentially the SEC decided to defer to the investment banks' own sophisticated models to determine appropriate leverage. More specifically, in June 2004 the SEC relaxed leverage limits for investment banks with more than $5 billion in assets and allowed the firms to police themselves so long as they agreed to groupwide examination by the SEC.[107] Unfortunately, the SEC made little effort to exercise the power granted it under the so-called Consolidated Supervised Entities Program. Instead, the SEC assigned seven staff members to supervise the five investment banks that had more than $4 trillion in assets and operations that spanned the globe. Soon after the SEC implemented this program of self-regulation, leverage soared to $33 of debt for every dollar of equity at Bear Stearns; 31.7 to one at Lehman Brothers; and at Merrill Lynch leverage doubled after the new SEC capital regimen. After Bear Stearns failed, the SEC inspector general found that the SEC's staff missed numerous red flags of too much risk at Bear Stearns—including too much leverage. Ultimately all five investment banks ceased to exist as investment banks: Two failed; Bank of America acquired Merrill; and Goldman Sachs and Morgan Stanley became banks. In late September 2008, SEC Chair Christopher Cox concluded that self-regulation "does not work," and the consolidated supervised entities program ended.[108]

Senator Schumer also advocated that the banking regulators loosen capital requirements for large banks. Even as late as June 2007, when subprime risks became manifest, he wrote to the Chair of the FDIC that "I do not agree that more capital is always better." Schumer wished the bank regulators to hasten their implementation of the Basel II capital regulation regimen.[109] Basel II essentially outsourced the capital regulation to the banks themselves and to the credit rating agencies. More specifically, highly rated (according to the models of the co-opted rating agencies, no less) debt paper counted as capital. And, the banks' own risk models form the basis of the Basel II regimen. Thus, Basel II outsourced capital regulation to private risk models as never before.[110] Even before Basel II, derivatives empowered many banks, such as Citigroup, to evade regulatory mandates through off–balance sheet entities. Ultimately, Citigroup obliged itself to repurchase derivatives in the form of special purpose entities based upon liquidity puts that allowed purchasers to put the interests back to Citigroup in the event of financial turmoil. Citigroup's financial statements did not reflect this obligation, which proved quite costly to Citigroup.

When the subprime losses emerged, America's largest financial institutions failed to weather the storm because they operated with too much debt on their balance sheets and not enough equity. The leverage contributed to firm profits while the party lasted, but when the inevitable hangover took hold, American banks toppled in unison.

The Shadow Banking System

The global shadow banking system also contributed to global financial instability when the crisis hit. The shadow banking system consists of a variety of institutions that facilitate lending but do not take retail deposits and therefore are not subject to traditional bank regulation. The institutions include investment banks, private equity funds, hedge funds, special investment vehicles, and asset conduits. Professor Gary Gorton zeroes in on the shadow banking system and its lack of regulation as a key cause of the subprime crisis of 2007–9. He argues that the shadow banking system operated as a key cog in the lending process by investing in a variety of securitizations and collateralized debt obligation funds. Basically, these are pools of debt instruments such as credit card receivables or mortgages. The shadow banking system became a key source of funding for traditional bank loans. Banks bundled up loans and sold them to the shadow banks rather than hold traditional loans in their portfolios.[111] Immediately prior to the crisis, the shadow banking system rivaled the traditional banks in terms of actual loan funding.[112]

Unfortunately, although the shadow banking system allowed banks to enhance their profits by maximizing loan volume, the system lacked any substantial legal and regulatory infrastructure. The economist Paul Krugman terms this "malign neglect."[113] Even though deposit insurance proved to be an effective means to stop bank runs, no such insurance applied to short-term claims held by investors within the shadow banking system. When the subprime crisis dawned, no investor in the shadow banking system could determine potential exposure to the rapidly depreciating value of subprime mortgage pools. Holders of short-term funds within the shadow banking essentially ran on the shadow banking system. The run did not make headlines because instead of panic-stricken depositors waiting in lines at banks, it all occurred electronically. It was the first e-run on a banking system. Like all runs, the shadow banks faced with huge demands for funds responded by selling assets. These sales led to fire sale prices.[114]

The shadow banking system included off–balance sheet special investment vehicles (SIVs) sponsored by traditional banks. When the e-run occurred in 2007–8, these SIVs often ended up on the balance sheets of such banks, and concomitant losses followed. Thus, in the fall of 2007, Citigroup took $55 billion in SIV assets back on its balance sheet, and the British bank HBOS took back $41 billion in SIV assets. Other banks absorbed smaller, but still multi-billion-dollar, losses.[115] Thus, the shadow banking system not only crashed in the face of the e-run, but it also inflicted huge losses on traditional banks after cratering. The problem with all banking relates to using short-term obligations to fund long-term assets.[116] If all depositors demand their funds at once, in response to some shock, then the bank will fail, as no bank ever has enough cash to pay all of its short-term obligations at once.

Deposit insurance accompanied by prudential regulation formed the foundation of a rare "quiet period" in U.S. banking. The period of 1934–2007 includes zero bank runs and financial panics. Professor Gorton proposes that the definition of banking include the full extent of institutions that can contribute to banking panics. In short, he calls for an expansion of the New Deal regulatory infrastructure to the full breadth of institutions that issue deposits or near-deposits to fund lending. Certainly, the extension of the New Deal approach to banking regulation to the shadow banking system could have operated to mitigate the financial crisis of 2007–9.[117]

Lender of Last Resort?

Every modern financial system includes an agency empowered to act as lender of last resort to banks. In the U.S., this function rests with the Fed.

A lender of last resort addresses the fact that banks lend over the long term and borrow short term. If financial markets fall into a panic, then liquidity could dry up to such an extent that even strong banks cannot roll over their liabilities or meet depositor demands for cash and thereby fail. A bank may face a liquidity crisis even though it holds plenty of solid collateral. The Fed long used its discount window to lend to solvent banks based upon adequate collateral.[118]

The financial crisis of 2007–9 saw the lender of last resort power of the Fed explode into a wholly new function without any legal charter to do so— propping up the entire global financial system. The Fed deserves some degree of credit for its vigorous action in the face of a historic financial collapse. Moreover, a bailout agency with an appropriate institutional design could well enjoy a sound economic rationale. Nevertheless, a central bank's use of its prodigious monetary policy powers to save politically powerful market participants from economic pain and accountability cannot be justified, and the Fed flirts with precisely this outcome. I take up the issue of bailouts in chapter 6. Here, I merely wish to spotlight the behavior of the Fed to serve political expediency rather than employ sound lender of last resort policies in the recent financial crisis.

The Fed bailouts commenced in early 2008 with a bailout of Bear Stearns. Bear borrowed heavily to fund investments in toxic loans and undertook further exposure in derivatives. Bear's failure consequently posed massive systemic risk. Creditors lost confidence in the ability of Bear to avoid insolvency, and an electronic bank run occurred on the investment bank. Fed Chair Ben Bernanke concluded that Bear could not be permitted to enter bankruptcy, or financial chaos would ensue. The Fed acted through JP Morgan Chase to arrange a subsidized merger between Chase and Bear.[119] The Fed used emergency powers to guarantee $30 billion of toxic Bear assets. The Fed's action left it in uncharted waters. It had never before used its lender of last resort powers to rescue a nonbank from insolvency.[120]

The Fed also undertook a series of extraordinary actions designed to keep the financial sector afloat. It committed to purchase $1.5 trillion in mortgage-backed securities, singlehandedly keeping the residential mortgage market functioning. It also purchased $500 billion in Treasury Securities. The additional demand generated through the Fed purchases increased the value of these securities; that, in turn, boosted the trading profits and balance sheets of every bank as banks hold trillions in aggregate in government securities and mortgage-backed securities. The Fed also now lends money to member banks at zero interest and at the same time pays interest on the excess reserves the banks hold. It is impossible to know the final cost of all of these initiatives.[121] These activities transcend the lender of last resort and traditional monetary policy functions.

The government bailouts actually commenced earlier than most may recall with the so-called shadow bailouts of the late summer of 2007. With the 2008 presidential election looming, Secretary of the Treasury Henry Paulson allowed the obscure Federal Home Loan Banks to provide billions in relief to the banking sector. For example, Countrywide borrowed $22.3 billion from the Federal Home Loan Bank of Atlanta in late 2007. At a time when increased bank failures suggested that the FDIC would bear the costs of higher deposit insurance payouts, Paulson also delayed increasing assessments on FDIC-insured banks. Of course the banks tend to make "massive contributions to political campaigns." Moreover, the public rebuke the Republican Party would face if financial chaos emerged would not help in the election. These factors effectively created incentives to hide all of this from public view.[122]

Paulson next took a fatal misstep. In 2007, the home mortgage market collapsed except for conforming Fannie and Freddie mortgages. Banks still held subprime MBS, but the market evaporated. Paulson, with the complicity of congressional Democrats, directed the firms to pump up their holdings of subprime MBS. As foreclosures ratcheted up, the GSE's very thin capital vaporized. Soon, foreign holders of Fannie and Freddie debt and conforming MBS panicked. An electronic run developed on the stock and debt issued by Fannie and Freddie. Paulson asked Congress for the power to nationalize the GSEs, which he received. Even that did not end the run. On September 8, 2008, Paulson exercised his authority to seize Fannie and Freddie and injected $200 billion in government equity. The "stealth bailout" failed. The seizure of Fannie and Freddie could not be concealed from the body politic. Directing Fannie and Freddie to invest in subprime MBS just as the market collapsed probably greatly increased the cost of the total bailout tab. The seizure of Fannie and Freddie on the eve of a presidential election also sent an unmistakable message to markets that serious trouble infected the U.S. financial system.[123]

When Lehman Brothers teetered, Paulson notified potential acquirers of Lehman that there would be no government money for a merger with Lehman. Only bankruptcy remained. The looming election figured prominently in Paulson's deliberations.[124] On September 15, 2008, Lehman filed for bankruptcy protection. Suddenly lenders perceived credit risk everywhere throughout the financial sector. Credit markets froze. Things devolved quickly from there.

AIG previously sold hundreds of billions in credit default swaps, including swaps that protected creditors from the failure of Lehman. A run started on AIG. The Fed again invoked its emergency powers to lend AIG $85 billion and took an 80 percent ownership stake in the world's largest insurance company. Later the Fed advanced billions more. The largest beneficiaries of the AIG bailouts were the counterparties to the billions and billions of risks it had underwritten through credit default swaps. Goldman Sachs (Paulson's former firm) raked in $13 billion, more than any other American financial institution. In all, the Fed ultimately extended a $185 billion line of credit to AIG.[125] The government left the market and market experts befuddled as a result of its ad hoc bailout policy.[126] These actions signify the most high-profile and expensive bailouts amidst a flurry of bailout activity prior to the passage of the TARP program (discussed in chapter 6).[127] All of these bailouts make a mockery of a sound and disciplined lender of last resort function for aid to otherwise solvent banks, and our democracy itself, as the Fed and others exceeded their traditional statutory charters.[128]

Taxpayers not only paid for the bailouts but also suffered through a capital-starved economy. Predictably, all of these programs failed to re-ignite lending or to revive the economy. Instead, the banks hoarded capital. Essentially, the rationale for the big bailouts can be found not in economics but in political power. As Joseph Stiglitz states, the "big banks used their political influence to get deregulation; they used their political influence to stop initiatives for new regulations to restrict their excessive risk taking in derivatives; and not surprisingly, they then used their political influence to get this massive unwarranted transfer of money from the American taxpayers."[129] The bailouts proved costly, ineffective, and deeply suboptimal precisely because the bailouts appeared politically driven. As former President of the Federal Reserve Bank of St. Louis William Poole puts it:

> Our current bailout world is an affront to democracy. . . .We know that many executives of financial firms, despite huge losses, have larger fortunes remaining than most of us can ever dream of enjoying. Taxpayers, in general, will pay for losses incurred by the insolvent, or nearly insolvent, firms these executives left behind. These bitter attitudes in our society today tend to be dismissed as "populist." That is a mischaracterization; no one, whatever his political persuasion, should be willing to accept without complaint wealth transfers of the sort now taking place.[130]

These bailouts posing as lender of last resort loans to otherwise solvent banks so far exceed the authority of government officials as to constitute lawlessness.[131]

This entire regulatory morass in the financial sector created the essential conditions for a "bursting asset bubble nourished on high leverage," which is a macroeconomic nightmare that can take a nation "to the very gates of hell itself." Basically, asset values plunge after the bubble bursts, and a sudden contraction in credit meets an overleveraged economy, creating years of economic pain.[132] The good times in capitalism naturally encourage more risk taking, and particularly more debt. Continued economic stability—ironically as the result of modern countercyclical macroeconomic tools such as monetary policy and fiscal policy—naturally serves as validation for previous risks taken. As past economic crises and disruptions fade, humans will naturally fall prey to the lure of higher returns with seemingly low risk. Regulators and policymakers are not immune to this cognitive dissonance, particularly when campaign contributions and lucrative positions await the true believers. Ultimately the level of risk becomes unsustainable and the system becomes unstable. Then comes a Minsky moment—named after the economist Hyman Minsky—when a sudden realization that too much credit and investment based upon too much risk will not generate sufficient cash flow to repay debts. Sudden capital withdrawal and deleveraging must follow.[133]

Economists have long recognized the inherent instability of capitalism, and as a matter of historic fact bubbles, manias, and panics plague capitalism.[134] The key problem with regulation over the past few decades revolves around the political influence of those controlling concentrated economic resources. The financial sector simply became too big and too reckless through the subversion of legal and regulatory infrastructure at great cost to the economy in general.[135]

Securing Regulatory Infrastructure in the Financial Sector

This all naturally raises this question: How can law secure sound regulation necessary to support market functioning against the twin threats of excessive and prolonged stability as well as elite influence? I posit that depoliticized regulation, robust private enforcement, professionalization (especially professional sanctions, standards, and competency and ethics requirements), and a reappreciation of fiduciary responsibility can operate to secure legal and regulatory infrastructure in the financial sector. These mechanisms of accountability and constraint should operate to mitigate the negative consequences of the huge wealth now controlled by corporate and financial elites.

The Potential of Depoliticization

The New Deal marks the birth of the modern Federal Reserve. It centralized monetary policy in the hands of the Federal Reserve Board of Governors, a federal agency. In 1935, Congress stated that this independence would permit the Fed to vindicate the "general public interest" and not indulge "the majority of special interests." Since 1935, Congress and the executive, with the insistence of financial markets, remain committed to Fed independence over monetary policy. Today the Fed enjoys self-funding, high staff salaries, long tenure for Governors, and post-employment job restrictions.[136] This institutional design permits the Fed to set monetary policy free of special interest influence.[137] Yet the power the Fed holds as monetary authority and lender of last resort may well be enough power in one agency. The Fed's performance as bank regulator in the subprime crisis rates poorly.

At the least, the Fed should be restructured to eliminate the influence of the privately held regional banks. Private bank interests participate in making monetary policy through the Federal Open Market Committee, which includes regional Federal Reserve Bank Presidents. This committee influences short-term interest rates through the purchase and sale of government bonds. The Federal Reserve member banks (pure private banks) elect regional bank directors and ultimately presidents. The proximity of the Fed Governors to the banking interest appeared tolerable until recently.[138] Today, the proximity of the banking industry creates the appearance of corruption.[139]

The recent financial crisis proves that the Fed struggles to be an effective regulator. The nonregulation of subprime mortgages alone justifies a restructuring. The Fed also played key roles in facilitating the massive consolidation of the financial sector, undercutting the regulation of derivatives, and allowing its lender of last resort function to become a politicized bailout facility. Two means of improving the Fed's structure would entail (1) eliminating the influence of the private banks through the abolition of the regional banks and (2) limiting the Fed's function to that of a pure monetary policy agency, to the extent practicable.[140] The Dodd-Frank Act originally moved in this direction but failed to change the institutional structure of the Fed in a meaningful way.[141]

The Fed holds too much power to act as both monetary authority and regulator. Fed Chair Alan Greenspan's faith in markets seemingly rendered him ideologically blind to the possibility that asset bubbles could develop in response to lax monetary policy, and this blindness no doubt contributed to the subprime debacle. In addition, Greenspan ardently pursued deregulation that again seemed ideologically driven and certainly contributed to the ongoing financial crisis.[142] These blind spots support an argument for limiting the regulatory power of the monetary authority. Bank regulation and monetary policy simply cannot rest upon the ideology of a single person.

Economists argue that the Fed's regulatory functions enhance its performance as monetary regulator. Yet the United Kingdom splits monetary power and regulatory power. This seems advantageous simply from the point of view of fragmenting power within our democracy. The main advantage of combining these functions appears to relate to access to the examination reports and ratings that a bank regulatory authority routinely enjoys. One study concludes: "The results in this paper indicate that, at a minimum, the conduct of monetary policy requires full access to supervisory information."[143] Monetary authorities, however, need not hold regulatory power in order to enjoy regulatory access. The key is simply to include the Fed within the zone of agencies and regulators that may routinely review bank supervisory information, including real-time access to examinations and discussions with regulatory personnel. Moreover, the Fed's lender of last resort function would continue to provide a window on the health of banks even if Congress moved its regulatory functions to an agency less intertwined with private banking interests.

The SEC also should become more depoliticized.[144] By the time of the subprime fiasco, the SEC resembled a toothless tiger. The SEC succumbed quickly to the pressure of the investment banking industry to eliminate meaningful capital limitations. It also failed to exercise meaningful supervision of the investment banking industry after it assumed supervisory and examination powers pursuant to the Consolidated Supervised Entities Program. The sophisticated models the investment banking firms used to value assets and by extension the firms' capital far outpaced the ability of the SEC to monitor the firms according to the SEC's own internal auditor.[145] The Division of Enforcement at the SEC botched the investigation into the most massive Ponzi scheme in history, perpetrated at a registered securities industry firm, Madoff Investment Securities. Professor Jill Fisch notes that the SEC's reaction to the current crisis evinces "limited responsiveness." Indeed, its suspension of short-selling financial stocks marks its most high-profile action, and by any measure this effort to protect the financial sector from market pressure failed.[146] These regulatory weaknesses substantially contributed to the financial crisis.

The SEC behaved as if industry interests had captured it. For example, in a stunning display of political power CEO John Mack of Morgan Stanley called Senator Charles Schumer to obtain a ban on short selling of major financial firms. Soon thereafter the SEC banned short selling in the shares of nineteen financial stocks.[147] The SEC stood by silently as the financial sector used political connections to bully the Financial Accounting Standards Board (which is regulated directly by the SEC) into relaxing accounting rules so that banks might show more capital on their financial statements than under preexisting mark-to-market accounting.[148] "A few choice words from politicians was all it took for the fearless members of the accounting watchdog to turn from staunch defenders of 'fair value' [accounting] to advocates of the more 'flexible' approach so beloved by banks."[149] The SEC actively opposed efforts to regulate derivatives and supported its own rule requiring disclosure of derivatives risks with half-hearted enforcement efforts that Professor Fisch terms "a strikingly light touch."[150] The SEC's legal structure must impose additional protection from political pressure exerted by those with economic power.

The bank regulators could also benefit from enhanced political independence. Regulatory competition poses a major threat to sound regulation, if regulatory competition does not benefit from appropriate legal infrastructure. Bank regulation creates direct competition for client banks to charter under either state or federal regulatory regimens. Indeed, as previously mentioned, the largest subprime originator, Countrywide Financial, switched charters specifically in search of more permissive regulation for its subprime activities. None of the federal regulatory agencies did much to discipline subprime lenders or securitizers. In addition, by permitting ever more complex trading in over-the-counter derivatives, the banking regulators basically suspended capital rules and permitted even more leverage in the financial sector because such derivatives get priced to models, not to markets. This throws open the door for manipulation of minimum capital levels.[151]

Former Treasury Secretary Lawrence Summers, who had a front-row seat during the Clinton administration's forays into financial deregulation, bemoans the lack of space between those regulators that big finance co-opts and regulators ignorant of finance's complexities. According to Summers, "We have a broad social problem that covers everything from finance to deep sea drilling and nuclear power . . . there is hardly anybody who is both knowledgeable and not co-opted."[152] The legal design of regulatory institutions can create a class of expert regulators that can resist ultimately serving the needs of the regulated. High salaries, secure tenure, and post-employment job restrictions logically operate to shut down the revolving door between the regulated and the regulators and to secure sophisticated regulation.

Expanding Federal Professionalization

The toxic assets of the Great Depression consisted of shares in corporations rather than subprime mortgages. During the boom of the 1920s, fully one-half of the total securities issued by corporate America turned out to be worthless. Restoring market trust and confidence formed a cornerstone to the New Deal. The basic concept amounted to this: "[U]nless constant extension . . . of a fiduciary relationship—a guarantee of 'straight shooting'—supports the constant extension of mutual confidence that is the foundation of a maturing and complicated economic system, easy liquidity of the resources in which wealth is held poses a danger rather than a prop to the system."[153] Investment and financial markets can be built only upon trust; otherwise, they are fertile grounds for panics and busts.

The Securities Exchange Act of 1934 subjected every securities professional to registration, professional standards, and membership in self-regulatory organizations, all under the watchful supervision of the SEC. Despite constant erosion of these New Deal protections—ranging from forgetful courts' declining to hold securities firms accountable for breach of duty to a somnolent SEC—these professionalization schemes enjoyed long success in preventing another round of macroeconomically significant retail brokerage fraud.[154] In 2002, this basic approach to raising business standards to inspire financial market trust resolved the problems revealed in the accounting industry by the collapse of Enron and other corporate scandals. Professionalization also implies liability for professional malpractice. This constitutes an effective and low-cost means of imposing professional standards. In essence, private litigation creates market incentives to enforce the law.[155]

Professors Engle and McCoy propose that mortgage brokers be subject to suitability requirements. They propose that Congress mandate that mortgage lenders and brokers belong to a self-regulatory organization (SRO), akin to those in the securities industry. The SRO would set and enforce industry standards. SRO enforcement would complement private and government enforcement efforts. Engle and McCoy argue in favor of broad remedies for borrowers of unsuitable subprime loans, including reformation, rescission, disgorgement of illicit profits, and extending the right of redemption to those already foreclosed upon. A government agency could supervise arbitration of suitability claims to extend rapid and low-cost relief.[156] They further argue that assignees should bear liability for this same obligation because of the central role of assignees in the process of securitizing predatory loans.[157] This extension of New Deal principles to the problem of predatory lending can only be termed sensible.

Professor Frank Partnoy argues for professionalizing the rating agencies. He proposes an independent agency termed the Credit Rating Agency Oversight Board (CRAOB) modeled upon the Public Company Accounting Oversight Board (PCAOB), created under the Sarbanes-Oxley Act of 2002.[158] The CRAOB would exercise registration, examination, and enforcement power over the ratings agencies. The agency would enjoy independent funding in the form of user fees and operate subject to SEC oversight. Board members of the CRAOB would possess expertise in financial markets. Post-employment job restrictions would shut down the possibility of a revolving door between the regulatory agency and the rating agency. It would impose broad disclosure requirements upon the rating agencies, even with respect to methodologies. Partnoy's proposal would specifically entail congressional action to resolve the conflicts implicit in the issuer-pays model of rating; for example, the rating agencies (similar to accountants regulated under the PCAOB) could be barred from receiving any other compensation from issuers.[159] Partnoy strengthens his regulatory approach through a backstop of civil liability for rating agency misconduct.

Liability and Private Enforcement of Accountability

Partnoy posits that because the ratings agencies enjoy *de facto* immunity from liability, they behaved as expected: engaging in more negligent, reckless, or fraudulent behavior than if they faced real threat of liability. He suggests that the rating agencies exploit this immunity from liability to enhance their operating profits (for example, skimping on staff) and pay larger compensation to their senior officers. Thus, he argues that Congress should roll back the ratings agencies' immunity and impose accountability for flawed ratings on par with that of accountants and lawyers.[160] The expansion of civil liability standards to incentivize financial sector professionalism draws support from the success of the New Deal.

The final element of the New Deal approach to pulling the financial sector out of its laissez-faire abyss involved broadening concepts of fiduciary obligation, particularly with respect to disclosure obligations. As President Franklin Roosevelt himself stated in his message to Congress accompanying the Securities Act of 1933, "This proposal adds to the ancient rule caveat emptor, the further doctrine 'let the seller also beware.' It puts the burden of telling the whole truth on the seller."[161] Efficient markets require perfect information. So, the idea of legally requiring truth in the sale of securities supports financial market functioning. As previously mentioned, the federal securities laws enjoy solid empirical support for their operation as the epitome of legal infrastructure. The subversion of private actions under the federal securities laws broke down traditional disincentives facing securities fraudfeasors. For the first time ever in our history, the federal securities laws operated to shield fraudfeasors from liability for fraud after the PSLRA and the SLUSA.

If the federal securities laws retained their traditional emphasis on private enforcement, fraudfeasors in the entire financial sector, from ratings agencies to mortgage originators to the issuers, would face private liability for selling the predatory loans at the core of the current crisis. The issuers of such securities would be liable for reckless misstatements upon general averments of intent to defraud. Congress should repeal the PSLRA as well as the SLUSA. Further, Congress should abrogate the 1994 Supreme Court decision that insulated those aiding and abetting fraud from liability. This principle, if available today, could ensnare predatory loan originators as well as the ratings agencies that rated the pools of mortgages (or interests derived from such mortgages) sold to investors across the globe. The core misconduct at the center of this crisis occurred in the wake of the evisceration of private liability under the federal securities laws during the 1990s. Today the entire global economy bears the costs of this indulgence of financial elite power.[162]

The New Deal ushered in an era of legal accountability for financial elites. For nearly seventy years thereafter, the U.S. economy did not suffer from a major economic contraction or financial crisis related to financial skullduggery. Since the dismantling of the many New Deal protections, the economy has suffered through the Enron scandals, the options-backdating scandals, and the subprime fiasco. The New Deal also highlights the importance of an agency's institutional design for resisting political pressure, particularly in the context of the Fed's administration of monetary policy. Finally, the New Deal, through the Glass-Steagall Act, proves the success of containing financial firm size and separating high-risk activities from commercial banking. I revisit this proposal in chapter 6, where I define the contours of bailout authority as a means of ending the last vestiges of the too-big-to-fail dynamic. Here, the point is that solutions to the challenge of financial sector regulation do not lack in number—instead, the challenge lies in the power of elites. The Dodd-Frank Act proves the degree of difficulty present in constraining corporate and financial elites.

The Dodd-Frank Wall Street Reform and Consumer Protection Act

The Dodd-Frank Wall Street Reform and Consumer Protection Act[163] (Dodd-Frank) could qualify as one of the most heavily lobbied bills in history. Sources indicate that between January 2009 and June 2010 financial firms spent $591 million lobbying Congress. Additionally, since 1989, these firms spent $112 million in campaign contributions to the members of the Conference Committee that held final sway over the legislation.[164] Moreover, the frenzy of influence peddling shifted to the administrative level where the Act as finally passed authorized 243 rulemakings and 67 studies. Financial and public firms appear willing to spare no expense to influence these administrative proceedings and dramatically increased lobbying activity at both the SEC and the CFTC.[165] Against this barrage, sound policy stands little chance.

The Act itself holds some hope. For example, the law outlaws predatory home loans and extends borrowers potentially powerful remedies for violations of this prohibition.[166] It also creates a Consumer Financial Protection Bureau charged with protecting consumers from abusive credit transactions.[167] Congress also saw fit to subject the credit rating agencies to liability under the federal securities laws to the same extent as lawyers and accountants.[168] Perhaps most important, the Act gives regulators the power to break up large banks, albeit under narrow circumstances that requires action of the Fed (and a two-thirds vote of the Financial Stability Oversight Council, which includes the Secretary of the Treasury as Chair), which can be tightly aligned to the financial sector.[169]

On the other hand, the Act calls for a "study" of the PSLRA but no rollback of its provisions that operate to insulate securities fraudfeasors from liability.[170] The Act also mandates a study of the issuer-pays model of ratings agency compensation in 2012 but leaves that model intact while imposing only uncertain liability.[171] The Act separates certain high-risk trading and hedge fund activity from commercial banks, but complete divestment may be delayed until 2022.[172] The restrictions regarding derivatives trading by banks include exemptions that may well prove to swallow the rule and do not take effect until July 2014 at the earliest.[173] The Act largely preserves the ability of the Fed to expand its lender of last resort function into a broad-based bailout regime.[174]

Perhaps most notably, the Act fails to restructure any administrative agency, fails to repeal the PSLRA and the SLUSA, fails to create any new professionalization regime for any element of the financial sector, and fails to mandate the breakup of any large financial institution. A final assessment of the Act depends upon the actions and rulemaking of numerous administrative agencies. The efforts of the financial industry to weaken the Act over time could greatly undermine its promise. As memories of the cataclysm of 2008 fade, the public is not likely to remain engaged. Time is on the side of the financial sector. Indeed, the 2010 election swept into the House of Representatives a Republican majority that ran on an antiregulation platform.[175] Thus, Dodd-Frank seems destined to fail to curb the power of Wall Street and prevent another market collapse.

Attacks on regulatory infrastructure caused the subprime fiasco, and that is evidenced by the erosion of basic and sound regulatory principles. Much of that erosion lacks even minimal levels of rationale. Power, not policy, untethered corporate and financial elites from traditional concepts of accountability and supervision. The rule of law broke down. Elites exploited the failure of law to rig the system so that they made millions for destroying their firms and inflicted tremendous macroeconomic costs. The reaction included an unnecessarily harsh contraction in credit. Unemployment soared. By early 2013 the supposed economic recovery seemed anemic at best. Furthermore, an even more painful debt crisis rooted in European sovereign debt loomed.

4

Rigged Globalization

[H]igh levels of economic and political inequality tend to lead to
economic and social arrangements that systematically favor the
interests of those with more influence. Such economic institutions
can generate economic costs. . . . Society, as a whole, is then likely
to be more inefficient and to miss out on opportunities for innovation and investment.
World Bank (2005)[1]

Globalization is a rigged game. The present construction operates to maximize elite power to lower wages and to free elites from regulatory restraint.[2]
The legal framework governing globalization encourages a race to the bottom whereby nation-states compete for transnational corporate patronage in
exchange for diluted regulatory infrastructure.[3] It fails to adequately mitigate
poverty and secure robust macroeconomic growth.[4] It fails to stem chronic
financial instability.[5] According to Joseph Stiglitz, former Chief Economist
of the World Bank, the course of globalization responded to "what seemed
a curious blend of ideology and bad economics, dogma that sometimes
seemed to be thinly veiling special interests."[6] The current approach suffers
from four fatal flaws: Globalization focused excessively on lowering wages
rather than on durable buying power; it relied upon excessive debt in the
U.S. (and Europe) to fuel global consumption; it ignored market development that keys growth; and it failed to impose a reasonable regulatory infrastructure. These flaws subverted the fundamental promise of globalization to
alleviate poverty and enhance macroeconomic growth.

In the short term, this approach to globalization generated massive profits for those in control of transnational corporations (especially financial firms). Over the long term, most Americans and global citizens enjoyed few if any gains.[7] By late 2006, despite soaring productivity, wages had stagnated to such an extent that wage income in the U.S. reached a record low while corporate profits reached highs not seen since the 1960s.[8] In fact, today in the U.S. corporate profits set sixty-year highs and wages set sixty-year lows, as a percentage of GDP.[9] Today, the current system of globalization generates serial crises and fails to achieve maximum economic growth.[10] Once again, concentrated economic resources short-circuited the potential of capitalism.[11] The flaws plaguing globalization played themselves out in the 2007–9 global financial crisis, which led to trillions in costs and impoverished 90 million more global citizens.[12]

This chapter highlights these links and proposes a reconstructed globalization founded upon more rational legal and regulatory infrastructure. Here again, the fundamental challenge revolves around how law can inveigh against concentrated economic power, and here again corporate and financial elites lie at the crux of the issue. Corporate and financial elites garnered massive profits from the current configuration of our global economy and will naturally use that wealth to oppose any deep reform.

Globalization under the Washington Consensus

Globalization evolved under the close supervision of the U.S. government, and many commentators refer to its core elements as the product of "the Washington Consensus."[13] In 2004, I wrote about the shortcomings of the laissez-faire Washington Consensus and posited that financial deregulation in particular poses "extraordinary risks" to global financial stability.[14] In 2006, I argued that a crisis of buying power made a financial crisis imminent because the global economy relied too much on consumption founded upon debt in the U.S.[15] In 2007, I termed the legal frameworks governing globalization "woefully inadequate" and stated that the global economy "[seemed] destined for catastrophe."[16] These shortcomings played a major role in the financial crisis of 2007–9 and greatly facilitated its propagation to the four corners of the globe.[17]

American Domination of Globalization

U.S. transnational corporations hold decisive influence over the course of globalization, and the legal framework governing free trade—ranging from preservation of domestic agriculture subsidies to patent protection for life-saving drugs—reflects this power.[18] First, the U.S. controls key institutional elements of the global economy, including the International Monetary Fund (IMF), the World Bank, and the World Trade Organization (WTO). Second, the political context within the U.S. is such that globalization issues are determined by transnational corporations and particularly their CEOs. The Department of the Treasury acts on behalf of financial firms; the Department of Commerce acts on behalf of industrial firms.[19] Therefore, given CEO primacy over the corporation, globalization has been structured to serve the interests of CEOs of transnational corporations.[20] Those interests revolve around short-term profits with little or no regard for long-term stability and growth.

With respect to the World Bank and the IMF, the U.S. exercises informal power to select the head of the World Bank and essentially exercises veto power over the IMF. Only the U.S. holds this kind of effective veto over the IMF.[21] These powers rest primarily with the Department of the Treasury. "The IMF and the World Bank were part of Treasury's turf, an arena [in] which . . . they were allowed to push their perspectives, just as other departments, within their domains, could push theirs."[22] The Department of the Treasury, in turn, tends to the interests of Wall Street firms.[23] Moreover, the U.S. also has a high degree of leverage over both the World Bank and the IMF as a result of its funding practices with regard to both of those agencies. Each time the IMF or World Bank requests funds, Congress uses the opportunity to threaten to withhold funds. Thus, the international financial institutions must placate not just the current administration but also Congress.[24]

The U.S. also possesses a high degree of informal power as the largest shareholder of the international financial institutions. The staffs understand that it is a waste of time to present any important recommendation without first clearing it with the U.S.[25] "In sum, the US has substantial capabilities to bring to bear in shaping the mandates, policies and *modus operandi* of [the] international financial institutions."[26] Thus, when the U.S. Treasury pushed for financial market liberalization, the IMF and World Bank pushed for financial market liberalization.[27] Deregulation, reduction of trade barriers, and an austere vision of government action came to define this version of globalization under the stewardship of the Washington Consensus.[28] The U.S. thus determines the core aspects of policy and structure within both the IMF and the World Bank.

With respect to the WTO, the U.S. enjoys disproportionate bargaining power in negotiations as a result of the size of its consumer market.[29] The former chief economist of the World Bank Joseph Stiglitz suggests that "in practice the United States, Europe and Japan have dominated" the consensus-driven WTO process.[30] This is because if the U.S. rejects a given trade agreement, then the trade agreement is rendered meaningless because of the size of the U.S. consumer market.[31] "The U.S. enjoys an unspoken veto over the appointment of the director general of the WTO and key staff."[32] The U.S. uses the WTO accession process to advance its foreign policy.[33] Further, few countries can match the administrative infrastructure and the resources that the U.S. can bring to bear in the context of any trade dispute.[34] Thus, it is fair to say that the U.S. also enjoys decisive influence over the WTO.[35]

The WTO arguably holds the most power of the three international financial institutions. The IMF and the World Bank are essentially limited to helping nations manage currency crises and to granting development loans, respectively. The WTO, on the other hand, has the power to adjudicate trade disputes that could bear on the domestic policies of member states.[36] One example of the scope of its power relates to its adjudication of a trade dispute over genetically modified foods. In 2008, the WTO prohibited Europe's effort to slow down the introduction of genetically modified foods on the grounds that the European Union's moratorium amounted to an unfair trade practice.[37] The WTO operates as referee of free trade and consequently wields tremendous influence over all aspects of the global economy.

The power of the U.S. over the WTO, and therefore over virtually all aspects of globalization, is exercised primarily through the president, the Congress, the State Department, the Treasury Department, and the Commerce Department.[38] Each of these entities responds to varied political pressures, yet the power of transnational corporations predominates on virtually all levels. The Commerce Department, for example, formulates trade policy in conjunction with an advisory committee that represents industry.[39] U.S. transnational corporations and the financial services sector enjoy ascendant political power as more of the nation's output is dependent upon free trade.[40] The course of globalization seldom ranks as a major political issue in U.S. elections because globalization (based upon market fundamentalism) enjoys deep bipartisan support.[41] Democratic processes do not affect the major elements of globalization. This political vacuum opened the door for corporate and financial elites and fueled the renewed policy emphasis on trade liberalization and laissez-faire global regulation.

This political reality led to a globalization constructed upon obsolete premises. Free market dogma formed the ideological basis for globalization. This free market mantra means an extremely limited role for government intervention in the economy of developing nations and the world economic system. Thus, the global economy rests upon a laissez-faire foundation (except for the freedom of people to move in response to higher wages). Finally, this extreme adherence to market fundamentalism means that trade barriers for goods and capital should always be eliminated immediately, and capital markets should be fully deregulated. The subprime mortgage debacle demonstrates the dangers of allowing this model of globalization to persist. In short, laissez-faire globalization conveniently generated massive profits for corporate and financial elites even while fomenting financial crises and economic disruptions.

Trade Imbalances, Job Losses, and Debt

Immediately prior to the financial crisis of 2007–9, the U.S. trade deficit stood at $788 billion. This means the U.S. consumed more than $2 billion more in foreign goods per day than it produced in exports. Financing the difference between exports and imports meant the U.S. rang up a current deficit of roughly the same amount and foreigners acquired that amount in claims—mainly debt claims—against the U.S. economy. Essentially the U.S. borrowed $2 billion a day to finance excessive consumption on the backs of mostly poorer developing nations. Even those taking an initially sanguine view of these imbalances ultimately concluded that the constant demand for and accumulation of U.S. debt instruments in connection with the trade deficit led to lower interest rates in the U.S. that "facilitated a boom in residential [real estate] and mortgage lending."[42] Others state that "epitomized by the China–U.S. bilateral trade relationship, these imbalances played at the very least an important supporting role in bringing on the financial crisis."[43] Nouriel Roubini and Stephen Mihm argue that these trade imbalances inherently destabilize the global economy and will lead to serial crises if not remedied.[44] Former Treasury Secretary Henry Paulson lists the trade imbalances as the first of four "crucial" issues driving the subprime crisis.[45]

The U.S. trade and current account imbalances metastasized from deep roots. After the historic East Asian currency crisis of the late 1990s, developing nations around the globe cut back on investment and consumption in order to save more and build foreign reserves, so that their currencies would stabilize.[46] Holding reserves in an easily converted currency like the dollar means that a nation could sell reserves in a crisis to constrict the global supply of its own currency and thereby protect its value. Holding reserves therefore provides ammunition to protect currency value, and to deter speculative attacks upon a currency. By 2006, China alone held nearly $1 trillion in dollar reserves and other East Asian countries held another $1.3 trillion—and most of these reserves are held in the form of (perceived) safe debt instruments.

This massive accumulation of dollar reserves created excess demand for dollar-denominated debt, strengthening the dollar, making imports cheaper, and lowering interest rates in America.[47]

The stronger dollar also allowed developing nations to export more to the U.S. A stronger dollar means Americans can buy more foreign goods. Unfortunately, a stronger greenback rendered the U.S. less competitive on global product markets and contracted U.S. manufacturing and exports because the stronger dollar meant that foreigners paid more for U.S. exports. Thus, the accumulation of dollar reserves exacerbated the loss of American jobs stemming from its higher-wage labor. Predictably, American wages for the vast majority of American workers stagnated for years leading up to the crisis. From 1999 to 2004, median household income plunged by 3 percent in real terms.[48]

After the crash of the tech bubble in stocks, foreign investors demanded lower risk assets. In response, the financial sector manufactured securities based on a wide variety of debt claims, particularly mortgage debt, traditionally viewed as low risk.[49] These constant and large capital flows lowered interest rates and depressed risk premia across the spectrum of American debt instruments.[50] Ultimately, "much of the U.S. housing bubble . . . was financed by non-residents—during the boom years they purchased more than half of the mortgage backed securities and collateralized debt obligations."[51] This influx of cheap capital, in turn, caused housing prices in the U.S. to soar. Americans felt wealthier and spent more. This meant even more debt for Americans.[52] After all, if home prices continued their upward trend, net worth could increase even if consumers accumulated more debt. By 2006, U.S. savings actually turned negative.[53] The Bush tax cuts of 2001–3 exacerbated this lack of savings, as the government swung into chronic fiscal deficit.[54]

Meanwhile, nations such as China happily obliged the debt binge. China's rapid expansion of manufacturing required a favorable exchange rate with the U.S. China engineered a favorable exchange rate through massive purchases of U.S. assets. This created higher demand for the dollar, which operated to buoy its value and make Chinese goods less expensive for American consumers. Basically, the U.S. acted as consumer of last resort fueling Chinese growth—as well as that of emerging markets around the world. Unfortunately, as wages stagnated in the U.S., consumption could only continue based upon debt.[55] By late 2007, just before the crisis, the U.S. consumed much more than it produced.[56] The resulting lofty debt levels imperiled even the dollar's status as reserve currency.[57]

The capital flows—from developing nations to fund consumption in developed nations—proved catastrophically large. On the cusp of the crisis, total estimated reserves approached $7.5 trillion.[58] Necessarily, these reserves mean an increase in debt across the globe—every creditor needs a debtor.[59] This excessive debt effectively buried durable buying power. The U.S. acted as the consumer of last resort accumulating vast debt to furnish unsustainable demand to the global economy. While the U.S. bore the brunt of these capital flows, the euro served as the secondary reserve currency.

The accumulation of euros also led to a concomitant loss of competitiveness and excessive debt in the eurozone. According to the European Central Bank, as of the end of 2010, euro-denominated assets constituted 26.3 percent of all reserves.[60] The huge cash flows from the developing world fueled debt accumulation in Greece, Spain, Ireland, Portugal, and the entire European Union. Once the crisis of 2007–9 crippled the global economy, these nations buckled under their own excessive debt loads.[61] The debt crisis inevitably moved from U.S. shores to engulf the eurozone.

Over a period of twenty years the U.S. went from the largest creditor nation to the largest debtor nation. External debt nearly doubled to 40 percent of GDP by 2008. This is on par with Argentina's debt levels prior to its financial meltdown in 2001.[62] Declining wages and job prospects within the U.S. rendered that level of debt unsustainable. Even prior to the subprime implosion, economists warned that "the current system is fraying at the edges." The essential problem arising from this dollar reserve system is that "the reserve currency country winds up getting increasingly into debt, which eventually makes its currency ill suited for reserves."[63] Moreover, there is "something unseemly about the poorest countries providing low interest loans to the richest."[64] With more than 2 billion souls subsisting on less than two dollars per day, it is simply impossible to justify $788 billion per year flowing to the U.S. to finance predatory lending of the disempowered there. Legal frameworks must operate to disrupt this economically and morally bankrupt reality.

Essentially the entire global economy leveraged growth upon the cheap labor of the developing world and the ever-increasing indebtedness of the developed world. A debt crisis seemed all but certain from this perspective. All this cheap debt triggered a global housing market bubble. In fact, Joseph Stiglitz, Nouriel Roubini, Robert Shiller, and other economists predicted a crisis arising from the bursting of the bubble and the excessive debt generated by globalization.[65] Throughout 2005–7, many experts raised alarms that the global economy faced a meltdown.[66] Former Fed Chair Paul Volcker projected a 75 percent probability of a financial crisis, and the chief economist of Morgan Stanley predicted financial "Armageddon."[67] *The Economist* warned in mid-2005 that a painful global housing crash appeared imminent and one year later that a global debt crisis loomed.[68]

The future looks even bleaker. The economist Alan Blinder, a former Vice Chairman of the Federal Reserve Board of Governors, analyzed precisely the degree to which American jobs and wages suffered under the cheap labor model of globalization. Blinder suggests that service jobs which traditionally were considered nontradable now are tradable through the advent of superior information and communications technology. He argues that service jobs will increasingly need to compete with lower-cost labor in increasingly educated nations such as China and India. Only jobs that require face-to-face interaction will be secure; all other jobs may move offshore. Blinder thus projects that all 14.3 million manufacturing jobs that remain in the U.S. are movable. He estimates that up to 42 million U.S. service jobs will be susceptible to offshoring in the electronic future. Nearly 60 million jobs could evaporate in the U.S. under the current regimen of globalization. Even in jobs not likely to flee, the U.S. will suffer from lower wages as workers flood into positions that cannot be offshored. This implies a major loss of durable buying power within the U.S. as wages decline and jobs flow to lower-wage locales. According to Blinder, nations must emphasize creativity in order to maintain high living standards. Blinder calls for new educational initiatives and enhanced adjustment assistance and social safety nets in the U.S. to help workers transition to a new global economy. Blinder suggests this process is just beginning and will take decades to wind down.[69]

I argued in 2006 that while economists like Blinder correctly assessed the massive impact of globalization on the U.S. economy, they generally failed to contend with the issue of stabilizing global consumption in the face of constant downward pressure on wages and the massive accumulation of dollar reserves. I noted that wages for the vast majority of workers in the U.S. stagnated for three decades under the cheap labor model of globalization while wages for those in the 99.99 percentile had increased 467 percent. Debt, meanwhile, exploded in the 1990s, with consumer debt alone increasing by 53 percent. This planted the seeds of the subprime debacle. Higher wages sustain higher debt; lower wages and higher debt cannot be sustained.[70] Thus, globalization urgently needs reform.

These huge trade imbalances hardly developed in stealth. This begs the question: Why did governing elites take zero action to address these imbalances before the collapse of the American consumer under the weight of massive subprime loans in 2007–8? Corporate and financial elites made a killing under this market fundamentalist perversion of globalization. The ability to manufacture in low-cost wage locales such as China and to sell in highly prosperous locales like the U.S. spelled easy money. Sustainability means little if CEOs focus more on annual bonuses tied to stock

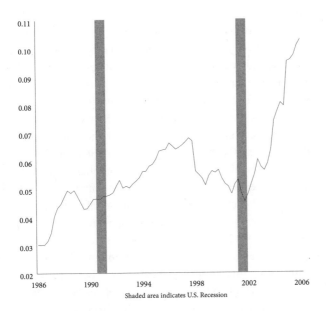

Figure 4.1 Corporate profits/GDP (Source: Federal Reserve Bank of St. Louis)

performance and the ever-present protection of golden parachute arrangements approved by board cronies. The easy money explains the structure of globalization—cheap wages and consumption on steroids fueled by excessive debt. As I stated in 2007, "CEOs have the motive and the means to increase their compensation notwithstanding the deleterious long term financial consequences."[71] The accompanying graph shows the enhanced profitability of corporations relative to GDP over the past twenty years of globalization on the cusp of the crisis.

Today, globalization furnishes yet another means by which corporate and financial elites use their political power to impose massive costs worldwide in order to boost their short-term compensation payouts (based upon higher profits).

Fundamentally, globalization as presently constructed means lower wages. The law governing globalization permits greatly enhanced mobility for jobs. Thus, more lost buying power seems inevitable. The nations receiving jobs cannot replace that lost buying power. By definition, the jobs move to low-cost locales. Further, these nations must save massive funds in order to continue to accumulate dollar reserves. China, for example, spends about one-half of what the U.S. spends on consumption relative to GDP.[72] As previously noted, many nations other than China accumulate dollar reserves, amounting to trillions more in lost demand.[73] Unsustainable debt replaced sustainable wage growth. Therefore, total wages suffer a net decline each time a job is moved to a lower-wage nation seeking to grow through exports, and more potential demand evaporates as a result of the excess savings implicit in the accumulation of dollar reserves.

This leads to debt-fueled consumption that leads to financial crises. Economists warned in 2005 that the U.S. faced an inevitable debt crisis.[74] The subprime debacle delivered on that prediction. After the stock market collapse of 2001–2, the huge capital inflows sought safe debt securities.[75] Mortgage debt appeared safe. So-called financial innovation channeled that debt into seemingly attractive securities backed by subprime mortgages.[76] Put simply, a classic Minsky credit cycle arose out of the model of globalization founded on cheap labor and the financial imbalances it spawned. Too much debt simply creates the conditions for a debt crisis and ensuing credit crunch.[77] Even today, debt accumulates at an alarming rate, although it finances tax cuts for the very wealthy rather than subprime mortgages.[78] The accompanying chart shows the continuation of the American current account deficit notwithstanding the crisis, and ever deeper debt arising from the current structure of globalization.

The U.S. still gorges on too much debt, even today. Indeed, the entire developed world gorged on excessive debt, and a sovereign debt crisis now seems imminent, threatening the economic viability of the eurozone.[79] This excessive debt finds its roots in the structure of globalization.

The first fatal flaw in the construction of globalization stems from its cheap labor bias.[80] The bias arises from the emphasis on free movement of both capital and goods, but no similar effort to allow the free movement of labor, as will be discussed in the next section.

The Problem with Free Movement of Jobs but Not People

If capital is empowered to move freely, then it will gravitate to the lowest-wage locale and flee high-wage locales. If labor lacks the ability to relocate out of low-wage locales, then the low-wage labor is locked in and cannot seek higher wages. This will enhance transnational corporate profitability. But consumption will dissipate. Every job that exits a high-wage locale and enters a low-wage locale destroys buying power, to the extent that labor payouts suffer relative to profit payouts in the form of dividends or bonuses to senior executives, who are unlikely to consume all their earnings. Further, every worker entering a high-wage locale creates productivity gains as

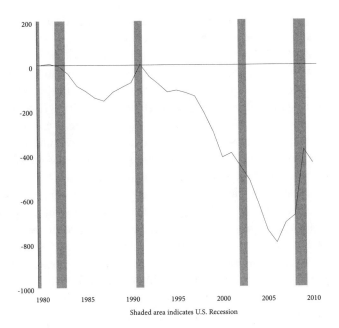

Shaded area indicates U.S. Recession

Figure 4.2 Balance on Current Account (Source: Federal Reserve Bank of St. Louis)

a result of greater demand for all goods and services, and therefore durable buying power.[81]

One important reform would entail empowering labor to move to its highest and best use, just as capital or jobs may move to more profitable locales. Free market capitalism supports the creation of a trade regimen that sought to vindicate gradually the right of people to move to their highest and best use. Capitalist theory long emphasized that all resources must be perfectly mobile in order for markets to allocate wealth efficiently.[82] Given the centrality of human capital to innovation-led growth, impediments to the free movement of labor entail great costs. Decades ago, economists estimated that global output could double under a free movement of labor approach.[83] More recently, economists put the cost of barriers to labor mobility at $55 trillion.[84] The benefits of free labor mobility include enhanced cultural diversity, which can operate to enhance cognitive functioning and support enhanced innovation.[85] Moreover, because of the value of labor complementarity, high-wage labor may increase its productivity when low-wage labor becomes more available.[86] Finally, enhanced market development associated with developed nations means that human capital is more productive in a prosperous environment than in an impoverished environment. Each of these factors should be considered in greater detail.

Complementary labor inputs do not compete but instead enhance total productivity. In fact, in a cross-country regression of per capita income on immigration, economists found immigration to be positively and causally related to per capita income gains in the destination country even for the great weight of native labor.[87] Not only does per capita income rise, but generally immigrants are a net fiscal positive by generating tax revenues that exceed government expenditures.[88] This all seems counterintuitive, as increasing the supply of labor should theoretically operate to lower wages. Nevertheless, if immigrant labor is complementary to native labor rather than redundant, then immigrant labor could furnish additional labor resources to relieve shortages—shortages that hold back native labor. This occurs when immigrant labor fills gaps rather than competes with native labor. Shortages will naturally create wage incentives that draw immigrants in the first instance.[89] Moreover, injecting low-cost labor into a high-cost locale can operate to discourage offshoring of jobs, because lower-cost domestic labor then competes with cheap foreign labor.[90] Thus, states with more immigration enjoyed more productive workers than states with lower levels of immigrants.[91] Apparently, immigrants free native labor to focus on the most productive tasks. Simply stated, complementary immigration enhances growth worldwide as well as in the receiving nation.

Allowing those workers located in low-wage locales to migrate to high-wage locales would effectively counteract the movement of jobs to low-wage nations by enhancing total labor productivity.[92] The same human capital immediately becomes more valuable (i.e., more productive) in a high-wage environment because of the deeper and broader market associated with high wages. In one study that used data from forty-two nations, the average gain in worker income from emigrating to the U.S. exceeded 400 percent, holding human capital constant.[93] Migrants enjoy higher wages, and nonmigrants enjoy higher wages as the labor supply contracts in the country sending migrant labor.[94] Studies suggest, for example, that wages in Mexico increased by 8 percent between 1970 and 2000, based upon emigration of workers.

While the sending country may face a possible "brain drain," it appears that nations invest more in human capital formation when emigration possibilities pose the opportunity for additional returns to human capital investments.[95] Further, migrating workers typically remit part of their earnings to relatives in their home country; these remittances support demand and further human capital formation in the home country.[96] Apparently, the major source of wage inequality in the world today is unequal returns to human capital rather than the accumulation of human capital; therefore, free movement of labor can generate out-sized gains through remediation of inefficient human capital distribution. Free movement of labor holds the promise of massive economic gains relative even to enhanced human capital investment.[97]

Immigration also spurs innovation through enhanced cultural diversity. In a recent study, economists found that in the U.S., immigrants patent at double the native rate. Moreover, based upon state data, immigrants spur patents sought by natives. States with higher levels of immigrants saw native patents jump by 15 percent.[98] This finding is consistent with studies finding that urban areas with a larger share of immigrants achieved higher growth. Thus, immigration operates not just to exploit well-developed markets but to contribute to well-developed markets through enhanced workforce cognition and innovation.[99] In the end, durable consumption rests upon enhanced worker productivity. The global economy of the 2000s needed more balanced consumption and production. Allowing the free movement of labor offers one possible solution to the huge imbalances that marred the global economy in the years prior to the debt crisis.

Developed nations learned from experience that capitalism can achieve high levels of macroeconomic growth only if regulatory infrastructure guides free markets and secures a robust middle class. Yet, corporate elites set globalization on a path toward a perverse form of laissez-faire that fundamentally empowered capital over people. This proved corrosive to a robust middle class and created a chronic crisis of buying power as elites chose short-term profits over sustainable globalization, a pattern further evidenced by the fate of economic human rights. Securing the right of labor to move freely in accordance with capitalist theory will add trillions in new wealth to the global economy. Other economic human rights can further secure a more robust global economy.

Global Market Development under Law

As demonstrated in chapter 2, the division of labor (or the specialization of labor) and the extent of effective buying power constitute the key drivers of growth. This suggests that globalization can charge transnational economic growth by extending markets. Instead of market development, corporate elites exploited the most well-developed consumer market in the world—the U.S. consumer market. The U.S. acted as the consumer of last resort worldwide, but globalization subverted the American consumer through the offshoring of jobs and cheap debt. In a classic tragedy of the commons episode, globalization drained jobs and buying power from the U.S. and substituted unsustainable debt to maintain the flow of profits today in exchange for a devastating debt crisis in the future.

Consumption worldwide suffers from stunted development relative to the potential implicit in a well-regulated consumer society supported by broad-based and durable macroeconomic growth. As referenced previously, China consumes at one-half the rate of the U.S., and the accumulation of dollar reserves represents a constant drain on durable buying power. Today, global currency reserves exceed $10 trillion.[100] This represents massive demand destruction as well as excessive debt subsidies at the heart of the global economy.

In mid-2006, I suggested that expanded protection for economic human rights could spur accelerated economic development worldwide and thereby spur more balanced global consumption.[101] Using the Universal Declaration of Human Rights as a template, I argued that universal basic education, accessible higher education based upon merit, decent health care, and strong social safety nets would both enhance macroeconomic performance and empower consumers worldwide.[102] Similarly, the International Covenant on Economic, Social and Cultural Rights seeks to secure rights to employment, wages sufficient for a "decent living," "healthy working conditions," "social security," "the widest possible protection and assistance" for families, "special measures of protection" for women and children, the right to be free from hunger, and the right to enjoy "the highest attainable standard of physical and mental health."[103]

The Universal Declaration of Human Rights passed the United Nations General Assembly on December 10, 1948, in the wake of World War II. Economic human rights became part of the Universal Declaration at the insistence of the Soviet Union. As such, economic rights bore a scarlet taint.[104] I posited, however, that economic rights serve to perfect capitalism insofar as such rights could break down oppressive realities and permit each individual to reach his or her full economic potential. Thus, the irony: The Soviet Union's push for economic human rights could serve to place capitalism on a more perfect foundation. Human rights, by definition, place human capabilities at the forefront of the nation-state's responsibilities. Human economic potential expands the concept of market ideals. As such, they pave the way for the realization of supplemented notions of perfect competition such as that articulated in chapter 2.

For example, the Universal Declaration articulates a broad vision of mass education by stating that "everyone" is entitled to a basic education and that advanced education should be "generally available" on the "basis of merit."[105]

"Researchers have found repeatedly that education plays a major role in economic growth."[106] Basic education is fundamental to economic performance; thus, raising literacy rates is a powerful means of achieving greater economic growth. "A country that achieves literacy scores one percent higher than average ends up . . . with labor productivity and GDP per capita respectively higher by 2.5 and 1.5 percent on average."[107] Higher education is crucial for innovation and is therefore a key driver of growth in developed and developing countries.[108] Indeed, expanding wage premiums for college graduates since World War II suggest that demand for educated workers outstrips supply. Yet, the transition to a knowledge-based economy that relies upon innovation to drive technological change requires more highly educated workers.[109]

A laissez-faire approach to education will fail to ensure that appropriate educational investments are made because of imperfect credit markets that allocate funds to those with collateral instead of to those with talent as well as the fact that education spurs positive spillovers that diminish individual incentives for investment. More specifically, because the poor have inadequate collateral they are credit-constrained and unable to develop their human capital; under such conditions, government could enhance growth and incentives by giving all children access to excellent educational opportunities.[110] As the World Bank notes, imperfect credit markets mean that highly capable poor children will not get basic education while wealthy children who are less able may go to college.[111] This "tyranny of collateral" invariably translates into a massive loss of economic opportunity and diminished growth.[112] These credit constraints compromise innovation-led growth and, ultimately, durable consumption.

Politically, education will get short shrift because of the extended period necessary for the full benefits of such investments to come to fruition.[113] Indeed, even public funding of education is subject to imperfections, as politically powerful elites will work to divert public funds from broad-based education.[114] One study found that funding on education is biased toward the rich and that "weak governance leads to intensified rent-seeking over public education funds, increasing inequality, reducing social mobility, and slowing growth."[115] As could be expected, in an environment with high political inequality, elites will diminish public education funding.[116] Thus, funding for education suffers financing infirmities.

Additionally, given the huge economic payoffs of appropriate education, facilitating deeper and broader education investments will lead to enhanced economic growth. As demonstrated previously, in chapter 1, skills development (rather than mere years of schooling) is powerfully associated with rapid economic growth. On the other hand, inequality in human capital formation operates to stunt growth. China achieved massive human capital investment at the same time it achieved very high economic growth. The World Bank found that the return on educational investments yields more than 25 percent for primary education and more than 17 percent for secondary education. Thus, there is a compelling need for vindication of an economic human right to education.[117]

Of course, it makes no sense to try to educate starving children, or to expect diseased citizens to be innovative. The Universal Declaration seeks to secure the right to an "adequate" standard of living, including "food, housing and medical care."[118] Included in this concept is a value of "special care and assistance" for mothers and children.[119] Yet according to the World Bank, global inequities in health care are massive, and today, in part because of the onset of the AIDS crisis, life expectancy gains from prior decades are being reversed.[120] Children in particular are suffering as even basic measures of childhood well-being—like infant mortality—differ radically between nations. In the U.S., "7 out of every 1000 American babies die in the first year of their lives, [while] 126 of every 1,000 Malian babies do."[121] These differences in basic life chances lack any economic justification.

Nor does the wanton destruction of human capital stop at birth. "Evidence supports the view that investing in early childhood [nutrition] has large impacts on children's health and readiness to learn and can bring important economic returns later in life—often greater than investments in formal education." For example, studies suggest that undersized Jamaican children suffered from "lower levels of cognitive development than those of normal height" but that enhanced nutrition and mental stimulation essentially wiped out the disadvantage over 24 months.[122] Again, societies that secure these rights for their citizens enjoy handsome dividends in terms of economic growth—amounting to several percentage points of GDP.[123] Other studies find that health capital accounts for about 22 to 30 percent of economic growth and that increasing life expectancy by one year may raise economic growth by up to 4 percent per annum. The World Bank specifically recognizes that strong social safety nets encourage household risk taking, which in turn can spur innovation. Because entrepreneurs generate social benefits that exceed private benefits and strong social safety nets encourages risk-taking, strong social safety nets can rightly be termed a meta-idea—that is, ideas which support the generation of more ideas. Apparently, strong social safety nets ensure that children can accumulate human capital and operate to encourage citizens to take risks that lead to innovations.[124] The size of gains from such investments suggests that societies are under-investing in social safety nets.

Moreover, weak social safety nets may also be associated with financial crises and disruptions. Professor Raghuram Rajan makes exactly this argument in his recent book *Fault Lines*. Rajan argues that in the U.S. political elites found it expedient to support consumption through wider access to credit rather than to invest in education, which has extended payoff periods—payoff periods that would include a time when such elites were no longer in office. Thus, in the face of declining wages, high inequality, and more difficult employment prospects, the U.S. gorged on debt. This high level of debt destabilized the economy and ultimately triggered a historic credit crunch. Rajan specifically argues that stronger safety nets would have relieved political pressure to maintain living standards through enhanced debt.[125]

The Universal Declaration also states that "everyone" is entitled to be free from discrimination, presumably based upon race, gender, caste, religion, class, or similar constructs.[126] Economists have long recognized that because these constructs have nothing to do with merit and operate to strip people of the opportunity to be as productive as their talents permit, discrimination based upon such elements reduces the output of a nation's labor force.[127] The World Bank documents the underlying dynamics of how artificial constructs destroy human capital.[128] In a recent study, the Bank found that lower-caste children in India taking cognitive tests scored lower than high-caste children when caste was announced but scored at parity when caste was concealed.[129] This study replicates the work of Professor Claude Steele in demonstrating the pernicious effects of "stereotype threat" on the performance of African Americans in the U.S.—as well as studies from around the world demonstrating compromised performance by oppressed minorities worldwide.[130]

All of these human rights ultimately prove conducive, even essential, to growth.[131] Unfortunately, human rights (including economic human rights) are enforced through moral suasion and embarrassing publicity rather than through more meaningful legal sanctions. Currently, economic human rights are enforced pursuant to annual reporting obligations to the Committee on Economic, Social, and Cultural Rights. This committee is charged with monitoring states' compliance with economic human rights and has the power to make recommendations for compliance. These recommendations do not have the force of law.[132] No transnational authority can mandate that any sovereign nation make any expenditure to support human rights.[133] Nor will such an authority emerge anytime soon. States value sovereignty too much to create such a broad and arguably intrusive array of enforceable economic human rights. Moreover, spending alone will not remedy human rights deficiencies arising within corrupt states. Governance matters, and sovereignty means that states enjoy autonomy to allocate funds for educational and other human rights expenditures. This can impede the effectiveness of government spending and therefore the realization of economic human rights.[134]

The World Bank, the International Monetary Fund, and the World Trade Organization, however, hold vast powers over the course of globalization, and these powers frequently impinge upon traditional notions of sovereignty. The World Bank exists for the purpose of promoting "long range balanced growth of international trade [and] for the development of productive resources of members, thereby assisting in raising productivity."[135] The IMF's purpose is to expand trade and promote high levels of employment.[136] The WTO promotes free trade and macroeconomic growth and stability.[137] Thus, each of these organizations certainly could conclude that economic rights are within the scope of its mission, given that such rights support macroeconomic growth. Nevertheless, none of these three institutions pursues economic human rights with the vigor that such rights deserve.

Instead, these institutions seem primarily concerned with serving the interests of transnational corporations, generally, and global banks, in particular. According to Professor Stiglitz, the IMF, the World Bank, and the WTO respond first and foremost to the interests of the financial and business community.[138] Thus, when the IMF lent to nations suffering financial disruptions, it would frequently insist that the nation raise interest rates and cut social spending as a condition to receiving IMF assistance. The World Bank essentially followed suit. The WTO, for its part, allows nation states to ascend to full membership with little concern for human rights and instead seems politically driven. More than anything, these institutions have used their clout to support market fundamentalism: maximum privatization, financial liberalization, fiscal austerity, and immediate elimination of all trade barriers. This completely subverted the reasons for their creation—to provide countercyclical global stimulus, to avert financial crises, and to facilitate growth through open trade.[139]

One means of securing more vigorous enforcement of economic human rights would involve a shift toward growth through individual empowerment within the IMF, World Bank, and the WTO. The fact that no single nation could fund the kind of massive human capital investments envisioned herein does not mean that the world economy lacks the resources to fund such economically compelling investments; the problem is one of organization, not resources, as China alone holds $3.2 trillion in foreign exchange reserves (mostly in dollars and the balance largely in European currencies).[140]

With global currency reserves now totaling more than $10 trillion, the world holds the resources to fund economic development on a grand scale that would dwarf the Marshall Plan or the GI Bill.[141] These resources currently subsidize excess consumption fueled by excess debt within the developed world—especially the U.S. and Europe—and operate to expose the global economy to serial financial crises. The global community could redeploy these resources to help finance a more sound global economy. If there were a global bank in which nations deposited their reserves safely (such as with the IMF) while such funds were productively invested in economic development (under the development expertise of the World Bank), then these massive reserves could support growth rather than unsustainable debt-driven consumption in the developed economies.

In other words, these resources could be banked, and therefore leveraged, to fund the most promising human capital and infrastructure investments within the developing world.[142] This could, in turn, create a durable foundation for more expansive and stable global consumption. Economists since John Maynard Keynes in 1944 have argued in favor of precisely this kind of support for durable global growth. Moreover, the IMF would need only extend modestly its current operations as global lender of last resort to provider of a global reserve currency.[143] The details admittedly involve a level of complexity beyond the scope of this book; nevertheless, the world clearly holds sufficient wealth to fund massive economic development perhaps exceeding $100 trillion (because of fractional reserve banking).[144] A gradual shift to such a regimen could stimulate immediate growth for decades.

The IMF currently pursues its mission of macroeconomic growth and stability through two primary channels. First, the IMF as international lender of last resort provides liquidity to nations to meet external financial obligations.[145] When the IMF bails out a nation, it imposes conditions—and thus far those conditions have generally mandated a market fundamentalism approach.[146] Second, the IMF undertakes annual "consultations" regarding the economic and financial condition of nations.[147] The outcome and nature of these "consultations" are crucial to the ability of most nations to raise external capital.[148] There is no reason why securing economic human rights cannot become central to both of these functions, pursuant to a clear and transparent policy, rather than its current approach, which too often seems driven by the needs of the developed world.[149] With respect to conditionality, the IMF should mandate that additional resources be devoted to economic human rights in appropriate contexts. This new emphasis on economic human rights would be in accord with the IMF's most fundamental mission of fostering global growth.

The World Bank shares a similar mission.[150] Unlike the IMF, however, the World Bank is not a crisis response agency; instead, its role is to assist in the funding of the construction of economic infrastructure. Naturally, this role gives the World Bank leverage for pursuit of human rights.[151] Instead, the World Bank has used its position as the world's development bank to pursue myriad interests other than human rights, including the propagation of market fundamentalism.[152] Recently, the World Bank reviewed its policy on conditionality—and economic human rights were given short shrift once again.[153] Thus, the World Bank seems to be doing little to implement the single legal framework that could secure its own vision of empowering the disempowered notwithstanding the interests of elites. Yet, like the IMF, the World Bank should use its powers to further economic human rights in a manner that the Bank itself has demonstrated is consistent with its chartered purposes of economic growth and development.[154]

Further, the developing world must subsidize more domestic growth. In the U.S., consumption amounts to 70 percent of GDP; in China, consumption accounts for about half of that. This means that China could contribute much more to global demand and instead draws too much of its economic growth from exports to other nations. Global imbalances simply reflect development strategies—export-led growth under the current construction of globalization necessarily means accumulation of currency reserves. Yet, those imbalances also just happen to fatten the profits of transnational corporations and megabanks. Transnational corporations enjoy lower labor costs as the accumulation of foreign reserves renders exports from developing nations more competitive. Financial conglomerates finance the massive flows of capital and sell dollar-denominated assets to developing nations— especially subprime mortgage backed securities from 2005 to 2006, when foreigners financed one-half of the subprime mania in the U.S.[155] Durable consumption must displace excess consumption based upon debt in the developed world, and funding economic human rights provides a template for the efficacious transitioning to that reality.

Another approach would require the WTO to embrace economic human rights as a core part of its operations. For example, the WTO exercises leverage over members of the global economy through its accession process.[156] Currently the process for WTO membership (which extends the full benefits of free trade) is politicized, ill defined, and nontransparent and subjects nations to differential treatment.[157] An alternative approach would emphasize a nation's commitment to share the benefits of free trade widely by requiring action to vindicate economic human rights.[158] The gains from free trade amount to hundreds of billions of dollars per year.[159] Requiring nations to invest a portion of such gains in the economic human rights of their citizens in the cause of global growth hardly seems unreasonable.

Arguably, people should possess the right to move freely in response to economic incentives as a human right. Regardless, the WTO should break down trade barriers applicable to the free movement of labor with the same zeal it applies to all other trade barriers. Given the gains to both the developed and the developing world, the WTO should pressure all nations to lift trade barriers on labor as a means of reviving the languishing Doha round of trade talks that initially focused on development issues. "The gains to poor people from relaxing the existing barriers to labor mobility are enormous relative to everything else on the development table."[160] Despite the not insignificant social costs of labor migration (loss of social cohesion, scapegoating, etc.), the economic benefits from labor liberalization suggest that an international accord to support free movement of people could spur rapid economic development.[161]

In September 2005, the World Bank released a report entitled *Equity and Development*.[162] The gist of the report is that market fundamentalism permits human potential to languish on the margins of the global economy. "The plea for a more level playing field in both politics and the economies of developing countries serves to integrate the World Bank's twin pillars of building an institutional climate conducive to investment and empowering the poor. . . . Greater equity can, over the long run, underpin faster growth."[163] Indeed, empirically laissez-faire too often leads to entrenched elites who will impose economic conditions that are hostile to maximum output and growth, rather than an optimized system of incentives and disincentives.[164] The World Bank report dramatizes the economically pernicious destruction of human capital that follows deep inequality and demonstrates the need to strip elites of the power to destroy human potential.

The report opens by introducing two young children born on the same day in 2000—Nthabiseng, born in Eastern Cape, South Africa; and Pieter, born in Cape Town. One is a black girl and the other is a white boy. After surveying their life circumstances, the Bank concludes that "the opportunities these two children face to reach their full human potential are vastly different from the outset, through no fault of their own." Further, the destruction of opportunities available to Nthabiseng will have societywide impact, as any brilliance or innovation she could have achieved is likely to go to waste.[165] In short, the World Bank challenges the law to secure human capital investments, at least to the extent that social payoffs exceed social costs, despite the harmful influence of growth-retarding elites.[166] This is now mainstream economic science, as empirical studies increasingly demonstrate the harm inequality inflicts upon macroeconomic performance and the role of elites in entrenching their privilege. Thus, Professor William Easterly found "high inequality to be a large and statistically significant hindrance to developing the mechanisms by which economic development is achieved."[167] According to Easterly, the causative elements linking inequality to diminished growth include weaker institutions (laws) and diminished investments in mass education.[168]

Unfortunately, elites will not necessarily seek to invest in the human capital of others, even if broader human capital development would enrich society.[169] And, the more "other" the others are, the deeper is the reluctance of elites to create conditions conducive to the economic betterment of all.[170] Race is an instrument by which the perceived distance between elites and others is maximized, and the power of elites to oppress others is therefore maximized.[171] Race is necessary for the Western conscience to permit 2.8 billion humans to live in deep poverty, as is the case today.[172] The realization of economic human rights, universally, would also serve to relieve the current manifestations of prior racialization and the destruction of human potential implicit in race and other similarly pernicious social constructions that operate to suppress human potential.[173]

Free market globalization operates to create a new transracialism that permits a growing distance between governing elites and the vast pool of laborers worldwide. This in turn operates to destroy human capital and impair human rights in a systematic fashion. There is evidence that very powerful elites are abandoning allegiance to any particular nation-state (and by extension their fellow citizens) in favor of a new global feudalism that concentrates power and resources among an increasingly narrow global elite.[174] A new transracialism seems central to this process.[175] Like race, transracialism involves the destruction of human potential and the sacrifice of economic output to the short-sighted and narrow interests of governing elites. I thus define transracialism as the wanton and pervasive destruction of human capital based upon the social and cultural difference between those with economic and political power and those who lack economic and political power. I contrast transracialism with traditional racism because transracialism need not turn upon any particular morphological features or hostility or hatred. Instead, transracialism simply requires a deep neglect of others based upon privilege. Today a transnational elite class has vigorously pursued a vision of globalization that "frees transnational corporations from the constraints of government" and leaves the mass of humanity to a "brutal and merciless . . . global market," based upon "social distance" and "class solidarity."[176]

Economic human rights (including the right to free movement of people) would operate to ensure opportunity for all regardless of political power, economic power, or cultural background. A truly robust global capitalism would ensure this minimum human capital development as a matter of sound economics. Legal and regulatory infrastructure should ensure the vindication of the economic values underlying the Universal Declaration of Human Rights through a reconfiguration of the IMF, the World Bank, and the WTO. Of course, the global economy needs other forms of legal and regulatory infrastructure to stabilize the global financial system.

The Need for a Global Regulatory Infrastructure

The lack of any reasonable regulatory infrastructure constitutes the final fatal flaw undermining globalization. Financial liberalization arose as a part of the deregulatory mantra of those controlling the destiny of our globalized economy. This meant that the global financial system ultimately resembled the patchwork regulation of the states prior to the New Deal's federalization of financial regulation in the U.S.[177] Developed nations learned from experience that capitalism can achieve high levels of macroeconomic growth only if regulatory infrastructure supports free markets. Financial regulation, deposit insurance, securities regulation, consumer protection, labor standards, social safety nets, bankruptcy protections, and environmental standards serve to secure the promise of free market capitalism. Elites set globalization on a path toward laissez-faire. Indeed, the course specifically prioritized financial market liberalization notwithstanding the fact that economic history taught that unregulated capital markets wobbled toward instability that fueled real economic crises.[178] That financial instability materialized with a vengeance in 2007–9 as debt securities emanating from the deregulated U.S. financial system flooded the global financial sector and nearly caused the greatest financial meltdown in history.

In late 2009, the United Nations entered the fray surrounding the causes and remedies of the global financial crisis of 2007–9 and the ensuing economic crisis. The UN commissioned a panel of experts (the Stiglitz Commission) to address the causes and make policy proposals to remedy the crisis, including economists and other experts from around the world with Joseph Stiglitz acting as Chair. The Stiglitz Commission found that the global economic architecture contributed to the crisis and needs reconfiguration. In particular, the current global financial system lacks any viable means of effective global regulation of the financial sector, thanks to the sway of special interest influence, backed by free market dogma.[179]

The Commission calls for a global financial regulatory body to advise the IMF, the WTO, and the World Bank and other international bodies on sustainable and responsible regulatory policies. "Economic globalization has outpaced the development of the political institutions required to manage it well."[180] In particular, the Commission advocates the creation of a Global Economic Coordinating Commission that functions to identify systemic risks, recommend actions to fill regulatory gaps, and facilitate harmonization of critical regulatory standards.[181] This entity would complement a Global Financial Authority that would coordinate general financial regulation.[182] The Commission also proposes to restructure many existing international agencies, including the IMF and the World Bank, to open their governance structures more widely to developing nations that too frequently lack substantial voice over policies that directly affect their people.[183]

In addition to suggesting new agencies and restructuring existing agencies, the Stiglitz Commission offers insights on elements of sound regulation. It attributes the long period of stable growth following World War II to the stringent regulatory regimen imposed by the New Deal, along with similar initiatives across the world. Market fundamentalism sought to unwind much of this regulation across the globe, and this effort in the financial sector led to the present crisis. In addition, regulatory agencies across the world suffered capture by the very interests they should regulate. Special interests further undermined education through the propagation of an ideology that supported their short-term interests. To the extent nations fail to pursue adequate regulatory policies, the entire world may suffer adverse economic consequences. All of these regulatory challenges led to a financial system that suffered from perverse incentives, the mispricing of risk, and a massive misallocation of resources leading up to the financial crisis of 2007–9. The lack of a global regulatory structure allowed this to infect the entire global economy.[184]

The Stiglitz Commission therefore proposes a comprehensive global regulatory regimen. The key parts of this regimen of financial regulation include safety and soundness regulation of all financial institutions, robust protection of consumers and investors, ensuring deep financial development and expanded access to sound finance, elimination insofar as possible of moral hazard, and the promotion of systemic stability. Further, such a regimen must strive to include an appropriate competition policy and sound corporate governance. This comprehensive approach to financial regulation must defeat any pressure for a global race to the bottom, mandating global coordination.[185] In short, the Stiglitz Commission's recommendations mirror many of the policy prescriptions he emphasized in 2002, in his book *Globalization and Its Discontents*.[186] He urged then and the Stiglitz Commission urges now that regulation evolve in accordance with the best economic science and learning available rather than in accordance with ideology or special interest influence. This yields a rather robust vision of financial regulation because of the sordid history of financial deregulation and the more benign history of the New Deal regulatory initiatives.

Other commentators argue in favor of global harmonization and central-ization of particular areas of law. For example, given that mortgage-backed securities lie at the center of the subprime crisis and that these securities landed in institutional portfolios across the world, one would expect some degree of reform energy on this front. Unfortunately, there has been a total absence of any initiative to reassess the legal framework governing the global distribution of securities. As discussed in chapter 1, securities regulation proved its economic benefits long ago. It seems that the global regulation of securities needs exactly that kind of New Deal reconstruction.[187]

Meanwhile, the legal academy languishes in an obsessive and narrow focus on free market efficiency. One cannot find a Law and Economics text that even discusses globalization, much less its central economic and ideological hypocrisies. The conventional learning on Law and Economics facilitates essentially the very market fundamentalism that Stiglitz and other economists hold is "bad economics" and ideologically driven.[188] Specifically, that ideological movement essentially rejects government intervention or disrupting those enjoying privileges at the expense of the disempowered to forgo the cauldron of competition. It seemingly rejects all manner of regula-tory infrastructure but the most basic elements of legal infrastructure—those relating to the enforcement of contracts and clear property rights. Until the Law and Economics movement recognizes the limits of free market doctrine, it will continue to lose touch with economic science and will ultimately be best termed law and pseudo-economics.[189] Unfortunately, this laissez-faire approach to financial regulation continues to mark global financial regula-tion—the Dodd-Frank Wall Street Reform and Consumer Protection Act fails to address trade imbalances, global financial regulation, or global mar-ket development at all.[190] I address this point more expansively in chapter 7.

This chapter traces the winners and losers under the current legal frame-work governing globalization and demonstrates that reconstructing global-ization can pay huge economic dividends. Those interested in robust mac-roeconomic growth and financial stability constitute the losers under today's globalization, and corporate and financial elites once again emerge as win-ners—winners with little or no downside risk or accountability. While a pre-cise accounting of the haul of the winners, and the money flowing out of the pockets of the 99.99 percent of us who do not sit at the apex of the financial and corporate sectors, cannot now be undertaken, it exceeds tens of trillions of dollars in forgone wealth. Economic disempowerment and economic privilege exact huge tolls on macroeconomic growth worldwide under the current approach to globalization. The next chapter spotlights the depths of disempowerment plaguing the American economy in particular.

5

The Costs of Economic Oppression

[S]omehow we're caught in an inescapable network of mutuality
tied in a single garment of destiny. Whatever affects one directly
affects all indirectly. For some strange reason, I can never be what
I ought to be until you are what you ought to be. You can never be
what you ought to be until I am what I ought to be.
Martin Luther King Jr. (1963)[1]

Throughout the world today, economic oppression exacts a painful economic toll on national economies and the global economy. Stripping an individual of the ability to reach his or her economic potential retards the extent
of the market available to support maximum innovation and specialized
knowledge for everyone. Stripping large groups of individuals of their ability
to reach their economic potential leads to grossly underdeveloped markets.
Here, Dr. King echoes Adam Smith: No person can reach his or her full economic potential if others are economically disempowered because markets
must be retarded if participants are irrationally excluded, or if their participation is irrationally diminished. Losses extend beyond market development losses. Impaired human capital formation means the loss of economic
potential in the form of ideas and innovation. Here, Dr. King echoes Paul
Romer: If ideas generate economic growth, then human mental capabilities
warrant protection as precious natural resources that must be nurtured, con-
served, and developed to the maximum extent possible.[2] So long as the world
permits 2.6 billion people to subsist on less than two dollars per day, the

economy languishes in a state of semi-development relative to its potential. This chapter seeks to demonstrate the costs of economic oppression, catalogue the means by which oppression continues to operate, and suggest the means by which law should disrupt such economic oppression and pursue individual economic empowerment.

The World Bank, in its *World Development Report 2006: Equity and Development*, highlights the losses to the global economy from persistent economic oppression. For example, the report warns that excessive economic inequality breeds too much elite privilege and a lack of resources for the disempowered to actualize their economic potential. Elite privilege goes hand in hand with irrational underdevelopment of human potential. Because of imperfect capital markets, the underprivileged will not enjoy access to education, and elite educational privilege further restricts access. Typically, societies construct economic disempowerment on foundations that transcend law but that operate through law. For example, across the globe disempowered groups score lower on standardized tests, and this can actually serve as a barometer of economic disempowerment. Test scores will reflect poor health outcomes, intergenerational deprivation of educational opportunities, inequality in primary and secondary educational facilities, and cultural mores and norms regarding disempowered groups. Social science experiments now isolate and explain elements of the so-called test gap around the world. Unfortunately, these standardized tests arouse a stereotype threat in the victims of economic oppression, whereby cultural attitudes can negatively influence test performance when such attitudes are internalized. Yet, law permits the continued use of these measures of oppression even in full view of their corrupt operation. In light of all of these mechanisms for the propagation of economic oppression, the World Bank suggests that policymakers take affirmative action to disrupt the economic losses that result.[3]

Continued economic oppression in the U.S. and throughout the world contributed to the subprime catastrophe on multiple levels. First, the crisis belies the so-called American meritocracy and reveals an economy dominated not by the best and the brightest but by the most reckless and irresponsible. This chapter seeks to prove the role of race and other constructs in fostering a corrupt meritocracy in America. Second, as discussed in the preceding chapter, the U.S. and the world suffered from retarded market development, leading to the U.S.'s acting as consumer of last resort based upon a mountain of debt. Better market development would operate to generate sustainable growth, and nowhere can market development proceed more rapidly than within deeply disempowered communities. Third, the most economically pernicious element of the subprime loan fiasco involved predatory loans that lacked a reasonable basis for repayment and that involved defrauding borrowers through various illegitimate machinations. If the U.S. endowed itself with more optimal mechanisms for human capital formation, this pool of disempowered borrowers would not exist. The predatory loans involved raw racial exploitation, in which the most powerful profited from the misery they imposed upon the most disempowered parts of the U.S. population. Fourth, the continued toleration of racial politics fundamentally obscured economic interests and allowed law to veer back to discredited laissez-faire policies that operate to empower elites to the maximum extent possible. In a society burdened with gaping economic inequalities, economic oppression will follow, and always this oppression entails massive economic losses, as the subprime crisis illustrates. America's racist legacy led to its dysfunctional meritocracy as well as subprime market development and regulation, human capital, and politics. These factors fueled all aspects of the subprime debacle.

The Mythological American Meritocracy

The tension between America's vaunted meritocracy and the reckless and irresponsible misconduct giving rise to the financial crisis of 2007–9 raises obvious questions that few wish to address. The financial oligarchs holding our economic destiny in their hands (along with their cronies in government) engaged in either grossly negligent misconduct or very corrupt misconduct. For example, Jamie Dimon, the CEO of JPMorgan Chase, told the FCIC that his bank "missed" the risks of high-risk mortgages.[4] That seems improbable, at best. The essential job of a banker involves identifying and managing risks. The alternative to missing such risks would be that bankers knowingly took massive risks on board to line their pockets at society's expense. In fact, according to the FCIC, Wall Street coined a new term for this: IBGYBG meaning: "I'll be gone, you'll be gone."[5] Either way, the meritocracy broke down at great cost to all but a handful of senior managers in the banking sector.

Race and other forms of irrational disempowerment fundamentally corrupt any putative meritocracy at work in America today. A meritocracy should operate much as other markets operate: to move human resources to their highest and best use so that the most able and trustworthy hold the most responsibility. "By excluding entire segments of the American population from equal access to opportunity, discrimination reduces competition" and allows privilege to fester instead of merit.[6] Further, a variety of other self-perpetuating mechanisms continue to operate to advantage white males. The combination of socioeconomic status and racial privileges and disadvantages explains our faulty meritocracy. The mythological meritocracy begins with college admissions.

According to *Wall Street Journal* investigative reporter Daniel Golden, white elites enjoy pervasive advantages in college admissions. Top universities rig admissions in favor of those with power through affirmative action for legacy applicants, affirmative action for large donors, affirmative action for applicants with wealthy parents who enjoy networks that include other wealthy parents, affirmative action for celebrity families, and affirmative action for participation in obscure sports like crew or polo. Few minorities relative to whites may take advantage of these affirmative action programs for children of the elite. The very modest affirmative action programs for the truly disadvantaged fail to counteract the massive privilege of white wealth. "While only a handful of low-income students penetrate the campus gates, admissions policies channel the children of the privileged into premier colleges, paving their way into leadership positions in business and government."[7] Another commentator studied admissions at Harvard, Yale, and Princeton and concluded that "Americans tolerate a system in which our most selective institutions of higher education routinely grant preference to the children of alumni and wealthy donors—a practice that viewed from a distance looks unmeritocratic at best and profoundly corrupt at worst."[8]

Most minorities and impoverished teens cannot overcome the huge advantages that wealthy whites hold even prior to college. For example, preparation courses, tutoring, and expensive coaching pad the standardized test scores of the wealthy.[9] It took years to implement desegregation mandates, and even today the U.S. maintains a high level of *de facto* racial segregation in its public schools. In fact, the U.S. regressed over the past few years to a level of segregation not seen since 1968.[10] This facilitates gross inequities in educational funding in the U.S. For example, during 2002–3 in New York City, with 72 percent students of color, per-pupil expenditures amounted to $11,627 versus $22,311 in a nearby suburban district in which 9 percent of the school population consisted of minority students.[11] Overall, the highest-spending districts can spend many times what the lowest-spending districts spend, and the higher-spending districts correlate to wealthy white areas and the lowest-spending schools tightly correlate to poor communities of color.[12] Private education can greatly exacerbate these inequalities by spending up to eight times what public schools spend.[13] These funding differentials that tightly correlate to wealth and race reflect raw economic power at work, not competitive capitalism.

Education marks the beginning of privilege, not the end. In an audit study involving fictitious résumés with white- and minority-sounding names, economists found that résumés with white-sounding names received 50 percent more callbacks than the résumés with minority-sounding names, after controlling for a variety of potential explanatory variables. The authors of the study conclude: "Our results must imply that employers use race as a factor in reviewing resumes."[14] Other studies suggest this dynamic operates with respect to female names—specifically, females with masculine-sounding names enjoy more opportunities than other females.[15] Similarly, women with children suffer career detriments while men with children benefit.[16] Even with respect to audit studies of apparently mundane transactions like taxicab tipping, scholars find evidence of a systematic bias in favor of whites.[17] Women and minorities also suffer weaker evaluations in terms of performance ratings than white males even when raters view videos of job performance that are specifically scripted to be identical.[18] A recent economic study on the effect of racism on the wage gap between African Americans and whites isolates the effect and concludes that 25 percent of the wage gap reflects the operation of racism.[19] The bottom line here is that white males enjoy significant economic privileges with respect to market outcomes relative to the 50 percent of the population that is female and the 40 percent of the population that is minority. No wonder 95 percent of the highest-paid senior managers of Fortune 500 companies are white, and 94 percent are male.[20]

Many Americans start life with precious few opportunities to excel economically. Because of the crisis, more American children live in poverty.[21] Now, about one in four young American children lives in poverty.[22] Thirty-nine percent of African American children and 36 percent of Hispanic children live in poverty.[23] Only an immoral nation that disfavored economic growth could tolerate such a waste of human resources. Indeed, even before the crisis, the U.S childhood poverty rate of 22 percent ranked near that of Mexico, at the bottom of rich nations, and well below those of wealthy nations such as Finland and Denmark, with childhood poverty rates of just 3 percent. In terms of fielding our best, brightest, and most responsible leaders, the U.S. is at the bottom of the ladder.[24] The American meritocracy utilizes only a fraction of its human resources and showers privileges upon a few. There is too much privilege and its mirror image, disempowerment, in the U.S. After all, in accordance with the theme of this book, every instance of elite privilege necessarily means a *pro tanto* degree of disempowerment. This chapter argues that disempowerment thereby reflects a *pro tanto* degree of privilege. Elites rigged the meritocracy just as they rigged law and regulation.

A dim or corrupt elite runs America. The so-called meritocracy failed to ensure that the best and most trustworthy enjoy the greatest responsibility.

As Joseph Stiglitz suggests, the problem posed is not just a few "rotten apples"; instead, the problem is that in the financial sector the whole "barrel [was] rotten."[25] The depths of the misconduct challenge the imagination. At Citigroup, a seasoned banker warned the Chair of the Executive Committee—board member Robert Rubin—that the bank dealt in risky mortgages and could face billions in losses. Even though he was proved correct, his warnings resulted in diminished pay, an effective demotion, and downgrades in his performance review. The Chief Risk Officer at Lehman Brothers warned the firm that it faced too much risk. Lehman shunted her aside and claimed the exit arose from "philosophical differences." At Ameriquest Mortgage, the nation's largest subprime lender, a senior investigator alerted management that he found fraud in the firm's mortgages within one month of starting his job. He faced demotion and layoff after other departments claimed he "looked too much" at the firm's lending practices. Even CEO Jamie Dimon "blames management teams 100% . . . and no one else."[26] Consequently, no real dispute remains regarding the culpability of senior managers in the financial crisis of 2007–9.

This irrationality of excessive privilege displacing meritocracy imposes tremendous costs. According to McKinsey & Company, the U.S. economy would expand by $1.3 trillion to $2.3 trillion per annum if it could close the education gap with nations such as Finland and South Korea. If the nation closed the gap between whites and children of color, the economy would enjoy between $310 billion and $525 billion in enhanced growth. Closing the gap between low-income and high-income students results in up to $700 billion annually in additional growth. "Put differently the persistence of these educational achievement gaps imposes the economic equivalent of a permanent recession."[27] This represents the baseline cost of wasting human resources.

It fails, however, to account for the cost of ineptitude and corruption of the leadership at the commanding heights of the American economy. Certainly, law and regulation permitted perverse incentives to take root in the financial sector. Yet commentators search for some rational explanation for the depths of the misconduct. *Fortune* ran a cover story about the new recklessness in banking that asked: "What Were They Smoking?"[28] Former Reagan administration official Peggy Noonan argues that use of widely prescribed antidepressants explains the bizarre recklessness or corruption engulfing the financial sector. She suggests that "maybe Wall Street was high as a kite" and failed to notice the "wildly imprudent" banking practices that led to our economic demise.[29] The reckless misconduct underlying our recent financial crisis reflects our corrupt meritocracy, and we should expect similar financial crises so long as we fail to impose accountability on the corporate and financial elites that proved their ineptitude or corruption by crashing their firms "like lemmings off a cliff."[30]

A World Awash in Economic Oppression

A world that permits 2.6 billion people to live on less than two dollars per day cannot possibly deploy its human resources to the maximum extent possible.[31] Yet, the global community seems oddly sanguine about this reality. The sheer randomness of the deep disempowerment of poverty ought to arouse suspicion that we live in a malconstructed world, wherein the luck of birth determines all and huge human potential simply festers, wasted and unknown. For example, in Mozambique, 15 percent of infants fail to survive their first year.[32] In the U.S., 7 of every 1,000 babies die before their first birthday. The average citizen of Luxembourg enjoys (adjusted for purchasing power parity) buying power that is 62 times higher than that of the average Nigerian. Sub-Saharan Africa achieves educational attainment of 5.4 years of schooling, while the developed world achieves 13.4 years in far better schools.[33] Yet for the most part little protest erupts as a result of these facts. If the fundamental injustice of this reality fails to arouse action, perhaps more widespread realization of the economic losses we each bear as a result of this deep disempowerment will.

According to the World Bank, too much inequality plagues the world economy. "Equity is complementary . . . to the pursuit of long-term prosperity. Institutions and policies that promote a level playing field—where all members of society have similar chances to become socially active, politically influential and economically productive—contribute to sustainable growth."[34] While too much equity can impede growth (as the communist experiment of the 20th century proved), too much inequality may reflect too much privilege and too much economic oppression, whereby a few enjoy insulation from competition through their control of law and others can never reach their full market potential because of deprivation of basic resources. Racial inequality and inequality in human capital opportunities constrict macroeconomic growth and impose costs on every citizen of the world.[35]

The World Bank argues that a combination of two inherently related realities grips the global economy and retards growth. First, too much economic potential languishes at the margin of the global economy, disempowered to innovate, produce, or contribute to a well-developed market to support a wider array of goods and services. Second, elites, holding sway over the construction of social policies and the distribution of wealth, too often work to entrench themselves instead of fostering macroeconomic growth. Indeed, the World Bank posits that high inequality contributes to stunted opportunities for the disempowered and too much privilege for elites because inequality leads to laws and regulations that systematically favor the powerful. If this occurs and property rights among the less powerful are enforced only selectively and the distribution of public expenditures favors the wealthy, then others end up with unexploited talent.[36] Thus, the global institution most involved in economic development, the World Bank, now holds that economic growth suffers from growth-retarding elites in accordance with the premise of this book. Although the World Bank's concerns predate the subprime fiasco and the ensuing financial crisis, I argued in 2006 that the World Bank's diagnosis of the global economy essentially heralded exactly the kind of crisis that emerged in 2007–9: a crisis in buying power arising from excessive debt.[37]

Of course, each nation suffers from its own evolution of economic oppression. In India, the role of caste operated to destroy human capital formation, stunt markets, and encourage predation. Ecuador's victims are the Quichua.[38] In Japan, economic oppression targets the Baraku and Koreans. In Sweden, Finns suffer marginalization. A disturbing transnational reality emerges from these divergent constructs. First, the telling measures of oppression take hold at birth—whether in the form of excess infant mortality or stunted prenatal health care, or impaired educational opportunities. Second, the cultural bombardment of the myth of inferiority takes hold. Third, the telltale differences in standardized test scores emerge. Here, the oppression is legitimized in admissions tournaments and other competitive gateways of opportunity. The creation of a subclass pivots on the destruction of human potential. The thin veneer of legitimacy results from the barometer of the oppression—standardized test scores that supposedly operate to identify potential but instead measure, transmit, and propagate oppression. The supposed impaired cognition of the disempowered arises from impoverished conditions, parental deprivations, and cultural messages of inferiority.

Those tests leave fingerprints of oppression. In Ecuador, students from the lowest 25 percent of the income strata score lower on cognitive development tests than students from the top 25 percent. But, tellingly, as time goes by, the gap widens. The scores begin to test the extent of oppression over time, not skills. The same dynamic holds with respect to maternal education. The gaps in test scores between those with highly educated mothers and those with lesser education expand over time.[39] Similarly, in India, when lower-caste children compete against higher-caste children in cognitive exercises they score very near (often above) the higher-caste children. But if caste is announced, the performance of the lower-caste students suffers; and if children are segregated according to caste, both the low-caste and high-caste children score even lower.[40] The oppressive reality of standardized tests can be relieved. If the minority Baraku move from Japan to the U.S., their scores equalize with those of other Japanese test takers.[41] When Finns emigrate from Sweden to Australia they perform on par with Swedes, as do Koreans relative to Japanese in America.[42] Other studies show that while childhood poverty lowers standardized test scores, removing children from poverty can restore cognitive test performance.[43] Thus, lifting conditions of social oppression eliminates disparities in cognition.

The World Bank makes specific suggestions for using law to relieve economic oppression. The Bank recognizes that one solution does not fit all nations and each country necessarily faces a different cultural context. Nevertheless, in general, nations should consider programs designed to facilitate early childhood development. The Bank argues that the acquisition of economic capabilities by children should not be dictated by "circumstances of their birth."[44] For example, the World Bank points out that an experiment in Jamaica focused on remedying nutritional requirements for undernourished children. After twenty-four months of both nutritional supplements and intellectual stimulation, the undernourished children virtually closed the cognitive development gap relative to that of well-nourished youth. According to the Bank, "[i]nvesting in the neediest people early in their childhoods can help level the playing field."[45]

Other areas the Bank identifies for productive investment include education, health care, and social safety nets. "Actions to equalize opportunities in formal education need to ensure that all children acquire at least a basic level of skills necessary to participate in society and in today's global economy."[46] Health care supports human capital formation and productivity; seriously ill children cannot learn and seriously ill workers cannot produce at their maximum capability. Social safety nets can "spur households to engage in riskier activities" such as innovation or business formation. While funding for these programs risks taxation that could prove economically harmful, the Bank concludes that broad-based consumption taxes and progressive income taxes could fund these programs.[47] More important, to the extent these programs support superior macroeconomic growth, they likely would generate more tax revenues greater than their costs, thereby leading to lower taxes over the long term. In fact, an economist found that generally higher tax rates to fund social spending along the lines recommended by the World Bank do not harm growth, and spending associated with enhanced worker productivity spurs growth.[48]

The absence of these programs (as well as no real mechanism for implementing economic human rights) means that economic oppression infects the world economy, stunting innovation and growth. Market development naturally suffers in the face of deep poverty. Combined with the capital flows discussed in chapter 4, which so distorted the world economy, this meant an even greater need for America to act as consumer of last resort. Economic oppression, unfortunately, also pervaded the American economy, and that too contributed to the crisis. Because of a world awash in oppression, it fell upon the U.S. to fully develop its human resources as a source of stable growth and durable consumption. Instead, the U.S. built a mountain of debt upon a stagnate middle class and ultimately upon the disempowered.

The Meaning of Race in America

Race is America's original sin, and it has bedeviled the nation since its founding. Race inflicts trillions in costs upon America, and yet our leaders propose few solutions for remediating this economic catastrophe. The definitive scientific explanation of race comes from the Human Genome Project:

> DNA studies do not indicate that separate classifiable subspecies (races) exist within modern humans. While different genes for physical traits such as skin and hair color can be identified between individuals, no consistent patterns of genes across the human genome exist to distinguish one race from another. There also is no genetic basis for divisions of human ethnicity. . . . [I]t has been proven that there is more genetic variation within races than exists between them.[49]

Geneticists find race as understood by most persons to be an arbitrary and scientifically indefensible concept. Random individuals from Ithaca and Albany, New York, evince greater genetic variation than a typical African American relative to a typical white person. Similarly, blood type holds more significance in terms of genetic variation than race.[50] Essentially, race as traditionally conceived is about as significant as shoe size.[51]

Race has never made sense. For example, consider the "one-drop of blood" rule. The rule worked quite well in terms of assuring that oppressed individuals could not mate their way out of their stigmatized status, as a means of avoiding, for instance, slavery in the American South prior to the Civil War or, for that matter, the death camps of Nazi Germany in the 1930s and 1940s. But there is no scientific basis for holding that a person with one of sixteen ancestors (or one of eight, or any at all) of a certain race is that race and no other. This rule rests on social necessity, not science. It kept the slaves in slavery and allowed no person to avoid genocide for their children, despite reproducing with a nontainted group. Thus, racial laws in the U.S. as elsewhere just made up racial categories out of whole cloth, legally constructed as opposed to founded on any science at all.[52]

Professor Ian Haney Lopez highlights the role of law—not science—in the social construction of race. Under law, only "white persons" could qualify for naturalized citizenship in the U.S. prior to 1967. So, the Supreme Court needed to define whiteness. Whiteness has no geographic reality behind it for there is neither a country called Whiteland nor a City of White. Ultimately the U.S. Supreme Court defined whiteness as an exclusive racial category to which only a privileged few could accede. It turned on anthropology when its doctrine performed an exclusive role. Yet it turned on the understanding of the "common man" when that performed a more exclusive role than anthropology. Thus whiteness was more about exclusivity than science. Indeed, the Court specifically recognized the futile efforts of science to even agree to the number of racial categories.[53] The legal construction of race once again was untethered to any scientific doctrine.[54] Instead, "[r]ace is revealed as historically contingent, socially mediated systems of meaning that attach to elements of an individual's morphology and ancestry."[55] In other words, race is made up—socially constructed—for social purposes unrelated to any science.

Specifically, race is one means by which those with power profit from artificial social distance. The Europeans who captured slaves from Africa to sell in the American South were not geneticists; they were greedy businessmen who saw a profit opportunity. They sold slaves to make money, not to vindicate any racial hierarchy. Everywhere and always the existence of artificial social distance exists to entrench the power of incumbents. Race followed profits, or the political needs of those with power. In sum, race is all about power.[56] As I mentioned in chapter 4, a new "transracialism" has dictated the course of globalization, which is specifically constructed in the wake of increasing social distance between economic elites and laborers throughout the global economy. Thus, the construction of globalization illustrates the point made here: Artificial social distance serves to enhance the power and profits of elites.

Invariably, groups subject to racial oppression suffer impaired human potential under law. Laws operate to prohibit or impede the education or actualization of human resources. For example, after the formal end of slavery, the so-called Black Codes delivered the former slaves into economic peonage, under local ordinances and law. Later in the Jim Crow era, African

Americans suffered deep economic disempowerment under law. In 1948, the Supreme Court finally held that southern states had to provide viable graduate educational programs to African Americans, without overruling the doctrine of separate but equal, which had operated to impose legally permissible educational inferiority.[57] Similarly, in primary and secondary education, America permitted segregated schools to operate until 1954, when the Supreme Court, in *Brown v. Board of Education,* finally abolished (in theory, at least) "separate but equal" schools.[58] Unfortunately, today the U.S. still suffers from an educational system that remains too segregated and too unequal. Education hardly stands alone in terms of enduring racial disparities.

For example, African Americans suffer a variety of negative health outcomes relative to whites. Infant mortality for African Americans greatly exceeds infant mortality for whites. "Although the overall infant mortality rate reached record low levels in 2000, the rate for African Americans remains twice that of Caucasians regardless of socioeconomic status, education, and/or health insurance status."[59] African Americans also suffer lower life expectancy. Experts find that excess deaths from continuing health disparities grew from 60,000 in 1980 to nearly 85,000 in 2005.[60] "There has been no sustained decrease in black–white disparities in age-adjusted mortality (death) or life expectancy at birth at the national level since 1945."[61] The constant stress of racial stereotype appears likely to contribute to hypertension in the African American community.[62]

America's policy of mass incarceration also follows racial construction. The U.S. leads the world in incarceration rates, almost exclusively because of the war on drugs. The U.S. locks citizens up at a rate that exceeds those of China and Iran. It locks up more of its people of color than South Africa did during apartheid. In cities like Washington, D.C., three out of four young black men will land in prison.[63] "The rate of ever having gone to prison among adult black males (16.6%) was over twice as high as among adult Hispanic males (7.7%) and over 6 times as high as among adult white males (2.6%)."[64] Professor Michelle Alexander highlights the costs of mass incarceration in terms of the destruction of human capital in *The New Jim Crow.* Specifically, she shows that the mass incarceration of young minority men taints them for life, closes economic opportunities, and bars them from exercising important civil rights such as the right to vote. Even though most drug users and dealers are white, and all Americans use drugs at similar rates, 75 percent of all those convicted of drug offenses are African American or Latino.[65] Thus, the war on drugs and America's policy of mass incarceration lead to the massive destruction of human capital and fall disproportionately upon communities of color.

All of these disparities necessarily mean restricted opportunities and messages from society regarding racial value. Thus, one would expect race to infect standardized test scores just as oppression infects so-called intelligence tests around the world. Social scientists have isolated stereotype threat (the internalization of society's racial norms and expectations) as a persistent and testable suppressant of standardized test scores for students of color in the U.S.[66] Moreover, the persistent racial disparities in health outcomes and poverty in the U.S. also likely operate to suppress performance on cognitive tests. After all, the World Bank highlighted how poor health negatively affected cognition tests for children in Jamaica.[67] The poverty rate for black children is more than three times as high as for white children in the U.S.[68] Students in ill health and suffering from poor nutrition will not score as high as their potential on standardized tests. Consequently, compelling evidence shows that so-called racial gaps in test scores both reflect and transmit oppression.

The combined impact of stereotype threat, poverty, the mass incarceration of youth of color, and disparate health outcomes such as life expectancy distorts incentives in communities of color. Hopelessness and impaired life expectancy deter human capital formation.[69] Cultural realities transmogrify over time into cultural norms and expectations. These racial disparities impose large macroeconomic costs, in terms of the diversion of massive funds from socially productive investments to the prison industrial complex that now exists to benefit from and encourage more incarceration. In short, the disparities in the U.S. reinforce themselves in a vicious cycle of economic oppression that mimics the pattern identified by the World Bank regarding the destruction of human capital through poverty and stereotype threat. Few of these socially significant racial disparities have materially diminished over the past thirty years.[70] Race clearly still pervades our society today.

The Costs of Economic Oppression Today in America

In 2004, I estimated the costs to America of continued racial oppression. I first reviewed the economic evidence showing that race continues to hold sway in America. For example, the Nobel Prize–winning economist Kenneth J. Arrow describes the empirical record showing the persistence of irrational racial discrimination as "decisive." "Especially striking are the audit studies on differential treatment in the housing and automobile markets."[71] Since then more compelling evidence has emerged that race still plays a powerful role in employment markets. These empirical studies stand in stark contrast to theoretical speculations that discrimination should be eliminated through the operation of market pressure in the long run.[72]

Given that race has no biological or genetic significance, all of the deep race-based disparities that persist in our society can be the consequence of social conditions only, as mediated through law. These disparities are so durable and deep in America today that these conditions can only be termed conditions of pervasive social oppression. In a landmark study of the economic costs of racial discrimination against African Americans, the economist Andrew Brimmer concluded that "the disparate treatment of blacks cost the American economy $241 billion in 1993. This figure is equal to roughly 3.8 percent of that year's gross domestic product (GDP)."[73]

Brimmer's analysis focuses upon two sources of diminished output: first, the lost economic output from the failure to exploit the existing education of African Americans; second, the lost output from a failure to appropriately improve upon the education of African Americans. With respect to the first source, Brimmer uses the fact that even today, after the promulgation of equal employment laws, "many blacks are still concentrated in positions which do not make full use of their talents. If . . . blacks could migrate more freely from low to high productivity occupations . . . total production would be increased."[74] With respect to the second source, Brimmer assesses the degree to which the under-investment in African American education compromises American economic performance.[75] This under-investment represents undeveloped human capital and thus restricted output.

There is little reason to think the picture has recently brightened in any material way. First, Brimmer has analyzed the economic consequence of continued racial discrimination through the same methodology for a number of years. The trends are discouraging. Brimmer's earliest study is from 1963, when he found the economic costs of discrimination against African Americans to amount to 3.5 percent of output. In 1967, the costs declined to 2.85 percent of GDP. Nevertheless, in 1973 and 1979 the costs rose again to 3.13 and 3.38, respectively. Thus, except for a slight dip from 1963 to 1967 (coinciding with the passage of the Civil Rights Act of 1964), the costs of American racial disparities in employment patterns and educational attainment have been remarkably durable and constant at around 3.5 percent of GDP. If anything, the costs of these disparities seem to be on the rise.[76]

Second, contemporary employment and educational data do not give any cause for optimism. Today, per capita income of African Americans amounts to just over $18,000 per year, and for whites it approximates $31,000 per year, while Hispanic per capita income amounts to about half of the income of whites.[77] Given the expanding African American and Hispanic population of 2010 of 100 million, this translates to about a $1.4 trillion loss of GDP annually, as manifested in labor markets. This update (and expansion to include

Hispanics) demonstrates that as our minority population expands, the continued persistence of disparities becomes more costly.[78] This estimate mirrors the assessment of McKinsey & Co. that closing the education gap between whites and minorities would expand U.S. GDP by 4 percent, which would today approach $600 billion in losses just from faulty human capital development alone (based upon estimated GDP of $14 trillion).[79] By any measure, the economy sustains staggering losses from the continuing disparities in economic opportunities.

Even these numbers, however, likely understate the costs of impeding people from actualizing their human capital in America. They do not include other racialized groups, such as Native Americans, and they do not include women, who continue to face a labor market that pays women laborers less than 80 percent of what men earn.[80] It also is limited to economic impact manifest in the labor market. Infant mortality, excess incarceration rates, life expectancy, and a host of other social maladies that disproportionately affect communities of color all take a macroeconomic toll that has not yet been quantified. Based upon the foregoing economic studies and data, it is certain that race and other forms of economic oppression portend a long-term multi-trillion-dollar American economic nightmare. These costs do not include the costs of an impaired meritocracy, discussed previously in the context of the subprime catastrophe, or the costs of exploitative conduct arising from power disparities and manifest by the predatory lending that drove the subprime crisis. Finally, the costs of economic oppression in the U.S. must include the impaired market development within the U.S. that led to an economy driven by debt rather than by innovation. Allowing a significant segment of the population to languish in poverty or jail limits the extent of the market.

The Power of Cultural Diversity

Of course, these losses constitute only the most direct costs of continuing to maintain a racialized society. Further costs include the losses relative to a society that not only takes affirmative action to resolve racial hierarchies but actually embraces the full potential of its human resources by seeking to harness cognitive diversity. Cultural diversity arises as a by-product of a racialized society, or from the different experiences of subgroups within a society, based upon a range of factors from gender to immigrant status. Cultural diversity can disrupt groupthink and affinity bias and can support superior creativity and cognition. Cultural diversity does not achieve these positive outcomes based upon morphological features but rather on different cognitive experiences and perspectives.

Social scientists identify groupthink as a problem of group decision making that arises from too much homogeneity. If groups are too similar and cohesive, they are more likely to adhere mindlessly to group norms and fail to question underlying assumptions that may operate to subvert sound decision making. Irving L. Janis wrote two volumes of case studies showing how groupthink led to flawed thinking and inferior outcomes at the apex of the American foreign policy establishment that persistently caused foreign policy elites to stumble into crises. Janis specifically identified group heterogeneity as one means by which groupthink may be disrupted and crises may be resolved.[81] Outsiders may well be more inclined to question underlying assumptions than those who may well place too high a value on group acceptance.

Similarly, affinity bias (or in-group bias) operates to cloud judgment in favor of a person based upon relatively trivial commonalities.[82] Compelling research over the past fifty years demonstrates that individuals hold a cognitive bias in favor of groups in which they enjoy membership. The bias operates even when group bonds seem arbitrary and meaningless, such as when coin flips define group membership.[83] In-group bias displays its greatest strength when the group is defined based upon membership in a privileged or advantaged group, such as race or ethnicity. As Professor Nilanjana Dasgupta explains, affinity bias seems driven most powerfully by "the tendency to prefer groups associated with the self as a confirmation of . . . positive self-esteem, and the tendency to prefer groups valued by the mainstream culture as a confirmation of the sociopolitical order in society."[84] Thus, in-group bias holds powerful sway in circumstances where race matters.[85] This necessarily means that in a variety of circumstances—ranging from boards of directors to judges—systematic errors can be expected anytime group membership may become salient, which is almost always.[86] On some levels humans seem hardwired to behave in this way, as group membership identification no doubt has contributed to survival.[87]

Homosocial reproduction operates to establish unified group membership based upon important social characteristics. People in power display a proclivity to select applicants who closely mirror their own background. Naturally, women and racial minorities must face homosocial reproduction as yet another barrier to success. Homosocial reproduction further impedes their ability to form valuable networks.[88] The payoff from homosocial reproduction for corporate elites lies in higher compensation driven by affinity bias.[89] Powerful evidence suggests that this factor corrupts the selection process at the very apex of American economic power—CEOs and directors of the public corporation.[90] Thus, affinity bias and homosocial reproduction operate together to cloud judgments and disrupt the operation of a true meritocracy at all levels of the American economy.

The disruption of groupthink, homosocial reproduction, and affinity bias may well serve to explain the findings of empirical studies showing superior outcomes from group decision making by diverse groups relative to homogenous groups. For example, racially diverse groups achieved higher quality and feasibility scores for marketing plans than more homogenous groups.[91] Similarly, with respect to boards of directors, financial studies find an association between board diversity and financial performance, even after controlling for firm size and industry and corporate governance practices.[92] Similarly, firms with more board diversity pursued less subprime lending and suffered lower losses.[93] A study from economics finds that the most diverse U.S. cities (measured by percentage of residents born in other countries) are the most productive cities measured by wages and rents.[94] In the world of higher education, a recent meta-analysis of seventeen studies of the link between diversity (racial as well as nonracial) and enhanced cognitive skills for the entire student population found that "the evidence for the cognitive benefits of college diversity experiences is quite strong."[95] Despite the limitations of empirical studies, this evidence paints a compelling picture that cultural diversity can help a society make better decisions and achieve superior cognitive outcomes. The subprime crisis shows that the U.S. must diversify its top leadership to achieve new heights of competence and to reduce homosocial reproduction as well as affinity bias.

Race, Economic Oppression, and the Subprime Debacle

While the Civil Rights Act of 1964 and *Brown v. Board of Education* removed the harshest elements of American apartheid, the U.S. still permits too much racial oppression. The U.S. never committed sufficient resources to resolve its racial hangover and instead continues to pursue policies that inflict serious damage on disempowered communities such as the so-called war on drugs. As a result, instead of rationally educating our youth, the U.S. expends $25,000 per year incarcerating many nonviolent youths of color.[96] The costs of pursuing such policies, as discussed previously, can be obscured because they tend to accrue silently in the form of lost economic opportunities and forgone output, rather than in dramatic financial calamities.

Occasionally, deep or persistent economic oppression can lead to crises, such as the subprime mortgage crisis. Even before the crisis, authoritative voices warned that the exploitation of vulnerable communities, including communities of color, through predatory lending posed a growing danger.

Assistant Secretary of Housing and Urban Development William Apgar tes-tified in 2000: "Predatory lenders target untold numbers of the most vul-nerable homeowners—focusing on the elderly, minorities, and low-income families, loading them down with debt, and stripping them of equity. In a growing number of cases, these predatory loan terms are too much to bear and, as a result, the family loses its home to foreclosure."[97]

Apgar's concerns echo Federal Reserve Governor Edward Gramlich's sim-ilar efforts to raise red flags about predatory lending. According to Gramlich, half of all subprime borrowers actually qualified for prime loans. Subprime loans carry interest rates that average 3.5 percentage points higher than prime loans—meaning that steering a prime borrower into a subprime loan can inflict hundreds of thousands in extra interest costs alone on a homeowner.[98] This renders default much more likely. In 2000, Gramlich tried to defuse the subprime time bomb through regulation, but Fed Chair Alan Greenspan sty-mied these efforts.[99] Audit studies confirmed that minority borrowers often faced steering pressures toward subprime and predatory loans that equally qualified whites did not.[100] Yet another study, based upon federally required information from lenders, found that "[e]ven at the highest income level, blacks are more than three times as likely to get their loans from a subprime lender as are others."[101] Consequently, well in advance of the subprime implo-sion, telltale signs showed that significant numbers of minority borrowers suffered unnecessary steering into costly subprime loans.

Once the subprime boom peaked in 2006 and 2007, these trends mani-fested themselves as key drivers of the crisis. The 2007 federal data showed that lenders subjected 54 percent of high-income blacks to high-cost loans versus 28 percent of low-income whites. Latino borrowers fared little better as nearly half of high-income borrowers ended up with high-cost loans.[102] Even after controlling for credit risk (through the use of a proxy variable based upon statistic similarity of borrowers to rejected applicants because federal law does not require lender disclosure of credit scores), blacks in 2006 faced 3.9 times the risk of white borrowers of placement in a subprime loan; Latinos faced 2.62 times the risk.[103] Lenders also steered minority borrowers away from low-cost FHA loans.[104] Another study combined data from federal sources with further data obtained from a proprietary database (including credit scores, loan-to-value ratios, etc.) and found that race played a major factor (e.g., up to 2.89 times the risk of higher cost loans) in the cost of loans: "[I]n multiple analyses that control for the major risk factors lenders explic-itly use to set prices, we find that borrowers' race and ethnicity continue to exert a statistically significant influence on the cost of their subprime mort-gages." Obviously, the possibility of an omitted variable looms; yet the authors controlled for credit scores, regulatory authority, and a majority of credit risk variables that lenders themselves identify as important.[105] Short of the lenders' opening up their entire loan files (which they have lobbied against), the best evidence available leads to only one conclusion: Lenders steered a huge number of minority borrowers into unnecessarily expensive loans.

This racial steering into subprime loans constitutes the most predatory type of lending, termed "reverse redlining," as mortgage brokers, lenders, securitizers, investment banks, and others knowingly extracted extra market profits through racial exploitation. The U.S. Department of Justice has initiated a wide-ranging probe into reverse redlining. These inquiries mirror pending cases in state courts.[106] Similarly, the Federal Trade Commission settled reverse redlining claims against Gateway Funding Diversified Mortgage Services. The FTC alleged (and Gateway stipulated) that this mortgage broker permitted its agents to levy surcharges against minority borrowers that caused such borrowers to pay more for loans solely based upon their race. In late 2011, in the largest fair lending settlement in U.S. history, Bank of America agreed to pay $335 million for discriminatory lending at Countrywide (which it had purchased) affecting 200,000 borrowers nationwide. Numerous similar cases are pending throughout the nation.[107] At this point, the question is not whether lenders steered minorities into predatory loans; the only question is how many hundreds of thousands of minority borrowers ended up overpaying for their loans and their homes.

Differential foreclosure rates suggest that a multitude did so. If a lender applies responsible and nondiscriminatory underwriting standards, then communities of color should have comparable foreclosure rates. Because of the losses implicit in foreclosure, even a few extra foreclosures out of one hundred borrowers could wipe out years of enhanced risk-adjusted interest for all one hundred loans. This means that although higher-risk loans may be expected to generate more foreclosures, highly divergent foreclosure rates suggest something else amiss. In Memphis, Tennessee (according to a lawsuit filed by several Tennessee municipal authorities), for example, 43 percent of Wells Fargo's foreclosures were in African American neighborhoods, where only 15 percent of its mortgages were made. Yet, white neighborhoods, where Wells made 60 percent of its loans, accounted for only 21.5 percent of foreclosures. Former Wells Fargo employees attest that Wells Fargo encouraged targeting black borrowers for subprime loans throughout the nation.[108] This pattern of racial differentials in foreclosures strongly suggests that Wells Fargo exploited communities of color in search of short-term profits (and higher bonuses for management). Wells ultimately settled a series of discriminatory lending cases for hundreds of millions in payments.

The banks exercised power over minority borrowers, in part, because of the continued exclusion of minority borrowers and their neighborhoods from prime loans. "At every income level blacks and residents of minority neighborhoods are more likely to turn to subprime lenders than are others."[109] Moreover, "[i]n the distorted world of subprime marketing[,] targeting racially . . . marginalized communities is an efficient, economically rational way to find consumers who feel excluded from mainstream credit markets, and are likely to be more vulnerable to deception and abuse."[110] In fact, the subprime boom occurred in specific geographic locations that coincide with both high loan rejection rates for prime loans and areas of historic minority marginalization—the Black Belt within the old Confederacy, Midwestern urban centers, and the Texas/Mexican border region. These factors persist even after controlling for a wide variety of lending factors, including creditworthiness.[111] A Federal Reserve study found that lenders specifically preyed upon the least sophisticated borrowers with the least ability to understand and compute mortgage costs.[112] Therefore, the story of who borrowed at subprime loan rates—with high costs and other oppressive features—seems more about where banks possessed the power to saddle borrowers with such loans than about specific credit characteristics of homebuyers.

Notably, no regulatory or law enforcement agency monitored the booming business of subprime and predatory lending. In mid-2005, the state of New York demanded information from a number of banks regarding their subprime lending activities, but the banks stymied the effort by arguing state power was preempted by the National Bank Act of 1864. The Bush administration joined these arguments, as did industry lobbying groups. The information the state requested was precisely the kind of information that would have revealed racial steering into subprime loans and predatory lending practices. The Department of Housing and Urban Development initiated only three fair lending investigations between 2006 and 2008—the period of the most reckless loans. The Department of Justice brought just one mortgage discrimination claim in all of 2007. The essential problem is that the regulators found regulation ideologically offensive. Meanwhile, as discussed in chapter 3, a wide variety of loans that previously were not legally permissible became very common.[113] This combination of lax regulation and enforcement proved toxic.

The subprime boom exploded after 2003. Subprime originations ballooned from $65 billion in 1995, to $332 billion in 2003, to $625 billion in 2006. Securitizations of subprime loans more than doubled to $425 billion between 2004 and 2006. At the same time, lenders pushed African American and Latino borrowers into subprime loans at a dramatically higher rate— nearly double in the case of Latinos. Yet, credit characteristics remained the same over this time. This all coincided with more rapid securitization of sub-prime loans and the peak of the "global savings glut" that Fed Chair Alan Greenspan identified as a key element underlying the subprime fiasco, as discussed in chapter 4. Put simply, the most reckless and exploitative phase of subprime lending appears to be driven not by the specific credit character-istics of the borrowers (or any other demand side element) but instead by the market power of the banks and the global demand for high-yielding product created by a fundamentally distorted global financial system. As more loans moved more quickly into the global financial sector, incentives for proper underwriting diminished and loan risks increased.[114] Minority borrowers were fleeced because the lenders could get away with fleecing them and the global financial sector demanded that they do so. The profitability, even if illusory, explains the subprime boom between 2004 and 2006, not a chari-table desire to help minority borrowers and the credit characteristics of the borrowers, which too often justified prime loans.

The economic impact of the subprime debacle on communities of color continues to devastate entire neighborhoods, cities, and families. The home ownership gap remains as high as ever: In 1940, for example, 23 percent more whites than blacks owned homes versus 28 percent more today. Whites con-tinue to enjoy easier access to conventional home loans, at all income levels. Even among high-income borrowers, three times more Latinos and African Americans service high-cost loans than white borrowers. Subprime loans carry a much higher risk of foreclosure. Today, 10 percent of African Ameri-cans face foreclosure versus 4 percent of white borrowers. With 9 million more foreclosures yet to come over the next three years, these trends mean massive destruction of wealth within communities of color. Thus far, the subprime crisis has destroyed between $164 billion and $213 billion of wealth within communities of color.[115]

Many warnings of misconduct in the subprime mortgage market emerged from 2000 to 2007. Regulators and lawmakers simply ignored all the signs of trouble. The explosive growth of subprime lending from 2000 to 2004 hardly occurred in secret. Further, the deregulatory mantra beginning in the 1980s also did not occur without warnings regarding the risks of precipitous deregulation of the financial sector. This raises the question of why the sys-tem responded in such a subdued, even invisible fashion.

Racial Politics and the Subprime Fiasco

The MIT economist Simon Johnson and James Kwak have written about the massive increase in the size of the financial sector in our economy. As part of this huge growth, the banks naturally accumulated more political influence. This explains much of the regulatory and legal history of the U.S. financial system over the past forty years.[116] The chain of causation from economic girth to political influence to enhanced compensation for financial elites seems clear. Still, the politics of race also played a role in enhancing the influence of financial elites. The economist Paul Krugman argues that the modern conservative resurgence—complete with its determination to redistribute wealth upward—took root as part of the GOP's "Southern Strategy," as perfected by Ronald Reagan. Substantial evidence supports Krugman.[117] Of course, financial deregulation took root beginning with the Reagan administration.[118]

On April 23, 2010, during a speech at DePaul University in Chicago, the Chairman of the Republican National Committee, Michael Steele, made a remarkable admission. "For the last 40-plus years we had a 'Southern Strategy' that alienated many minority voters by focusing on the white male vote in the South."[119] Steele became the second Republican chairman to admit to the GOP's race-based "Southern Strategy." In 2005, then-Chairman Ken Mehlman stated at the NAACP National Convention that since at least 1970, "Some Republicans gave up on winning the African American vote, looking the other way or trying to benefit politically from racial polarization. I am here today as the Republican chairman to tell you we were wrong."[120] Apparently, after at least forty years of using racial polarization to build a political coalition and attract southern white voters, the GOP regrets its success. The injection of race into the body politic could only amplify the trends identified by Johnson and Kwak regarding the political power of financial elites.

The era of deregulation started in 1980 with the election of Ronald Reagan. Following his nomination, Reagan kicked off his 1980 presidential campaign in Philadelphia, Mississippi, a small rural town. The only significance of Philadelphia for such an event is this: An infamous race-related crime occurred in Philadelphia. After midnight, on June 21, 1964, white supremacists killed three civil rights workers on a road outside of Philadelphia. Reagan, in 1980, stated the following: "I believe in states' rights. . . . I believe we have distorted the balance of our government today by giving powers that were never intended to be given in the Constitution to that federal establishment." He promised "to restore to states and local governments the power that properly belongs to them." While controversy surrounds the events of 1980 in Philadelphia, even those defending former President Reagan's intent agree that "it's obviously true that race played a role in the G.O.P.'s ascent."[121] That is the core point. The so-called Reagan Revolution imposed nothing less than discredited laissez-faire thinking on the U.S. economy without a fair debate; the fair debate essentially suffocated in Philadelphia, a victim of the so-called Southern Strategy.

To be fair, Reagan hardly needed the Southern Strategy in the end, as he swept not only the South but also the West, the Midwest, and the Northeast in a landslide victory over President Jimmy Carter. Yet, the consequences of his vision of highly limited government immediately paved the way for much of the predatory lending at the root of the subprime crisis. In 1982, he signed the Garn–St. Germain Depository Institutions Act,[122] which operated to expand the availability of adjustable rate mortgages and eliminated mandatory loan-to-value ratios and negative amortization loans.[123] In 1984 the Secondary Mortgage Market Enhancement Act[124] became law, clearing the way for more expansive private securitization of mortgages (including predatory mortgages) by preempting state securities law and authorizing a variety of financial institutions to invest in such securities.[125] It is hard to imagine that the large numbers of working-class whites (even in northern cities) who voted for Ronald Reagan really supported these laissez-faire predicates to the subprime fiasco, as opposed to feeling that the Democratic Party was too closely aligned with the interests of African Americans and other minorities. The work of the pollster Stanley B. Greenberg illustrates the point: He found that many of the so-called Reagan Democrats deserted the Democratic Party because they identified the Democrats as the party of the poor and minorities.[126] Indeed, these voters "expressed a profound distaste for blacks."[127]

Race operates in other ways to distort politics. The economist Glenn Loury, in *The Anatomy of Racial Inequality*, carefully studied the mechanisms that produce racial inequality even in the absence of an intent to discriminate on the basis of race. One mechanism he identifies is racial stigma. Racial stigma arises from deeply held but largely unspoken attitudes of racial inferiority or superiority. These attitudes do not cause any particular harm, except for the effect on the nation's political discourse. Thus, for example, Loury posits that the sanguine response of the American body politic to the incarceration rate in the U.S., including the very large number of youths of color in the criminal justice system, could be accepted only by voters who supposedly value justice, freedom, and fair opportunity for all, because of notions of racial inferiority. Our society incarcerates African American males at seven times the rate of white males, and this patent injustice warrants nary a blip on the radar of the body politic. Only a powerful social construct like race can explain the cognitive dissonance of society on this issue.[128]

Predatory lending similarly failed to register at all with the American body politic. For example, in 2004, neither the Republican nor the Democratic platform even mentioned predatory lending, subprime lending, racial inequality in loan terms, or financial regulation. Instead, the Democrats urged "tough punishment" for crime and a "crack down on gang violence and drug crime."[129] The Republican platform similarly failed to mention anything about financial reform or subprime lending, although the GOP did stand for an expanded death penalty.[130] In March 2008, the Bush administration's Department of the Treasury released its *Blueprint for a Modernized Financial Regulatory Structure*. To its credit, the report suggests many constructive changes to the regulatory framework governing subprime lending. However, by March 2008 the global financial system meltdown had reached an advanced stage—Bear Stearns collapsed on March 14, 2008. In any event, the report makes no mention of race or racial disparities in mortgage lending and mentions predatory lending only in a paragraph that suggests Federal Reserve rule making to prevent predatory loans.[131] Given the damage to the economy from subprime lending (and particularly from predatory lending), the inherent racial inequity in predatory lending from historic patterns of economic oppression, and the patent warnings well in advance of the crisis, it seems that more visibility for this issue may well have proved helpful. Certainly, the election of 2004 left much time to forestall the brewing crisis.

Notably, political pressure for more subprime lending regulation did emerge at the state level. North Carolina passed a law as early as 1999 that limited loan flipping (constant refinancing for the same borrower) and prepayment penalties. Georgia, New York, and New Jersey each passed similar laws aimed at cracking down on predatory loans in 2002.[132] The Office of the Comptroller of the Currency, the primary regulator for national banks, and the Office of Thrift Supervision, the primary regulator of the savings and loan industry, each ruled that these state laws did not apply to federal depository institutions because federal regulation preempted state regulation for federally chartered banks and thrifts.[133] The U.S. Supreme Court, as part of its continuing crusade for laissez-faire, upheld the exercise of preemptive power of the banking regulators and thereby missed yet another opportunity to help prevent the financial meltdown of 2007–9.[134] Perhaps if the Supreme Court recognized the subprime debacle it would rule differently.

Racial politics tends inherently to lack transparency. Politicians rarely if ever admit to using racial divisions strategically. Similarly, proof that an issue would receive more attention but for racial stigma will always be impossible. Thus, it is unknowable whether a completely race-free America would have averted or mitigated the subprime crisis and the ensuing financial crisis. Nevertheless, given the racial disparities driving predatory lending and its key role in the height of the subprime boom, it seems likely that America's racialized politics played a substantial role in bringing about the crisis and amplifying its destructiveness.

In sum, race contributed to the subprime debacle in four fundamental ways. First, as discussed in chapter 4, elites rigged globalization to rely upon consumption centered in the U.S. and founded on debt, yet global economic oppression and the construct of race in America precluded any broader market development and human capital formation to secure consumption. Second, race prevented full actualization of human resources in the U.S. and allowed an elite produced by pervasive privilege and unaccustomed to real competitive pressures to game the financial sector the same way they gamed the college admissions process—they win no matter what, and the rest of us lose. Third, the continued sway of race left a disempowered subclass in place that invited exploitation, and predatory lending followed. Finally, race fundamentally polluted the body politic so that laissez-faire could grip our system without the body politic's really bargaining for it—instead, these voters voted against a party seen as too closely aligned with the interests of minorities, and the GOP exploited this for forty years to the maximum extent possible, as admitted by two party chairmen. Furthermore, the body politic seems not to have reacted appropriately to warnings of race-based predatory lending.

As emphasized throughout this book with respect to every putative cause, race did not exclusively cause the subprime debacle. Many factors combined for the crisis of 2007–9. Those peddling a single explanation to the crisis risk simplistic and reductionist explanations. Most notably, extreme conservatives frequently blame the government's efforts to further affordable housing and home ownership as the exclusive cause of the crisis. At times, these arguments flirt with outright racial scapegoating.[135] A Federal Reserve study found that only 6 percent of all subprime loans qualified to fulfill bank obligations under the Community Reinvestment Act.[136] As previously stated, Fannie Mae and Freddie Mac invested in nonprime MBS, but losses on these investments from 2008 to 2011 total only $3 billion.[137] These losses pale in comparison to losses suffered in the riskiest lending and can mean only that Fannie and Freddie did not invest much in the highest-risk mortgages.

Three of the four Republican members (and all of the Democratic members) of the Financial Crisis Inquiry Commission declined to attribute primary or exclusive causation to the CRA, affordable housing goals, or the government-sponsored enterprises at the heart of the home mortgage market—Fannie Mae and Freddie Mac. Instead, all nine of these Commissioners concur that Fannie and Freddie played only a modest role and attribute the crisis primarily to an extended list of other causes.[138] Thus, the view that affordable housing goals somehow caused bankers to gorge on risk (and incidentally find hundreds of millions in compensation payments in their pockets) can only be termed a far-right position. Charity did not drive the bankers—quite the opposite.

This crisis resulted from a complex of legal and regulatory deficiencies. It is impossible to quantify the role of race. We simply cannot know whether in a perfectly de-racialized America a crisis would have stricken the financial sector. These imponderables, however, should not mask the key point of this chapter: Race played a significant role in the crisis and contributed as a substantial factor to either creating the economic meltdown or worsening its effects. Only an optimal economic rule of law would have certainly prevented this crisis. And, as will be explored in chapter 7, imposing a durable economic rule of law or economic constitution is no simple undertaking.

Remediating Race

In light of the foregoing, expanding antidiscrimination law under the Fourteenth Amendment of the U.S. Constitution and Civil Rights Act of 1964, as well as affirmative action, appears eminently sensible. These suggestions complement the findings of the World Bank regarding the dangers that mass disempowerment pose to growth. A number of legal scholars argue in favor of exactly such expansion. To the extent such arguments included recognition of "entrenched inequalities" that mainstream scholars ignored, these arguments seem prescient in suggesting that many Americans still are shut out from economic opportunities and that the nation suffers a less competent and responsible governing elite.[139] Other scholars argued that Title VII assumed the operation of a meritocracy that in fact was more myth than reality, as non-overt discrimination pervaded the work world in the U.S.[140] Nevertheless, the Supreme Court in recent decades has evinced persistent hostility to combating race-based discrimination in the absence of compelling evidence of discriminatory intent that usually cannot be produced in the real world. The Court seems determined to maintain vestigial white privilege. In a so-called postracial political climate, reform on these fronts may prove difficult.[141]

In the past, I have argued that the law should facilitate a broader and deeper embrace of our culturally diverse human resources. Diversity can operate as a source of richer cognitive perspectives that arise from differing experiences in our racialized society. Because these cognitive resources arise independently of the morphological features associated with race, embracing these facilities to create more diverse workgroups across the entire range of society does not implicate antidiscrimination law strictures or constitutional limitations regarding race-based decision making. This could prove economically valuable in generating ideas because diverse workgroups consistently outperform nondiverse workgroups in accordance with Irving R. Janis's groupthink theory. In addition, diversity should operate to disrupt affinity bias in areas where elites entrench themselves through homosocial reproduction.[142] I proposed a range of legal innovations to support wider embrace of cultural diversity including a safe harbor under Title VII antidiscrimination law.[143] Most notably I proposed that diversity in the boardroom of the publicly held firm could lead to superior corporate governance outcomes as shown in numerous empirical studies. Given the importance of embracing diversity for profit, I argued that the federal securities laws should mandate that public firms disclose their diversity policies.[144]

Lani Guinier and Gerald Torres, in *The Miner's Canary*, argue that a transracial coalition of those oppressed by holders of concentrated economic and political power should come together to achieve reform. They suggest that the Texas plan to admit the top 10 percent of every high school class to the state's flagship university epitomizes the potential for this type of coalition.[145] Professor Richard Delgado challenges this vision of a transracial coalition to achieve racial reform. According to Delgado, "coalition is likely to founder on cultural misunderstandings or historical grievances, and to encounter internal defections and efforts by the dominant group to split the coalition."[146] History certainly suggests that Delgado is right. Yet the election of 2008 resulted from a broad coalition of voters of color that propelled an African American into the White House even though a majority of white voters cast their votes against Barack Obama. In chapter 7, I will address this issue in greater depth. Right now, I wish merely to suggest that deep social reform, of the kind needed to address the underlying causes of the great market meltdown of 2008, is likely to require a vast array of interests to oust the very concentrated interests that I posit have rigorously entrenched themselves at the apex of our economic and political system. In other words, I ultimately seek to extend the Guinier and Torres approach beyond race and into broader legal and regulatory reform.

At some level, law simply cannot change the power dynamics within any society—including the constructs of race and economic disempowerment. Instead, a cultural suspicion of deep economic disempowerment must emerge. People must recognize that disempowerment of others means constricted demand for their own services and money out of their own pockets. Instead of feeling threatened by the disempowered, a cultural consensus of citizens must emerge that understands the threats of concentrated economic power. Citizens must recognize the extreme unlikelihood that the disempowered are harming their interests. Voters must become suspicious of the rich and powerful rather than the least threatening and most disempowered elements of society. At some point the costs of indulging elite privilege become intolerable. At that point the law can operate to create durable frameworks, such as economic human rights, that limit elite power and create a more powerful macroeconomy at once. Moreover, law can sway cultural attitudes over the long run by memorializing how concentrated economic power has damaged economic opportunity for all.

The central point of this chapter is to explore the ways in which elites benefit from racial and economic oppression. Economic oppression, along with constructs like race, enhances elites' ability to rig the system in their favor and to insulate themselves from fair competition. This tendency imposes economic costs upon the macroeconomy. These costs can total trillions in forgone output and must include episodic financial crises which result from the rigged system that elites embrace and pursue.

6

The Crisis in Crisis Management

Dismissing financial crisis on the grounds that bubbles and bust cannot take place because that would imply irrationality is to ignore a condition for the sake of a theory.
Charles P. Kindleberger (2000)[1]

The history of capitalism proves that financial crises can be eliminated only with superior legal and regulatory infrastructure, if then. The MIT economist Charles Kindleberger, in his classic *Manias, Panics and Crashes*, shows that aside from a thirty-year period of stability, from 1945 through 1975, "speculative excess," such as manias or panics, is "if not inevitable, at least historically common."[2] Professor Hyman Minsky takes Kindleberger's argument a step further: "turbulence—especially financial instability—is normal in a capitalist economy." Minsky's key insight relates to the centrality of the financial sector to growth and the optimism engendered by stability and growth. Speculative finance will naturally follow stability, especially in a laissez-faire financial system. Sooner or later the system will gorge on risk. Manias, crashes, and bubbles are therefore inherent to capitalism.[3] According to Minsky, capitalism is rigged toward instability; even periods of stability breed excessive risk.

Monetary policy fails to resolve this essential challenge. The Nobel laureate Robert Lucas famously declared severe economic disruptions an historic relic, slayed by modern monetary policy.[4] Unfortunately, monetary policy relies upon bank lending. If lenders prefer safety above all else, a liquidity trap will render monetary policy impotent. Further, monetary policy cannot induce stable growth in the context of a debt crisis accompanied by a bursting asset bubble, because firms and consumers will seek to minimize debt loads (deleverage) and make contractionary debt repayments.[5] Indeed, the current debt crisis facing the U.S. highlights the problems with excessive reliance upon monetary policy as the near-exclusive government response to economic crises and downturns. The trajectory of the debt burden since 1980 within the American economy and the recent debt crisis involving subprime mortgages suggest that debt cannot always be used to resolve every economic disruption. "Such turmoil is a sign that debt is not the instant solution it was made out to be."[6]

Modern finance creates new sources of uncertainty and risks that regulators may not foresee and comprehend. In May 1998, Alan Greenspan, Chairman of the Federal Reserve, delivered a startling speech. Greenspan stated that although the sophisticated financial system that spanned the globe promised higher living standards, the "high-tech financial system" outstripped our understanding and threatened "a systemic disruption beyond our degree of comprehension or our ability to respond effectively."[7] Essentially the Chairman of the Federal Reserve Board admitted (ten years before the current crisis) that a massive financial crisis beyond the mitigatory capacity of monetary policy increases in probability as our financial system becomes more complex. This means that regardless of regulatory fastidiousness, the possibility of a financial meltdown can never be fully discounted. Twice in the past century, at least, markets confirmed Greenspan's point. In both the 1930s and 2008, financial markets suffered near-total collapses, inflicting massive macroeconomic losses. The events of 9/11 highlight the possibility of market meltdown arising from geopolitical tensions. The Dow Jones Industrial Average registered its largest one-day loss in the immediate aftermath of the 9/11 attacks.[8] Financial crises cannot always be averted any more than mass panic can be averted.

John Maynard Keynes famously posited that financial markets ultimately move in accordance with "animal spirits."[9] Minsky further argued that the combination of financial innovation and a return to laissez-faire deregulation threatened debt deflation.[10] Minsky shows that extended stability invites manias and bubbles that lead to financial crises. Minsky claimed that a "sophisticated, dynamic and complex financial system" requires more regulation because it is bound to generate greater instability. "Capitalism is unstable because it is a finance and accumulating system with yesterdays, todays and tomorrows." Yesterday's profits invariably lead to an underpricing of risk today, with a consequent crash tomorrow when risk becomes an adverse reality.[11] In short, the Minsky thesis essentially predicted the subprime debacle.

Regulators and policymakers should therefore assume that markets tend toward instability, as history certainly proves this central point. Government regulation must err on the side of caution as well as impose redundant systems to ensure the stability of the system. Since the date of Greenspan's speech, the complexity of the global financial system has increased. Consequently, the need for ever more optimized legal frameworks to secure government's crisis management efforts is ever more compelling. This chapter articulates legal frameworks securing precisely these kinds of government-sponsored stabilization efforts.

In modern capitalistic societies, government must respond to financial crises and other economic disruptions or risk economic contractions and the wrath of voters. This implies massive government intervention into the economy. This reality means that law faces a challenge to organize government's economic interventions through optimized legal and regulatory frameworks.[12] Once again, this chapter demonstrates that excessive economic and political power corrupts sound policy in the absence of legal limits, at great expense to growth and stability and by extension to society generally.

In terms of stabilization policies, government enjoys three channels of influence: monetary policy, fiscal policy, and firm bailouts. Monetary policy relies upon expansion of the money supply, usually through expanded bank credit, to stoke demand and quell economic downturns. Fiscal policy seeks to replace slack in demand with enhanced government spending. Bailouts involve the use of government resources to stop economic contagion and control systemic risk from the failure of large or interconnected firms. In the crisis of 2007–9, each of these stabilization instruments played a prominent role in the government's response. Moreover, each of these instruments suffered from a suboptimal institutional structure as well as inappropriate political subversion.

In what can only be termed an epic effort, the government deployed massive financial resources to stemming the downturn, particularly during the fall of 2008 and the spring of 2009. The government assumed potential obligations of $23 trillion and made massive outlays that continue through today and long into the future.[13] The Federal Reserve extended more than $16 trillion in loans to save the entire global financial system.[14] It also purchased $1.25 trillion in mortgage-backed securities from the financial sector to prop up real estate values.[15] Furthermore, Congress provided $700 billion through the Troubled Asset Relief Program to recapitalize the banking sector. Even before the fall of 2008, the Federal Home Loan Bank Board (the central bank for the thrift industry) quietly acquired hundreds of billions of dollars in mortgages from troubled savings banks and savings and loans.[16] Finally, once the mortgage market collapsed in 2007, Fannie Mae and Freddie Mac, under the supervision of Treasury Secretary Henry Paulson, continued to purchase hundreds of billions of dollars' worth of mortgages, effectively shifting losses from the private financial sector to the government, which ultimately backstopped Fannie and Freddie.[17] These extraordinary and unprecedented actions to keep the financial sector afloat often stretched beyond the contemplation of the legal powers Congress granted to these agencies.[18]

Unfortunately, these expenditures suffered from severe political distortions.[19] The U.S. government deserves credit for averting a repeat of the Great Depression in 2009–10. Yet many of its actions sow the seeds for crises down the road.[20] In particular, the government's conduct created firmer incentives for reckless misconduct in the financial sector. Moreover, the government failed to deal with the debt overhang from as early as the 1980s and thereby consigned the economy to an exceedingly high risk of a period of economic stagnation and instability.[21] The U.S. taxpayer thus bears the burden of massive expenditures that may well have averted disaster only at the cost of serial crises as well as a long-term decline in American living standards. The government simply did not get enough bang for its buck because too much wealth flowed to those holding political power and too little to those most victimized.[22] Legal and regulatory frameworks failed to secure a scientifically based response unadulterated by concentrated economic influence. The sordid story starts with monetary policy.

Monetary Policy

Debt generally stimulates growth by facilitating more consumption or investment than could otherwise occur if financed only through current income. By definition, however, it also creates claims on future output. Moreover, excessive debt burdens will lead to curtailed credit conditions and, by extension, diminished output. Monetary policy depends upon debt creation, which through fractional reserve banking creates money to fuel expanded demand to support greater growth. Fractional reserve banking means that banks need not hold as reserves the full amount of demand deposit accounts. If they lend by creating a demand deposit account for the borrower, they need not reserve for the full amount of the loan, even though that demand deposit account may immediately support borrower spending.[23] Banks therefore act as a key "transmission belt" of monetary policy.[24] If banks lend, then more money can be spent to support economic activity.

The Federal Reserve can induce more borrowing through interest rate cuts. When interest rates fall, loan demand increases. The Federal Reserve maintains direct control of a bank's cost of funds through its control of the Federal Funds rate. That rate governs the costs of loans made through short-term interbank loans. The Federal Reserve also influences interest rates through its open market operations conducted through the Federal Open Market Committee. When it buys government bonds, it injects reserves into the banking system, and buying bonds on the open market increases the demand for such instruments, causing bond prices to go up and yields on such bonds to fall. Yields fall because the increased demand for government bonds means more buyers, who will accept lower yields in order to obtain bonds in demand. Lowering yields (i.e., interest rates) on debt and injecting more reserves into the banking system spur lending. This gives the Fed tremendous power over the pace of economic activity.[25]

Modern monetary policy dates to the Great Depression. One traditional explanation for the depths and persistence of the Great Depression involves the Federal Reserve's sloppy administration of monetary policy.[26] Commentators have long maintained that the Fed followed an expansionary policy prior to the Depression that fed the speculative frenzy, and a contractionary policy after the onset of the Depression. In particular, the Fed apparently raised interest rates in order to enhance bank earnings, as banks held vast amounts of bonds. This increase in interest rates caused a continued contraction in economic activity.[27] Thus, an essential part of the New Deal involved placing monetary policy on a firmer legal framework that could resist special interest influence, and particularly the influence of the banking industry.[28]

More specifically, after the New Deal banking reforms, the governors of the Federal Reserve Board enjoy fourteen-year terms, the staff of the Federal Reserve System earns competitive salaries, and the Federal Reserve Board may levy assessments on member banks—meaning that the Fed is a self-funded administrative agency unbeholden to economic interests or the political branches. Prior to the New Deal, the Secretary of the Treasury and the Comptroller of the Currency served on the Federal Reserve Board, but the Banking Act of 1935 terminated their membership. The New Deal reforms aimed to reduce the influence of special interests on monetary policy. For the most part, monetary policy since these reforms appears driven by economic science and expertise.[29]

Nevertheless, the Fed may benefit further from an explicit charter to lean against dangerous asset bubbles. Mass mania inheres in the creation of an asset bubble; by definition, a bubble involves widespread belief that asset values may rise above traditional indicia of fundamental value. Political support in favor of government action against bubbles will therefore necessarily fade as the bubble becomes more dangerous.[30] The Fed currently lacks power to burst asset bubbles. Recently, the President of the Federal Reserve Bank of New York, William Dudley, called upon central banks to fight bubbles with regulation rather than with monetary policy. Dudley claims that monetary policy broadly affects the economy and therefore would prove too costly for combating bubbles in terms of forgone output and more unemployment.[31]

In 2002 in the wake of the stock market bubble of the 1990s, I argued that the Fed's chartering statute should provide explicit power to burst bubbles through control of credit on a targeted basis. Specifically, I suggested that the Fed's enabling statute include the responsibility to "discourage incipient asset bubbles." Further, I argued that credit controls aimed at specific asset classes could forestall asset bubbles without broad-based damage to the real economy implicit in raising interest rates generally.[32] Professor Timothy Canova suggests that targeted credit controls could operate to control many asset bubbles across asset classes, including loan-to-value ratios for real estate as well as margin requirements for securities.[33] The subprime debacle shows that debt-driven bubbles can devastate an economy when they burst as a result of the dual impact they have on wealth of investors and financial sector solvency. Therefore, the Fed should also be given broader power to rein in the speculative excesses of financial institutions by restricting leverage throughout the financial sector or on a targeted basis. Certainly, given the trillions in costs from the current crisis, such a legal innovation makes sense—perhaps with even more robust targeted credit controls. Since the bursting of the housing bubble, no legislative proposal to endow the Fed with this power has emerged. Targeted credit controls promise to reduce the threat of bubbles without general interest rate increases that affect the general economy and risk economic slowdowns.

Another problem with the current legal framework governing monetary policy in the U.S. is the relationship of the Fed to the banking industry. The Federal Reserve System actually consists of multiple entities. At the apex of the system sits the Federal Reserve Board of Governors, an administrative agency of the U.S. government based in Washington, D.C. The President appoints Governors to fourteen-year terms. The chair holds office for four years. The Senate confirms all appointments. Under the Board of Governors sit the regional Federal Reserve Banks, formed as private corporations that are owned by the member banks of the Federal Reserve System. Despite their private status, the Board of Governors appoints three of nine board members of each regional Federal Reserve Bank and retains approval power of each regional bank's president. The presidents of the regional banks hold five of twelve positions on the Federal Open Market Committee, which oversees one element of monetary policy—the purchase or sale of government bonds in the open market.[34] Thus, the Board of Governors dominates monetary policy, not the regional banks.

Nevertheless, the banking industry itself plays a powerful role in the Federal Reserve System. The members of the Federal Reserve System—which are all private commercial banks—elect a majority of each regional bank board. These boards then elect regional bank presidents—all of whom are attendees of each Federal Open Market Committee, and five of whom actually cast votes at such meetings. At the very least, this raises the specter of cognitive capture, as the representatives of the banking industry mingle freely as peers with the Federal Reserve Board of Governors at the critical FOMC meetings, and beyond. Professor Minsky argues that it is "difficult to discover or invent a serious reason for the existence of twelve Federal Reserve Banks."[35] Essentially, one Federal Reserve Bank should act as an agency of the Federal Reserve Board, with a completely public governance structure. This reform negates the prospect of agency capture inherent in private ownership of the Federal Reserve Banks. The current influence of private banks smacks of corruption.[36]

To be fair, the Fed needs to comprehend the dynamics facing the banking industry in order to conduct monetary policy, for banks act as the transmission belt of monetary policy through their lending activities. Such a facility exists separate and apart from the Federal Reserve Bank system. The Federal Advisory Council (FAC) exists for the very purpose of creating a forum for bankers to exchange information with the Fed. Scholars studied whether the FAC operated as a means of inappropriate industry influence over monetary policy and concluded that it did not.[37] Thus, the FAC, rather than the Federal Reserve Bank System, should function as the focal point of exchange between the Fed and the banking industry. Indeed, the Fed itself identifies this as the primary role of the FAC.[38] This approach seems more likely to avert cognitive capture than the current approach.

That potential for capture traditionally seemed immaterial to the conduct of monetary policy, as both the Federal Reserve Board and the banking industry possessed broadly aligned interests in a sound currency, low inflation, and macroeconomic stability, if not full employment. The financial meltdown of 2008 illustrated the dangers of the position of industry representatives at the heart of the Federal Reserve System. For instance, the Fed commenced paying interest on bank reserves held within the Federal

Reserve System on October 8, 2008, just as the economy swooned. So, at a time when zero-risk Treasury securities paid zero interest, banks could earn at least some interest on their zero-risk reserves held at the Fed. This subsidized the financial sector but contracted the money supply at a most inopportune time. Paying interest on reserves exerts a contractionary influence on the economy because it creates incentives for banks to hold reserves rather than increasing lending, particularly when the economy is gripped with fear like that which gripped the economy in October 2008. Two economists, Robert Hall and Susan Woodward, thus term the Fed's decision to pay interest on bank reserves at the depth of an historic economic contraction "utterly inexplicable."[39] Another economist calls the decision "one of the most significant errors in [the Fed's] 95 year history."[40] Bank reserves at the Fed subsequently soared, and lending fell at an epic pace.[41] Soon businesses realized that credit availability was constrained, and they reacted by hoarding cash, which as of 2012 had reached record levels.[42] Yet for the banking industry the decision enhanced profitability—the Fed essentially provided a liquid, risk-free instrument for banks at a higher yield than any other investor could obtain. This decision subsidized the financial sector at the expense of the general macroeconomy.[43]

In sum, the two major flaws apparent in light of the subprime crisis relate to the Fed's lack of a mission to prevent bubbles through targeted credit controls and its closeness to the banking industry. Leaning against bubbles naturally requires political insulation, and the Fed enjoys a large degree of political insulation, so it would be a natural locus for such power, which seems sorely needed after the bursting of the subprime bubble. The exercise of its extraordinary bailout powers and payment of interest on reserves raise the question of cognitive capture of the Federal Reserve Board. The twelve Federal Reserve Banks create an unnecessary appearance of proximity that calls into question the Fed's use of its powers to benefit the banks so handsomely during the height of the crisis. These reforms hardly rate as radical ideas. In fact, one is supported by the President of the New York Fed. The second, elimination of the regional banks, seems like a minor evolutionary adjustment of the Fed's structure given that the regional banks serve virtually no economic purpose.

A third problem arises from the excessive use of monetary policy to manage economic downturns. Monetary policy may rescue an economy from the Minsky credit cycle or other exogenous economic shocks such as the 9/11 attacks. But this comes at the cost of more debt and the prospect of reigniting the unstable credit boom and bust again. Indeed, the catastrophe of 9/11 and the bursting of the dot-com bubble in 2000 to 2001 led to easy money policies at the Fed that spawned the credit bubble of 2003 to 2007. The trajectory of gross debt within the U.S. since 1980—from 160 percent of GDP to as high as 375 percent of GDP prior to the crisis—shows that overreliance on monetary policy entails real risks in the form of excess debt.[44] Much controversy surrounds the issue of whether the Fed kept rates too low for too long. Between 2004 and 2008, the Fed lost control of long-term interest rates, including mortgage rates. Even when the Fed raised short-term rates, long-term rates declined based upon diminished inflationary expectations.[45] As explained in chapter 4, much of the problem here relates to the massive flow of capital from China and other surplus countries into the U.S., where it funded and subsidized unsustainable consumption fueled by a mountain of debt.[46] In the next section, however, I argue for a more robust fiscal policy function that could help reduce reliance upon debt-driven monetary policy.

Fiscal Policy

Professor Hyman Minsky argued that "[p]eriods of stability (or of tranquility) of a modern capitalist economy are transitory."[47] Additionally, "the inherent instability of capitalism is due to the way profits depend upon investment . . . and investment depends upon the availability of external financing. But the availability of financing presupposes that prior debts and the prices that were paid for capital assets are being validated by profits."[48] Thus, debt destabilizes an economy, and the more debt an economy holds, the more dangerous the potential destabilization. The reliance of monetary policy upon the accumulation of more debt means that monetary policy cannot operate as the sole means of meeting economic disruptions.

First, the excessive accumulation of debt within the financial system itself creates instability. As debt burdens increase, debt's stimulative effect weakens because more must service prior debt.[49] At some point, investors deem debt accumulation unsustainable, and the supply of credit contracts rapidly. Minsky theorized in *Stabilizing an Unstable Economy* that credit cycles driven by natural human psychology inhere to capitalist economies. The credit bubble and housing bubble exemplify Minsky's focus on the excessive optimism, validated through the realization of profits, which in turn feeds into a more optimistic outlook. Nonetheless, a crash is the ubiquitous outcome for every asset bubble. Suddenly credit disappears even for worthy borrowers as an excessively pessimistic view takes hold.[50] Thus, 2003–7 gave rise to 2008–10, in accordance with Minsky's thesis.

Second, at some point, because of a major disruption such as the failure of a systemically important financial institution or a bursting asset bubble or a botched rescue of the financial system, risk aversion could turn so severe that a liquidity trap results. A liquidity trap occurs when investors prefer money or near-money to actual lending or investing. Such a reality became most pronounced in the immediate aftermath of the failure of Lehman Brothers on September 15, 2008.[51] Shortly after that cataclysm a money market fund—supposedly a safe oasis in a storm—announced it could not pay out the full amount of funds deposited with it and severe risk aversion took hold.[52] The interest rate on short-term Treasury securities—the ultimate refuge in a financial maelstrom—fell below zero, meaning that purchasers sought safety above all else.[53] No investor wanted any risks. Under these circumstances, monetary impotence results, and lending cannot stimulate the economy no matter how hard the central bank tries to ignite economic activity through traditional means.[54] Indeed, even rates of zero may fail to ignite the economy.

This condition means that monetary policy has run into the zero-rate bound. One could deem this an extraordinary condition, but it plagued Japan throughout the 1990s, as the work of the Nobel laureate Paul Krugman demonstrates.[55] It has its theoretical roots in Keynes's *General Theory of Interest Rates and Employment*, where he explained the same condition during the Great Depression.[56] In fact, one central reason for the current economic malaise, even in the face of massive government stimulation efforts, directly relates to the banking sector's cash hoarding and consequent monetary impotence, as discussed in chapter 3. Therefore the law should secure an additional means of stimulating a recessing economy beyond monetary policy alone. Government spending provides the only means of replacing the lost demand during a crisis, in accordance with the teachings of John Maynard Keynes.

Fiscal policy can operate to supplement monetary policy, particularly in the context of a liquidity trap, at zero long-term cost.[57] Keynes suggested that fiscal policy can replace lost investment arising from severe risk aversion. Keynes seemingly took several steps further: "[A] somewhat comprehensive socialisation of investment will prove the only means of securing . . . full employment."[58] Minsky offered a comprehensive regimen of public investment in the wake of a credit bust.[59] He contended that deficits hold maximum stimulative firepower when the government normally runs offsetting surpluses. This protects government creditworthiness and acts as a brake on inflation in good times.[60] Minsky also argued that government stimulation should act first to stem damaging unemployment. He proposed a variation on New Deal programs like the Civilian Conservation Corps to develop human resources, provide environmental protection services, and place a floor on the labor market that would obviate the need for minimum-wage legislation.[61] Within these broad outlines, Minsky encouraged more thinking about how to secure an effective government-stabilization program like those the government administered "in the not too distant past" because "Big Government is here to stay if we are to avoid great depressions."[62]

Virtually all commentators agree that fiscal policy operated to end the Great Depression when World War II triggered massive government expenditures. Furthermore, compelling evidence shows that in the postwar period countercyclical fiscal policy operated to blunt downturns in investment in 1974–75 and 1981–82. Notably, corporate profits benefited from countercyclical fiscal policy during these downturns and suffered in 1929–30 when government surpluses exacerbated a downturn in investment.[63] The economist Richard Koo demonstrates the powerful benefits of steady fiscal stimulus during the 1930s in Germany—when unemployment plunged from 26 percent to just over 2 percent.[64] More recently, in the crisis of 2007–9, China responded quickly to a potential crisis in its incipient capitalist system with a classical Keynesian approach—a massive fiscal stimulus in the form of infrastructure investment. Indeed, China pursued "perhaps the biggest peacetime stimulus ever."[65] Chinese Premier Wen Jiabao states that "from both the near and long-term perspective and in both the real economy and the fiscal and financial field, our stimulus package, policies and measures are timely, forceful, effective and suited to China's realities." Further, the stimulus package "will bring benefits to both the current and future generations and serve the interests of the world."[66] This has resulted in a continued boom in China that proves again the utility of fiscal stimulus in the face of a downturn.[67]

Notably, this vision of government-sponsored investment in the face of falling private investment ought to result in self-liquidating government expenditures. More specifically, the government's expenditures as investor of last resort, if properly structured under law, should result in outlays that enhance future productivity and future tax revenues.[68] If the government can direct its investments into projects that yield aggregate benefits in excess of government costs (including its cost of capital, which should be low as a result of the aforementioned risk aversion), then government's investor-of-last-resort activities should be costless while simultaneously reducing the long-term risk that investors face arising from recessions. Empirically, little doubt remains that properly structured government interventions may enhance worker productivity and thereby generate more growth than outlays.[69] Indeed, programs like the GI Bill educational benefits prove that government tax revenues alone may exceed government outlays by many times.[70] Because of the centrality of ideas and human capital to economic growth, it comes as no surprise that economists also find that investment in transportation and communication infrastructure consistently correlates to enhanced growth.[71] Simply put, it pays to enhance the productivity of people.[72] In *The Wealth of Nations* Adam Smith stated that government should provide "public institutions" and "public works" that are "in the highest degree advantageous to a great society" but which may throw off insufficient benefits for any single private economic actor to justify the investment.[73] Government should seek to provide key economic infrastructure that serves to lower the cost of capital or raise the return to capital—like an educated and healthy workforce or a superhighway.

Basically, the structure of government spending matters, and consistent with the theme of this book, spending that unleashes human productivity operates in the long run to sustain growth. Koo states that in a globalized economy, developed nations must use "fiscal policy to upgrade the education system and build the research and development capabilities necessary for [them] to maintain their technological lead."[74] Pursuing these productivity-enhancing programs in a countercyclical manner enhances their benefits through macroeconomic stabilization while minimizing their costs through the lower cost of capital that generally prevails in a slowdown.[75] In the U.S., the structure of federal spending shifted from productivity-enhancing investment (like the GI Bill or the interstate highway system) to less productive expenditures like transfer payments. Yet, in the not too distant past, the U.S. facilitated growth through massive public investment.

The evidence suggests a massive public investment deficit in the U.S. today. A hurricane devastated New Orleans in 2005 because known weaknesses in its preparedness and infrastructure failed to attract public funds, at a cost of billions. A major interstate highway fell into the Mississippi River in Minneapolis in 2007, after an inspection found the bridge "structurally deficient" in 1990.[76] The returns to higher private education soar year after year, demonstrating an economy that thirsts for highly educated workers.[77] Other nations appear far ahead of the U.S. in developing such potentially powerful new economic platforms as alternative energy and stem cell research.[78] Twenty-eight nations now rank higher than the U.S. in Internet downloading speed.[79] The U.S., despite controlling massive resources in the form of the world's largest economy, suffers from chronically impaired public investment that is bound to relegate it to long-term decline in favor of nations that invest in their people to enhance productivity and in critical infrastructure.[80]

Arguably, once deep risk aversion or deleveraging takes root in an economy, only massive fiscal stimulus will re-ignite "animal spirits" and lead to a self-sustaining recovery. After all, the shock and awe of World War II pulled the entire global economy out of a depression. Richard Koo suggests that

this type of fiscal shock and awe maximizes the fiscal multiplier of government expenditures because it breaks the deflationary conduct of consumers
and businesses that cause them to prefer building cash reserves or repaying
debts.[81] Under this view, perhaps the greatest contribution of massive fiscal
stimulus (like World War II) is that it inspires those hoarding cash to employ
it productively. Unfortunately, Koo also shows that fiscal policy (and accompanying deficits) inspires political opposition because leaders rarely get
credit for averting a disaster and because half-measures, in particular, can be
portrayed as wasteful government expenditures that will lead to larger taxes
at some point.[82] Governing elites thus face temptation to favor long-term tax
minimization rather than long-term growth.

Indeed, the U.S. suffers from a leadership crisis in that its governing elites
refuse to support economic growth and invest in the public goods every
economy needs to remain competitive. According to the OECD, the U.S.
pays less in taxes than any other developed nation except for Mexico, Chile,
and Turkey. Nations that rate higher than the U.S. in the United Nations
Human Development Index (Norway, Australia, and the Netherlands) pay
more in taxes.[83] These nations also do not bear the heavy burden of defense
expenditures that the U.S. economy bears. The U.S. spends nearly $700 bil-
lion annually on defense, more than the next ten highest-spending nations
combined.[84] Historically, the U.S. paid more in taxes than it does today.
Today the U.S. pays about 24 percent of its GDP in taxes. In 2000, the U.S.
paid nearly 30 percent of its GDP in taxes at the same time that employment
in the U.S. reached a historic peak. In 1965, the U.S. paid the same proportion of its GDP in taxes as the OECD average; today, the U.S. pays 10 percent
less than other developed nations.[85] Amazingly, despite this modest sense of
public obligation and patriotism, after the election of 2010 the political leadership of the U.S. extended the Bush tax cuts to flirt with another debt crisis.[86] Elites in the U.S. evince more commitment to low taxes than to funding
macroeconomic growth.

Unfortunately, the U.S. never imposed a disciplined or rationalized legal
framework for government investment. In 2002, I proposed that the U.S.
create a new legal framework for fiscal policy that extended the depoliticized legal framework governing monetary policy to countercyclical fiscal
expenditures. I suggested a depoliticized agency with the power to direct
government investment to the highest and most productive use based upon
economic science (instead of purely politicized allocation from Congress)
and to modulate expenditures in response to macroeconomic conditions.
This would ensure that government investments benefited from a low cost
of capital and packed the largest macroeconomic punch possible. It would

also minimize the likelihood that government investment would crowd out private investment. Beyond this rationalized government investment framework, the government would be required (except in a national emergency such as war or severe economic downturns) to maintain a balanced budget. Our history suggests that a balanced budget amendment (or similar mechanisms) to the U.S. Constitution can discipline federal spending.[87] A depoliticized agency for managing government investment and the use of debt would simply extend these historic instances of success.[88]

During the crisis of 2007–9, the U.S. government effort to use fiscal stimulus helped avert a catastrophe according to nonpartisan assessments. The use of fiscal policy saved jobs and arrested the economic downturn.[89] The consensus of economists holds, however, that the nation needed a larger stimulus.[90] The stimulus also included too much focus on tax cuts, which in a deleveraging environment will likely fund contractionary debt repayments.[91] In a risk-averse environment, fiscal policy outlays should focus on productivity-enhancing infrastructure and maximizing employment.[92] That alone ensures that fiscal outlays pay for themselves through a maximum multiplier effect, relative to a baseline scenario of a self-reinforcing risk aversion and vicious cycle of debt repayments.[93] Thus the U.S. obtained insufficient "bang for the buck" as a result of its stimulus.[94]

Bailouts

When a firm faces insolvency, the rules of capitalism hold that the firm enter bankruptcy or, in the case of a bank, FDIC receivership. Either result carries unpleasant consequences for management and unsecured creditors (except bank depositors). If a bank fails (or becomes "critically undercapitalized"), then the FDIC seizes control and ousts management.[95] Managers who hold any further claim against the bank (severance payments, pensions, etc.) generally get paid nothing. Typically, the FDIC pays off insured depositors and therefore enjoys priority in the distribution of assets over uninsured depositors. General unsecured creditors take deep losses. Shareholders stand last in line and generally get wiped out.[96] The failure of Washington Mutual in September 2008 illustrates the soundness of this resolution regime. Although it was the largest bank failure in U.S. history, it cost the government insurance fund nothing, and its assets were immediately transferred to another bank. While general unsecured creditors took large losses, there is little evidence that Washington Mutual's failure led to more widespread instability.[97]

Bankruptcy applies to all firms other than banks. Bankruptcy can be triggered at the instance of creditors or the firm itself. Unsecured creditors typically fare poorly in bankruptcy too—their claims are subject to an automatic stay and are usually paid out in the form of newly issued equity securities by the reorganized firm.[98] Thus, bankruptcy proceedings eliminate issues of moral hazard as unsecured creditors are put at risk of loss, and management contracts (for bonuses, golden parachutes, and deferred compensation such as retirement) are treated as just another creditor claim. On the other hand, bankruptcy should not be confused with liquidation; in fact, Chapter 11 reorganization specifically promotes the ongoing operations of the firm by staying collection activity (which may otherwise prove disruptive) and making special financing available.[99] Neither bankruptcy nor FDIC receivership law contemplated the enormous bailouts of 2008–9.

Firms often seek protection outside of these regimes. Capital from the government can always spare a firm from failure. Economically, government assistance to private businesses may produce benefits that exceed costs, at least in theory. Temporary market paralysis can deprive a business of capital resources in unpredictable, even irrational ways. These conditions could destroy firms with positive net present value but for severe market turbulence. Thus, in the past, the government successfully bailed out firms such as Chrysler and even earned a profit on its investment. But even if the government earns a profit from a bailout it may still create perverse incentives that prove very costly throughout the economy for an extended time period. Specifically, the government should never reward inept or reckless firm management and the government should never shield unsecured creditors from the market discipline that the risk of loss engenders. Thus, a critical element of a rationalized bailout regime must punish managers for steering their firms into insolvency and impose risks of loss on creditors. Without these elements bailouts can operate to entrench politically powerful corporate elites and force competitors to operate at a disadvantage in terms of cost of capital.[100] Manifestly, government assistance for failed management teams and risk-insensitive creditors operate to reward ineptitude in defiance of capitalist norms.

In the crisis of 2007–9, bailouts played a central role. Arguably, the most stunning development of the crisis of 2008–9 involved the massive deployment of government resources to save the financial sector. The bailouts started with the Federal Reserve's facilitation of JP Morgan Chase's acquisition of Bear Stearns in March 2008—at a taxpayer cost of $35 billion. Next, in September 2008 the government assumed control of Fannie Mae and Freddie Mac, at great cost to taxpayers (up to $685 billion) and great benefit to banks that held the great weight of securities issued by the government-sponsored entities.[101] This failed to reassure markets, and a few days later

Lehman filed for bankruptcy, destabilizing markets worldwide. The failure of Lehman locked up credit markets worldwide. Investors reacted with a massive risk aversion that sent short-term Treasury obligations soaring in price while yields flirted with zero or below.

Unable to stomach the prospect of further uncontrolled systemic risk, the Fed and the Treasury quickly cobbled together a bailout for AIG, the world's largest insurance company. AIG sold credit default swaps on pools of securitized assets (including subprime mortgages) to many other financial institutions throughout the world. This meant that many banks shifted the risk of default on pools of asset-backed securities from their balance sheets to AIG. The government feared that if AIG failed, it would take many other large financial institutions with it. Such a financial collapse would engender panic throughout the global financial system and freeze capital markets. In response to this realization, the government rescued AIG through commitments totaling $180 billion and ultimately became the largest shareholder in the company. Next came the biggest bailout in history, the Troubled Asset Relief Program—the TARP.[102]

On September 18, 2008, the Chairman of the Federal Reserve Board, Ben Bernanke, and the Treasury Secretary, Henry Paulson, stunned the world. At a meeting with senior congressional leaders, the two economic chieftains stated that unless Congress approved a massive bailout of the financial sector, economic collapse would ensue. Congress ultimately approved a $700 billion bailout of the most powerful but grossly inept bankers in the world. TARP resulted in hundreds of billions of dollars of government capital injections into the financial sector. Even TARP failed to quell the panic, and tens of billions more in targeted bailouts proved necessary to keep Citigroup and Bank of America afloat. A citadel of laissez-faire—the financial sector—obtained huge socialized investments from the government during a period when private capital sources totally shut down.[103] All of these efforts were only the most public bailout efforts. The government also pursued massive stealth bailouts amounting to potentially massive costs down the road. These bailouts essentially took the form of various government-backed agencies' purchasing trillions in mortgage-backed securities prior to the election of 2008.[104] "Never before had so much taxpayer money been dedicated to save an industry from the consequences of its own mistakes."[105]

Congress enacted the TARP bailouts in an intense political cauldron, with an election looming in just a few weeks. Under these conditions and with financial conditions deteriorating daily, the environment proved detrimental to sound law making. Indeed, the market plunged when an earlier version of TARP failed in the House of Representatives.[106] Campaign contributions played a key role in determining the likelihood of a given congressional representative's supporting the bill, along with the presence of financial services businesses in a given representative's district.[107] These conditions demonstrate the need for a formal bailout regime to displace the possibility that Congress might face the possibility of a legislative shakedown.

The bailouts as structured enjoyed little support from mainstream economics. The former IMF Chief Economist Simon Johnson asserted that the megabanks simply exercised their excessive political power to obtain "grossly favorable" terms in the bailouts.[108] The NYU economist Nouriel Roubini claimed that the bailouts amounted to "socialism" for the benefit of the "rich and well-connected."[109] Joseph Stiglitz maintained that the bailouts would worsen the "preserve incentives" that precipitated the crisis.[110] The key problem, according to economists such as Paul Krugman, revolves around the ability of the bailed-out banks to supply credit to the economy; so-called "zombie banks" will hoard capital rather than lend. Krugman as well as others did not claim that the government rescue itself created the problem.[111] The challenge always revolved around how to structure the financial rescue, and economists offered a range of options, such as creating new well-capitalized banks that could ignite lending and ultimately be sold to private investors. Only new banks with new managers and "pristine" balance sheets can restore normal credit flows to the economy.[112]

In fact, economic science demonstrated the elements of successful financial rescues. Managers should never benefit from rescues; instead, the bankers should be dismissed, so that full loss recognition may proceed. If management retains its control of the firm it is apt to cover up losses to maintain the veneer of success to the extent possible and to avert deeper insolvency. New management will want a clean slate and will therefore face incentives to write down all possible losses, which will be charged to the conduct of prior management. Moreover, if new management recognizes losses today, such losses will not be charged against future profits.[113] Loss recognition means that borrowers can negotiate with lenders based upon reality rather than upon obstinate refusal to recognize losses. Forcing banks into bankruptcy or receivership thus facilitates deleveraging—first, creditors are forced to reckon with losses, and then the bank can forgive debts that realistically are not recoverable. Investor (shareholders and unsecured creditors other than depositors) claims should be wiped out in order to free bank assets for new lending. The quicker this resolution process occurs, the quicker lending can return to normal. In the bailouts of 2008–9, the government "did not force out a single CEO of a major commercial or investment bank, despite the fact that most of them were deeply implicated in the misjudgments that nearly brought them to catastrophe."[114]

Instead, the U.S. created zombie banks uninterested in lending and determined to hoard capital. Trillions in government support therefore did little to restore lending. Indeed, through the beginning of 2010, bank lending fell at an epic pace not seen since 1942.[115] Banks instead maintained huge balances of idle reserves with the Fed, amounting to well over $1 trillion through 2010 alone.[116] Even as of mid-2012, banks still hoard more than $1.5 trillion in excess reserves.[117] Thus, the economy suffers from a dysfunctional financial sector even today.

Bailouts of managers and unsecured creditors destroy capitalism. When a firm is insolvent, government should not come to the rescue because if government does so then creditors will gravitate to firms perceived to be "too big to fail" (TBTF). They will enjoy a lower cost of capital and possess an unfair competitive advantage over smaller firms. Further, if firm managers perceive themselves to be TBTF they will face a moral hazard: If they fail, the costs will be borne by the government, but if succeed, they will enjoy the profits. This type of moral hazard naturally leads to more risk taking, just as the lower cost of capital provides more capital to fund more risky ventures. Further, managers of firms perceived to be TBTF will also enjoy inappropriate subsidies. Their personal compensation agreements, which amount to millions, will become effectively guaranteed by the government. Once again, their incentive will be to rack up large profits through excessively risky activities and allow the government to clean up the mess when the risks sink the firm. Thus, the TBTF problem can lead to excessive risks from a range of sources. Indeed, the subprime catastrophe illustrates the kind of excessively risky business inspired by TBTF.[118]

Politicians face real challenges, however, in imposing market discipline upon large firms. No politician wishes to have voters identify his or her behavior as a key part of an economic catastrophe. Moreover, the large wealth held by firms deemed TBTF generally means that such firms hold vast economic and political power.[119] Finally, the failure of Lehman Brothers in late 2008 suggests that often the costs of allowing large or economically interconnected firms to fail far exceed the costs of bailing out firms in the short-term world of political calculus. The collapse of short-term credit markets in late September 2008 shows that some firms simply cannot be allowed to fail—or allowed to become TBTF in the first instance.[120] The costs of Lehman's bankruptcy in terms of economic growth and stability vastly exceed the costs of saving Lehman, which in turn vastly exceed the costs of breaking Lehman up before it could be TBTF.[121] Thus, the key question posed by the potential of government-sponsored bailouts revolves around how bailouts are structured and when government bailouts are triggered.

Government-sponsored bailouts should provide certain disincentives for firms to avert government bailouts. As shown in chapter 2, in the U.S., public firms (the largest firms in the American system) tend toward CEO primacy. In other words, the CEO exercises a large degree of autonomy over a firm's operations. Consequently, no firm is likely to become so big that TBTF applies without the acquiescence of the CEO. Bailouts should be structured to ensure that senior managers avoid the temptation of becoming TBTF. There is, after all, no economic compulsion for a firm to be TBTF. Empirical data suggests that economies of scale vanish well before a firm becomes TBTF.[122] For example, in the banking sector, economies of scale disappear after a bank reaches about $10 billion in assets.[123] Therefore, firm CEOs can keep a firm below the TBTF threshold without compromising economic performance.

One means of assuring that CEOs face proper incentives to avoid TBTF status is to require the termination of all the senior managers and board members of any bailed-out firm. Typically, termination of senior management means that the vast majority of workers at a firm remain in place. The senior managers can hardly be deemed essential to the continuing operations of the firm; in fact, these are the very managers that destroyed the firm. Moreover, if highly paid senior management is retained, senior management's incentive would be to cover up the extent of their recklessness to keep the firm on the government dole. New managers would want to recognize all losses immediately so that future earnings would not be diminished by buried losses. This would facilitate a rapid return to health and avoid the problems posed by "zombie" firms. Zombie firms exist only as a result of government largesse. Such firms become highly risk averse because they understand the problems hidden within their balance sheets and hoard capital to protect against future expected losses.[124] Many Western banks—in the U.S. and Europe—qualify today as zombie banks.[125]

Another means of discouraging managers from seeking TBTF status would be to discharge employment agreements between bailed-out firms and senior managers and directors. Employees should not attain windfalls at the expense of the taxpayer. Senior managers did not bargain for government guarantees and therefore should never receive protection from the government for compensation agreements. The alternative would create perverse incentives: As business sags, the senior managers would prefer insolvency in order to achieve government-guaranteed payouts. Further, such an arrangement creates yet another asymmetric incentive for risk. Senior managers could create large profits from risky business practices knowing that they enjoy government insulation from the downside of risks. To remove any such danger, senior managers should never benefit directly from insolvency, and therefore all their compensation agreements should be discharged as a matter of law once the government bailout occurs. Unfortunately, much TARP money funded excessive CEO compensation.[126]

Given the amount of damage firms may inflict upon the economy through TBTF, as illustrated in the fall of 2008, a compelling need exists to deter recklessness within such firms. The entire economy depends upon prudence within the financial sector (which now clearly forms the preponderance of TBTF risks), and if the largest players within that sector engage in reckless business transactions, the government may well need to expend trillions in support to save the economy. Therefore, any person who recklessly causes a TBTF firm to suffer a large loss—say, more than $10 million—should face stiff criminal and civil sanctions. Apparently, the bailouts of 2008–9 led to only minimal criminal and civil consequences. As such, the law is not deterring socially pernicious conduct but actually affirms such behavior by lying idle while the reckless retain the fruits of their misconduct.

Finally, the very nature of conduct resulting in TBTF bailouts suggests that the policy bases for certain insulating legislation vanish in the TBTF context. For example, the Private Securities Litigation Reform Act of 1995 is based upon the idea that class actions too often benefit class counsel rather than shareholders and that shareholders too often pay for their own recovery out of corporate funds. Yet when the government steps in to bail out a firm, the shareholders are wiped out and the government may or may not be made whole. Thus, personal liability should definitely be restored in this context, at least. No policy basis justifies the insulation of managers of a TBTF firm from securities fraud liability. Similarly, the government should be able to sue managers for negligently causing the demise of the firm. In the failed bank context, the FDIC specifically benefits from a statutory repeal of provisions such as section 102 (b) (7) of the Delaware general Corporation Law and instead imposes liability for gross negligence.[127] Because we now know that the failure of TBTF firms exacts macroeconomic costs far in excess of the failure of a single community bank, there is no basis for holding managers of TBTF firms to more permissive standards of liability than less dangerous managers of community banks bear. The government should step into the shoes of former shareholders and retain the right to sue management for securities fraud and ordinary negligence.

The upshot of this regimen aims to remove the profitability to managers of navigating their firms into TBTF status. Instead, managers flirting with

TBTF status face real economic costs to achieving such size and complexity that the government faces economic compulsion to shield their firm from the full consequences of its own misconduct. Managers will no longer seek to become TBTF. We know that managers frequently lead their firms into value-destroying mergers and acquisitions. We know that compensation structures frequently encourage this economically inefficient behavior because managers of large firms are paid more. We also now know that such firms can threaten the entire global economy. Yet managers greatly benefit from TBTF. The regimen articulated herein should operate to disrupt this pernicious behavior by directly altering the incentives managers face to become TBTF.[128]

So why have no proposals for such financial reforms emerged? According to Senator Dick Durbin of Illinois, the Majority Whip, the banking industry is the "most powerful lobby" in Congress and "they frankly own the place."[129] Congressman Collin C. Peterson of Minnesota, the chair of the House Agriculture Committee, maintains that bank regulation is problematic in Congress because "[t]he banks run the place."[130] President Obama pledged that his administration would include no lobbyists and then promptly waived his own new rules so that a former Goldman Sachs lobbyist could be the Chief of Staff for the Secretary of the Treasury.[131] In the election of 2008, the banking and investment banking industry contributed to both the Democratic and Republican candidates: According to Opensecrets.org, Senator John McCain's top five campaign contributors were all large financial institutions.[132] Senator Barack Obama received even more contributions, from essentially the same financial firms, totaling more than $3.5 million.[133] Financial interests as a whole spent $450 million to lobby policymakers in 2008.[134] In 2009, after receiving massive government support, they spent hundreds of millions more, increasing their spending by 12 percent over 2008.[135]

Lobbying expenditures and campaign contributions do not tell the complete tale of the influence of the large banks. The revolving door between Wall Street and the government spins elites back and forth between the regulated and the regulators at a dizzying pace. Consider just the movement of people from Goldman Sachs to government over the past three administrations: Robert Rubin, Treasury Secretary under President Bill Clinton; Henry Paulson, Treasury Secretary under President George W. Bush; Senator Jon Corzine of the Senate Banking Committee to governor of New Jersey; Neel Kashkari, the head of the Troubled Asset Relief Program (TARP); Joshua Bolten, Director, Office of Management and Budget and Chief of Staff to President Bush; Stephen Friedman, Director, National Economic Council under President Bush; Gary Gensler, Undersecretary of Treasury under President Clinton; Robert Steel, Undersecretary of Treasury under President

Bush; and William Dudley, the current President of the New York Federal Reserve Bank. Robert Rubin left government to become Vice Chairman of the Board at Citigroup, and Robert Steel went on to become CEO of Wachovia Bank. When the same people run Washington and New York, the problem is not just cognitive capture; it is cognitive identity.[136]

The benefits of power are lucrative. Goldman Sachs garnered $12.9 billion in benefits just from the government's bailout of AIG. Consider the capital injected into the banking system as a result of the TARP bailout. The TARP Oversight Panel found that compared with private sector capital contributions, the government overpaid for its rights by nearly $80 billion.[137] As a further example of the scale of government subsidies, the megabanks now enjoy a huge advantage in their cost of funds relative to smaller banks: 0.78 percentage points, up from 0.50 percentage points from 2000. The market understands that the government will stand with the megabanks even while relegating smaller banks to conventional FDIC receiverships.[138] This constitutes a huge operating subsidy to megabanks.

Politics tainted all of these bailouts. The market lacked any rationalized framework for predicting which firms would be permitted to fail and which ones were "too big to fail."[139] Some claimed that political connections predominated over economic rationales for determining which firms should be bailed out.[140] The most reckless banks received bailouts regardless of solvency, but other banks like Washington Mutual faced FDIC receivership. The media later reported that as the government made key decisions regarding bailouts, politically influential firms like Goldman Sachs held an inordinate degree of attention of key policymakers.[141] Long after the AIG bailout, AIG disclosed that Goldman Sachs received the greatest benefit of the government funds injected into AIG.[142] Ultimately, the risk of financial contagion after Lehman Brothers failed drove the political system to fund a massive bailout of the financial system. But not a single bank manager faced termination under the government bank bailouts.

This meant that the U.S. greatly expanded its debt to entrench reckless bank managers at the very time when the appetite to lend was at a historic low point. Politics should play no role in determining which firms are bailed out. The true costs of saving the bankers may not be known for years. Nevertheless, in the two years following the crisis U.S. debt increased by $3 trillion, almost all of which is attributable to the financial crisis and the actions taken in response to the financial crisis.[143] Moreover, the crisis may well enter a new more painful phase as the U.S. government appears to face limits on its ability to expend trillions to bail out elites.[144] Prospectively, the law can do better.

Simply stated, to avoid future bailouts, bailouts must be highly punitive to senior mangers.

A modern economy requires an advanced legal framework for crisis management. This framework must achieve four primary goals. First, the legal system must create a framework for rationalizing the government assistance so that only firms (including banks) that will generate sufficient long-term profits to justify support can obtain government assistance. Second, firms which fail to meet that economic viability threshold must be liquidated in an orderly process under law so that their assets may be transferred (free of equity and debt claims) to the highest bidder, and deleveraging may proceed. This is especially necessary in the financial sector, where risk-averse banks are likely to block effective monetary stimulus policy. Third, managers must be accountable for reckless or unsafe and unsound practices that compromise the viability of their firms. Fourth, an advanced economy needs a depoliticized authority to oversee any bailouts backed with government resources. Combined with the disincentives applicable to managers, discussed previously, bailouts will return to relative rarities reserved for extreme market conditions.

The political energy for these reforms would by definition be weak. If bailouts are doled out in accordance with political power, a depoliticized regimen will not attract much in political support. Similarly, a depoliticized fiscal policy function would strip significant power from the political leaders currently presiding over fiscal policy. Nevertheless, in the 1980s the savings and loan crisis was resolved largely free of political influence and in a manner that controlled the cost to the government and minimized disruptions to credit markets. Moreover, the resolution of the savings and loan crisis exacted retribution on errant managers.

Throughout the crisis, the megabanks grew. Bank of America grew by a third to $2.7 trillion in assets. JP Morgan Chase grew by 25 percent to $2 trillion. This girth opened up new avenues for profits. Indeed, volatility itself, like bubbles, generates huge profits (and bonuses) to the megabanks and their senior managers. In 2009, the stock market crashed to new lows in March and then marched back rapidly thereafter. Combined with all their subsidies, the market volatility paid off handsomely for the banking elite. In the first half of 2009, Goldman Sachs set aside $11.4 billion for bonuses, or the equivalent of $750,000 per annum per employee. This return to business as usual, with the U.S. taxpayer subsidizing the risks of the financial sector, threatens more market instability into the future, as the financial sector seems certain to pursue ever more risk. This cannot be termed capitalism—instead, it constitutes a corrupted economic system rigged at the top for elite enrichment only.

The Dodd-Frank "Reforms"

With respect to crisis management, Dodd-Frank does much but changes very little. There is no restructuring of the Fed, and the regional banks remain private. The Fed still lacks authority to fight bubbles. It may still fatten bank profits and create disincentives to lending through the payment of interest on reserves. Congress did not change so-called fiscal policy, such that the U.S. economy remains hobbled and exposed to the excesses and impotence of monetary policy alone. Government investment still takes a back seat to tax cuts for the wealthy and powerful. But, most important for financial elites, every American taxpayer continues to subsidize the megabanks and stands ready to pay for the risks gone bad in the financial sector.

The Dodd-Frank Act includes some provisions that address the TBTF issue in a positive way. For example, it includes an orderly liquidation authority that would permit regulators to place large financial firms into receivership similar to the FDIC receivership process. Management would suffer termination. Unsecured creditors could face the risk of loss. Managers would face expanded personal liability, at least for gross negligence. The orderly liquidation authority also operates to minimize the risk of taxpayer loss with respect to firms placed into the orderly liquidation regimen.[145] Therein lies the rub.

In order for a firm to enter receivership under the orderly liquidation regimen, the Treasury Secretary, the Fed, and the FDIC must concur. Both the Fed and the FDIC must approve the receivership by two-thirds votes of their governing boards.[146] Basically, Congress rigged the Dodd-Frank Act so that no megabank need fear that it will end up in orderly liquidation. The process is purely politicized as the executive branch, in the person of the Treasury Secretary (think Andrew Mellon, Robert Rubin, Henry Paulson, and other scions of Wall Street), must join the supermajority votes of both the Fed and the FDIC. None of these regulators really showed much desire to usher a megabank into bankruptcy (where unsecured creditors would presumably face losses), so why would any of them now wish to usher a megabank into orderly liquidation (where unsecured creditors would presumably face losses)? In fact, in 2009, Treasury Secretary Timothy Geithner simply ignored President Obama's decision to liquidate Citigroup with impunity.[147] Only an entirely different set of regulators from those of recent vintage could reasonably be expected to pull the trigger on the orderly liquidation authority—and that may occur only after decades of the scourge of TBTF.

So rather than an orderly liquidation, the same disorderly bailouts of the fall of 2008 will repeat themselves in the event of a megabank solvency crisis. Dodd-Frank facilitates this through formal authorization for both the Fed and the FDIC to assist foundering megabanks outside of the orderly liquidation authority. Indeed, the Act directs the FDIC to put a "widely available program to guarantee obligations of solvent insured depository institutions or solvent depository institution holding companies (including any affiliates thereof) during times of severe economic distress" in place "as soon as practicable."[148] The Fed must create emergency programs with "broad-based eligibility" for loan facilities "as soon as practicable."[149] Thus, every bailout that occurred in 2008 may continue to take place after Dodd-Frank pursuant to these expanded bailout powers.

Perhaps the behavior of the credit markets demonstrates this best. Since Dodd-Frank the credit ratings agencies continue to give the megabanks a multi-notch upgrade based upon the prospect of government assistance for such banks. According to Thomas Hoenig, President of the Federal Reserve Bank of Kansas City, the credit rating agencies give the five largest megabanks an upgrade of up to eight notches based upon perceived government backing, and the average of the five largest banks is a four-notch upgrade. This saves the banks 360 basis points (3.6 percent) on debt with a maturity of seven years. This amounts to a multi-billion-dollar federal subsidy for the megabanks.[150] This subsidy took root at a time when the funding needs for economic growth suffer deep neglect and 25 percent of our children live in poverty. This government subsidy epitomizes the corruption of our government, our moral vacancy, and the economic backwardness of the U.S., all at once. This lawlessness undermines the rule of law itself, as market participants see these wild indulgences of elite power for what they are: an unlevel playing field.

In conclusion, when it comes to monetary policy, fiscal policy, and bailout authority, those seeking to profit from bubbles, low taxes, and TBTF subsidies won the day with Dodd-Frank, and economic rationality perished. The highly profitable status quo prevailed—for a small handful of financial elites.

7

The Potential for an Economic Rule of Law

The history of human improvement is the record of a struggle by which inch after inch of ground has been wrung from . . . maleficent powers, and more and more of human life rescued from the iniquitous dominion of the law of might.
John Stuart Mill (1850)[1]

This book argues that those with economic "might" subverted law and regulation in the years leading up to the financial meltdown of the fall of 2008. They rigged law to loot the American economy with impunity.[2] Between 1986 and 2008, constraints on economic power ranging from liability under the federal securities laws to the duty of care for directors of public firms to the limits on the size of financial institutions vanished, freeing corporate and financial elites to pocket huge windfalls for economically pernicious misconduct. Further, new activities and frameworks fundamentally left elites with the power to impose massive costs upon society in general while reaping huge paydays, ranging from the nonregulation of derivatives to the construction of our globalized economy. The law unleashed the powerful to prey upon the disempowered through predatory mortgage lending. When the collapse came, the government bailed out the reckless, proving the lack of accountability under law. Today, the same elites remain at the pinnacle of our economy, where they continue to collect record bonuses. Indeed, in December 2010, our politicians extended tax cuts for these elites.[3]

All of this legal indulgence, at variance with tradition and policy, occurred as historically high economic inequality took hold in the U.S. Corporate elites leveraged their new-found economic power to seize more power over the commanding heights of our capitalist system—the public corporation. Shortly thereafter, they seized the commanding heights of the commanding heights—the largest financial firms in the U.S. Now, a few dozen CEOs hold the reigns of economic power in the U.S., including those of economic regulation and law.[4] The Dodd-Frank Act leaves those in control of the financial sector undisturbed. The recent Supreme Court decision in *Citizens United v. Federal Election Commission* promises to further concentrate power in these very few hands.[5]

The "triple whammy" of concentrated economic power—income inequality, the concentration of CEO power over the public firm, and the concentration of power within the financial sector—created an unprecedented concentration of economic power in very few hands. As predicted by economists and political scientists, the breakdown of law and regulation followed shortly thereafter. Then, capitalism nearly collapsed in the U.S. and globally.[6] Simply put, the closest flirtation with total financial collapse followed the highest degree of economic concentration in our history.[7] Today, that concentration of economic power continues unabated and threatens further economic pain.

The Dodd-Frank Act suggests that notwithstanding further financial crises and economic disruptions, governing elites will steadfastly resume their flirtation with and indulgence of concentrated economic power. This all stands at great variance with American economic and legal history, as well as traditional American suspicion of concentrated power as manifest in our Constitution, which effectively diffuses political power among three co-equal branches and among dual state and federal sovereigns.[8] In fact, American history stands as a monument to John Stuart Mill's insight that all human progress finds its roots in power constrained by law.

Consider the New Deal. It imposed unprecedented accountability upon power. It broke up J. P. Morgan's megabank.[9] It imposed for the first time broad disclosure obligations and liability upon corporate and financial elites. It empowered workers and more than doubled the number of college graduates between 1940 and 1950.[10] Never before did the American legal system so dramatically transform economic and political power in America, and seventy years of prosperity followed.[11] Only when elites exploited fading memories and the power of race in America (most notably in 1980 with the election of Ronald Reagan and the perfection of the so-called Southern Strategy) did the New Deal fail and did economic power reach pre-Depression levels of concentration and beyond.[12] A new inequality founded upon bipartisan tax cuts in the late 1970s and 1980s took hold.[13]

This chapter assesses the Mills insight regarding progress, law, and the control of power versus the only other legal philosophy (Social Darwinism) that can support the devolution of law in the U.S. I argue that any society seeking to maximize economic growth will necessarily impose legal and regulatory frameworks that control concentrated economic power. Next, the chapter examines the means by which law can operate to quell the negative influence of concentrated economic power. Any given society will get only the rule of law its people demand. While law may facilitate the control of power, in the end a cultural suspicion of concentrated economic power must take root to support law.

The Dodd-Frank Act suggests that Americans believe the current distribution of economic power poses no threat to growth and that only very marginal reform will repair the financial system. This chapter demonstrates that Dodd-Frank will prove woefully inadequate. In the end, if the U.S. legal system is not capable of controlling unfettered economic power, it will suffer "a doomsday cycle of booms, busts, and bailouts" while other nations pursue economically rational policies to build a sound macroeconomy without excessive economic power concentrations.[14] The chapter concludes by highlighting the stark choice before the American body politic: Either pursue deep economic reform that strips corporate and financial elites of the ability to sabotage growth for their own short-term interests or prepare for deeper financial disruptions leading to a painful American economic decline.[15] Americans must insist upon the imposition of a durable economic rule of law marked by universal accountability and limited power of corporate and financial elites to change rules in their favor or face descent into Third World status.

Visions of an Economic Rule of Law

Perhaps the best summary of the approach to economic regulation in the U.S. today can be found in the thinking of former Supreme Court Justice Oliver Wendell Holmes Jr. wrote in 1873, "[W]hatever body may possess the supreme power for the moment is certain to have interests inconsistent with others which have competed less successfully. The more powerful interests must be more or less reflected in legislation; which like every other device of man or beast, must tend in the long run to aid the survival of the fittest."[16] Holmes openly endorsed class warfare, stating that "[t]he objection to class legislation is not that it favors a class" but that "it fails to benefit the legislators, or that it is dangerous to them because a competing class has gained in power, or that it transcends the limits of self-preference, which are imposed by sympathy." All that law can do is to "modify itself in accordance with the will of the *de facto* supreme power in the land." Holmes essentially viewed law as a zero sum game between competing economic classes, and therefore he maintained that law simply acted as an instrument of class domination.[17] Holmes's endorsement of class warfare through law presents a myriad of problems.

First, the Holmes approach to law drips with cynical dishonesty. It directly contradicts the rhetoric and ideals of the law. Indeed, the ultimate monument to the American legal system, the U.S. Supreme Court building, promises every citizen "Equal Justice under Law."[18] This basic principle of American law itself can find its roots in the teachings of the Greek orator Pericles that Greek law knows no "class considerations" or any "bar" based upon poverty.[19] Ours is "a government of laws, and not of men."[20] Holmes's vision promotes law as a power play, with lawmakers constantly taking measure of each participant's economic firepower so that they can know which class to favor in the contest. Law schools do not teach this mode of legal reasoning, judges do not clothe their decisions on these grounds, and politicians do not run for office on the promise of identifying the most powerful and fostering their entrenchment. Thus, this vision of law devolves quickly into survival of the most treacherous, not the "fittest." This view of the law is nothing short of rule by fraud instead of law. If law operates to promote only the interests of the most politically or economically powerful, then the rhetoric of the law must change. Otherwise, it becomes impossible to identify the "fittest" as opposed to the most entrenched and the most sinister. Only a level economic arena can identify the "fittest."

Second, as shown throughout these pages, the subversion of legal and regulatory infrastructure for profit, the exploitation of the disempowered, the festering of class privilege and class disadvantages, and the neglect of economically rational human capital development and market development are not zero sum games but deeply negative sum realities for the entire economy. In short, Holmes's views entail an economic catastrophe. Modern economics teaches that growth follows legal institutions that operate directly opposite of the Holmes vision. As the economist Daron Acemoglu highlights, growth requires "good institutions" that are marked by "constraints on the action of elites," including "property rights for a broad cross section of society" and "some degree of equal opportunity for broad segments of society."[21] Human capital formation, regulatory infrastructure, and market development must be secured by the rule of law, if macroeconomic considerations form a goal of policymakers. Given the key role that macroeconomic growth plays in human well-being and its ability to expand opportunities for all, macroeconomic considerations rightfully hold a central role in legal policy deliberations.

Third, history demonstrates that law need not limit itself to the role of scrivener or courtesan to elite influence. The founders instituted a new political regime that fundamentally altered the identity of the holder of "*de facto* supreme power in the community*" from kings and nobility to elected leaders. This they accomplished through law, and it proved sustainable based upon legal innovations such as the separation of powers and judicial review.[22] The founders brought concentrated political power to heel before the rule of law. The American experience also includes legal innovations intended to fragment economic power.

The New Deal imposed a new constitutional order upon the American economy almost overnight (at least in the famous Hundred Days).[23] The New Deal certainly redistributed economic power from a regimen based upon the false hopes and premises of laissez-faire capitalism to a regimen based upon massive federal intervention into the economy. As President Franklin Roosevelt stated: "The day of enlightened administration has come. . . . As I see it the task of government in its relation to business is to assist the development of . . . an economic constitutional order."[24] This redistribution of economic power lasted for sixty years, before memories of the costs of unbridled markets faded and elites imposed a new laissez-faire that generated massive profits for themselves regardless of any reasonable notion of merit and regardless of costs upon society generally.

The Holmes vision of law as mere scrivener to elite power rather than actor to limit power actually operates merely as rule by law and permits all state oppression throughout history as its close companion. Professor Brian Tamanaha exhaustively studied various concepts of the rule of law. No broad consensus of the meaning of the rule of law exists. At its "thinnest" conception, the rule of law demands only that the government act pursuant to law, which effectively means that every government adheres to this vision of the rule of law.[25] Even such outlaw states as Nazi Germany acted under law. Thus, this thin version of the rule of law allows the state to engage in any oppression or immoral action so long as it acts under law.

The economist Freidrich Hayek articulated a corollary to the austere vision of the "thinnest" version of the rule of law, requiring only that the rule of law be fixed and announced in advance.[26] Hayek's austere vision presents two major problems. First, it fails to account for oppressive legal regimes that destroy economic output through the destruction of human potential, like the Jim Crow South. Second, it fails to address the possibility of law operating as an instrument of elite interest to the detriment of the common-weal. In short, Hayek's vision of rule by law fails to secure macroeconomic growth and stability. Although Hayek moves beyond the thinnest rule of law, his vision is still consistent with feudalism, genocide, and mass disempower-ment. Hayek and Holmes both countenance a rule of law consistent with the vast weight of state-sponsored oppression, even genocide, seen throughout human history. This vision of the rule of law proves both economically and morally bankrupt.

The Chinese legal scholar Li Shuguang argues for a rule of law that curbs the abuse of power and suggests that the rule of law should be distinguished from the rule by law in that the rule by law permits "the law [to] serve as a mere tool that suppresses in a legalistic fashion."[27] In the economic sphere, this vision of the rule of law should operate to limit opportunities for irra-tional deviations from accountability for the violation of traditional market norms. It should also operate to limit severe power imbalances that prove macroeconomically corrosive and morally objectionable. Such an eco-nomic rule of law would impose accountability in a way that is not demo-cratically negotiable, and it should operate to curb the abuse of economic power to harm human capital development. This vision of minimal levels of accountability inspires popular support by holding even the most powerful to account. It limits the ability of concentrated economic interests to abuse power by disempowering or exploiting others.

Professor Tamanaha argues in favor of a less expansive rule of law. Tama-naha recognizes that the rule of law cannot function in a society that per-vasively questions the even-handedness of the legal system. Without a firm belief in the fairness of the law, citizens will disregard the law when opportu-nities to flout the law present themselves. This in turn corrodes the ability of the rule of law to rule. Thus, the rule of law requires that citizens believe in the rule of law, and this perception will not hold if the law suffers from wide-spread bias in application.[28] Presumably, under this approach law tolerates economic abuses under law so long as the mass of people continue to adhere to the rule of law because they believe in the rule of law. Thus, the Jim Crow South may persist as an exemplar of the rule of law so long as its citizens firmly believe in the fairness of the legal system.

The "thickest" vision of the rule of law emerged from an international gathering in New Delhi in 1959 of more than 185 judges, lawyers, and law professors from 53 countries. At its "thickest,"

the Rule of Law is a dynamic concept for the expansion and fulfillment of which jurists are primarily responsible and which should be employed not only to safeguard and advance the civil and political rights of the individual in a free society, but also to establish social, economic, educational and cultural conditions under which his legitimate aspirations and dignity may be realized.[29]

This expansive notion of the rule of law flirts with a society ruled by the judiciary, as the broad rights secured and the central role of judicial review contemplated by this vision of the rule of law leaves too little to be politically or democratically negotiated. This type of judicial domination may not be appropriate within the context of a well-functioning, culturally embedded democratic society. Presumably, a well-educated body politic would insist upon such rights in any event through democratic or republican rule rather than through the judiciary. Further, judges simply lack many institutional capabilities to order the enforcement of positive rights, and judges and litigation do not naturally favor the disempowered. Judges hail from elite backgrounds, and the powerful retain skilled attorneys.[30]

Still, a more durable economic rule of law, consistent with both notions of human rights as well as macroeconomic growth, seems within the reach of the law. The law should operate to stem economic despotism, which can harm social well-being as much as political despotism. This means law must secure economically rational human capital investment, until costs exceed benefits (if ever); otherwise, too many citizens suffer the despotism of impoverishment.[31] Government should secure market development to further empower all citizens and entrepreneurs; this at least ensures a minimum if not optimal macroeconomic opportunity for all. Further, the law should secure important legal and regulatory infrastructure from elite subversion; the law can thereby avert economic meltdowns. Longstanding norms of accountability must remain intact so that no individual may act above the law. This places real limits on the economically mighty to impose massive costs on others and society generally through the abuse of economic power.

Such a rule of law would meet the minimal definition proposed by Professor Tamanaha as well as the more robust vision of Li Shuguang. It would stem abuses of power and inspire confidence that the economy secured fair competition for all. Nevertheless, it also demands more. Not only must the law prevent abuses of power, but individuals must enjoy protection from morally reprehensible and economically objectionable outcomes—that is, no individual should suffer stunted education or arbitrarily suffer from economic despotism. Under political despotism, individuals may suffer arbitrary incarceration, lawless confiscation of property, or even death. Under economic despotism, individuals may suffer seriously impaired health and the economic death of impoverishment. This more demanding rule of law would yield great economic benefits in terms of growth and stability even beyond averting crises.[32]

Economists know that the rule of law plays a crucial role in macroeconomic performance. Yet they admit to failing to define the rule of law.[33] The Nobel laureate Robert Lucas, a pioneer of the study of economic growth, along with others previously mentioned, holds that no other economic issues rivals growth in terms of its potential impact on human welfare. As previously shown, growth means more resources to meet challenges such as global warming, environmental degradation, starvation, infant mortality, and disease. Because the keys to growth involve human capital formation, market development, and economically rationalized legal and regulatory infrastructure, the path to maximum growth fundamentally runs through an optimal rule of law that constrains elite action to impair growth for their own benefit. History and economics prove that these elements of growth cannot take hold unless secured by law. The increasing attraction of economists to growth becomes easy to understand once one ponders the stakes for humanity. The value of growth should drive visions of an economic rule of law because otherwise those with power may use the law to irrationally impose massive costs on all others. In the end, this vision of an economic rule of law secures the same values as a political rule of law: individual autonomy, integrity, and freedom. The neglect of these values led to exploitation and economic catastrophe at the same time during the subprime debacle.[34]

These failures of law to stem the abuse of power and economic despotism cost trillions. The cost of the resulting financial crisis of 2007–9 may not be known with certainty for years to come, but it will certainly amount to trillions of dollars in financial losses and forgone economic growth, as well as massive government expenditures and bailouts. Since the end of 2008, U.S. debt increased by trillions as the government strove mightily to save the financial sector and revive the economy.[35] Globally this failure of law led to trillions in additional debt across the world, threatening another, more dangerous crisis arising from sovereign debt defaults.[36] A more robust economic rule of law can prevent such crises by limiting the ability of governing elites to subvert legal and regulatory infrastructure, exploit the disempowered, and neglect market development through the maintenance of a broad middle class.

The U.S. remains far from this vision of an economic rule of law. Abundant evidence proves that the U.S. economy suffers from a second-rate legal system akin to that of Third World countries. Our economic system suffers from corporate and financial elites untethered to legal accountability and able to bend law for their private profit. Remarkably, the crisis of 2008–9 led to very little accountability under criminal law, despite all of the reckless lending and reckless sale of mortgage-backed securities, backed with recklessly originated mortgages. For example, two central figures from the crisis completely escaped criminal accountability despite apparent evidence of securities fraud and other misconduct.

In early 2011, the government apparently terminated its criminal inquiry against Countrywide Financial CEO Angelo Mozilo. Mozilo raked in $521 million from 2000 through 2008, even as he crashed his firm through predatory loans that he himself recognized as toxic and poisonous. The SEC leveled against Mozilo civil claims of securities fraud that he settled on the eve of trial for $70 million (with a total personal expenditure of $22.5 million).[37] His leadership of Countrywide's residential mortgage business later resulted in the largest predatory lending settlement in history.[38] A private civil fraud action led to a settlement payment of $600 million (paid by Bank of America, which acquired Countrywide). Yet Mozilo retains the hundreds of millions he garnered in compensation as well as his liberty, and criminal authorities seem uninterested in charging Mozilo with criminal fraud.[39] Of course, Mozilo and Countrywide generously funded (and gave favorable mortgages to) leaders of both political parties.[40]

The government similarly terminated a criminal inquiry against Joseph Cassano, the head of AIG Financial Products, a subsidiary of AIG. AIG Financial Products wrote hundreds of billions in credit default swaps on mortgage instruments.[41] When the mortgage market collapsed, AIG, the world's largest insurance company, also collapsed, resulting in a $182 billion federal bailout.[42] Cassano assured investment analysts in December 2007 that "it is very difficult to see how there can be any losses" arising from the CDS positions.[43] One year later, AIG posted the largest loss in corporate history as a direct result of the CDS.[44] Indeed, at the very time of the statement to investment analysts, according to the Financial Crisis Inquiry Commission, AIG had already posted $2 billion in collateral to Goldman Sachs to cover losses that Goldman projected on securities guaranteed by AIG; Cassano and AIG failed to disclose this payment to investors.[45] AIG paid Cassano $315 million for his gambling, including a $1 million per month consulting agreement after termination.[46] Cassano and AIG also showered both political parties with contributions.[47]

These two examples constitute only the most high-profile instances of the failure of legal accountability. Not one senior manager at any of the firms at the center of the crisis suffered even an indictment under the Obama administration. Instead of bringing criminal actions, Obama administration officials actually lobbied state authorities to refrain from pursuing wrongdoing.[48] Financial elites cognitively and culturally captured the Obama White House.[49] The savings and loan crisis of the 1980s spawned nearly 1,000 felony convictions.[50] Given the massive costs imposed by this crisis, only a failure of law explains such a failure of justice. As one commentator stated in mid-2010, "[T]he American people should now get the justice we deserve, in the form of prosecuting the people on Wall Street who had major roles in causing the financial crisis in the first place."[51] Simple accountability disintegrated in this crisis, and restoring the rule of law to finance will require criminal convictions of those responsible for the lawlessness in our banks.[52] This historic pacification of criminal accountability will dilute disincentives for criminal profits for decades to come. But the lack of criminal accountability forms just one element of the breakdown in law.[53]

The bailouts effectively socialized losses while privatizing profits. This amounts to an unprecedented betrayal of capitalism.[54] The former Chief Economist of the IMF Simon Johnson called the bank bailouts "the Quiet Coup," because the bailouts as structured deviated so dramatically from the best economic science regarding assistance to the financial sector.[55] I argued that the bailouts inexplicably left the errant (perhaps even corrupt) financial elites at the helm of the financial sector and therefore extended windfalls to the least meritorious based only upon political power. All of the bailouts fail even the Hayek version of the rule of law because the bailouts did not arise from fixed rules announced in advance.[56]

The revelation of lawlessness within the financial sector reached new heights in late 2010, when the foreclosure crisis demonstrated that financial and corporate elites not only acted recklessly in underwriting and packaging subprime mortgage-backed securities but also acted recklessly in documenting their mortgage rights. One court characterized the banks' misconduct as "utter carelessness."[57] For example, the banks filed massive numbers of fraudulent affidavits in support of foreclosure, apparently expecting impunity.[58] Further, the banks filed mortgages with recorders' offices across the nation that named fictitious mortgagees to evade the need to record the actual beneficial owners and incur additional transaction costs in the form of filing fees.[59] Finally, the banks failed to ensure the proper transfer of promissory notes under the law of commercial paper.[60] All of this created unprecedented uncertainty in American property rights, prompting experts to predict an even more extended recession.[61] Economists quickly held this fiasco up as an example of the deterioration of the economic rule of law in America.[62]

Earlier, other signals suggested the rule of law needed reinvigoration in the U.S. A recent global assessment of the rule of law co-sponsored by the American Bar Association found that the U.S. ranked near the bottom among wealthy nations.[63] The U.S. ranked near the bottom for absence of corruption. The U.S. further suffers from inadequate access to justice, particularly for marginalized communities, and ranks dead last on this element of the rule of law among wealthy nations. This fact reflects a huge gap between rich and poor in the perceived fairness of justice in America.[64] Essentially the poor and middle class face real barriers in asserting their legal rights.[65] Other assessments rate the U.S. even weaker in terms of the rule of law: The Fund for Peace in 2010 rated the U.S. the same as Mauritius and a bit higher than Belize with respect to "Suspension or Arbitrary Application of the Rule of Law and Widespread Violation of Human Rights."[66] The entire subprime crisis percolated in the shadow of a broken justice system that permitted the rich and powerful to trample upon the legal rights of most Americans with little prospect of accountability.[67] According to the World Governance Indicators, the U.S. legal system rates ranks alongside those of Chile, Slovenia, and Uruguay in terms of controlling corruption.[68] Unlike that of other nations, however, the corruption of the rule of law in the U.S. can "impact the world's financial stability and overall growth prospects, as demonstrated by the costly repercussions of the recent financial crisis that started on Wall Street."[69] Thus, a compromised rule of law in America taxes the entire global economy.

The U.S. must face a new truth: It has a second-rate legal system, at best, and a very weak rule of law in the economic sphere. This will economically hobble the U.S. far into the future.[70] The World Economic Forum recently highlighted this fact when it dropped its rating of the U.S. economy to fourth from second in terms of competitiveness. More disturbing than the loss of competitiveness, the U.S. ranked fortieth in property rights protections, fiftyfourth in distrust of politicians, fifty-fifth in government favoritism, and sixty-eighth in wastefulness of government resources. This suggests a failure to control corruption through law on par with Gambia. Among other things, the World Economic Forum uses surveys of the public and of business leaders to assess competiveness.[71] This demonstrates a plunge in the American public's faith in its legal institutions.

In light of the foregoing, the American people should be forgiven if they hold the perception that our economy devolved at some point into a rigged game. This reality means a real economic loss in terms of the corrosion of the rule of law. If a population abandons the rule of law—in the sense that the vast majority of the population no longer follow the law unconditionally based upon a belief that they benefit from the rule of law—economic costs follow. Without a well-functioning rule of law, economic actors cannot be sure that contracts will be executed without resort to courts, they cannot predict the behavior of others, and they will avoid transactions with many people out of fear that they will suffer noncompensable losses. A compromised rule of law can impair investment in particular and destroy an economy.

The rule of law should operate to move society toward the expanded theoretical model of perfect competition I articulated earlier—a model that recognizes the macroeconomic toll of disempowerment and privilege. The failure of the rule of law to control concentrated economic power will entail economic costs, including the likelihood of severe financial crises as elites erode important regulatory and legal infrastructure for their own profit and neglect important props to stable growth. In short, law, policy, regulation, and politics must view large concentrations of economic power with suspicion. Laws that favor the powerful must suffer a presumption of illegitimacy and laws in favor of the disempowered must enjoy a presumption of political approval, as Adam Smith suggested long ago. Such a rule of law will support both macroeconomic growth as well as a more robust humanity by securing both the durability and quality of life in terms of life expectancy, educational attainment, creativity, and prosperity.

The Basic Contours of the Economic Rule of Law

The concept of an economic constitution or an economic rule of law revolves around the principle of political non-negotiability and insulation. Political non-negotiability always involves a broad consensus that the law should protect core values against mere transitory political goals. Constitutional values form the paradigm of political non-negotiability to the extent that constitutional rights enjoy protection from political infringement. Since the New Deal, monetary policy operated largely free of political interference because of the political structure of the Fed. Certain other issues, such as civil liability, evolve under the auspices of the judiciary, long considered the least democratic branch of government, and consequently enjoy some degree of political insulation. Similarly, professional associations historically regulate important economic functions free of excessive political influence. The protection of these core economic values helped the U.S. develop economically, particularly in the decades following World War II. This chapter assesses the means and likelihood that the U.S. could continue this leadership, which will necessarily require an expansion of the core economic values removed from the political arena through law.

Constitutional Protections

Values secured under constitutional principles typically rely upon judicial review for protection. Judicial review requires judges—and ultimately

a state or federal court of final review—to stand ready to set aside a popu-
larly enacted law or regulation. It also further depends upon the executive
branch to enforce judicial orders. Usually, the executive does enforce judicial
decrees, and so judicial review functions well to protect many core values.
But, the threat of non-enforcement (and, less, actual non-enforcement) chills
judicial review. In the realm of individual rights the judiciary approved of
concentration camps for U.S. citizens of Japanese descent during World War
II,[72] allowed *de jure* racial segregation until 1971,[73] and failed to secure *habeas
corpus* during the Civil War.[74] Judicial review fails most during war, or in
resisting powerful and widespread cultural norms such as racial hierarchies.

In 2004, I argued for a reinvigoration and expansion of the constitutional
protections articulated in *Brown v. Board of Education*. Instead of extending
Brown since 1954, our society has allowed racial disparities in educational
opportunities to fester. This entailed massive macroeconomic costs and
flirted with dangers inherent in all inequality, including economic instability and subverted legal infrastructure. There is no acceptable rationale for
persistent racial inequality other than corrupted legal frameworks.[75] Today,
racial disparities in education and segregation within the American educational system remain at historic highs.[76] Thus, constitutional protections
enforced through judicial review offer slim hope for durable protection of
economic rights. Indeed, the U.S. Supreme Court often seems determined
to entrench concentrated economic power through law even in the face of
overwhelming evidence of the macroeconomic costs of allowing corporate
and financial elites to subvert law and regulation.[77]

Although far from perfect, judicially protected constitutional rights can
secure certain elements of a rational economy notwithstanding the political
power of elites. In *Montoy v. State*, the Kansas Supreme Court used the state
constitution to persuade the legislature to appropriate an additional $755 mil-
lion to ensure an adequate education for children in Kansas.[78] At least in the
hands of a judiciary that understands economics and the widespread benefits of education, constitutional protections can create enforceable rights to
enhanced funding for superior and more equitable human capital development.[79] On the other hand, the U.S. Supreme Court leaves such issues largely
to the political process.[80] This amounts to macroeconomic abdication rather
than any appreciation for the economic rule of law. For reasons discussed
earlier, the political process will not favor the disempowered, even though
investment in the most disempowered by definition will yield the highest
investment returns.

Constitutional recognition of economic human rights would move the
U.S. toward a more ideal capitalism by assuring that all citizens may access

sufficient resources to compete and contribute economically. This necessarily diminishes the burdens of privilege. If the Constitution protected basic rights to adequate education, universal health care, and decent housing, excessive concentrations of wealth would not do as much economic harm.[81] A well-educated populace could check elite political power at the polls. Empowered citizens do not fall prey to elite overreaching as U.S. citizens did during the subprime debacle. Unfortunately, neither the courts nor legal elites in the U.S. see fit to pursue this vision of human rights even though other nations, such as South Africa, do judicially enforce such rights.[82] In the recent past, the U.S. Supreme Court appeared inclined to move in this direction, but political shifts short-circuited the recognition of any positive rights.[83] Constitutionally recognized economic human rights could operate to mitigate economic power imbalances and may diminish the likelihood of another financial crisis rooted in legal subversion and predation. The current majority in control of the Supreme Court, however, appears intent upon maintaining the current economic status quo.

Depoliticizing Regulatory Agencies

Law can secure core values without express constitutional provisions. Thus, for example, the Federal Reserve Board's administration of monetary policy exemplifies depoliticized regulation and the potential for a hardened regulatory agency that can resist the influence of the regulated. The SEC, on the other hand, illustrates the paradigm of a captured regulatory agency. As Harry Markopolos puts it, "The SEC . . . has suffered through decades of sloth, abysmal leadership, underfunding and benign neglect."[84] While this section focuses upon the Fed and the SEC, the core point, that institutional design matters in terms of resisting the efforts of growth-retarding elites to subvert regulatory infrastructure, could well apply to each regulatory agency responsible for financial regulation. Overall, the regulatory state failed in the U.S., even though sound regulation must guide the economy, as it successfully did for several decades after the New Deal.[85]

The Federal Reserve Board enjoys the highest degree of political insulation for purposes of monetary policy. Congress endowed the Fed with a self-funding mechanism (levies on member banks), which means that Congress does not control its purse strings. Members of the Federal Reserve Board, the ultimate governing authority within the Federal Reserve System, serve for fourteen years. The Fed also pays relatively high salaries for government agencies. It need not concern itself with regulatory competition as it is the sole authority with respect to monetary policy. All of this gives the Fed the highest degree of insulation from the politics of the moment. Of course, Congress may always abolish the Fed. This ultimate source of accountability reflects the mandates of a true republican form of government.[86] No lawmaking organ can ever achieve complete insulation from politics. The Fed's structure, however, operated well during the subprime crisis with regard to monetary policy. Most observers agree that "U.S. monetary policy may have contributed to the credit bubble but did not cause it."[87]

Still, neither the Fed nor its legal structure operated optimally during the subprime crisis with respect to regulation. The Fed played a central role in providing trillions in bailout funds without any democratic input and arguably in defiance of its statutory powers.[88] The Fed also has fumbled its regulatory responsibilities at least since the mid-1980s, when it greased the regulatory skids for banks to expand in size and scope with little or no appreciation of the risks implicit in government guarantee of their failure.[89] The Fed waited from 1994 until the summer of 2008 to exercise important regulatory powers over the residential mortgage market.[90] By that time, predatory lending had metastasized throughout the global financial system, and financial collapse loomed.[91] Although critics target the Fed for lax monetary policy, the Fed actually lost control of monetary policy in that even when the Fed raised rates in 2005, long-term rates went down in the face of diminished inflationary expectations.[92] Nevertheless, the Fed certainly indulged banking interests it supposedly regulated and insulated the banks from the market consequences of their own folly.

The Federal Reserve System features an archaic relic that allows private banking interests to hold sway both formally and informally—the regional Federal Reserve Banks.[93] Banks control each regional Federal Reserve Bank and elect the president of the regional banks. The presidents hold five of the twelve votes on the all-important Federal Open Market Committee (FOMC), which plays a key role in the formulation and implementation of monetary policy. Critics charge that the regional banks give private banking interests too much sway within the Federal Reserve system and have called for additional limitations on the regional banks or even the abolition of the regional banks.[94] Joseph Stiglitz suggests that the admixture of public and private interests within the governing structure of the Federal Reserve system creates at least the appearance of corruption.[95] The regional Federal Reserve banks open an avenue for cognitive capture to take hold through their presence on the collegial FOMC.[96] The Fed sorely needs a new institutional structure, and the elimination of the regional banks from the FMOC, as some favor, would at least reduce the opportunities for cognitive capture.

The SEC, for its part, reached such unprecedented levels of docility that it missed a massive Ponzi scheme that grew to previously unimaginable proportions right under its regulatory nose.[97] With respect to subprime mortgage-backed securities, the SEC admitted that it practically never reviewed prospectuses and offering materials.[98] Indeed, in the face of a financial scandal featuring widespread securities fraud, the SEC filed no enforcement actions against any major issuer or seller of mortgage-backed securities until after the crisis even though the FCIC found indicia of securities fraud.[99] Further, according to the SEC's own Inspector General, the SEC knowingly allowed the nation's largest investment banks to gorge on debt and take huge risks on board, and it took no regulatory action.[100] Thus, this key regulatory agency, like the Fed, botched its regulatory duties in a way that facilitated key elements of the crisis.

Even prior to the subprime crisis, powerful evidence proved that the SEC could not resist corporate influence.[101] Indeed, former SEC Chair Arthur Levitt wrote an entire book cataloging his efforts to impose sound regulation in the face of determined and well-heeled corporate and financial interests.[102] Business luminaries like Enron CEO Ken Lay lobbied to stop the SEC from enhancing auditor independence—and ultimately Enron crashed in an accounting storm that showed the mythological nature of auditor independence. Congress eagerly supported business interests over the efforts of the SEC.[103] During the battle with corporate America over the PSLRA, senators threatened to "turn off the lights" at the SEC if it did not support corporate interests.[104] For decades, politicians held SEC funding hostage to special interests, and influential voices advocated self-funding.[105] According to Levitt, one problem (which would be predicted by Mancur Olson's *Theory of Collective Action*) is that investors simply lack a lobbying organization that can compete with corporate wealth.[106] Furthermore, the SEC long suffered from a regulatory revolving door that too often caused staffers to work hard not to "rock the boat" in the very industry in which they may ultimately seek employment.[107]

Regulatory competition also plagues U.S. financial regulation. Financial firms hold discretion to pick their regulator to a significant degree. This means that regulators cannot assume a stricter posture than competing agencies without facing the risk of regulatory migration. For example, Countrywide Financial switched from a bank charter to a thrift charter, effectively trading the OCC and the Fed for the OTS as its primary regulator. The OTS actually recruited Countrywide. Countrywide told public investors that it sought a more housing-focused regulator. Internal memoranda show that Countrywide thought the OTS would conduct fewer and less intrusive examinations and generally lacked sophistication. The OTS promised to permit pay-option mortgages, which the Fed resisted, while the OCC took a stricter view of appraisal requirements.[108] Recall that the OTS's lack of sophistication also facilitated AIG's credit default swap business, as discussed in chapter 3. Regulatory competition simply creates damaging incentives for regulators to cater to the regulated and for the regulated to avoid more demanding regulation.

No administrative agency can or should enjoy complete political insulation. Nevertheless, "buffers can be put in place to reduce unwarranted political pressure that can harm the public interest."[109] These buffers include freeing the agency from the congressional appropriations process; imposing post-employment restrictions upon agency staff; ensuring that the agency need not contend with regulatory competition; ensuring competitive salaries for staff; qualification requirements for agency leadership; geographic and background diversity; and a political commitment to the independence of an agency.[110] These kinds of protections can create a system of hardened administrative regulation that can resist concentrated economic power. In an era of high inequality combined with concentrated power over public firms and concentration within the financial sector, a compelling necessity for such measures arises. In the U.S. today, financial regulatory agencies, from the SEC to the Fed and beyond, face intense pressure to indulge corporate and financial elites who can manipulate Congress, offer jobs, and hire lawyers and lobbyists to press their interests. Moreover, other areas of law and regulation, such as corporate governance, need the expert administrative regulation that a properly structured agency can provide to displace excessive political influence. I argue that a depoliticized and optional federal incorporation regime can finally remedy the flaws apparent in corporate governance and can effectively resist political influence.[111] Between the Great Depression and the subprime debacle, the administrative regulation of finance proved largely successful.

The key to reviving the regulatory capability of the government is to restructure key financial regulatory agencies. At the very least, the SEC's flawed response to the subprime crisis suggests that Congress should endow it with a self-funding mechanism. Furthermore, the Fed system should not permit private interests to enjoy a regulatory voice—Congress should abolish the regional banks. Finally, financial regulation must be consolidated to avoid unnecessary regulatory competition.

Professionalization

As an economy becomes more complex, it requires more professional management in key positions of responsibility. Professionals face professional licensing requirements and professional discipline. The twin mandates of professional competency and ethics form the foundational elements of a profession. Dean of Harvard Law School Roscoe Pound posited that professionals as a group "pursu[e] a learned art as a common calling in the spirit of public service, its work no less a public service because it is also a means of a livelihood."[112] Ideally, "professions, if sufficiently free and independent, provide individual citizens with a buffer against authoritarian and overreaching governmental power."[113] The creation of professional mandates, supervised through an appropriately supervised self-regulatory organization, forces professionals to subordinate self-serving, short-term needs to the possibility of disbarment. High standards of professional conduct can lead to higher client trust and higher profits. Professionals as a group thus become vested in maintaining high standards to preserve the pricing power that trust may inspire. Once a profession is created, a built-in constituency seeks its preservation, and the dilution of professional standards can become politically difficult.

Professionalization regimens rely upon an important subset of regulatory tools to enforce economic norms. For example, stockbrokers must adhere to broad professional regulation, backed by the coercive powers of the federal government. They must pass qualification exams, register with the SEC, adhere to a professional code of conduct, and face professional discipline. Sanctions for violations of professional conduct standards can result in fines, suspensions, and even expulsion from the industry. Stockbroker misconduct played a role in the Great Depression. In the nearly eighty years since the advent of professionalization of the securities business, broker misconduct in regulated markets has never again figured in a financial disruption.[114]

Politics rarely intrudes in this professional regulation. Similarly, common law tort liability—including professional malpractice, fraud, and negligent misrepresentation—traditionally imposed broad norms of professional accountability under the expertise of the judiciary. These norms applied to all professional actors regardless of political connections. Professional malpractice requires the testimony of a peer professional. This gives the professions the ability to police themselves as an additional form of self-regulation.[115] This privilege of self-regulation and enhanced protection from liability compensates for the need to adhere to professional competence and ethics.

The subprime fiasco cries out for expanded professionalism. Mortgage brokers made loans that can only be termed predatory for borrowers and suicidal for the financial system.[116] CEOs and boards took on risks that put either their competence or their ethics at issue.[117] Credit rating agencies faced no incentive for rating securities other than in accordance with their own profit motives and with no penalty for ineptitude.[118] In a highly interdependent economy, where one person's ineptitude leads to another person's failing in business because of a sudden and excessive tightening of credit, professional competence and ethics can be the difference between depression and prosperity. Moreover, the essential merit-based elements of professional competence and ethics operate to directly diminish privileges and to move toward the expanded notion of perfect competition whereby merit, not wealth or power, determines economic outcomes. Senior managers of public firms and directors hold power over the fortunes of millions of citizens. Their ineptitude and unethical behavior costs the entire global economy trillions, and each global citizen therefore faces an impaired ability to excel. Why not impose competency and ethical norms and penalize reckless and corrupt behavior with disbarment, fines, and banishment from the industry? The same logic supports professionalizing credit rating agency staff, mortgage brokers, and supervisors of such firms. Put simply, "a systematic breakdown in accountability and ethics" caused the financial crisis, and professional accountability and ethics can avert a similar crisis.[119]

Entitlements

Entitlement funding mechanisms add a degree of political insulation that ordinary government appropriations do not possess. Specifically, once a beneficiary pays into a system that provides social benefits, the continuation of the program comes with a built-in constituency, in addition to current beneficiaries. Entitlements form a sturdy bastion of politically hardened social welfare in the U.S. Such entitlement expectations give beneficiaries and future beneficiaries a fairness stake that beneficiaries of other government programs lack. Thus, President Franklin Roosevelt insisted that funding Social Security through payroll taxes would create real, paid-for entitlements that proved to be politically non-negotiable. He did this because he did not want any "damn politician" to undercut benefits and expenditures in the future.[120]

Military or other service to the nation can also support a sense of entitlement, and the broader the service requirement, the more durable the entitlement becomes politically. If all youth faced a mandatory national service requirement, perceptions of privilege and disempowerment could give way to a new cultural norm of service and sacrifice shared by all. In the past, all families contributed to war efforts, for example, and the nation enjoyed far more responsible leadership than that on display in the years leading up to the financial crisis. All four of President Franklin Roosevelt's sons served in World War II and saw heavy action, and President Eisenhower's son John served in Korea.[121] Perhaps mandatory service requirements can at least serve to deter unnecessary wars, if not inculcate national service norms among our key leaders. Insisting upon national service certainly provides a forum for testing individual merit and can thereby help restore the American meritocracy that seems ever more mythological.[122] The subprime crisis impugns the quality of American leadership and calls the very nature of our so-called meritocracy into question.[123]

In exchange for such a service requirement, upon honorable discharge each youth could be entitled to a four-year college education at an institution of his or her choice. Currently there is no universal service requirement, and too many of our youth face incarceration rather than service with the promise of education. The key point, economically, is that every child could attain a college education at no cost—much like the GI Bill in place after World War II. This would diminish inequality, develop our human resources, and eliminate the type of deep disempowerment that drove the predatory lending underlying the subprime debacle. Solid empirical evidence demonstrates that such a program would pay for itself, as the GI Bill yielded up to $12.50 for each dollar expended.[124] In a nation in which one in four children languishes in poverty, this kind of entitlement program could empower millions in potential competitors to reduce the sway of privilege in our economy and move toward a more perfect competition.[125] Once a broad percentage of Americans serve, it would be politically challenging to substantially reduce funding for their educational entitlement.

Securing Accountability through Civil Liability

While the New Deal used experimentation as the basis for many of its innovations, it also relied upon "ancient" principles of accountability to restore faith in the financial system.[126] The pre–New Deal securities markets made little sense economically. Corporations owed no obligation to provide any information to their shareholders. Without basic information, America's securities markets resembled a casino more than a crucial mechanism for the allocation of capital. As John Maynard Keynes put it, "When the capital development of a country becomes a by-product of the activities of a casino, the job is likely to be ill-done."[127] Investors understandably lack confidence in securities if they lack basic information regarding their investments. This creates markets prone to panic. Any sound vision of capitalism includes the free flow of reliable information.

The New Deal responded to this bizarre form of capitalism with a mandatory-disclosure regime providing for the periodic dissemination to shareholders of all material information regarding a firm, accompanied by broad investor remedies. Chapter 2 reviewed evidence of the economic benefits of a mandatory-disclosure regimen. Chapter 3 discussed the dilution of the private right of action as one candidate among many playing a key role in the subprime mortgage crisis through diminished accountability. Here the important point is how private rights of action impose accountability upon corporate and financial elites regardless of politics. Private litigation costs the government almost nothing. More important, private litigation does not respond to lobbying expenses or campaign contributions. Plaintiffs' attorneys generally seek monetary rewards, not political favor or post-employment positions. As such, they respond primarily to market incentives. Thus, private litigation exemplifies a depoliticized means of holding elites, no matter how powerful, to account. Private securities litigation serves as an indispensible deterrent to financial misconduct, and rather than limit the deterrent effect of private claims, Congress should seek to restructure such litigation to ensure that it operates in accordance with its underlying policy bases.[128]

Restoring accountability to the financial sector through the use of broad private remedies for securities fraud would be simple. First, Congress should abrogate the U.S. Supreme Court decisions to curtail aiding and abetting liability under the securities laws. In *Central Bank of Denver, N.A. v. First Interstate Bank of Denver, N.A.*[129] and in *Stoneridge Investment Partners, LLP v. Scientific-Atlanta*,[130] the Supreme Court held that only persons and entities speaking directly to investors are liable for securities fraud, not those merely aiding and abetting a fraudulent scheme with full knowledge of the fraud. This insulated important corporate gatekeepers such as accountants and lawyers from liability for securities fraud. Prior to these cases, courts consistently held for decades that those lending substantial assistance to securities fraud with knowledge of the fraud could be liable along with the primary fraudfeasors.[131] Such liability arose from deep roots in common law fraud and benefited from years of congressional acquiescence.[132] Nevertheless, the Court determined that liability for those merely aiding fraudulent conduct would be vexatious.[133] In *Stoneridge*, Justice John Paul Stevens dissented, stating, "I respectfully dissent from the Court's continuing campaign to render the private cause of action under [the federal securities fraud] toothless."[134] Bloomberg News trumpeted the Court's most recent decision with the following headline: "Investors Lose Again."[135]

Bloomberg also suggested that the Supreme Court sounded like the U.S. Chamber of Commerce, which spent years trying to eviscerate the federal securities laws and largely succeeded. The Chamber believes accountability for securities fraud raises the cost of capital. Justice Anthony M. Kennedy parroted this position, arguing that expanding private claims "may raise the cost of being a publicly traded company under our law and shift securities offerings away from domestic capital markets."[136] The Court seemed oblivious to the possibility that the destruction of shareholder rights is not costless and will operate to raise the cost of capital. Even shareholders with no desire ever to file a claim may perceive that our securities markets lack fairness. Diminished investor confidence entails a higher cost of capital. Justice Kennedy's approach seems destined to shrink American capital markets, as the best economic evidence available suggests that "both extensive disclosure requirements and standards of liability facilitating investor recovery of losses are associated with larger stock markets."[137] Aiding and abetting liability required corporate gatekeepers—accountants, attorneys, and other consultants—to ensure truthful disclosures in accordance with "several hundred years" of common law precedent. Thanks to the Supreme Court's dilution of accountability, investors in U.S. stocks should expect more fraud.[138] The ultimate irony of Justice Kennedy's rhetoric is that it immediately preceded a historic meltdown in the American financial sector related to subprime mortgage securities that operated to destroy global confidence in the honesty of American financial markets.

Second, Congress should repeal the Private Securities Litigation Reform Act of 1995. That Act extended special protections unknown in common law to securities fraudfeasors. Securities fraudfeasors do not deserve special protections; instead, securities fraud should carry enhanced sanctions because of the key role that securities markets play in economic growth and stability. No policy supports encouraging fraud in the nation's securities markets through indulgent law. At the very least, Congress should repeal the provision imposing enhanced pleading requirements for scienter (prior to discovery) and the safe harbor for forward-looking frauds. Since 1995, scandals have become endemic in the securities markets. The Internet bubble, the options-backdating scandals, and the subprime mortgage crisis all counsel against laws protecting those who commit securities fraud.

The essential problem is that legal elites began to believe that the securities laws "may be a waste of time." Since 1975, the Supreme Court has relentlessly narrowed the scope of private rights of action under the federal securities laws, contending that "that litigation under Rule 10b-5 presents a danger of vexatiousness different in degree and in kind from that which accompanies litigation in general."[139] This refrain appears again and again in the Court's rulings on private securities fraud claims.[140] The Court's current attitude represents a dramatic departure from the approach of justices with a less remote acquaintance with the reality of the Great Depression. Prior to 1975, the Supreme Court sought to interpret the federal securities laws to achieve their broad remedial purposes. Thus, the Court recognized an implied right of action for misleading proxy statements in *J.I. Case Co. v. Borak.*[141]

The subprime crisis furnishes an example of the costs society can expect to bear in the absence of traditional norms of accountability as expressed in the common law (and reflected in the federal securities laws). Unregulated hedge funds reportedly pioneered a trade strategy involving subprime mortgages that helps explain why banks made so many loans with so little prospect of repayment.[142] This strategy became widely known as the Magnetar Trade—named after a hedge fund that aggressively used the strategy.[143] The Magnetar Trade involved sponsoring pools of debt obligations like mortgages in an instrument known as collateralized debt obligation funds ("CDOs"), investing in the so-called equity tranche (the riskiest part of the CDO), and then shorting the less risky and much larger tranches. The Magnetar Trade allowed the sponsor to profit from the collapse of the CDO.[144] The Trade would even permit the sponsor to help select the mortgage securities for the pool.[145] When the mortgages defaulted, the sponsor would lose money on the small equity portion but make much more money by purchasing credit default swaps on the larger so-called senior tranches.[146] So, the structure of the Magnetar Trade created an incentive for the sponsor to select the riskiest mortgages.[147] These facts often went undisclosed to investors in the CDO.[148]

Investors naturally concluded that a highly rated senior tranche appeared safe, given that the sponsor purchased even more risky equity tranches that would be paid only if senior tranches paid out first. The investors surely did not realize that the sponsor would sell them something the sponsor knew to be toxic. Nor would the investor appreciate that the sponsor loaded the CDO up with the riskiest mortgages in order to profit when the securities sold defaulted and created massive losses. The investors invested only because of material nondisclosures. In short, sponsoring a pool of securities designed to fail and not disclosing that fact constitutes securities fraud. According to industry experts, this trading strategy "is arguably the most important influence on subprime bond issuance in 2006–2007."[149] The Financial Crisis Inquiry Commission found that "of all the CDOs issued in the second half of 2006 more than half of the equity tranches were purchased by a hedge fund that also shorted the other tranches."[150]

Reportedly, Magnetar and its founder gave large political contributions to Rahm Emanuel, the future Chief of Staff for the Obama administration.[151] No criminal action resulted from this trading strategy. The SEC brought civil claims against the promoters of some CDOs that involved similar misconduct.[152] One such case resulted in the largest fine ever paid to the SEC.[153] Yet the SEC never pursued similar misconduct on a large-scale basis. Elite subversion of regulatory agencies means that private actions must play an essential role in deterring misconduct.[154] Private actions could serve to deter future instances of manifestly deceptive practices on such a systematic basis, with such devastating macroeconomic consequences.[155] Fraud, negligent misrepresentation, breach of fiduciary duty, professional malpractice, and the duty of good faith and fair dealing must robustly operate to ensure appropriate market incentives and accountability.

Private civil claims hold a key advantage over law enforcement claims. Private plaintiffs' attorneys do not typically run for office, do not solicit campaign contributions, and would face disbarment if they ever accepted any side payment from a defendant they pursued. Private attorneys face incentives for aggressive pursuit of claims in the form of large contingency fees that may be earned if a case results in a large recovery. Further, private claims do not require government expenditures, and tight budgets do not reduce the number of private attorneys prepared to pursue civil claims. Thus, a society that takes accountability seriously will provide for generous private claims in accordance with common law notions of responsibility. Indeed, this is a traditional mechanism by which capitalism protects property rights of all—even Ayn Rand, the legendary libertarian, condemned fraud.[156] The real question is why the Supreme Court (and Congress) seems so eager to make securities fraud profitable.[157] Securities fraud covers the full breadth of the financial sector, and beyond; thus, the diminution of this source of accountability will plague our entire economy for years.

The crisis arose from a breakdown in accountability and ethics.[158] Our business system and our entire economy rely upon trust. People will not invest if they face a substantial risk of a fleecing. Law must secure transparency, good faith and fair dealing, accountability, and responsibility. Even the most powerful financial elites must face legal sanction for the kind of misconduct that drove every phase of this historic crisis.[159] The failure of law to restore historic norms of accountability in the name of indulging elite power will ruin the American economy and sentence our children to life in a Third World economy.

Restoring Legal Accountability and Suspicion of Concentrated Power

The Great Depression rocked the foundations of the American economy and American society. Unemployment soared to 25 percent and output dropped by 33 percent. This means that the Great Depression inflicted economic pain to a much greater extent than the crisis of 2007–9 when unemployment topped at 10 percent and output shrank only by a small percentage of the output lost from 1929 to 1933. Voters desperately sought change. In the depths of the Great Depression more voters than ever supported the Socialist and Communist parties. President Franklin D. Roosevelt therefore benefited from a powerful political consensus for his reform programs.[160] Over the years, as memories faded, political commitment to controlling concentrated economic power similarly faded.

Ferdinand Pecora predicted such a breakdown in accountability. Chief Counsel to the Senate Committee on Banking and Currency in 1933 and 1934, Pecora participated in investigative hearings on the Securities Act of 1933 and the Securities Exchange Act of 1934. In his book regarding those hearings, Pecora recognized that the moneyed interests in favor of laissez-faire would not vanish. Moreover, Pecora recognized that these interests would always assert that untethering them from traditional notions of accountability would foster prosperity. He predicted that powerful interests would wish to return to laissez-faire markets that would allow the powerful to act without constraint.[161] Reform enacted in the wake of a crisis will suffer from erosion from the influence of concentrated elites with concentrated resources over time. Reformers must therefore construct legal and regulatory infrastructure with this fact in mind. When reform possibilities arise, reformers must design reform with attention to durability. Law should memorialize the dangers of excessive economic power and thereby facilitate cultural suspicion of such power. Otherwise, public demands for reform will fade, and policymakers will fail to take on board lessons from history that they did not live.

Those reform possibilities seem certain to arise. As Professor Minsky showed in great analytic detail, capitalism suffers from inherent stability. Keynes referred to the "animal spirits" that drive investment. Pecora simply adds to this basic psychological source of instability the fact that the memories of the crisis giving rise to regulatory and legal reform will naturally fade. The inevitability of crises in the face of eroding or imperfect legal infrastructure creates the possibility of reform. Unfortunately, the reform possibility itself can fade if the crisis ends. In 2010, apparently, pressure toward reform proved insufficient to impose meaningful, much less durable, reform. In fact, rather than view concentrated economic power as suspect, the body politic extended the so-called Bush tax cuts, which disproportionately benefited the wealthiest.[162] Yet the lack of reform may simply mean that a deeper crisis is inevitable. The crisis of 2007–9 will turn out to be dormant rather than resolved.

International economic competition can also fuel reform. Derrick Bell recognized long ago the importance of marshaling elites behind reform. Bell argued that fundamental reforms—like *Brown v. Board of Education*—result from the convergence of interests between elites and the disempowered. That convergence arose in terms of civil rights from the competition between the U.S. and the Soviet Union for the hearts and minds of people of color around the world. Segregation blighted American claims to liberty and freedom.[163] The Bell theory of interest convergence now enjoys broad support both empirically and from the development of similar theories in economics and political science.[164] Richard Delgado extends Bell's insight to argue that marshaling elite support paves the way for reform.[165] Usually this convergence arises from crisis conditions that generate fear among those with economic and political power.

Thus, for example, the fear of communism and the need for the U.S. to project itself as a just society in Africa, South America, and Asia played a key role in the outcome of *Brown v. Board of Education*, as Professor Bell predicted.[166] The GI Bill, which helped double the number of college graduates between 1940 and 1950, arose from the fear that 16 million returning war veterans would trigger mass unemployment, a possible depression, and social unrest, as occurred after the wind-down from World War I.[167] When the Soviets launched their *Sputnik* satellite in 1957, a shocked U.S. prompted the Eisenhower administration to counter the threat of Soviet technological superiority with a massive federal investment in science education, as well as the creation of a new agency to coordinate scientific research (ultimately leading to the creation of the Internet).[168] The Marshall Plan sprang from the possibility of widespread economic strife in Europe and fear of Soviet-style states taking root there, a prospect it quelled by assuring the creation of prosperous mixed economies founded upon markets.[169] Major economic reforms or development initiatives require a crisis to generate the fear needed to bring otherwise entrenched elites to the table to negotiate for broad-based growth efforts. International competition may serve to bring out the best in American capitalism. In fact, since the end of the Cold War no similar effort of the same scale as the massive investments discussed here occurred.

The nation that constantly strives to perfect its economic rule of law will achieve superior macroeconomic performance. Global competition to optimize legal and regulatory infrastructure should create pressure for constant improvements in law. The American brand of capitalism overcame these pressures and imposed a neoclassical regimen upon the world economy, seemingly rigging the process in favor of laissez-faire outcomes. This constipated the development of the economic rule of law worldwide. Fast-growing nations, such as China, ignored the insistence upon laissez-faire, opting instead for a highly interventionist approach.[170] By definition, laissez-faire means that the government takes no action to disrupt the status quo regardless of economic power imbalances.

In fact, it appears that the Chinese economy actually benefited from the crisis, as its rapid growth continued unabated and it mustered the resources to stimulate its economy in a fundamentally pro-growth direction.[171] The Chinese economy actually grew rapidly in 2009 and 2010 in a dramatic proof of the Keynesian proposition that enhanced government spending can avert a slowdown.[172] The Chinese economy threatens now to generate substantial inequalities that may outweigh its history as a hardened state that could resist elite domination.[173] Nevertheless, China's very rapid growth and its commitment to investment and human capital formation suggest that it could furnish a competitive threat to the U.S. that could encourage the development of a more robust economic rule of law in the U.S. as well as globally. Indeed, China evinces a greater commitment to the eradication of poverty than the U.S.[174] Increasingly, Americans view China as a competitive threat and therefore will seek to respond to the Chinese model of massive investment in human capital and infrastructure.[175] The hope is that the U.S. sees these policies as an avenue for empowering individuals to succeed economically, as China apparently realizes.[176]

This pressure from abroad to rationalize the economic rule of law in America could become supercharged after a transition to a free movement of labor regimen. Assuming that the most productive individuals will gravitate to the nation where they may maximize the value of their output, then labor would move magnetically to the nation with the most optimized economic rule of law to support growth and stability. Nations would need to compete—not just by offering cheap labor and regulatory laxity as they do under the present structure of globalization but by offering macroeconomic dynamism backed by law. In short, the nation that offers the more perfect meritocracy will attract the most meritorious individuals. Nations that permit elites to entrench themselves will repel the most competitive individuals. Thus, the free movement of people may well prove a political game changer for controlling elites (which serves to explain its absence).

Education extends another means by which a greater cultural appreciation for controlling economic power may take root. Because the returns to education seem inexorably upward, it could be expected that additional pressures toward a more educated populace are inevitable in the long run.[177] Ultimately, a more educated body politic will also exert a positive influence on law. Economic complexity requires a more educated electorate. Indeed, given the time constraints voters face, even highly educated voters may face challenges in staying fully informed regarding the state of law on a wide range of financial regulatory issues from "too big to fail" to derivatives regulation to the shadow banking system. Education could nevertheless mitigate the impact of elite domination of the economy. Certainly, in general, a college graduate likely could fully understand these issues with greater ease than a person with only an eighth-grade education. Thus, mass higher education may well serve to create additional pressure for reform and for a rationalized economic rule of law. Indeed, it may well be time to expand mandatory education beyond age sixteen.

Another means of enhancing the prospects for a durable economic rule of law would be enhanced primary and secondary education in the specific areas of economics and business. The U.S. benefits from a sophisticated capitalist economy. Informed capitalist participation should constitute a fundamental value in such an economy. Capitalism works best when informed decision makers make intelligent economic choices. Much evidence suggests that in the world's largest capitalist economy, many citizens simply lack the necessary understanding to participate in the economy constructively.[178] In the subprime debacle, unsophisticated borrowers suffered from deep exploitation by sophisticated lenders. In short, uninformed traders in a capitalist system can impose broad societal costs.[179] Therefore, the already strong case for enhanced financial and economic education efforts now enjoys overwhelming support.[180]

Finally, legal academics must train tomorrow's leaders to appreciate the role of law and regulation in securing conditions conducive to growth. Today, our leadership suffers from delusions about self-correcting markets that are deeply rooted in our culture. The default reaction of our governing elites still tends toward the approach of virtually all Law and Economics texts—laissez-faire efficiency. Our judges similarly harbor misconceptions about economic growth like the misguided conclusions of Justice Kennedy regarding how law fosters enhanced capital market development. The fact that his rhetorical position goes unchallenged in the Supreme Court stands as testament to the flawed approach of the legal academy to the intersection of Law and Economics. Laissez-faire lives on among legal elites in the U.S. despite overwhelming evidence that it remains an economic dead end, just as it was proven to be in the Great Depression. The hope is that Judge Richard Posner's epiphany regarding the need for regulation constitutes the first step in a reconfiguration of Law and Economics to include evidence regarding the relationship of law and regulation to growth and stability.[181]

America needs to adjust its economic constitution—that is, the laws, regulations, and cultural frameworks that govern economic activity. The U.S. is uniquely suited to this effort because of its political and economic history.

The U.S. Constitution revolutionized the legal disruption of concentrated political power. The U.S. economy is also the world's largest and most developed. It enjoys the greatest historic experience with modern free market economics and the quest for an optimal legal infrastructure. The Law and Economics of the challenge are straightforward. Elites must be disempowered to disempower others through distorted law and regulation, because one disempowered individual means a constricted demand for everyone else's goods and services. In the end, if elites hold power to change law in their favor, then all others lose by being forced to compete in a rigged market. The subprime debacle constitutes a preview of the costs of a pervasively rigged economy.

In the final analysis, the subprime crisis of 2007–9 proves that the rule of law in America fails to constrain adequately those with concentrated wealth. Whatever society develops a rational suspicion of concentrated economic power—on par with the deep-seated suspicion Americans harbor for monarchies—will be the society that will best use law to channel economic power, just as the U.S. Constitution has operated to channel and limit political power. This central point stands alone from the specific content of that law. Law needs to curb power, and a modern economy needs an economic rule of law. Indeed, the analysis in this book fully demonstrates the costs inherent in permitting corporate and financial incumbents to subvert law and to entrench their power.

The Dodd-Frank Act in Perspective

The Dodd-Frank Act stands as the primary legal reform effort in the wake of the 2007–9 financial crisis. Indeed, the midterm elections of 2010 marked the reversal of many of the Dodd-Frank reforms, particularly through lack of funding for reform.[182] Consequently, the Dodd-Frank Act constitutes the sole legislative response to the flaws in the legal and regulatory frameworks revealed during the crisis. Unfortunately, the Act reflects complete ambivalence with respect to the pernicious impact of historically high economic inequality on the rule of law. Dodd-Frank does nothing to change the underlying political, economic, and regulatory realities that drove every phase of the crisis.

For example, further consolidation within the financial sector during the crisis leaves the U.S. with more concentrated economic wealth than ever before. The Act fails to fragment this power, as discussed in the prior chapter. Instead, the institutionalization of "too big to fail" promises further distorted incentives toward excessive risk. Dodd-Frank does nothing to disrupt or reverse the political and economic power of the megabanks, which will continue to receive massive government subsidies.

There are other flaws with Dodd-Frank, many discussed in earlier chapters. Dodd-Frank leaves the SEC's institutional structure unchanged, despite its sordid record manifest failures with respect to the subprime debacle. The current SEC Chair, Mary Schapiro, argued for a self-funding mechanism for the SEC.[183] The Fed similarly continues with the same institutional structure that failed the nation. Indeed, Dodd-Frank, as shown previously, gives the Fed even more power. Thus, a regulator with a manifestly flawed institutional structure now has more power. This invites further crises. The Act does nothing to change the incentives facing senior managers of public firms in a meaningful way or in a meaningful time frame.[184] The Act does nothing to disrupt a global economy that elites rigged in their favor and operates to burden the U.S. with ever more debt without regard to adverse economic consequences.[185] Dodd-Frank allows the megabanks to continue to gamble in the derivatives and securities markets far into the future.[186] In short, the Act will prove ineffective in stemming the next financial crisis.

Fundamentally, this outcome arises from the Dodd-Frank Act's determined effort to do as little as possible to alter the current distribution of economic and political power. More specifically, it leaves a handful of large banks and corporations largely in the hands of a few men with even more political and economic power that they held prior to the crisis. Under this reality, one outcome remains certain: These corporate and financial elites will continue relentlessly to subvert regulatory and legal infrastructure in their favor.

The Dodd-Frank Act suggests that Americans still harbor odd delusions regarding their economy. Many seem more threatened by the economically weak than by the very powerful—a rather backward outlook on reality. The powerless by definition cannot harm society as much as the powerful. Rather than demand that government hold economic power to account, in the election of 2010 voters seemed determined to disempower government to impose rational regulation. The most noteworthy outcome of this bizarre turn is that the American people demanded that political elites cut the taxes of their friends, the corporate and financial elites at the center of the crisis, leaving ordinary Americans facing a fiscal nightmare.[187] The extension of the Bush tax cuts in early 2011, with broad bipartisan support, even for the very wealthiest in our society, strongly demonstrates that the deep economic crisis that took root in the fall of 2008 created insufficient pain for the body politic to muster the will to constrain the economic power of corporate and financial elites. Simply put, they crashed global capitalism, and the politicians cut their taxes. The reform energy that so influenced the election of 2008 had completely dissipated by 2010.[188]

This remarkable and rapid reversal of political heat no doubt arises from complex factors. One major intervening development, however, towers above all others. The Supreme Court fundamentally restructured American democracy by judicial fiat. In *Citizens United v. Federal Election Commission*, the Supreme Court enhanced the power of senior management of public corporations to influence elections without any semblance of concern for the implications of giving CEOs even more power over the economy.[189] This book shows that the Supreme Court certainly undermined the ability of the American economy to operate under a rational economic rule of law by vesting even more political power in the corporate and financial elites who engineered the financial crisis.

Legal scholars argue that the decision violated basic principles of judicial restraint. For example, Professor Richard Hasen stated that the Supreme Court "had to go out and grab this one" and extend the decision far beyond the traditional limits of Supreme Court decision making.[190] The issue of why and whether a corporation (created for economic service to the state and society) holds any Constitutional rights or First Amendment rights separate and apart from its shareholders never apparently warranted a full judicial resolution.[191] Other commentators term the decision "intellectually irresponsible."[192]

In the aftermath of *Citizens United*, the role of money took hold in political outcomes as never before. According to a recent report by Public Citizen (a consumer advocacy organization), spending by outside groups jumped to $294.2 million in the 2010 election cycle, almost four times the amount spent during the last midterm elections, in 2006. Nearly half of this spending came from just ten groups, and the origins of many of these groups cannot be traced. The candidate benefiting most from outside spending won the race in almost eighty congressional races.[193] "In one swift and radical decision, five justices on the U.S. Supreme Court turned back the clock on the American legislative process a century, reminiscent of the days when the Robber Barons largely dictated the legislative agenda of Congress."[194] Indeed, the *Citizens United* case and its impact reflect such a profound change in our democracy that even former Supreme Court Justice Sandra Day O'Connor publicly voiced criticism of the decision and her former colleagues.[195]

Little doubt remains that these massive expenditures profoundly influence law in a pro-corporation (or, more precisely, pro-CEO) direction, at both the judicial and legislative level. A recent empirical study found that judges who are elected in partisan races favor corporations significantly more than appointed judges in employment disputes. In mandatory employment arbitration appeals, the study found that when partisan-elected judges review arbitration decisions, employees win only 32.1 percent of the appeals; when appointed or nonpartisan elected judges decide such cases, employees win 52.7 percent of the time.[196] Studies long ago demonstrated that campaign spending (especially television advertising) enhances the chances of victory in legislative elections.[197] Economists recently developed more sophisticated models to focus on the effectiveness of campaign contributions in influencing legislative behavior that demonstrates the expected outcome: Money influences legislators and thus law.[198] The passage of the TARP bailout bill proves that special interests may purchase even unpopular legislation.[199] Thus, "[s]eating judges that are hostile to workers and cozy to corporate interests will surely be a byproduct of *Citizens United*" and "[e]lecting legislators that are passionate laissez-faire capitalists and antagonistic toward common sense corporate regulation will surely be a byproduct of *Citizens United*, despite a clear failure of capitalism in the recent financial market crisis."[200]

Professor Hasen suggests that "supporters of campaign finance reform may have to wait another generation and [for] a change in Supreme Court personnel for the opportunity to overturn *Citizens United*."[201] I disagree. While the *Citizens United* case will certainly operate to entrench the very corporate and financial elites who lie at the core of the entire financial crisis of 2001–9, it also lays the foundation for another crisis arising from America's second-rate economic rule of law. Dodd-Frank and *Citizens United* take America into economically uncharted waters and raise an urgent question: How much economic pain can hyper-concentrated economic power untethered to the rule of law cause? My supposition is that a massive economic crisis will prompt the American body politic to denude corporate and financial elites of their unmerited and pernicious control of our economy and lead to a massive realignment in the distribution of economic and political power on a scale beyond the New Deal.

Noted jurists recognize that adherence to the principles of Holmes led our legal system into "the embarrassing valuelessness in which American jurisprudential theory finds itself wallowing today."[202] The vision of an economic rule of law offered herein seeks to replace this valuelessness in law with a new value that focuses upon maximum and broadly distributed economic empowerment of individuals by resisting privilege. Such empowerment will maximize the resources available to society to secure a more robust humanity in terms of life expectancy, educational attainment, health outcomes, prosperity, creativity, and environmental sustainability. In short, this vision of maximal empowerment maximizes the excellence of life. Under this approach, law must inveigh against high inequality that undermines individual empowerment or spawns privilege and thus compromises growth, harming each individual with any economic stake in society. Once law secures economic empowerment and minimizes privilege to the full extent of economic logic, inequality becomes irrelevant. The subprime debacle vividly demonstrates the alternative to empowerment as a legal value—that is, concentrated economic power and privilege run amok.

Optimized Legal Infrastructure and the End of Scarcity

The economist Paul Romer theorized in 1993 that, given the number of elements in the universe, the possibilities for innovation by putting things together in new ways may be finite but are definitely enormous.[1] The key to exploiting this fundamental reality is to create as many innovators as possible—that is, to create institutions through law to support the creation of more ideas.[2] In particular, Romer suggests that investment in children will be the key driver to explosive growth.[3] John Maynard Keynes wrote in 1930 that the fundamental problem with the global economy in 1930 arose from too much productive capacity requiring ever-decreasing amounts of labor. He called this "technological unemployment," and it gave way to "the enormous anomaly of unemployment in a world full of wants."[4] Yet he could foresee an end to capital scarcity and an era of abundance.[5]

Recently, the advent of additive manufacturing holds the possibility of creating mass quantities of objects at very low cost, as easy as hitting the Print button on a computer.[6] Technology promises to ultimately vindicate the post-scarcity prophesies of Keynes and Romer. From an economic perspective, the concept of scarcity seems more constructed than real. It may well be that deficient legal and regulatory frameworks constitute the primary barrier to any post-scarcity vision.

This book focused upon the economic carnage wrought by flawed legal and regulatory frameworks. During the years 2003 to 2007, trillions of dollars in capital flowed into senseless real estate loans that ultimately destroyed families, communities, and the primary source of middle-class wealth in America. Deeply suboptimal incentives under law and regulation drove these flows. One answer that this book proffers to the question of how this occurred in an ostensibly modern global economy is that law failed to secure adequate growth to make alternative capital investments more profitable; more specifically, law failed to secure adequate human capital and market development. Another answer is that elites rigged the financial system so that they achieved high payouts even if the pernicious capital flows generated huge losses for everyone else, including their own firms; here, law failed to secure basic market incentives and disincentives from subversion by corporate and financial elites. Massive predatory lending generated untold millions in compensation for a few and untold trillions in costs for the global economy. In the end, this story reckons that law itself permitted, even facilitated, this massive waste of social wealth. Preventing a recurrence therefore requires repairing the economic rule of law and reimposing rationalized incentives and disincentives.

This book, however, also scratches the surface of what the world would look like if an optimized rule of law took root. If all people could innovate and reach their highest and best use, a virtual treasure trove of unprecedented economic growth seems attainable and sustainable. In the end, environmental innovations and economic innovations are inextricably linked. Thus, we could double global output simply by empowering people to move freely in accordance with economic incentives for meeting shortages with skills. That amounts to $65 trillion in forgone output.[7]

McKinsey and Co. estimates that the U.S. could enhance growth by up to $2.3 trillion annually if it simply educated all of its children on par with other leading developed nations.[8] Given that the U.S. constitutes less than 5 percent of world population, that number would grow astronomically if the same human resource development program empowered all the children of the world. If ideas fuel growth, the world today wastes human ingenuity on a global scale.

Economists show that getting corporate governance right could generate "enormous" economic benefits.[9] If corporate governance could reduce the manipulation of risk for profit by financial and corporate elites, the global economy would be more free of the costs and risks of substantial financial disruptions. Given the costs of the subprime debacle, this too is likely a multi-trillion-dollar issue.

These issues are just a few ways that law can enhance innovation and therefore growth. An optimized rule of law would unlock tremendous economic growth and pave the way to any kind of post-scarcity world. Such a world begins with maximum human empowerment.

Indeed, it is difficult to imagine any other way to achieve the highest possible economic growth. People and ideas certainly play a central role in economic growth. Allowing all people to compete to achieve their highest and best use should axiomatically form the core function of an economic rule of law. Privilege and disempowerment corrode human incentives to compete. Privilege also threatens law. Those holding concentrated economic resources will naturally seek to entrench their power through subverted law and regulation. This will operate to create uneven playing fields. Thus, law should inveigh against excessive privilege and disempowerment. Law should similarly inveigh against elite power to subvert legal and regulatory infrastructure. Achieving optimal human capital development, optimal market development, and optimal legal and regulatory infrastructure law operates to maximize economic growth. It also creates the shortest path to a post-scarcity world.

Even a cursory scan around the world reveals massive economic potential locked into idle or near-idle resources. American banks, in fear of their own insolvency, hoard $1.5 trillion in excess reserves.[10] America's corporations, in fear of another credit collapse, hoard another $2 trillion.[11] Emerging nations hold more than $10 trillion in currency reserves.[12] These reserves operate to fund excess consumption and dangerous debt levels in the entire developed world.[13] On the human side, 2.6 billion souls subsist on less than two dollars per day. The awesome scale of wasted resources across the world proves the costs of allowing elites to lawlessly run riot across the global economy. A new cultural abhorrence of wasted economic potential must take root. People should abhor the mass disempowerment of people because it necessarily means that all humans suffer economically from wasted and underutilized economic resources. Optimized legal infrastructure with optimized incentives for all would minimize economic waste. Ultimately, a suboptimal economic rule of law takes a huge, almost unimaginable economic toll on everyone, relative to a world with a sound economic rule of law.

NOTES

PREFACE

1. Andrew Jackson, *Bank Veto Message to the Senate* (July 10, 1832), *reprinted in* 2 A Compilation of the Messages and Papers of the Presidents 576, 590 (James D. Richardson ed., 1897).
2. Andrew Ross Sorkin, Too Big to Fail 2, 3 (2009).
3. *Id.* at 401 and 409–10.
4. Simon Johnson and James Kwak, 13 Bankers 165 (2010).
5. Steven A. Ramirez, *Subprime Bailouts and the Predator State,* 35 Dayton L. Rev. 81, 87 (2009) (citing Joe Nocera, *As Credit Crisis Spiraled, Alarm Led to Action*, N.Y. Times, Oct. 1, 2008, at A1 (quoting Federal Reserve Chairman Ben Bernanke) and *Frontline: Inside the Meltdown* (PBS television broadcast, Feb. 17, 2009), available at http:// www.pbs.org/wgbh/ pages/frontline/meltdown/etc/synopsis.html).
6. Emergency Economic Stabilization Act of 2008, Pub. L. No. 110-343, 122 Stat. 3765 (2008) (codified in scattered sections of 12, 15, 26, and 31 U.S.C.).
7. Ramirez, *supra* note 5, at 86–90. *See also* Thomas Ferguson and Robert Johnson, *Too Big to Bail: The "Paulson Put," Presidential Politics, and the Global Financial Meltdown*, 38 Int'l J. Pol. Econ. 3, 25–27 (2009) (discussing Secretary Paulson's efforts to pursue a "shadow bailout" outside of public view by directing the Federal Home Loan Banks (a lender of last resort for thrifts), Fannie Mae, and Freddie Mac to purchase mortgages from banks and thrifts).
8. Gretchen Morgenson, *The Rescue That Missed Main Street,* N.Y. Times, Aug. 28, 2011, at BU1.
9. Ramirez, *supra* note 5, at 86–90. Ultimately, the government essentially socialized the mortgage market and directly funded nearly all mortgages through its wards Fannie Mae and Freddie Mac. Zachary A. Goldfarb & Dina El Boghdady, *Mortgage Market Bound by Major U.S. Role*, Wash. Post, Sept. 7, 2009, at A01 (noting that 90 percent of all home mortgages were funded or guaranteed by the government, including Fannie Mae and Freddie Mac).
10. American Recovery and Reinvestment Act of 2009, Pub. L. No. 111-15, §§ 1101, 1302, 123 Stat. 115 (2009).
11. Sorkin, *supra* note 2, at 440.
12. John C. Dugan, Comptroller of the Currency, Remarks before the Exchequer Club, at 6 (Jul. 21, 2010), available at http://www.occ.gov/news-issuances/speeches/2010/pub-speech-2010-84a.pdf (stating that "the recent financial crisis was caused by a number of factors [including] at the heart of it all, the worst mortgage underwriting in our nation's history").
13. Roger Lowenstein, The End of Wall Street 18 (2010).
14. David Reilly, *U.S. Banks Get Boxed in on Foreclosures*, Wall St. J., Oct. 9–10, 2010, at B16.

15. Gretchen Morgenson and Andrew Martin, *Battle Lines Forming in Clash Over Foreclosures*, N.Y. Times, Oct. 21, 2010, at A1.
16. Gretchen Morgenson, *One Mess That Can't Be Papered Over*, N.Y. Times, Oct. 24, 2010, at BU1.
17. Sorkin, *supra* note 2, at 4, 14, and 81.
18. Financial Crisis Inquiry Commission, Financial Crisis Inquiry Report 111 (2011).
19. *Id.* at 175.
20. Sorkin, *supra* note 2, at 159 and 359.
21. *See* Steven A. Ramirez, *Market Fundamentalism's New Fiasco: Globalization as Exhibit B in the Case for a New Law and Economics*, 24 Mich. J. Int'l. L. 831 (2003).
22. Project Censored, U.S. Congress Sells Out to Wall Street (2010), http://www.projectcensored.org/top-stories/articles/1-us-congress-sells-out-to-wall-street-sources/.
23. Johnson and Kwak, *supra* note 4, at 164.
24. *Id.* at 3.
25. William Greider, *Paulson Bailout Plan a Historic Swindle*, Nation, Oct. 6, 2008, http://www.thenation.com/article/paulson-bailout-plan-historic-swindle.
26. William Poole, Senior Fellow at Cato Inst., Moral Hazard: The Long-Lasting Legacy of Bailouts, Address at the 27th Annual Monetary and Trade Conference 3 (Apr. 29, 2009), *available at* www.interdependence.org/docs/Bill-Poole-Speech.pdf.
27. Michael R. Crittenden and Marshall Eckblad, *Lending Falls at Epic Pace*, Wall St. J., Feb. 24, 2010, at A1.
28. Eugene Robinson, *Lawyers Got It Right on the Foreclosure Mess*, Wash. Post, Oct. 22, 2010, http://www.washingtonpost.com/wp-dyn/content/article/2010/10/21/AR2010102104846.html.
29. Jim Puzzanghera, *Mortgage Database's Murky Legal Status Adds Another Wrinkle to Foreclosure Mess*, L.A. Times.com, Oct. 21, 2010, http://www.latimes.com/business/la-fi-mortgage-foreclosure-20101021,0,1416690,full.story.
30. Peter Coy et al., *How Joseph Lents Dodged Foreclosure for Eight Years and Started a Movement*, Bloomberg.com, Oct. 21, 2010, http://www.bloomberg.com/news/2010-10-21/how-joseph-lents-dodged-foreclosure-for-eight-years-and-started-a-movement.html.
31. Peter Coy, *Mortgages Lost in the Cloud*, Bloomberg.com, Oct. 14, 2010, http://www.businessweek.com/magazine/content/10_43/b4200009860564.htm?chan=rss_topStories_ssi_5 (quoting Hernando de Soto).
32. Hernando de Soto, The Mystery of Capital 163 (2003).
33. Paul Krugman, *The Mortgage Morass*, N.Y. Times, Oct. 15, 2010, at A33.
34. Ramirez, *supra* note 5, at 85 n.37.
35. Joseph E. Stiglitz, Freefall 1 (2010).
36. Gretchen Morgenson, *This Bailout Is a Bargain? Think Again*, N.Y. Times, Apr. 18, 2010, at BU1, BU4.
37. Johnson and Kwak, *supra* note 3, at 282–83.
38. *See* Joseph E. Stiglitz, *How to Make the Best of the Long Malaise*, FT.com, Aug. 11, 2011, http://www.ft.com/intl/cms/s/0/c864cd58-c1d1-11e0-bc71-00144feabdc0.html#axzz1VvfzFAHn; Paul Krugman, *The Third Depression*, N.Y. Times, June 27, 2010, at A19.
39. Nouriel Roubini, *Is Capitalism Doomed?*, Aug. 15, 2011, Project Syndicate, http://www.project-syndicate.org/commentary/roubini41/English.
40. Emma Coleman Jordan, *A Fair Deal for Taxpayer Investments* 1 (2009), http://www.americanprogress.org/issues/2009/09/pdf/public_directors.pdf.

41. Lucian Bebchuk et al., *The Wages of Failure: Executive Compensation at Bear Stearns and Lehman 2000–2008*, 27 Yale J. Reg. 257, 259 (2010).
42. Aaron Luchetti and Stephen Grocer, *On Street, Pay Vaults to Record Altitude*, WSJ.com, Feb. 2, 2011, http://online.wsj.com/article/SB10001424052748704124504576118421859347048.html; Liz Rappaport et al., *Wall Street Pay: A Record $144 Billion*, Wall St. J., Oct. 12, 2010, at C1.
43. Gretchen Morgenson, *Attorney General of N.Y. Is Said to Face Pressure on Bank Foreclosure Deal*, N.Y. Times, Aug. 21, 2011, at B1; Gretchen Morgenson and Louise Story, *In Financial Crisis, No Prosecutions of Top Figures*, N.Y. Times, Apr. 14, 2011, at A1.
44. Financial Crisis Inquiry Commission, Financial Crisis Inquiry Report xxii (2011).
45. Jacob S. Hacker and Paul Pierson, Winner-Take-All Politics 1–4 (2010).
46. Raghuram G. Rajan and Luigi Zingales, Saving Capitalism from the Capitalists 312 (2004).
47. Jonathan Weil, *Zombie Banks Have Us Right Where They Want Us*, Bloomberg.com, Sept. 15, 2010, http://www.bloomberg.com/news/2010-09-16/zombie-banks-have-us-right-where-they-want-us-jonathan-weil.html.
48. Joseph E. Stiglitz, *Obama's Ersatz Capitalism*, N.Y. Times, Mar. 31, 2009, at A31.
49. Pub. L. No. 111–203, 124 Stat. 1376 (2010).
50. Daniel Kaufmann, *Financial Regulatory Reform: Less Than Meets the Eye on Financial Institutions, More Than Meets the Eye on Oil Companies?*, Brookings, July 16, 2010, http://www.brookings.edu/opinions/2010/0716_financial_reform_kaufmann.aspx.
51. Pew Research Center, Wealth Gaps Rise to Record Highs Between Whites, Blacks and Hispanics 1 (2011), *available at* http://pewsocialtrends.org/files/2011/07/SDT-Wealth-Report_7-26-11_FINAL.pdf.
52. *Schumpeter: The Daughter also Rises*, Economist, Aug. 27, 2011, at 58.

INTRODUCTION

1. Robert E. Lucas Jr., *On the Mechanics of Economic Development*, 22 J. Mon. Econ. 5 (1988).
2. Joseph E. Stiglitz, *Justice for Some*, Project Syndicate, Nov. 4, 2010, http://www.project-syndicate.org/commentary/stiglitz131/English.
3. Joseph E. Stiglitz, Freefall 225 (2010).
4. United Nations Development Project, Human Development Report 135 (2011).
5. World Economic Forum, Global Competitiveness Report 2010–2011 18, 23 (2010).
6. United States Census Bureau, Income, Poverty, and Health Insurance Coverage in the United States: 2010 14 (2011).
7. Stiglitz, *supra* note 3, at 225–26.
8. *See* Raghuram Rajan, Fault Lines 43 (2010).
9. The World Bank, World Development Report 2006: Equity and Development 1–2 (2005); *see also* Daron Acemoglu and James A. Robinson, Why Nations Fail 3–4 (2012) (arguing that poverty results from narrow elites' rigging society in their favor to the detriment of all others and that prosperity results when elite power is broken and economic power is broadly distributed).
10. Mancur Olson, The Logic of Collective Action 165–66 (rev. ed. 1971). Olson's theory transcends economic issues and applies generally to the political arena—even to matters of war and peace. *Id.* ("The taxpayers are a vast group with an obvious common interest, but in an important sense they have yet to obtain representation." Further, "[t]here are multitudes with an interest in peace, but they have no lobby to match those of the 'special interests' that may on occasion have an interest in war").

11. Charles P. Kindleberger, Manias, Panics and Crashes 220–21 (4th ed. 2000) ("Dismissing financial crisis on the ground that bubbles and bust cannot take place because that would imply irrationality is to ignore a condition for the sake of a theory").

12. Ragurham G. Rajan and Luigi Zingales, Saving Capitalism from the Capitalists 312 (2004).

13. George Athan Billias, American Constituionalism Heard Round the World, 1776–1989 6–7 (2009).

14. *See* Brian Z. Tamanaha, On the Rule of Law: History, Politics, Theory 141 (2004).

15. *E.g.*, Rick Brooks and Ruth Simon, *Subprime Debacle Traps Even Very Credit-Worthy*, Wall St. J., Dec. 3, 2007, at A1 (reporting on a *Wall Street Journal*–commissioned study which found that 61 percent of all subprime borrowers in 2006 qualified for lower-cost prime mortgages).

16. *E.g.*, Elvin K. Wyly, *The Subprime State of Race*, *in* The Blackwell Companion to the Economics of Housing: The Housing Wealth of Nations 381 (S. Smith and B. Searle, eds., 2010) (finding that in 2006 blacks faced 3.9 times the risk of a subprime loan and Latinos faced 2.6 times the risk of equally qualified white borrowers).

17. *E.g.*, Financial Crisis Inquiry Commission, Financial Crisis Inquiry Report 192 (2011) (an FCIC survey found that one-half of all collateralized debt obligation funds sold in the second half of 2006 were sponsored by hedge funds that actually shorted the senior tranches, meaning they had incentives to include mortgage loans destined to default because the more defaults in the loan package the more profits they would make on their short positions).

18. Federal Reserve Board of Governors, Press Release, July 20, 2011, http://www.federalreserve.gov/newsevents/press/enforcement/20110720a.htm.

19. *Id.*

20. Lucian Bebchuk et al., *The Wages of Failure: Executive Compensation at Bear Stearns and Lehman 2000–2008*, 27 Yale J. Reg. 257 (2010).

21. Nouriel Roubini and Steven Mihm, Crisis Economics: A Crash Course in the Future of Finance 176–81 (2010).

22. Pub. L. No. 111–203, 124 Stat. 1376 (2010).

23. John Rawls, A Theory of Justice 65–73 (rev. ed. 1999).

24. John C. Bogle, The Battle for the Soul of Capitalism 28 (2005).

25. Stiglitz, *supra* note 3, at ix.

26. Amartya Sen, Development as Freedom 3 (1999).

27. Adam Smith, The Wealth of Nations 137 (Prometheus Books 1991) (1776).

28. *Id.* at 151.

29. *Id.* at 474.

30. *Id.* at 488.

CHAPTER 1

1. Adam Smith, The Wealth of Nations 24 (Prometheus Books 1991) (1776).

2. *Id.* at 263.

3. *Id.* at 151.

4. *Id.* at 83.

5. Paul M. Romer, *Increasing Returns and Long Run Growth*, 94 J. Poli. Econ. 1002 (1986).

6. Paul Krugman, *Increasing Returns, Monopolistic Competition, and International Trade*, 9 J. Int'l Econ. 469 (1979).

7. Charles I. Jones, *Ideas and Growth*, *in* The Handbook of Economic Growth 1063–111 (P. Aghion and S. Durlauf, eds. 2005).

8. Douglass C. North, Institutions, Institutional Change, and Economic Performance 3 (1990).

9. Daron Acemoglu et al., *Institutions as the Fundamental Cause of Long Run Growth, in* Handbook of Economic Growth 385 (P. Aghion and S. Durlof, eds. 2005).

10. Douglass C. North, Structure and Change in Economic History 20–32 (1981).

11. Daron Acemoglu, *Root Causes: A Historical Approach to Assessing the Role of Institutions in Economic Development,* Fin. & Dev., June 2003, at 27.

12. Daron Acemoglu and James A. Robinson, Why Nations Fail 428–62 (2012); Daron Acemoglu et al., *Understanding Prosperity and Poverty: Geography, Institutions and the Reversal of Fortunes, in* Understanding Poverty 19, 20–21 (A. Banerjee, ed., 2006).

13. J. Bradford Delong, *Confessions of a Deregulator,* Project Syndicate, June 30, 2011, http://www.project-syndicate.org/commentary/delong115/English.

14. Joseph E. Stiglitz, Freefall 27 (2010).

15. *E.g.,* Steven A. Ramirez, *Market Fundamentalism's New Fiasco: Globalization as Exhibit B in the Case for a New Law and Economics,* 24 Mich. J. Int'l L. 831, 853 (2003).

16. Robert Solow, *Technical Change and the Aggregate Production Function,* 39 Rev. Econ. Stat. 312 (1957).

17. Robert Lucas, *Making a Miracle,* 61 Econometrica 251, 270 (1993).

18. Paul Romer, *Economic Growth, in* Fortune Encyclopedia of Economics 183, 188 (1993).

19. Philippe Aghion & Peter Howitt, Endogenous Growth Theory 1 (1999).

20. Edward B. Barbier, A Global Green New Deal: Rethinking the Economic Recovery 4 (2010).

21. Eban S. Goodstein, Economics and the Environment 119–21 (4th ed. 2007).

22. Joseph A. Schumpeter, The History of Economic Analysis 571 (1954).

23. Robert J. Gordon, Two Centuries of Economic Growth: Europe Chasing the American Frontier, CEPR Working Paper, Mar. 24, 2004, *available at* http://www.ifs.org.uk/conferences/bob_gordon.pdf.

24. Michelle Alexander, The New Jim Crow 4–7, 18, 92–94, 185, 218 (2010).

25. U.N. Dev. Program, Human Development Report 2011 (2011).

26. David N. Weil, Economic Growth 3, 9 (2009).

27. *Id.* at 3.

28. Benjamin M. Friedman, The Moral Consequences of Economic Growth 79–102, 147–48, 267–94 (2005).

29. Weil, *supra* note 26, at 2–3, 17, 158, and 174.

30. David Romer, Advanced Macroeconomics 145 (3rd ed. 2006).

31. Peter Saunders, Capitalism 14–17, 96–98 (1995).

32. Joseph A. Schumpeter, Capitalism, Socialism and Democracy 118 (3rd ed., 1950).

33. Jeffrey J. Pompe and James R. Rinehart, Environmental Conflict: The Search for Common Ground 68–70 (2002).

34. *See* Paul Krugman, *Here Comes the Sun,* Nov. 6, 2011, N.Y. Times, http://www.nytimes.com/2011/11/07/opinion/krugman-here-comes-solar-energy.html.

35. *See* Robert Kunzig, *Carbon Capture: Scrubbing the Skies,* Nat'l Geog., Aug. 2010, at 30 (reporting on new technology to extract carbon dioxide from of the atmosphere through the use of artificial trees).

36. David Warsh, Knowledge and the Wealth of Nations 370–82 (2006).

37. Weil, *supra* note 21, at xv–xvi.

38. Paul M. Romer, *Increasing Returns and Long Run Growth,* 94 J. Poli. Econ. 1002 (1986).

39. Paul M. Romer, *Endogenous Technological Change,* 98 J. Poli. Econ. S71 (1990).
40. Commission on Growth and Development, The Growth Report: Strategies for Sustained Growth and Development 37–41 (2008).
41. Philippe Aghion and Peter Howitt, Endogenous Growth Theory 4 (1999).
42. Elhanan Helpman, The Mystery of Economic Growth 36–46 (2004).
43. Bronwyn Hall, *The Private and Social Returns to Research and Development, in* Technology, R&D, and the Economy 140–83 (Bruce Smith and Claude Barfield, eds., 1995).
44. Edwin Mansfield, *Basic Research and Productivity Increase in Manufacturing,* 70 Am. Econ. Rev. 863–73 (1980).
45. Jungsoo Park, *Dispersion of Human Capital and Economic Growth,* 28 J. Macroeconomics 520 (2006).
46. B. Zorina Khan and Kenneth L. Sokoloff, *Institutions and Democratic Invention in 19th Century America,* 94 Am. Econ. Rev. 395 (2004).
47. Schumpeter, *supra* note 32.
48. Antonio Ciccone and Elias Papaioannou, *Human Capital, the Structure of Production, and Growth,* 91 Rev. Econ. Stat. 66 (2009).
49. Mark L. Rogers, *Directly Unproductive Schooling: How Country Characteristics Affect the Impact of Schooling on Growth,* 52 Euro. Econ. Rev. 356 (2008).
50. Erik A. Hanushek and Ludger Woessmann, *The Role of Cognitive Skills in Economic Development,* 46 J. Econ. Lit. 607, 608, 657 (2008).
51. Enrico Moretti, *Workers' Education, Spillovers and Productivity: Evidence from Plant-Level Production Functions.* 94 Am. Econ. Rev. 656 (2004); Daron Acemoglu and Joshua Angrist, *How Large Are Human-Capital Externalities? Evidence from Compulsory Schooling Laws,* 15 NBER Macroeconomics Ann. 9–74 (2001).
52. Enrico Moretti, *Estimating the Social Return to Higher Education: Evidence from Longitudinal and Repeated Cross-Sectional Data,* 121 J. Econometrics 175, 209 (2004).
53. Lance Lochner and Enrico Moretti, *The Effect of Education on Crime: Evidence from Prison Inmates, Arrests and Self-Reports,* 94 Am. Econ. Rev. 155, 157–58 (2004).
54. Janet Currie and Enrico Moretti, *Mother's Education and the Intergenerational Transmission of Human Capital: Evidence from College Openings,* 118 Q. J. Econ. 1495 (2003).
55. Angel de la Fuente and Rafael Domenech, *Human Capital in Growth Regressions: How Much Difference Does Data Quality Make?,* 4 J. Euro. Econ. Assn. 1 (2006).
56. Francois Bourguignon and F. Halsey Rogers, *Global Returns to Higher Education: Trends, Drivers, and Policy Responses, in* Higher Education and Development 15–40 (J. Lin and B. Pelskovic, eds. 2008).
57. Daniele Checchi, The Economics of Education 30 (2006).
58. Ralph Stinebrickner and Todd R. Stinebrickner, *Effect of Credit Constraints on the College Drop-Out Decision: A Direct Approach Using a New Panel Study,* 98 Am. Econ. Rev. 2163, 2178–79 (2008).
59. National Center for Education Statistics, Youth Indicators 2005 51 (2005).
60. Samuel Bowles and Herbert Gintis, *The Inheritance of Inequality,* 16 J. Econ. Persp. 3 (2002).
61. Katharine Bradbury and Jane Katz, Trends in U.S. Family Income Mobility, 1967–2004, Working Paper 09-7, Federal Reserve Bank of Boston, Aug. 20, 2009, *available at* http://papers.ssrn.com/sol3/papers.cfm?abstract_id=1475309.
62. Wojciech Kopczuk et al., *Earnings Inequality and Mobility in the United States: Evidence from Social Security Data since 1937,* 125 Q. J. Econ. 91 (2010).

63. Organisation for Economic and Cooperation Development, Economic Policy Reforms 2010: Going for Growth 181–98 (2010). *See also* Jason DeParle, *Harder for Americans to Rise from Lower Rungs*, N.Y. Times, Jan. 5, 2012, at A1.

64. Susana Iranzo and Giovanni Peri, *Schooling Externalities, Technology, and Productivity: Theory and Evidence from U.S. States*, 91 Rev. Econ. Stat. 420 (2009).

65. Organization for Economic and Cooperation Development, Eduation at at Glance: Highlights 21 (2011).

66. Daniel Golden, The Price of Admission 6–7 (2006).

67. Peter Sacks, Tearing Down the Gates: Confronting the Class Divide in American Education 161 (2007).

68. Atila Abdulkadiroğlu et al., *Accountability and Flexibility in Public Schools: Evidence from Boston's Charters and Pilots*, 111 Q. J. Econ. 699 (2011).

69. *E.g.*, Michael Heller, The Gridlock Economy 49–78 (2008).

70. Lawrence Lessig, Remix 294 (2008).

71. Paul Romer, *When Should We Use Intellectual Property Rights?*, 92 Am. Econ. Rev. 213 (2002).

72. Joan-Ramon Borrell and Mara Tolosa, *Endogenous Antitrust: Cross-country Evidence on the Impact of Competition-enhancing Policies on Productivity*, 15 App. Econ. Letters 827 (2008).

73. Romer, *supra* note 71.

74. Barry M. Leiner et al., A Brief History of the Internet, www.isoc.org/internet/history/brief.shtml (last visited August 30, 2010).

75. Organisation for Economic Co-operation and Development, Education at a Glance: Highlights 17 (2011).

76. *Id.*

77. *The Great Schools Revolution*, Economist, Sept. 17, 2011, http://www.economist.com/node/21529014; QS World University Rankings 2011/12, http://www.topuniversities.com/university-rankings/world-university-rankings/2011 (last visited Apr. 15, 2012).

78. Mark Whitehouse, *Economists' Grail: A Post-Crash Model*, WSJ.com, Nov. 30, 2010, http://online.wsj.com/article/SB10001424052702303891804575576523458637864.html.

79. *E.g.*, Paul Krugman, *Scale Economies, Product Differentiation, and the Pattern of Trade*, 70 Am. Econ. Rev. 950 (1980).

80. Paul Krugman, *Increasing Returns and Economic Geography*, 99 J. Poli. Econ. 483 (1991).

81. Haiwen Zhou, *The Division of Labor and the Extent of the Market*, 24 Econ. Theory 195 (2004). *See also* James K. Galbraith, Inequality and Instability 169, 270 (2012) (highlighting evidence that links more egalitarian income distribution with innovation).

82. Diana Weinhold and Usha Nair-Reichert, *Innovation, Inequality and Intellectual Property Rights*, 37 World Dev. 889 (2009); Zorina Khan and Kenneth L. Sokoloff, *The Early Development of Intellectual Property Institutions in the United States*, 15 J. Econ. Persp. 233 (2000). *See also* Mark D. Partridge, Does Income Distribution Affect U.S. State Economic Growth?, 45 J. Reg. Sci. 363 (2005) (finding that states with more robust middle classes outgrew states with higher inequality over the long run).

83. A Cost-Benefit Analysis of Government Investment in Post-Secondary Education Under the World War II GI Bill, Subcommittee on Education and Health of the Joint Economic Committee, December 14, 1988.

84. Edward P. St. John & Charles I. Masten, *Return on the Federal Investment in Student Financial Aid: An Assessment for the High School Class of 1972*, J. Student Fin. Aid, Fall 1990, at 4, 19.

85. Katherine Kiemle Buckley and Bridgid Cleary, *The Restoration and Modernization of Education Benefits under the Post-9/11 Veterans Assistance Act of 2008*, 2 Vet. L. Rev. 185 (2010); Laura W. Perna and Chunyan Li, *College Affordability: Implications for College Opportunity*, J. Student Fin. Aid, Jan. 2006, at 7–24.

86. Steven A. Ramirez, *The Law and Macroeconomics of the New Deal at 70*, 65 Maryland L. Rev. 515 (2003).

87. Suzanne Mettler, Soldiers to Citizens 123, 156 (2005).

88. Weinhold and Nair-Reichert, *supra* note 82, at 899.

89. Peter Howitt, *Health, Human Capital, and Economic Growth: A Schumpeterian Perspective* in Health and Economic Growth 19 (G. Lopez-Casasnovas et al., eds. 2005).

90. Kwabena Gyimah-Brempong & Mark Wilson, *Health, Human Capital and Economic Growth in Sub-Saharan Africa and OECD Countries*, 44 Q. Rev. Econ & Fin. 296 (2004).

91. William Easterly, *The Middle Class Consensus and Economic Development*, 6 J. Econ. Growth 317 (2001).

92. Elinor Ostrom et al., *Revisiting the Commons: Local Lessons, Global Challenges*, 284 Science 278 (1999).

93. Galbraith, *supra* note 81 at 1–9; Raghuram Rajan, Fault Lines 21–46 (2010).

94. Steven A. Ramirez, *Bearing The Costs of Racial Inequality: Brown and the Myth of the Equality/Efficiency Trade Off*, 44 Washburn L.J. 87, 93 (2004).

95. Steven A. Ramirez, *The Law and Macroeconomics of the New Deal at 70*, 62 Maryland L. Rev. 515 (2003).

96. Michael Greenstone et al., *Mandated Disclosure, Stock Returns, and the 1964 Securities Acts Amendments*, 121 Q. J. Econ. 399, 447 (2006).

97. Richard Posner, The Economic Analysis of Law 482 (2007).

98. Gary Gorton, Slapped by the Invisible Hand 5, 17, 41, 123 (2010).

99. Angela de la Fuente and Rafael Domenech, *Human Capital in Growth Regressions: How Much Difference Does Data Quality Make?*, 4 J. Euro. Econ. Ass'n. 1 (2006). *See also* Serge Coulombe et al., International Adult Literacy Survey: Literacy Scores, Human Capital and Growth Across Fourteen OECD Countries 6 (2004) ("raising the average literacy and numeracy skill level of the workforce, and reducing the proportion of workers at the lowest level of skill, could yield significantly higher levels of growth in GDP per capita").

100. Yan Wang and Yudong Wao, *Sources of Chinese Economic Growth 1952–1999: Incorporating Human Capital Accumulation*, 14 China Econ. Rev. 32, 34, 47 (2003).

101. Joseph E. Stiglitz, *Some Lessons from the East Asian Miracle*, 11 World Bank Res. Obs. 151, 152, 153 154, 162 (1996).

102. Thomas Ferguson and Robert Johnson, *Too Big to Bail: The Paulson "Put," Presidential Politics, and the Global Financial Meltdown*, 38 Int'l. J. Poli. Econ. 3, 6, 11–14 (2009).

103. Laura de Dominicis et al., *A Meta-Analysis on the Relationship Between Income Inequality and Economic Growth*, 55 Scottish J. Poli. Econ. 654 (2008).

104. *See* David N. Weil, Economic Growth 354–66 (2nd ed. 2009) (explaining why governing elites often pursue policies harmful to growth); Raghuram Rajan, *Rent Preservation and the Persistence of Underdevelopment*, 1 Amer. Econ. J.: Macroeconomics 178 (2009) (demonstrating that in an unequal society competitive rent preservation may lead to suboptimal economic outcomes for all); *see also* Oscar Vilhena Vieira, *Inequality and the Subversion of the Rule of Law*, 6 Int'l. J. Human Rights 27 (2007) (arguing that high inequality undermines legal impartiality, demonizes those arguing for assistance to the poor, and leads to immunity for the privileged).

105. Oded Galor and Omer Moav, *From Physical to Human Capital Accumulation: Inequality and the Process of Development,* 71 Rev. Econ. Stat. 101 (2004).

106. Amparo Castello and Rafael Domenech, *Human Capital Inequality and Economic Growth: Some New Evidence,* 112 Econ. J. C187, C199 (2002).

107. Oded Galor et al., *Inequality in Landownership, the Emergence of Human-Capital Promoting Institutions, and the Great Divergence,* 76 Rev. Econ. Stud. 143 (2009); Alberto Choonny and Mark Gradstein, *Inequality and Institutions,* 8a Rev. Econ. Stat. 454 (2007); Stanley L. Engerman and Kenneth L. Sokoloff, *Factor Endowments, Inequality and Paths of Development Among New World Economies,* 3 Economia 41 (2002) .

108. Edward Glaeser, Jose Scheinkman, and Andrei Shleifer, *The Injustice of Inequality,* 50 J. Monetary Econ. 199, 2154–216 (2003). *See also* William Easterly, *Inequality Does Cause Underdevelopment: Insights from a New Instrument,* 84 J. Dev. Econ. 755 (2007) (demonstrating causal direction running from inequality to impaired growth by showing that if initial conditions demanded large plantations rather than family farms, initial high inequality led to inferior rule of law).

109. Brown v. Bd. of Educ., 347 U.S. 483 (1954); Brown v. Bd. of Educ. (Brown II), 349 U.S. 294, 301 (1955).

110. Steven A. Ramirez, *Bearing the Costs of Racial Inequality:* Brown *and the Myth of the Equality/Efficiency Trade-Off,* 44 Washburn L.J. 87, 96, 99 (2004).

111. Deitrich Vollrath, School Funding and Inequality in the United States, Jan. 6, 2010, at 21, available at http://sites.google.com/site/dietrichvollrath/Home/proptax. *See also* Era Dabla Norris & Mark Gradstein, The Distributional Bias of Public Education: Causes and Consequences, IMF Working Paper, Nov. 2004, at 14, *available at* http://papers.ssrn.com/sol3/papers.cfm?abstract_id=879039 (finding that spending on education is biased toward the rich and that "weak governance leads to intensified rent-seeking over public education funds, increasing inequality, reducing social mobility, and slowing growth").

112. Chad Turner et al., *Education and the Income of the States of the United States 1840–2000,* 12 J. Econ. Growth 101 (2007).

113. Catalina Gutierrez and Ryuchi Tanaka, *Inequality and Education Decisions in Developing Countries,* 7 J. Econ. Inequality 55 (2009).

114. Oded Galor et al., *Inequality in Land Ownership, the Emergence of Human Capital Promoting Institutions, and the Great Divergence,* 76 Rev. Econ. Stud. 143 (2009).

115. Mancur Olson, The Logic of Collective Action 1–2, 11–12, 165–66 (rev. ed. 1971).

116. Edward J. McCaffery and Linda R. Cohen, *Shakedown at Gucci Gulch: The New Logic of Collective Action,* 84 N.C. L. Rev. 1159, 1233 (2006).

117. Thomas Piketty and Emmanuel Saez, *Income Inequality in the United States 1913–1998,* 118 Q. J. Econ. 1 (2003).

118. Emmanuel Saez, Striking It Richer: The Evolution of Top Incomes in the United States, Aug. 5, 2009, available at http://elsa.berkeley.edu/~saez/saez-UStopincomes-2007.pdf; Thomas Piketty & Emmanuel Saez, *The Evolution of Top Incomes: A Historical and International Perspective,* 96 Am. Econ. Rev. 200, 201, 204 (2006).

119. World Economic Forum, The Global Competitiveness Report 363 (2011).

120. Simon Johnson and James Kwak, 13 Bankers 64–90, 90–100, 113, 203 (2010).

121. Steven A. Ramirez, *Lessons from the Subprime Debacle: Stress Testing CEO Autonomy,* 54 St. Louis U. L.J. 1 (2009).

122. Jacob S. Hacker and Paul Pierson, Winner-Take-All Politics 1–8, 12–13, 22–23, 27–28, 46, 48 (2010).

123. Peter Howitt, *Growth and Development: A Schumpeterian Growth Perspective on the Canadian Economy*, C.D. Howe Institute Commentary, Apr. 2007, at 1, 13, available at http://www.cdhowe.org/pdf/commentary_246.pdf.

124. Daron Acemoglu and James A. Robinson, *Why Nations Fail* 421–432 (2012); Daron Acemoglu and James A. Robinson, *Economic Backwardness in Political Perspective*, 100 Am. Poli. Sci. Rev. 115 (2006).

125. Joseph A. Schumpeter, The Theory of Economic Development 66 (1936).

126. Maria Petrova, *Inequality and Media Capture*, 92 J. Pub. Econ. 183 (2008).

127. Konstantin Sonin, *Why the Rich May Prefer Poor Protection of Property Rights*, 31 J. Comp. Econ. 715 (2003).

128. Pranab Bardhan, *Democracy and Development: A Complex Relationship*, *in* Democracy's Values (I. Shapiro and C. Hacker-Cordon, eds. 1999).

129. Michael Kumhof and Romain Rancière, Inequality, Leverage, and Crises, IMF Working Paper 10/268, Nov. 2010, http://www.imf.org/external/pubs/ft/wp/2010/wp10268.pdf.

130. *See* Alberto Chong and Mark Gradstein, *Inequality and Institutions*, 89 Rev. Econ. Stat. 454 (2007) (finding that inequality and poor institutions reinforce each other).

131. Antonio Savoia, Joshy Easaw, and Andrew McKay, *Inequality, Democracy, and Institutions: A Critical Review of Recent Research*, 38 World Dev. 142 (2010).

132. Owen Fiss, *Trebilcock's Heresy*, 60 U. Toronto L.J. 511 (2010).

133. George Priest, *Michael Trebilcock and the Past and Future of Law and Economics*, 60 U. Toronto L.J. 155, 155 (2010).

134. Steven A. Ramirez, *Market Fundamentalism's New Fiasco: Globalization as Exhibit B in the Case for a New Law and Economics*, 24 Mich. J. Int'l. L. 831 (2003).

135. Richard A. Posner, *Creating a Legal Framework for Economic Development*, 13 World Bank Res. Obs. 1, 9 (1998).

136. Richard A. Posner, *Creating a Legal Framework for Economic Development*, 13 World Bank Res. Obs. 1, 9 (1998)

137. *E.g.*, Ronald H. Coase, *The Problem of Social Costs*, 3 J. L. Econ. 1 (1960).

138. Joseph E. Stiglitz, Globalization and Its Discontents 219 (2002).

139. *Id.*

140. Richard A. Posner, Economic Analysis of Law 3 (7th ed. 2007).

141. Richard A. Posner, Economic Analysis of Law 3 (5th ed. 1998).

142. *Id.* at 569.

143. *Id.* at 30.

144. Jeffrey L. Harrison, Law and Economics: Positive, Normative and Behavioral Perspectives 34–43 and 59–62 (2nd ed. 2007).

145. Richard A. Posner, A Failure of Capitalism xii, 75, 115, 286–87 (2009).

146. *See* Richard A. Posner, Economic Analysis of Law 34–35, 445–53, 608–12, 613–21, 634–36 (8th ed. 2011) (attributing crisis primarily to financial deregulation and a failure to address underlying causes of massive inequality and concomitant entrenchment through subversion of law).

147. *Id.* at xxiii, 22 and 616–21.

148. Edwin Mansfield, Microeconomics 249–50, 417–18 (3rd ed. 1979).

149. *Id.* at 522.

150. Amartya Sen, *Markets and Freedoms: Achievements and Limitations of the Market Mechanism in Promoting Individual Freedoms*, 49 Oxford Econ. Papers 519 (1993).

151. John Rawls, A Theory of Justice §§ 13, 14 (rev. ed. 1999).

152. Amartya Sen, Development as Freedom 18–20, 41, 70–86 (1999).

153. David N. Weil, Economic Growth 3 (2nd ed. 2009).

154. Geraldine Fabrikant, *At Elite Prep Schools, College-Size Endowments*, N.Y. Times, Jan. 26, 2008, at A1.

155. Raghuram Rajan, Fault Lines 25 (2010).

CHAPTER 2

1. John C. Bogle, Founder and Former Chief Executive, The Vanguard Group, Ethical Principles and Ethical Principals (Nov. 1, 2006), http://www.vanguard.com/bogle_site/sp20061101.htm.

2. John C. Bogle, The Battle for the Soul of Capitalism 28 (2005). *See also* Carl C. Icahn, *The Economy Needs Corporate Governance Reform*, Wall St. J., Jan. 9, 2009, at A13 ("Lax and ineffective boards, self-serving managements, and failed short-term strategies all contributed to the entirely preventable financial meltdown").

3. Lucian Bebchuk and Yaniv Grinstein, *The Growth of U.S. Executive Pay*, 21 Oxford Rev. Econ. Pol'y 283, 287 (2005).

4. *See* Lucian A. Bebchuk et al., *The Wages of Failure: Executive Compensation at Bear Stearns and Lehman 2000–2008*, 27 Yale J. Reg. 257 (2010) (finding net payouts to senior executives at Bear Stearns and Lehman to be decisively positive despite losses on shareholdings); Sanjai Bhagat & Brian Bolton, *Investment Bankers' Culture of Ownership* 4–5, 18–20, http://ssrn.com/abstract=1664520 (Aug. 2010) (last visited Apr. 15, 2012) (reviewing compensation arrangements of the CEO at the fourteen largest firms involved in the financial meltdown and concluding that the compensation structures created incentives for excessive risk taking that resulted in positive payoffs for the CEOs while shareholders experienced negative returns).

5. George W. Dent Jr., *Academics in Wonderland: The Team Production and Director Primacy Models of Corporate Governance*, 44 Hous. L. Rev. 1213, 1240, 1245–50, 1273 (2008) ("the evidence is overwhelming that most boards are passive, dominated by CEOs who exert their power in their own interests").

6. Steven A. Ramirez, *The End of Corporate Governance Law: Optimizing Regulatory Structures for a Race to the Top*, 24 Yale J. Reg. 313–20, 327 (2007).

7. Raghuram Rajan, *Bankers' Pay Is Deeply Flawed*, Fin. Times, Jan. 8, 2008, at 11, http://us.ft.com/ftgateway/superpage.ft?news_id=ft0010920081142101282.

8. *E.g.*, James L. Bicksler, *The Subprime Mortgage Debacle and Its Linkages to Corporate Governance*, 5 Int'l J. Disclosure & Governance 295, 295 (2008). *See also* John Cassidy, *Wall Street Pay: Where's the Reform?*, The New Yorker Online, July 23, 2010 ("Despite widespread anger on the part of the public, and a rare consensus among economists that faulty compensation structures were partly responsible for the financial crisis, the U.S. political system has failed to rise to the challenge"), http://www.newyorker.com/online/blogs/johncassidy/2010/07/wall-street-pay.html#ixzz1sF1vDYv3. The OECD also concluded that "to an important extent" the financial crises arose from "failures and weaknesses in corporate governance," particularly in the areas of compensation incentives and risk management. Organisation of Economic Co-operation and Development, The Corporate Governance Lessons from the Financial Crisis 2 (2009) (report drafted by Grant Kirkpatrick).

9. Paul Krugman, *Banks Gone Wild*, N.Y. Times, Nov. 23, 2007, at A37 (describing how the system of executive compensation encourages high-risk decision making).

10. Interview by Neil Conan with Joseph Stiglitz, Professor, Columbia University, *Talk of the Nation: Economists Explain How to Save Capitalism* (NPR radio broadcast Oct. 20, 2008), http://www.npr.org/templates/story/story.php?storyId=95906243.

11. Douglas W. Diamond and Ragurham G. Rajan, *The Credit Crisis: Conjectures about Causes and Remedies*, 99 Am. Econ. Rev. 606, 607 (2009).

12. Ronald Suskind, Confidence Men 20 (2011).

13. Financial Crisis Inquiry Commission, Financial Crisis Inquiry Report xviii–xx (2011).

14. Ross Levine and Sara Zervos, *Stock Markets, Banks, and Economic Growth*, 88 Am. Econ. Rev. 537 (1998).

15. Maurice Obstfeld, *Risk-Taking, Global Diversification and Growth*, 84 Am. Econ. Rev. 1310 (1994).

16. Raghuram G. Rajan & Luigi Zingales, *Financial Dependence and Growth*, 88 Am. Econ. Rev. 559 (1998).

17. Rafael La Porta et al., *The Economic Consequences of Legal Origins*, 46 J. Econ. Lit. 285, 294 (2008).

18. Margaret M. Blair, *Locking in Capital: What Corporate Law Achieved for Business Organizers in the Nineteenth Century*, 51UCLA L. Rev. 387, 389–90, 454 (2003).

19. Henry Hansmann and Reinier Kraakman, *The Essential Role of Organizational Law*, 110 Yale L.J. 387, 393 (2000).

20. American Law Institute, Principles of Corporate Governance: Analysis and Recommendations § 2.01(a) (1994).

21. Hyman P. Minsky, Stabilizing an Unstable Economy 351–52 (2008).

22. *See* Reinier Kraakman et al., The Anatomy of Corporate Law: A Comparative and Functional Approach 5 (2004).

23. *Id.* at 6–9.

24. Lawrence E. Mitchell, Corporate Irresponsibility: America's Newest Export 49, 53, 276–78 (2001).

25. Douglas Litowitz, *Are Corporations Evil?*, 58 U. Miami L. Rev. 811, 829 (2004).

26. Larry Catá Backer, *From Moral Obligation to International Law: Disclosure Systems, Markets and the Regulation of Multinational Corporations*, 39 Geo. J. Int'l. L. 591 (2008).

27. Paul Romer, *Economic Growth, in* Fortune Encyclopedia of Economics 183, 188 (David R. Henderson ed., 1993).

28. Blair, *supra* note 18, at 437 n. 198 (quoting Nicholas Butler, Why Should We Change Our Form of Government 82 (1912)).

29. John Micklethwait and Adrian Wooldridge, The Company: A Short History of a Revolutionary Idea xv (2003).

30. Steven A. Ramirez, *Rethinking the Corporation (and Race) in America: Can Law (and Professionalization) Fix "Minor" Problems of Externalization, Internalization and Governance?*, 79 St. John's L. Rev. 977 (2005).

31. Michael C. Jensen & William H. Meckling, *Theory of the Firm: Managerial Behavior, Agency Costs and Ownership Structure*, 3 J. Fin. Econ. 305, 308 (1976).

32. *Id.* at 312–13 and 357.

33. Sarbanes-Oxley Act of 2002, Pub. L. No. 107-204, 116 Stat. 745 (2002).

34. Ramirez, *supra* note 6, at 321–23.

35. D. Quinn Mills, Wheel, Deal and Steal: Deceptive Accounting, Deceitful CEOs, and Ineffective Reforms 183 (2003).

36. Douglas Guerrero, *The Root of Corporate Evil*, Internal Auditor, Dec. 2004, at 37.

37. Charles Forelle & James Bandler, *Matter of Timing: Five More Companies Show Question-able Options Pattern—Chip Industry's KLATencor Among Firms with Grants Before Stock-Price Jumps—A 20 Million-to-One Shot*, Wall St. J., May 22, 2006, at A1 (quoting former SEC Chair Arthur Levitt). *See also* Jesse M. Fried, *Option Backdating and Its Implications*, 65 Wash. & Lee L. Rev. 853, 886 (2008) ("secret backdating, which was generally illegal . . . boosted and camouflaged managerial pay. Secret backdating thus provides further support for the view that managerial power has played an important role in shaping executive compensation arrangements").

38. M. P. Narayanan et al., *The Economic Impact of Backdating of Executive Stock Options*, 105 Mich. L. Rev. 1597, 1601 (2007).

39. Paul Gompers et al., *Corporate Governance and Equity Prices*, 118 Q. J. Econ. 107, 145 (2003).

40. Lucian Bebchuk et al., *What Matters in Corporate Governance?*, 22 Rev. Fin. Studies 783 (2009). *See also* Thuu-Nga T. Vo, *To Be or not to Be Both CEO and Board Chair*, 76 Brooklyn L. Rev. 65, 126–27 (2010) (finding that evidence strongly supports limiting CEO power by splitting the board chair position from the CEO position and that many of the firms at the center of the financial crisis combined the two positions).

41. Charles P. Himmelberg et al., *Investor Protection, Ownership and the Cost of Capital* 38–39 (World Bank Policy Research, Working Paper no. 2834, 2002), *available at* http://ssrn.com/abstract=303969.

42. Inessa Love, *Corporate Governance and Performance around the World: What We Know and What We Don't*, 26 World Bank Res. Obs. 42 (2010).

43. Raghuram G. Rajan, Fault Lines 139 (2010).

44. Steven A. Ramirez, *Lessons from the Subprime Debacle: Stress Testing CEO Autonomy*, 54 St. Louis U. L.J. 1 (2009).

45. *Id.* at 23–25.

46. Financial Crisis Inquiry Commission, Financial Crisis Inquiry Report 20 (2011).

47. David Wighton, *Prince of Wisdom*, Fin. Times, Nov. 4, 2007, http://www.ft.com/cms/s/0/fce88e10-8b12-11dc-95f7-0000779fd2ac.html.

48. Ramirez, *supra* note 44, at 23–27.

49. FCIC, *supra* note 46, at 19.

50. *Economic and Budget Challenges for the Short and Long Term: Hearing Before the S. Budget Comm.*, 111th Cong., 3 (2009) (statement of Ben Bernanke, Chairman, Board of Governors of the Federal Reserve System).

51. Ramirez, *supra* note 44, at 28–31.

52. FCIC, *supra* note 46, at 272–74.

53. *See* Ramirez, *supra* note 44, at 27–28 and 31. For example, a detailed and bipartisan Senate investigation of Washington Mutual (WaMu) found that "WaMu's CEO received millions of dollars in pay, even when his high-risk loan strategy began unraveling, even when the bank began to falter, and even when he was asked to leave his post." Indeed, "[i]n 2008, when he was asked to leave the bank, [the CEO] was paid $25 million, including $15 million in severance pay." Over five years, WaMu paid its CEO about $100 million—plus multi-million-dollar retirement benefits. United States Senate, Permanent Subcommittee on Investigations, Wall Street and the Financial Crisis: Anatomy of a Financial Collapse, Majority and Minority Staff Report, Apr. 13, 2011, available at http://www.hsgac.senate.gov/download/?id=273533f4-23be-438b-a5ba-05efe2b22f71. Amazingly, these huge compensation payments occurred even after WaMu's chief risk officer told the bank's

executive committee in early 2005 that it was making too many high-risk mortgages, at just the wrong time. *Id.* at 109–12. They also continued even after an internal audit team alerted the bank in 2005 that employees engaged in "an extensive level of loan fraud" at times infecting up to 83 percent of all loans tested. *Id.* at 95–101. WaMu lost billions on its way to becoming the largest bank failure in American history. *Id.* at 48.

54. Gretchen Morgenson, *Gimme Back Your Paycheck*, N.Y. Times, Feb. 22, 2009, at BU1.

55. *Id.*

56. *Id.*

57. *Id.*

58. FCIC, *supra* note 46, at 111.

59. *Id.* at 18.

60. Lucian A. Bebchuk et al., *The Wages of Failure: Executive Compensation at Bear Stearns and Lehman 2000–2008*, 27 Yale J. Reg. 257, 259–60 (2010); Sanjai Bhagat & Brian Bolton, *Investment Bankers' Culture of Ownership* 4–5, 18–20, http://ssrn.com/abstract=1664520 (Aug. 2010) (last visited Apr. 15, 2012) (reviewing compensation arrangements at the fourteen largest firms involved in the financial meltdown and concluding that the compensation structures created incentives for excessive risk taking that resulted in positive payoffs for the CEOs while shareholders experienced negative returns).

61. Adolf A. Berle Jr. and Gardiner C. Means, The Modern Corporation and Private Property 238 (1932).

62. Steven A. Ramirez, *The Special Interest Race to CEO Primacy and the End of Corporate Governance Law*, 32 Del. J. Corp. L. 345, 348–49 (2007).

63. William L. Cary, *Federalism and Corporate Law: Reflections upon Delaware*, 83 Yale L.J. 663 (1974).

64. Ralph K. Winter Jr., *State Law, Shareholder Protection, and the Theory of the Corporation*, 6 J. Legal Stud. 251, 254–62 (1977).

65. *See* Michael E. Murphy, *The Nominating Process for Corporate Boards of Directors: A Decision-Making Analysis*, 5 Berkeley Bus. L.J. 131, 148–49 (2008).

66. andré douglas pond cummings, *"Ain't No Glory in Pain": How the 1994 Republican Revolution and the Private Securities Litigation Reform Act Contributed to the Collapse of the United States Capital Markets*, 83 Neb. L. Rev. 979 (2005).

67. *See* Edward J. McCaffery & Linda R. Cohen, *Shakedown at Gucci Gulch: The New Logic of Collective Action*, 84 N.C. L. Rev. 1159, 1161 (2006) (citing Mancur Olson, The Logic of Collective Action: Public Goods and the Theory of Goods (1965)).

68. *Id.* at 1233–35 (finding that Congress exploits special interests by stringing issues along and having repeated votes without resolving anything on issues such the repeal of the estate tax).

69. Edward Glaeser et al., *The Injustice of Inequality*, 50 J. Mon. Econ. 199 (2003).

70. Steven A. Ramirez, *The Special Interest Race to CEO Primacy and the End of Corporate Governance Law*, 32 Del. J. Corp. L. 345, 367 (2007).

71. Lucian A. Bebchuk & Zvika Neeman, *Investor Protection and Interest Group Politics*, 23 Rev. Fin. Studies 1089 (2010).

72. Joel Seligman, *The Case for Minimum Federal Corporate Law Standards*, 49 Md. L. Rev. 947, 949 (1990).

73. *Id.* at 949–72.

74. Roy C. Smith & Ingo Walter, Governing the Modern Corporation: Capital Markets, Corporate Control, and Economic Performance 116–17 (2006).

75. Securities Act of 1933, ch. 38, 48 Stat. 74 (codified as amended at 15 U.S.C. §§ 77a-77aa (2000)).

76. Securities Exchange Act of 1934, ch. 404, 48 Stat. 881 (codified as amended at 15 U.S.C. §§ 78a-78mm (2000)).

77. Cynthia A. Williams, *The Securities and Exchange Commission and Corporate Social Transparency*, 112 Harv. L. Rev. 1197, 1221–22 (1999).

78. Louis D. Brandeis, Other People's Money and How the Bankers Use It 92 (1914).

79. Marc I. Steinberg, Understanding Securities Laws §10.07 (5th ed. 2009); Melvin Aron Eisenberg, Corporations and Other Business Organizations 269–74 (9th ed. 2005).

80. Herman & MacLean v. Huddleston, 479 U.S. 375, 386 (1983) (citing SEC v. Capital Gains Research Bureau, 375 U.S. 180 (1963)).

81. Steven A. Ramirez, *Arbitration and Reform in Private Securities Litigation: Dealing with the Meritorious as Well as the Frivolous,* 40 Wm. & Mary L. Rev. 1055, 1083–84 (1999).

82. Rafael La Porta et al., *What Works in Securities Laws?*, 61 J. Fin. 1, 5 (2006).

83. Merritt B. Fox et al., *Law, Share Price Accuracy, and Economic Performance: The New Evidence,* 102 Mich. L. Rev. 331 (2003).

84. Michael Greenstone et al., *Mandated Disclosure, Stock Returns, and the 1964 Securities Acts Amendments,* 121 Q.J. Econ. 399, 447 (2006).

85. Private Securities Litigation Reform Act of 1995, Pub. L. No. 104-67, 109 Stat. 737 (1995) (codified at 15 U.S.C. §§ 77a, k(f), t, z, z-2, 78a, j-1, u-4, u-5, 771, and 18 U.S.C. § 1964(c)).

86. Brian D. Hufford, *Deterring Fraud vs. Avoiding the "Strike Suit": Reaching an Appropriate Balance,* 61 Brook. L. Rev. 593, 641 (1995).

87. Ramirez, *supra* note 81, at 1087 n.156.

88. Douglas M. Branson, *Running the Gauntlet: A Description of the Arduous and Now Often Fatal Journey for Plaintiffs in Federal Securities Laws Actions,* 65 Cin. L. Rev. 3, 58 (1996).

89. 15 U.S.C.A. § 78u-4(b)(2).

90. Fed. R. Civ. P. 9(b).

91. Charles W. Murdock, *Corporate Corruption and the Complicity of Congress and the Supreme Court—The Tortuous Path from* Central Bank *to* Stoneridge Investment Partners, 6 Berkeley Bus. L.J. 131 (2009).

92. 15 U.S.C. §§ 77z-2(c)(1)(A)(i) and 78u-5(c)(1)(A)(i) (2006).

93. Ramirez, *supra* note 81, at 1076 (quoting Columbia University law professor John C. Coffee Jr.).

94. Pub. L. No. 105-353 (1998).

95. *See* 15 U.S.C. § 78bb(f)(1)(A) (2006).

96. Lisa M. Fairfax, *The Future of Shareholder Democracy*, 84 Ind. L.J. 1259, 1307–8 (2009).

97. Joel Seligman, *A Modest Revolution in Corporate Governance*, 80 Notre Dame L. Rev. 1159, 1162–68 (2005).

98. 17 C.F.R. § 14(a)(8)(i)(8) (2009).

99. Anil Shivdasani & David Yermack, *CEO Involvement in the Selection of New Board Members: An Empirical Analysis,* 54 J. Fin. 1829, 1852 (1999); *see also* Jonathon B. Cohn et al., On Enhancing Shareholder Control: A (Dodd-) Frank Assessment of Proxy Access, July 14, 2011, at 23–24, http://papers.ssrn.com/sol3/papers.cfm?abstract_id=1742506 ("Our evidence suggests that reforms allowing greater shareholder control (via increased proxy access) are associated with increases in firm value for those firms with shareholders who were more likely to take advantage of that access").

100. *See* Security Holder Director Nominations, 68 Fed. Reg. 60,784 (proposed Oct. 23, 2003) (not codified); Shareholder Proposals Relating to the Election of Directors, 72 Fed. Reg. 70,450 (proposed Dec. 11, 2007) (not codified).

101. Amy Borrus, *SEC Reforms: Big Biz Says Enough Already*, Bus. Wk., Feb. 2, 2004, at 43; Amy Borrus & Mike McNamee, *A Legacy That May not Last*, Bus. Week, June 13, 2005, at 38.

102. Business Roundtable v. S.E.C., 647 F.3d 1144 (D.C. Cir. 2011).

103. Lucian A. Bebchuk, *The Myth of the Shareholder Franchise*, 93 Va. L. Rev. 675, 732 (2007).

104. *See* James D. Westphal & Edward J. Zajac, *Who Shall Govern?: CEO/Board Power, Demographic Similarity, and New Director Selection*, 40 Admin. Sci. Q. 60, 77 (1995) (finding that CEOs will exercise power to select demographically similar directors and achieve high pay).

105. Steven A. Ramirez, *Games CEOs Play and Interest Convergence Theory: Why Diversity Lags in America's Boardrooms and What to Do About It*, 61 Wash. & Lee L. Rev. 1583, 1613 (2004).

106. Antony Page, *Unconscious Bias and Director Independence*, 2009 Univ. Ill. L. Rev. 237, 248–49.

107. Alliance for Board Diversity, Missing Pieces: Women and Minorities on Fortune 500 Boards☒2010 Alliance for Board Diversity Census 1, 5, 7 (2011).

108. Maureen I. Muller-Kahle and Krista B. Lewellyn, *Did Board Configuration Matter? The Case of US Subprime Lenders*, 19 Corp. Gov.: An Int'l. Rev. 405 (2011).

109. *Id.* David A. Carter et al., *Corporate Governance, Board Diversity and Firm Value*, 38 Fin. Rev. 33, 36 (2003); Claude Francoeur et al., *Gender Diversity in Corporate Governance and Top Management*, 81 J. Bus. Ethics 83 (2008). *See also* David A. Carter et al., *The Gender and Ethnic Diversity of US Boards and Board Committees and Firm Financial Performance*, 18 Corp. Gov.: An Int'l. Rev. 356 (2010) (finding no evidence of statistically significant positive impact for board diversity from 1998 to 2002). Board diversity also enhances firm innovation and reputation and thus financial performance. Toyah Miller and Maria del Carmen Triana, Demographic Diversity in the Boardroom: Mediators of the Diversity Firm Performance Relationship, 46 J. Mgmt. Stud. 755 (2009).

110. 17 C.F.R. § 229.407(c)(2)(vi) (2010).

111. Pub. L. No. 101-73, Title II, s 212(k), 103 Stat. 243 (1989) (codified at 12 U.S.C. § 1821(k) (1994)).

112. *E.g.*, Bates v. Dresser, 251 U.S. 524 (1922).

113. Atherton v. FDIC, 519 U.S. 213 (1997).

114. Steven A. Ramirez, *The Chaos of 12 U.S.C. Section 1821(k): Congressional Subsidizing of Negligent Bank Directors and Officers?*, 65 Fordham L. Rev. 625, 682–88 (1996).

115. H.R. Rep. No. 73-85, at 1–2 (1933).

116. Ramirez, *supra* note 114, at 630 n. 19 and 631 n. 26.

117. Lawrence A. Hamermesh, *The Policy Foundations of Delaware Corporate Law*, 106 Colum. L. Rev. 1749, 1779–80 (2006).

118. Ramirez, *supra* note 44, at 34–38.

119. Joseph W. Bishop Jr., *Sitting Ducks and Decoy Ducks: New Trends in the Indemnification of Directors and Officers*, 77 Yale L.J. 1078, 1099–101, 1103 (1968).

120. Bernard Black et al., *Outside Director Liability*, 58 Stan. L. Rev. 1065, 1070–71 (2006).

121. Smith v. Van Gorkom, 488 A.2d 858 (Del. 1985).

122. Michael Bradley & Cindy A. Schipani, *The Relevance of the Duty of Care Standard in Corporate Governance*, 75 Iowa L. Rev. 1, 43 n. 317 (1989).

123. Del. Code Ann. tit. 8, § 102(b)(7) (2007).

124. Marc I. Steinberg, *The Evisceration of the Duty of Care*, 42 Sw. L.J. 919 (1988).

125. Steven A. Ramirez, *The Chaos of* Smith, 45 Washburn L.J. 343, 352 (2006).

126. *Id.* at 865–70.

127. Smith v. Van Gorkom, 488 A.2d 858, 898–99 (Del. 1985) (motion for reargument).

128. *Id.* at 871–82.

129. In re *Walt Disney Company Derivative Litigation,* 906 A.2d 27, 62–67 (Del. 2006).

130. *See* In re *Citigroup, Inc. Shareholder Derivative Litigation,* 964 A.2d 106 (Del. Ch. 2009).

131. Miriam A. Cherry and Jarrod Wong, *Clawbacks: Prospective Contract Measures in an Era of Excessive Executive Compensation and Ponzi Schemes,* 94 Minn. L. Rev. 368, 378 (2009).

132. Lucian A. Bebchuk & Jesse M. Fried, Pay Without Performance: The Unfulfilled Promise of Executive Compensation 15–41 (2004).

133. Joel Seligman, *Rethinking Private Securities Litigation,* 73 Cin. L. Rev. 93, 113–15 (2004).

134. Institute for Policy Studies and United for a Fair Economy, Executive Excess 2006, August 30, 2007, at 31, http://www.faireconomy.org/files/ExecutiveExcess2006.pdf.

135. Yuka Hayashi and Phred Dvorak, *Japanese Wrestle with CEO Pay as They Go Global,* Wall St. J., Nov. 28, 2008, http://online.wsj.com/article/SB122782362228562381.html.

136. Restatement (Third) Agency §§ 8.03, 8.09, 8.08, 8.11 (2006).

137. Charles W. Murdock, *Why Not Tell The Truth? Deceptive Practices and the Economic Meltdown,* 41 Loyola U. Chi. L.J. 801 (2010).

138. *E.g.,* Mary K. Ramirez, *Criminal Affirmance: Going Beyond the Deterrence Paradigm to Examine the Social Meaning of Declining Prosecution of Elite Crime,* Apr. 13, 2012, at 82, http://papers.ssrn.com/sol3/papers.cfm?abstract_id=2039785 ("The affirmance effect appears evident in . . . the financial market crisis of 2007–2009" as notwithstanding "the generous fees and bonuses awarded for creating a financial Armageddon [and] the fraudulent loan documentation to support foreclosures" there has been a "failure to pursue criminal charges against any of the major actors or their legions of supporters in the legal, accounting, and credit rating fields, despite evidence of financial fraud"); Gretchen Morgenson, *Case Said to Conclude Against Head of A.I.G. Unit,* N.Y. Times, May 22, 2010, at A15.

139. Ramirez, *supra* note 44, at 10–14.

140. Joel Seligman, *The Case for Minimum Federal Corporate Law Standards,* 49 Md. L. Rev. 947, 971–74 (1990).

141. *But see* Brian R. Cheffins, *Did Corporate Governance "Fail" During the 2008 Stock Market Meltdown? The Case of the S&P 500,* 65 Bus. Law 1 (2009) (arguing that firms removed from S&P 500 exhibited acceptable corporate governance practices but failing to consider impact of systemic legal frameworks and legal indulgences).

142. *See* Joel Seligman, *Rethinking Securities Litigation,* 73 U. Cin. L. Rev. 95 (2004).

143. Raghuram G. Rajan, Fault Lines 154–55 (2010).

144. Steven A. Ramirez, *The Professional Obligations of Securities Brokers Under Federal Law: An Antidote for Bubbles?,* 70 U. Cin. L. Rev. 527 (2002).

145. Ira M. Milstein, *The Professional Board,* 50 Bus. Law. 1427 (1995).

146. A Working Group of Concerned MBA Candidates Enrolled in the Harvard Business School, Public Policy Proposal for the Corporate Governance College, Apr. 1, 2009, available at http://papers.ssrn.com/sol3/papers.cfm?abstract_id=1413286.

147. Rakesh Khurana & Nitin Nohria, *Management Needs to Become a Profession,* Fin. Times, Oct. 20, 2008, http://www.ft.com/cms/s/0/14c053b0-9e40-11dd-bdde-000077b07658.html.

148. *See* Harald Hau et al., *Bank Governance and the Crisis: Did Board (In)competence Matter for Bank Performance During the Recent Crisis?,* Euro. Fin. Rev., Feb./Mar. 2011, at 38, 40 ("Our

data confirm that a lower supervisory board competence in finance is related to higher losses in the financial crisis").

149. George Dent, *For Optional Federal Incorporation,* 39 J. Corp. L. 499 (2010).

150. Steven A. Ramirez, *The End of Corporate Governance Law: Optimizing Regulatory Structures for a Race to the Top,* 24 Yale J. Reg. 313, 313–20, 327 (2007).

151. Arthur Levitt, Take on the Street 106–15 (2002).

152. Liz Moyer, *How Regulators Missed Madoff,* Forbes.com, Jan. 27, 2009, http://www.forbes.com/2009/01/27/bernard-madoff-sec-business-wall-street_0127_regulators.html; Elizabeth Williamson and Kara Scannell, *Family Filled Posts at Industry Groups,* Wall St. J., Dec. 18, 2008, at A16.

153. David Lieberman et al., *Investors Remain Amazed over Madoff's Sudden Downfall,* USA Today, Dec. 15, 2008, http://www.usatoday.com/money/markets/2008-12-14-ponzi-madoff-downfall_N.htm.

154. David Stout, *Report Details How Madoff's Web Ensnared S.E.C.,* N.Y. Times, Sept. 3, 2009, at B1.

155. Ramirez, *supra* note 150, at 347–58.

156. Melvin Aron Eisenberg, Corporations and Other Business Associations 561 (9th ed. 2005).

157. Ramirez, *supra* note 81, at 1078–79.

158. Steven A. Ramirez, *Rethinking the Corporation (and Race) in America: Can Law (and Professionalization) Fix "Minor" Problems of Externalization, Internalization and Governance?,* 79 St. John's L. Rev. 977, 999–1000 (2005).

159. George W. Dent Jr., *Academics in Wonderland: The Team Production and Director Primacy Models of Corporate Governance,* 44 Hous. L. Rev. 1213, 1228 (2008).

160. *See* Steven F. Cahan & Brett. R. Wilkinson, *Board Composition and Regulatory Change: Evidence from the Enactment of the New Companies Law in New Zealand,* 28 Fin. Mgmt. 32 (1999) (finding that the more rigorous demands of the New Companies Act in New Zealand did not lead to a reduction in outside director representation).

161. *See generally* Sarbanes-Oxley Act of 2002, 15 U.S.C. § 78j-1 (2006).

162. Ramirez, *supra* note 44, at 42.

163. 15 U.S.C § 78j-1(m)(3)(A).

164. 15 U.S.C § 78j-1(m)(3)(B).

165. 15 U.S.C. § 78j-1 (2006).

166. 15 U.S.C. § 7265 (2006). The SEC promulgated regulations implementing this section. 17 C.F.R. §§ 228, 229, 249 (2008).

167. *E.g.,* Ronald C. Anderson et al., *Board Characteristics, Accounting Report Integrity, and the Cost of Debt,* 37 J. Acct. & Econ. 315, 340 (2004) (finding that independent audit committees are associated with a lower cost of debt).

168. Joseph V. Carcello et al., Audit Committee Financial Expertise, Competing Corporate Governance Mechanisms, and Earnings Management 32–33 (Feb. 2006) (unpublished manuscript), *available at* http://papers.ssrn.com/sol3/papers.cfm?abstract_id=887512 (finding that independent audit committee members facilitate higher-quality audits); Daniel A. Cohen et al., Trends in Earnings Management and Informativeness of Earnings Announcements in the Pre- and Post–Sarbanes Oxley Periods 30 (Feb. 2005) (unpublished manuscript), *available at* http://papers.ssrn.com/sol3/papers.cfm?abstract_id=658782.

169. *See, e.g.,* Donald Nordberg, Waste Makes Haste: Sarbanes-Oxley, Competitiveness and the Subprime Crisis 21–23 (May 10, 2008) (unpublished manuscript), *available at* http://papers.ssrn.com/sol3/papers.cfm?abstract_id=1131674.

170. Ramirez, *supra* note 44, at 40–53.

171. *Id.*

172. 130 S.Ct. 876 (2010).

173. Dodd-Frank Wall Street Reform and Consumer Protection Act, Pub. L. No. 111-203, §§ 951, 952, 953, 957, 971, 124 Stat. 1376 (2010).

174. *Lawmakers Seek Update From "Overwhelmed" Regulators,* SFGate, Sept. 29, 2010, http://www.sfgate.com/cgi-bin/article.cgi?f=/g/a/2010/09/29/bloomberg1376-L9J2771A1I4H01-55N1GM8LNI1JSSA71OJUPJK33U.DTL.

175. Eric Lichtblau, *Ex-Regulators Get Set to Lobby on New Financial Rules,* July 28, 2010, N.Y. Times, at B1.

176. *Banks See Midterms as FinReg Opportunity,* Sept. 10, 2010, Newsweek.com, http://www.newsweek.com/2010/09/10/banks-see-midterms-as-finreg-opportunity.html.

177. Business Roundtable v. S.E.C., 647 F.3d 1144 (D.C. Cir. 2011).

CHAPTER 3

1. John Maynard Keynes, The General Theory of Employment, Interest and Money 161–62 (Great Minds ed., 1991) (1936).

2. Charles P. Kindleberger et al., Manias, Panics, and Crashes 26–39, 298 (6th ed. 2011); Hyman P. Minsky, Stabilizing an Unstable Economy 131–36 (1986) (McGraw-Hill ed. 2008).

3. David Ratner, Securities Regulation in a Nutshell § 11 (2d ed. 1982).

4. Joel Seligman, The Transformation of Wall Street 79 (1983).

5. Simon Johnson and James Kwak, 13 Bankers 6–8, 92 (2010) (quoting Senator Dick Durbin that the banks are the most powerful lobby in Washington and that they "frankly own the place").

6. Thomas Ferguson and Robert Johnson, *Too Big to Bail: The "Paulson Put," Presidential Politics, and the Global Financial Meltdown (Part I),* 38 Int'l. J. Poli. Econ. 3, 6 (2009).

7. Timothy A. Canova, *Financial Market Failure as a Crisis in the Rule of Law: From Market Fundamentalism to a New Keynesian Regulatory Model,* 3 Harv. J. L. & Pol'y 369, 385–86 (2009).

8. Bradley Keoun, *Citigroup Names Obama's Orszag Vice Chairman of Investment Bank,* Bloomberg.com, Dec. 9, 2010, http://www.bloomberg.com/news/2010-12-01/citigroup-said-to-discuss-hiring-former-white-house-budget-director-orszag.html.

9. Simon Johnson and James Kwak, 13 Bankers 91–92 (2010).

10. Ferguson and Johnson, *supra* note 6, at 17.

11. Johnson and Kwak, *supra* note 9, at 6 and 221.

12. Nouriel Roubini and Stephen Mihm, Crisis Economics 221–23 (2010).

13. Garn–St. Germain Depository Institutions Act of 1982, Pub. L. No. 97-320, 96 Stat. 1469 (codified as amended at 12 U.S.C. 1823(c) (1994)).

14. Depository Institutions Deregulation and Monetary Control Act of 1980, Pub. L. No. 96-221, 94 Stat. 132 (codified as amended in scattered sections of 12 U.S.C. and 15 U.S.C.).

15. Canova, *supra* note 7, at 376–77.

16. *E.g.,* Secondary Mortgage Market Enhancement Act of 1984, Pub. L. No. 98-440, 98 Stat. 1689 (1984).

17. Dorit Samuel, *The Subprime Mortgage Crisis: Will New Regulations Help Avoid Future Financial Debacles?,* 2 Alb. Gov't L. Rev. 217, 232–43 (2009).

18. Assistant Treasury Secretary Sheila Bair, Mortgage Reform and Predatory Lending: Addressing the Challenges, Assistant Treasury Secretary Sheila Bair Remarks to the

Women in Housing and Finance Fall Symposium Willard Inter-Continental Hotel, Nov. 8, 2001, http://www.treasury.gov/press-center/press-releases/Pages/po772.aspx.

19. Edmund L. Andrews, *Fed Shrugged as Subprime Crisis Spread*, N.Y. Times, Dec. 18, 2007, at A1.

20. Pub. L. 103-325; 108 Stat. 2190 (1994) (codified as amended in scattered sections of the Truth in Lending Act, 15 U.S.C. §§ 1601–67).

21. 15 U.S.C. § 1639(l)(2) (2006).

22. Truth in Lending, Final Rule, 73 Fed. Reg. 44522 (July 30, 2008).

23. Patricia A. McCoy et al., *Systemic Risks Through Securitization: The Result of Deregulation and Regulatory Failure*, 41 Conn. L. Rev. 493, 500, 511, 517–20 (2009).

24. *Mortgage Lending: Subprime Subsidence*, Economist, Dec. 16, 2006, at 33.

25. Bair, *supra* note 18.

26. Interview by Frontline of Sheila Bair, Chair, FDIC, Frontline, *Inside the Meltdown* (PBS, Feb. 17, 2009), http://www.pbs.org/wgbh/pages/frontline/meltdown/interviews/bair.html.

27. Kristopher Gerardi et al., Financial Literacy and Subprime Mortgage Delinquency: Evidence from a Survey Matched to Administrative Data, Federal Reserve Bank of Atlanta, Working Paper no. 2010-10, Apr. 2010, http://www.frbatlanta.org/documents/pubs/wp/wp1010.pdf.

28. Office of the Comptroller of the Currency, Bd. of Governors of the Fed. Res. Sys., Fed. Deposit Ins. Corp. & Office of Thrift Supervision, Supervision and Regulation Letter 01-4, Expanded Interagency Guidance for Subprime Lending Programs (2001), http://www.federalreserve.gov/boarddocs/srletters/2001/sr0104a1.pdf.

29. The Financial Crisis Inquiry Commission, The Financial Crisis Inquiry Report 191–93 (2011).

30. Jesse Eisinger and Jake Bernstein, *The Magnetar Trade: How One Hedge Fund Helped Keep the Bubble Going*, ProPublica, Apr. 10, 2010, http://www.propublica.org/article/the-magnetar-trade-how-one-hedge-fund-helped-keep-the-housing-bubble-going/single.

31. Press Release, Securities and Exchange Commission, Citigroup to Pay $285 Million to Settle SEC Charges for Misleading Investors About CDO Tied to Housing Market (Oct. 19, 2011), http://www.sec.gov/news/press/2011/2011-214.htm.

32. Jean Eaglesham and Suzanne Kapner, *Citigroup to Pay $285 Million to Settle Fraud Charges*, Oct. 20, 2011, Wall St. J., http://online.wsj.com/article/SB10001424052970204618704576640873051858568.html.

33. Kathleen C. Engle and Patricia A. McCoy, *A Tale of Three Markets: The Law and Economics of Predatory Lending*, 80 Texas L. Rev. 1255, 1259–70 (2002).

34. Rick Brooks and Ruth Simon, *Subprime Debacle Traps Even Very Credit-Worthy*, Wall St. J., Dec. 3, 2007, at A1.

35. Brian M. McCall, *Learning from Our History: Evaluating the Modern Housing Finance Market in Light of Ancient Principles of Justice*, 60 S.C. L. Rev. 707, 723 (2009).

36. Claudia Coulton et al., Pathways to Foreclosure, June 2008, at 1 http://blog.case.edu/msass/2008/06/23/Pathways_to_foreclosure_6_23.pdf.

37. Gerardi et al., *supra* note 27, at 4.

38. Christopher L. Peterson, *Fannie Mae, Freddie Mac, and the Home Mortgage Foreclosure Crisis*, 10 Loyola J. Pub. Int. L. 149, 168 n. 128 (2009).

39. Steven A. Ramirez, *The Real Subprime and Predatory Fraud (Fannie and Freddie Acquitted Again and Again II)*, The Corporate Justice Blog (Nov. 6, 2011, 6:41 PM), http://corporate-justiceblog.blogspot.com/2011/11/real-subprime-and-predatory-fraud.html. This post will be updated on the Corporate Justice Blog as more predatory lending comes to light.

40. Peterson, *supra* note 38, at 156–58.

41. HUD's Housing Goals for the Federal National Mortgage Association (Fannie Mae) and the Federal Home Loan Mortgage Corporation (Freddie Mac) for the Years 2005–2008 and Amendments to HUD's Regulation of Fannie Mae and Freddie Mac, 69 Fed. Reg. 63,580, 63,741 (Nov. 2, 2004).

42. Carol D. Leonnig, *How HUD Mortgage Policy Fed the Crisis*, Wash. Post, June 10, 2008, http://www.washingtonpost.com/wp-dyn/content/article/2008/06/09/AR2008060902626.html.

43. Charles Duhigg, *Pressured to Take More Risk, Fannie Reached Tipping Point*, N.Y. Times, Oct. 4, 2008, at A1.

44. Federal Housing Finance Agency, Conservator's Report on the Enterprises' Financial Performance Second Quarter 2011 14 (2011).

45. Peterson, *supra* note 38, at 168.

46. Nouriel Roubini and Stephen Mihm, Crisis Economics 63–64, 76, 81 (2010).

47. McCoy et al., *supra* note 23, at 514–15 and 516.

48. Watters v. Wachovia Bank, N.A., 127 S. Ct. 1559 (2007).

49. Gretchen Morgenson, *Countrywide to Set Aside $8.4 Billion in Loan Aid*, N.Y. Times, Oct. 5, 2008, at B1.

50. Steven A. Ramirez, *Lessons from the Subprime Debacle: Stress Testing CEO Autonomy*, 54 St. Louis U. L.J. 1, 24–26 (2009).

51. Kathleen C. Engle and Patricia A. McCoy, *Turning a Blind Eye: Wall Street Finance of Predatory Lending*, 75 Fordham L. Rev. 101, 123–32 (2007).

52. In re 2007 Novastar Financial Inc., Securities Litigation, 579 F.3d 878 (8th Cir. 2009).

53. Sharenow v. Impac Mortg. Holdings, Inc., 385 Fed.Appx. 714 (9th Cir. 2010).

54. Footbridge Ltd. v. Countrywide Home Loans, Inc., Slip Copy, 2010 WL 3790810 (S.D.N.Y. 2010).

55. In re Citigroup Inc. Securities Litigation, 753 F.Supp.2d 206, 2010 WL 4484650 (S.D.N.Y. 2010).

56. Richard Bitner, Confessions of a Subprime Lender 45 (2008).

57. Dorit Samuel, *The Subprime Mortgage Crisis: Will New Regulations Help Avoid Future Financial Debacles?*, 2 Alb. Gov't L. Rev. 217, 232–43 (2009).

58. Richard Bookstaber, A Demon of Our Own Design 156, 250 (2007).

59. Procter & Gamble Co. v. Bankers Trust Co., 925 F. Supp. 1270, 1290 (S.D. Ohio 1996).

60. Leslie Wayne and Andrew Pollack, *The Master of Orange County: A Merrill Lynch Broker Survives Municipal Bankruptcy*, N.Y. Times, July 22, 1998, at D1.

61. *Frontline: The Warning* (PBS television broadcast, October 20, 2009).

62. Commodity Futures Modernization Act of 2000, Pub. L. No. 106-554, 114 Stat. 2763 app. E (2000) (codified as amended in scattered sections of 7, 11, 12, and 15 U.S.C.).

63. andré douglas pond cummings, *Still "Ain't No Glory in Pain": How the Telecommunications Act of 1996 and other 1990s Deregulation Facilitated the Market Crash of 2002*, 12 Fordham J. Corp. Fin. L. 467, 530 (2007).

64. Interview of Joseph Stiglitz by Frontline, Professor of Economics, Columbia University, *The Warning* (PBS, Feb. 17, 2009), http://www.pbs.org/wgbh/pages/frontline/warning/interviews/stiglitz.html.

65. Letter from Warren E. Buffet, Chairman of the Board, Berkshire Hathaway, Inc., to Shareholders of Berkshire Hathaway Inc. 14 (Feb. 21, 2003), http://www.berkshirehathaway.com/letters/2002pdf.pdf.

66. Masaki Kondo, *Derivatives Market Growth Accelerates to 18%, BIS Says*, Bloomberg Businessweek, Nov. 15, 2011, http://www.businessweek.com/news/2011-11-15/derivatives-market-growth-accelerates-to-18-bis-says.html.

67. Canova, *supra* note 7, at 388.

68. Art Patnaude et al., *European Debt Markets Hammered*, WSJ.com, Sept. 22, 2011, http://online.wsj.com/article/SB10001424053111903703604576586120331116288.html.

69. Ian Talley, *European Banks Risk New Global Financial Crisis, IMF Warns*, WSJ.com, Apr. 18, 2012, http://blogs.wsj.com/economics/2012/04/18/european-banks-risk-new-global-financial-crisis-imf-warns/; *U.S. Banks Face Contagion Risk from Europe Debt, Fitch Says*, Bloomberg Businessweek, Nov. 15, 2011, http://news.businessweek.com/article.asp?documentKey=1376-LURTMK6S972B01-3J2SJP583VQ9LRSQECBEGUA18G.

70. John Maynard Keynes, The General Theory of Employment, Interest, and Money 159 (1936).

71. Frank Partnoy, *Enron and the Derivatives World, in* Enron Corporate Fiascos and Their Implications 169–86, 175 (Nancy B. Rapoport and Bala G. Dharan eds. 2004).

72. *Id.* at 186.

73. Henry M. Paulson Jr., On the Brink 222–34 (2010).

74. Frank Partnoy, Rethinking Regulation of Credit Rating Agencies: An Institutional Investor Perspective, Apr. 2009, at 2–5 (Council of Institutional Investors White Paper), http://www.cii.org/UserFiles/file/CRAWhitePaper04-14-09.pdf.

75. Thomas J. Fitzpatrick IV and Chris Sagers, *Faith Based Financial Regulation: A Primer of Oversight of Credit Ratings Agencies*, 61 Admin. L. Rev. 557, 573 (2009).

76. *Id.* at 573 n. 57.

77. Henry M. Paulson Jr., On the Brink 477 (2010).

78. Fitzpatrick and Sagers, *supra* note 75, at 586.

79. Gretchen Morgenson, *Tamed or Caught Napping,* N.Y. Times, Dec. 6, 2008, at A1.

80. SEC, Summary Report of Issues Identified in the Commission Staff's Examinations of Select Credit Rating Agencies (2008), *available at* http://www.sec.gov/news/studies/2008/craexamination070808.pdf.

81. County of Orange v. McGraw-Hill Cos., 245 B.R. 151 (C.D. Cal. 1999).

82. Fitzpatrick and Sagers, *supra* note 75, at 602–3.

83. Frank Partnoy, *The Paradox of Credit Ratings, in* Ratings, Rating Agencies and the Global Financial System 65, 79 (Richard M. Levich et al. eds. 2002).

84. Eric Lipton and Raymond Hernandez, *A Champion of Wall Street Reaps Benefits*, N.Y. Times, Dec. 14, 2008, at A1.

85. Pub. L. No. 109-291, § 4(a), 120 Stat. 1329 (2006) (codified at 15 U.S.C. § 78o-7(i)(1) (2006)).

86. 15 U.S.C. § 78o-7(c)(2).

87. Fitzpatrick and Sagers, *supra* note 75, at 595.

88. Barbara Black, *Protecting the Retail Investor in an Age of Financial Uncertainty*, 35 U. Dayton L. Rev. 61, 68–71 (2010).

89. Henry M. Paulson Jr., On the Brink 63, 106, 201, 231–34, 264, 277 (2010).

90. Gary H. Stern & Ronald J. Feldman, Too Big to Fail: The Hazards of Bank Bailouts 2, 17, 20–42 (2004).

91. Steven A. Ramirez, *Lessons from the Subprime Debacle: Stress Testing CEO Autonomy*, 54 St. Louis U. L.J. 1, 25–29 (2009).

92. Steven A. Ramirez, *Subprime Bailouts and the Predator State*, 35 Dayton L. Rev. 81, 83, 93, 100–12 (2009).

93. *Id.*

94. *Id.* at 95–99; Simon Johnson, *"Citi Weekend" Shows Too-Big-to-Fail Endures: Simon Johnson*, Bloomberg Bus. Wk., http:// www.businessweek.com/news/2011-01-17/-citi-weekend-shows-too-big-to-fail-endures-simon-johnson.html.

95. Joseph E. Stiglitz, Freefall 138 (2010).

96. Gary H. Stern & Ronald J. Feldman, Too Big to Fail: The Hazards of Bank Bailouts 66 (2004).

97. Financial Services Modernization Act of 1999 (also known as the Gramm-Leach-Bliley Act), Pub. L. No. 106-102, 113 Stat. 1338 (codified at 15 U.S.C. §§ 6801-6809, 6821-6827 (2006)).

98. Banking Act of 1933 (Glass-Steagall Act), Pub. L. No. 73-65, §§ 16, 20, 21, 32, 73 Stat. 184–85, 188–89, 194.

99. Stiglitz, *supra* note 64.

100. Joseph Karl Grant, *What the Financial Services Industry Puts Together Let No Person Put Asunder: How the Gramm-Leach-Bliley Act Contributed to the 2008–2009 American Capital Markets Crisis*, 73 Alb. L. Rev. 371, 385–98 (2010).

101. *Id.* at 400–3; Kim Chipman and Christine Harper, *Parsons Blames Glass-Steagall Repeal for Crisis*, Bloomberg, Apr. 19, 2012, http://www.bloomberg.com/news/2012-04-19/parsons-blames-glass-steagall-repeal-for-crisis.html ("To some extent what we saw in the 2007, 2008 crash was the result of the throwing off of Glass-Steagall").

102. Arthur E. Wilmarth Jr., *The Dark Side of Universal Banking: Financial Conglomerates and the Origins of the Subprime Financial Crisis*, 41 Conn. L. Rev. 963, 1044 (2009).

103. Arthur E. Wilmarth Jr., *The Transformation of the U.S. Financial Services Industry, 1975–2000: Competition, Consolidation and Increased Risks*, 2002 U. Ill. L. Rev. 215.

104. William E. Kovacic, *The Modern Evolution of U.S. Competition Policy Enforcement Norms*, 71 Antitrust L.J. 377, 441 (2003).

105. Robert Scheer, *Robert Rubin's Great Misfortune*, Pittsburgh Post-Gazette, Mar. 23, 2000, at A21.

106. McCoy et al., *supra* note 23, at 503–4.

107. Alternative Net Capital Requirements for Broker-Dealers That Are Part of Consolidated Supervised Entities, 69 Fed. Reg. 34,428, 34,451 (June 24, 2004).

108. McCoy et al., *supra* note 23, at 524–26.

109. Letter from Senator Charles Schumer to FDIC, June 27, 2007, available at http://graphics8.nytimes.com/images/2008/12/12/business/SchumerFDIC.pdf.

110. Erik F. Gerding, *Code, Crash, and Open Source: The Outsourcing of Financial Regulation to Risk Models and the Global Financial Crisis*, 84 Wash. L. Rev. 127, 155–58 (2009).

111. Gary B. Gorton, Slapped by the Invisible Hand 38–45 (2010).

112. Paul Krugman, The Return of Depression Economics and the Crisis of 2008 162–64 (2009).

113. *Id.*

114. Gorton, *supra* note 111, at 45–59.

115. *Id.* at 150–52.

116. It's a Wonderful Life (Republic 1947).

117. Gorton, *supra* note, at 111 and 170–73.

118. Andrew Campbell and Rosa Lastra, *Revisiting the Lender of Last Resort*, 24 Banking & Fin. L. Rev. 453, 490 (2009).

119. Henry M. Paulson Jr., On the Brink 94–121 (2010).

120. Campbell and Lastra, *supra* note 118, at 492–94.

121. Steven A. Ramirez, *Subprime Bailouts and the Predator State*, 35 Dayton L. Rev. 81, 83, 93, 100–12 (2009).

122. Thomas Ferguson and Robert Johnson, *Too Big to Bail: The "Paulson Put," Presidential Politics, and the Global Financial Meltdown (Part I)*, 38 Int'l J. Poli. Econ. 3, 24–27 (2009).

123. *Id.* at 5, 12, 13, and 17–18.

124. Paulson, *supra* note 119, at 177, 181, 183, 184–86, 189, and 192. Paulson apparently allowed a negotiating ploy to kill any deal involving public money, which he now claims he was actually willing to do. *Id.* at 181. Apparently, Lehman Brothers declared bankruptcy because of a miscommunication.

125. Ramirez, *supra* note 85, at 29–32.

126. Anna Jacobson Schwartz, *Man Without a Plan*, N.Y. Times, July 25, 2009, at WK12.

127. Ramirez, *supra* note 121, at 89–92.

128. *See* Christian A. Johnson, *Exigent and Unusual Circumstances: The Federal Reserve and the U.S. Financial Crisis*, __Euro. Bus. Org. L. Rev.__ (2010).

129. Stiglitz, *supra* note 64.

130. William Poole, Senior Fellow at Cato Inst., Moral Hazard: The Long-Lasting Legacy of Bailouts, Address at the 27th Annual Monetary and Trade Conference 7 (Apr. 30, 2009), available at http://www.interdependence.org

131. Ramirez, *supra* note 115, at 82–83.

132. Ferguson and Johnson, *supra* note 122, at 7.

133. Hyman Minsky, Stabilizing an Unstable Economy (1986).

134. Charles P. Kindleberger, Manias, Panics and Crashes: A History of Financial Crises 220–21 (4th ed. 2000).

135. Simon Johnson and James Kwak, 13 Bankers 6, 36, 59, 92 133, 221 (2010).

136. Rachel E. Barkow, *Insulating Agencies: Avoiding Capture Through Institutional Design*, 89 Texas L. Rev. 15, 62–63 (2010).

137. Steven A. Ramirez, *Depoliticizing Financial Regulation*, 41 Wm. & Mary L. Rev. 503, 522–32 (2000).

138. *Id.* at 538–54.

139. Shahien Nasiripour, *Stiglitz, Nobel Prize–Winning Economist, Says Federal Reserve System "Corrupt,"* Huffington Post, Mar. 8, 2011, http://www.huffingtonpost.com/2010/03/03/stiglitz-nobel-prize-winn_n_484943.html.

140. Charles Goodhart and Dirk Schoenmake, *Should the Functions of Monetary Policy and Bank Supervision Be Separated?*, 47 Oxford Econ. Papers 539 (1995).

141. Timothy A. Canova, *The Federal Reserve We Need*, Am. Prospect, Oct. 10, 2010.

142. Ferguson and Johnson, *supra* note 122, at 10 and 12–13.

143. Joe Peek et al., *Is Bank Supervision Central to Central Banking?*, 114 Q. J. Econ. 629, 651 (1999).

144. Nouriel Roubini and Stephen Mihm, Crisis Economics 219–24 (2010).

145. Sec. & Exch. Comm'n, Office of Inspector Gen., SEC's Oversight of Bear Stearns and Related Entities: The Consolidated Supervised Entity Program, at ix–xi (Report No. 446-A, Sept. 25, 2008) http://www.sec-oig.gov/Reports/AuditsInspections/2008/446-b.pdf.

146. Jill E. Fisch, *Top Cop or Regulatory Flop? The SEC at 75*, 95 Va. L. Rev. 785, 786, 790–95, 803–5 (2009).

147. *Schumer's Stands*, N.Y. Times, Dec. 12, 2008, http://www.nytimes.com/interactive/2008/12/12/business/20081214-schumer-table.html.

148. Fisch, *supra* note 146, at 806–7.

149. Francesco Guerrera, *Don't Eat Wall Street's Big Fudge—It's a Dog's Breakfast*, Fin. Times, Apr. 4, 2009, at 15.

150. Fisch, *supra* note 146, at 807–10.

151. Ferguson and Johnson, *supra* note 122, at 16.

152. Institute for New Economic Thinking, Larry Summers and Martin Wolf on New Economic Thinking, Bretton Woods Conference, Apr. 8, 2011, http://ineteconomics.org/video/bretton-woods/larry-summers-and-martin-wolf-new-economic-thinking.

153. H.R. Rep. No. 73-1383, at 5 (1934).

154. Steven A. Ramirez, *The Professional Obligations of Securities Brokers Under Federal Law: An Antidote for Bubbles?*, 70 U. Cin. L. Rev. 527, 535, 560, 567–68 (2002).

155. Steven A. Ramirez, *Fear and Social Capitalism: The Law and Macroeconomics of Investor Confidence*, 42 Washburn L.J. 31, 65 (2002).

156. Engle and McCoy, *supra* note 33, at 1337–58.

157. Engle and McCoy, *supra* note 51, at 151.

158. Sarbanes-Oxley Act of 2002, § 101, Pub. L. No. 107-204, 116 Stat. 745 (codified as amended in scattered titles of U.S.C.).

159. Partnoy, *supra* note 74, at 7–13.

160. *Id.* at 2, 13–16.

161. H.R. Rep. No. 73-85, at 2 (1933) (quoting letter from President Franklin Roosevelt).

162. Steven A. Ramirez, *Arbitration and Reform in Private Securities Litigation: Dealing with the Meritorious as Well as the Frivolous*, 40 Wm. & Mary L. Rev. 1055, 1069–70, 1075–76, 1081–93 (1999).

163. Pub. L. No. 111-203, 124 Stat. 1376 (2010).

164. Jennifer Liberto, *Lobbyists Swarm as Wall Street Bill Talks Start*, CNNMoney.com, June 10, 2010, http://money.cnn.com/2010/06/10/news/economy/Wall_Street_Reform/index.htm.

165. Amanda Becker, *Multitudes of Lobbyists Weigh in on Dodd-Frank Act*, WashingtonPost.com, Nov. 22, 2010, http://www.washingtonpost.com/wp-dyn/content/article/2010/11/19/AR2010111906465.html.

166. Dodd-Frank Act §§ 1411, 1413.

167. Dodd-Frank Act §§ 1011–14.

168. Dodd-Frank Act § 933.

169. Dodd-Frank Act § 121.

170. Dodd-Frank Act § 929Z.

171. Dodd-Frank Act § 939; Aline Darbellay and Frank Partnoy, *Credit Rating Agencies Under the Dodd-Frank Act*, Bank. & Fin. Serv. Pol'y Report, Dec. 2011, at 3.

172. Dodd-Frank Act § 619; Jesse Eisinger, Volcker Rule Gets Murky Treatment, N.Y. Times, DealBook, Apr. 18, 2012, http://dealbook.nytimes.com/2012/04/18/interpretation-of-volcker-rule-that-muddies-the-intent-of-congress/ ("The path to gaming the Volcker Rule has always been clear: Banks will shut down anything with the word 'proprietary' on the door and simply move the activities down the hall").

173. Dodd-Frank Act § 716; Roger Lowenstein, *Derivatives Lobby Has U.S. Regulators on the Run*, Bloomberg, Apr. 17, 2012, http://www.bloomberg.com/news/2012-04-17/

derivatives-lobby-has-u-s-regulators-on-the-run.html ("The derivatives industry is squeezing Washington like a python. Desperate to control the tone and thrust of derivatives regulation, industry lobbyists have been swarming over the Commodity Futures Trading Commission and the Securities and Exchange Commission, each of which is writing derivatives rules as mandated by the Dodd-Frank reform law").

174. Dodd-Frank Act § 1101.

175. Clea Benson and Phil Mattingly, *Firms That Fought Dodd-Frank May Gain Under New House*, Bloomberg.com, Nov. 3, 2010, http://www.businessweek.com/news/2010-11-03/ firms-that-fought-dodd-frank-may-gain-under-new-house.html.

CHAPTER 4

1. The World Bank, World Development Report 2006: Equity and Development 1–2 (2005).

2. Oxfam, Rigged Rules and Double Standards: Trade Globalization and the Fight Against Poverty 5–6 (2002).

3. Eric C. Chafee, *Finishing the Race to the Bottom: An Argument for Harmonization and Centralization of International Securities Law*, 40 Seton Hall L. Rev. 1518 (2010).

4. Joseph E. Stiglitz, Making Globalization Work 11 (2007).

5. Nouriel Roubini and Stephen Mihm, Crisis Economics 26–37 (2010).

6. Joseph E. Stiglitz, Globalization and Its Discontents xiii (2002).

7. Raghuram G. Rajan, Fault Lines 23 (2010).

8. Steven Greenhouse and David Leonhardt, *Real Wages Fail to Match a Rise in Productivity*, N.Y. Times, Aug. 26, 2006, http://www.nytimes.com/2006/08/28/business/28wages. html?_r=1&pagewanted=all.

9. *Corporate Profits' Share of Pie Most in 60 Years*, MarketWatch, July 29, 2011, http://www. marketwatch.com/story/corporate-profits-share-of-pie-most-in-60-years-2011-07-29.

10. Roubini and Mihm, *supra* note 5, at 7–11, 276–301.

11. Stiglitz, *supra* note 6, at 191 and 103–32.

12. Danny Leipziger, *Globalization Revisited*, *in* Globalization and Growth 23 (M. Spence and D. Leipziger, eds. 2010).

13. Paul Krugman, The Return of Depression Economics 34–35 (2009).

14. Steven A. Ramirez, *Market Fundamentalism's New Fiasco: Globalization as Exhibit B in the Case for a New Law and Economics*, 24 Mich. J. Int'l L. 831, 841 (2004).

15. Steven A. Ramirez, *Endogenous Growth Theory, Status Quo Efficiency, and Globalization*, 17 Berkeley La Raza L.J. 1, 19 (2006).

16. Steven A. Ramirez, *American Corporate Governance and Globalization*, 18 Berkeley La Raza L.J. 47, 63 (2007).

17. Financial Crisis Inquiry Commission, The FinancialCrisis Inquiry Report xxv–xxvi, 419–20 (2011). Notably, the dissent and the majority differ regarding the degree of causation attributable to global capital flows. *Id.*

18. *See* Joseph E. Stiglitz & Andrew Charlton, Fair Trade for All 46–49, 77, 84, 100, 174–77 (2005).

19. Stiglitz, *supra* note 6, at 63–64, 70, and 173–76.

20. Ramirez, *supra* note 15, at 59–63.

21. Stiglitz, *supra* note 6, at 12 and 19.

22. *Id.* at 80.

23. Jagdish Bhagwati, *The Capital Myth: The Difference Between Trade in Widgets and Dollars*, Foreign Aff., May–June 1998, at 7, 10–12 (describing "a definite network of like-minded luminaries among the powerful institutions—Wall Street, the Treasury Department, the State Department, the IMF, and the World Bank . . . which may aptly, if loosely, be called the Wall Street–Treasury Complex").

24. Nagire Woods, *The US, the World Bank and the IMF, in* US Hegemony and International Organizations 93, 102 (Rosemary Foote et al., eds. 2003).

25. *Id.* at 107.

26. *Id.* at 113.

27. Stiglitz, *supra* note 6, at 102.

28. Paul Krugman, The Return of Depression Economics 34–35 (2009).

29. Guatam Sen, *The US and the GATT/WTO System, in* US Hegemony and International Organizations 116 (Rosemary Foote et al., eds. 2003).

30. Stiglitz, *supra* note 4, at 225–26.

31. *See id.*

32. Sen, *supra* note 29, at 131.

33. Stiglitz & Charlton, *supra* note 18, at 159 and 165.

34. *Id.*

35. Sen, *supra* note 29, at 115 and 131.

36. *Id.*

37. *See Europe "Stopped GM Food Imports,"* BBC News, Feb. 7, 2006, http://news.bbc.co.uk/1/hi/business/4688686.stm.

38. Woods, *supra* note 24, at 101–2; Sen, *supra* note 29, at 125.

39. Sen, *supra* note 29, at 125.

40. *Id.* at 134–35.

41. Ramirez, *supra* note 15, at 61–62.

42. Richard N. Cooper, *Understanding Global Imbalances in* Globalization and Growth 95, 107 (M. Spence and D. Leipziger, eds. 2010).

43. Dani Rodrik, *Growth after the Crisis in* Globalization and Growth 125, 126 (M. Spence and D. Leipziger, eds. 2010).

44. Nouriel Roubini and Stephen Mihm, Crisis Economics 238–55 (2010).

45. Henry M. Paulson Jr., On the Brink 439 (2010).

46. Roubini and Mihm, *supra* note 44, at 240–47.

47. Joseph E. Stiglitz, Making Globalization Work 245–68 (2007).

48. *Id.* at 45 and 250–54.

49. Raghuram G. Rajan, Fault Lines 132–33 (2010).

50. Stiglitz, *supra* note 47, at 247–48.

51. Roubini and Mihm, *supra* note 44, at 247.

52. Barry Eichengreen, Globalizing Capital 213–14 (2008).

53. Council of Econ. Advisers, Economic Report of the President 24 (2007), available at http://www.gpoaccess.gov/eop/2007/2007_erp.pdf.

54. Eichengreen, *supra* note 52, at 213.

55. Stiglitz, *supra* note 47, at 10–11, 251, 265, and 270–72.

56. Rajan, *supra* note 49, at 21–45.

57. Barry Eichengreen, Global Imbalances and the Lessons of Bretton Woods 123–24 (2010).

58. IMF, Currency Composition of Official Foreign Exchange Reserves (COFER), Mar. 30, 2012, http://www.imf.org/external/np/sta/cofer/eng/cofer.pdf.

59. Eichengreen, *supra* note 57, at 5.

60. European Central Bank, The International Role of the Euro 10 (2011) *available at* http://www.ecb.int/pub/pdf/other/euro-international-role201107en.pdf.

61. Nouriel Roubini and Stephen Mihm, Crisis Economics 255 (2010).

62. Jeff Faux, Global Class War 192 (2006).

63. Stiglitz, *supra* note 47, at 254.

64. *Id.* at 265.

65. *Id.* at 254–60 and 265; Roubini and Mihm, *supra* note 61, at 1–4.

66. Roubini and Mihm, *supra* note 61, at 1–4. *See also* Paul Krugman, *Running Out of Bubbles*, N.Y. Times, May 27, 2005, http://www.nytimes.com/2005/05/27/opinion/27krugman.html ("the national housing market as a whole looks pretty bubbly").

67. Faux, *supra* note 62, at 192.

68. *After the Fall*, Economist, June 21, 2005, http://www.economist.com/node/4079458?story_id=4079458; *The Dark Side of Debt*, Economist, Sept. 21, 2006, http://www.economist.com/node/7943243. *See also In Come the Waves*, Economist, June 16, 2005, http://www.economist.com/node/4079027?story_id=4079027 ("The worldwide rise in house prices is the biggest bubble in history. Prepare for the economic pain when it pops").

69. Alan S. Blinder, *Offshoring: The Next Industrial Revolution*, Foreign Affairs, Mar./Apr. 2006, at 113–28.

70. Steven A. Ramirez, *American Corporate Governance and Globalization*, 18 Berkeley La Raza L.J. 47, 53–56 (2007).

71. *Id.* at 61–63.

72. Roubini and Mihm, *supra* note 61, at 286.

73. *Id.* at 246–47.

74. Brad Setser & Nouriel Roubini, *How Scary Is the Deficit?*, Foreign Affairs, July/Aug. 2005, 194, 195.

75. Ricardo J. Caballero and Arvind Krishnamurthy, *Global Imbalances and Financial Fragility*, 99 Am. Econ. Rev. 584 (2009).

76. Douglas W. Diamond and Ragurham Rajan, *The Credit Crisis: Conjectures about Causes and Remedies*, 99 Am. Econ. Rev. 606 (2009).

77. Hyman Minsky, Stabilizing an Unstable Economy 281 (2d ed. 2008) ("Over an expansion, new financial instruments and new ways of financing activity develop. Typically, defects of the new ways and new instruments are revealed when the crunch comes").

78. Simon Johnson, *Tax Cutters Set Up Tomorrow's Fiscal Crisis: Simon Johnson*, Bloomberg.com, Dec. 22, 2010, http://www.bloomberg.com/news/2010-12-23/tax-cutters-set-up-tomorrow-s-fiscal-crisis-commentary-by-simon-johnson.html.

79. Matthew Lynn, Bust 243–62 (2011). *See also* Carmen M. Reinhart & Kenneth Rogoff, This Time Is Different: Eight Centuries of Financial Crises 170 (2009) (finding that the "true legacy of banking crises is greater public indebtedness" and that "debt typically increases by 86 percent on average (in real terms) during the three years following the crisis").

80. Faux, *supra* note 62, at 137.

81. Giovanni Peri, *The Effect of Immigrants on U.S. Employment and Productivity*, FRBSF Econ. Ltr., Aug. 2010, at 1–5, available at http://op.bna.com/dlrcases.nsf/id/kpin-88u2nq/$File/SFfedreport.pdf.

82. Edwin Mansfield, Microeconomics 249–50 (1979).

83. Bob Hamilton and John Whalley, *Efficiency and Distributional Implications of Global Restrictions on Labour Mobility: Calculations and Policy Implications,* 14 J. Dev. Econ. 61, 70 (1984).

84. Jonathon W. Moses & Bjorn Letnes, *The Economic Costs to International Labor Restrictions: Revisiting the Empirical Discussion,* 32 World Dev. 1609, 1610 (2004).

85. Gianmarco I.P. Ottaviano and Giovanni Peri, *The Economic Value of Cultural Diversity: Evidence from US Cities,* 6 J. Econ. Geography 9 (2006).

86. Tyler Cowen, *How Immigrants Create More Jobs,* NY Times, Oct. 30, 2010, at BU6.

87. Gabriel J. Felbermayr et al., *Does Immigration Boost Per Capita Income?,* 107 Econ. Letters 177 (2010).

88. Ronald Lee & Timothy Miller, *Immigration, Social Security, and Broader Fiscal Impacts,* 90 Am. Econ. Rev. 350, 351 (2000).

89. Gianmarco I.P. Ottaviano and Giovanni Peri, Rethinking the Effects of Immigration on Wages, NBER Working Paper No. 12497, Aug. 2006, http://www.nber.org/papers/w12497.pdf.

90. Gianmarco I.P. Ottaviano et al., Immigration, Offshoring and American Jobs, NBER Working Paper No. 16439, Oct. 2010, http://papers.nber.org/papers/w16439.

91. Giovanni Peri, *The Effect of Immigrants on U.S. Employment and Productivity,* FRBSF Econ. Ltr., Aug. 30, 2010, http://www.frbsf.org/publications/economics/letter/2010/el2010-26.html.

92. Joseph E. Stiglitz and Andrew Charleton, Fair Trade for All 247–51 (2005).

93. Lant Pritchett, *The Cliff at the Border, in* Equity and Growth in a Globalizing World 263, 271–75 (M. Spence and R. Kanbur, eds. 2010).

94. Gordon H. Hanson, *International Migration and Development, in* Equity and Growth in a Globalizing World 229, 230 (M. Spence and R. Kanbur, eds. 2010).

95. *Id.* at 239.

96. Stiglitz and Charleton, *supra* note 92, at 247–48.

97. Mark R. Rosenzweig, *Global Wage Inequality and the International Flow of Migration, in* Equity and Growth in a Globalizing World 205, 226 (M. Spence and R. Kanbur, eds. 2010).

98. Jennifer Hunt and Marjolaine Gauthier-Loiselle, *How Much Does Immigration Boost Innovation?,* 2 Am. Econ. Rev.: Macroeconomics 31 (2010).

99. Gianmarco I.P. Ottaviano and Giovanni Peri, *The Economic Value of Cultural Diversity: Evidence from US Cities,* 6 J. Econ. Geography 9 (2006).

100. IMF, *supra* note 58.

101. Steven A. Ramirez, *Taking Economic Human Rights Seriously After the Debt Crisis,* 42 Loyola U. Chi. L.J. 713 (2011).

102. Universal Declaration of Human Rights, G.A. Res. 217A (III), at 71, U.N. GAOR, 3d Sess., U.N. Doc. A/810 (Dec. 12, 1948).

103. International Covenant on Economic, Social, and Cultural Rights, opened for signature Dec. 16, 1966, entered into force Jan. 3, 1976, 993 U.N.T.S. 3.

104. Paul Gordon Lauren, The Evolution of Human Rights: Visions Seen 237, 246–47 (1998).

105. Universal Declaration of Human Rights, *supra* note 102, at art. 26.

106. Elhanan Helpman, The Mystery of Economic Growth 41 (2004).

107. Serge Coulombe, Jean Francois Tremblay, & Sylvie Marchand, Literacy Scores, Human Capital and Growth Across Fourteen OECD Countries 31 (2004), *available at* http://www.nald.ca/fulltext/oecd/oecd.pdf.

108. Helpman, *supra* note 106, at 41.

109. *Id.* at 94-100.

110. Philippe Aghion and Peter Howitt, Endogenous Growth Theory 1, 283, 317 (1999).

111. The World Bank, World Development Report 2006: Equity and Development 2 (2005).

112. Raghuram G. Rajan & Luigi Zingales, Saving Capitalism from the Capitalists 28–33, 43 (2003).

113. Raghuram G. Rajan, Fault Lines 34 (2010).

114. Oled Galor et al., *Inequality in Land Ownership, the Emergence of Human Capital Promoting Institutions, and the Great Divergence,* 76 Rev. Econ. Stud. 143 (2009); Dietrich Vollrath, Wealth Distribution and the Provision of Public Goods: Evidence from the United States, University of Houston, Economics Working Paper, 2008-04, Nov. 11, 2008, at 21 (finding inequality to be negatively associated with education funding based upon a cross-sectional analysis of U.S. county-level data in 1890).

115. Era Dabla-Norris & Mark Gradstein, The Distributional Bias of Public Education: Causes and Consequences, IMF Working Paper, Nov. 2004, at 14, *available at* http://papers.ssrn.com/sol3/papers.cfm?abstract_id=879039. Racial and ethnic divisions exacerbate the distributional bias in favor of the rich of funding for education. Mark Gradstein, The Political Economy of Public Spending on Education, Inequality, and Growth, World Bank Working Paper, Nov. 2003, *available at* http://www-wds.worldbank.org/external/default/WDSContentServer/WDSP/IB/2003/12/05/000160016_20031205145559/additional/120520322_20041117150550.pdf.

116. Daron Acemoglu et al., *Economic and Political Inequality in Development: The Case of Cundinamarca, Colombia, in* Institutions and Economic Performance 181 (E. Helpman, ed. 2008).

117. Chris Bramall, Sources of Chinese Economic Growth 1978–1996 107 (2000).

118. Universal Declaration of Human Rights, *supra* note 98, at art. 25.

119. *Id.*

120. World Bank, *supra* note 111, at 6.

121. *Id.*

122. *Id.* at 11.

123. Kwabena Gyimah-Brempong & Mark Wilson, *Health Human Capital and Economic Growth in Sub-Saharan Africa and OECD Countries,* 44 Qrtl'y Rev. Econ. & Fin. 296 (2004).

124. *See* Joseph E. Stiglitz & Andrew Charleton, Free Trade for All 29, 39 (2005).

125. Rajan, *supra* note 113, at 118.

126. Universal Declaration of Human Rights, *supra* note 96, at arts. 2 & 23. The International Covenant for Economic, Social and Cultural rights specifies that all rights articulated therein shall be extended "without discrimination of any kind as to race, colour, sex, language, religion, political or other opinion, national or social origin, property, birth, or other status." International Covenant on Economic Rights, *supra* note 99, at art. 2, sec. 2.

127. Steven A. Ramirez, *What We Teach About When We Teach About Race: The Problem of Law and Pseudo-Economics,* 54 J. Leg. Ed. 365 (2004).

128. The World Bank, World Development Report 2006: Equity and Development 8 (2005).

129. *Id.*

130. *See* Steven A. Ramirez, *A General Theory of Cultural Diversity,* 7 Mich. J. Race & L. 33, 56 n. 148 (2001).

131. Irv Garfinkle et al., Wealth and Welfare States: Is America a Laggard or a Leader? 31–35 (2010).

132. Peter Straub, *Farmers in the IP Wrench—How Patents on Gene-Modified Crops Violate the Right to Food in Developing Countries*, 29 Hastings Int'l Comp. L.J. 187, 206 (2006).

133. Paul Gordon Lauren, The Evolution of Human Rights: Visions Seen 237–59 (1998).

134. Emanuele Baldacci et al., *Social Spending, Human Capital, and Growth in Developing Countries*, 8 World Dev. 1317 (2008).

135. Articles of Agreement of the International Bank for Reconstruction and Development, opened for signature, Dec. 27, 1945, 60 Stat. 1440, T.I.A.S. No. 1502, 2 U.N.T.S. 134, as amended Dec. 16, 1965, 16 U.S.T. 1942, T.I.A.S. No. 5929, at art. I (iii), available at http://siteresources.worldbank.org/EXTABOUTUS/Resources/ibrd-articlesofagreement.pdf.

136. Articles of Agreement of the International Monetary Fund, art. I, Dec. 22, 1945, 60 Stat. 1401, 2 U.N.T.S. 39 available at http://www.imf.org/external/pubs/ft/aa/aa.pdf.

137. Agreement Establishing the World Trade Organization, Apr. 15, 1994, at art. XII, available at http://www.wto.org/english/docs_e/legal_e/04-wto.pdf.

138. Joseph E. Stiglitz, Globalization and Its Discontents 91–92,173–76, 207 (2002).

139. *Id.* at 11–13.

140. Tom Orlick and Bob Davis, *Beijing Diversifies Away from U.S. Dollar*, Wall St. J., Mar. 12, 2012, at A1; *China's Currency Reserves Rise to Record, Domestic Lending Exceeds Target*, Bloomberg, Jan. 11, 2011, http://www.bloomberg.com/news/2011-01-11/china-s-currency-reserves-rise-to-record-domestic-lending-exceeds-target.html; Michael Kitchen, *China Reserves 65% in Dollars, 26% in Euro: Report*, MarketWatch.com, Sept. 3, 2010, http://www.marketwatch.com/story/china-reserves-65-in-dollars-26-in-euro-report-2010-09-03.

141. The Marshall Plan contributed approximately $100 billion for the rebuilding of Europe after World War II. Lawrence Korb & Arnold Kohen, *A Marshall Plan for the Third World*, Boston Globe, Nov. 15, 2005, at A17. For an overview of the scale of the GI Bill, both in terms of outlays as well as consequences, see Steven A. Ramirez, *The Law and Macroeconomics of the New Deal at 70*, 62 Md. L. Rev. 515, 557–59 (2003).

142. *See* Bruce C. Greenwald and Judd Kahn, Globalization 156–60 (2009).

143. Joseph E. Stiglitz, Making Globalization Work 260–68 (2007).

144. *See* Barry Eichengreen, *Out of the Box Thoughts about the International Financial Architecture*, 1 J. Comm. Econ. Pol'y 1, 7 (2010) ("For the SDR to become a true international currency, in other words, the IMF would have to become more like a global central bank and international lender of last resort").

145. *See* Articles of Agreement, *supra* note 130, art. IV, sec. 3(b).

146. Catherine H. Lee, *To Thine Ownself Be True: IMF Conditionality and Erosion of Economic Sovereignty in the Asian Financial Crisis*, 24 U. Pa. J. Int'l Econ. L. 875, 880 (2003).

147. Articles of Agreement, *supra* note 132, at art. IV, sec. 3.

148. Daniel D. Bradlow, *The World Bank, the IMF, and Human Rights*, 6 Transnat'l L. & Contemp. Probs. 47, 50 n. 13 (1996).

149. *See* Ariel Buira, *An Analysis of IMF Conditionality, in* Challenges to the World Bank and IMF 55, 62 (Ariel Buira, ed., 2003).

150. *See* Articles of Agreement of the International Bank for Reconstruction and Development, opened for signature, Dec. 27, 1945, 60 Stat. 1440, T.I.A.S. No. 1502, 2 U.N.T.S. 134, as amended Dec. 16, 1965, 16 U.S.T. 1942, T.I.A.S. No. 5929, available at http://siteresources.worldbank.org/EXTABOUTUS/Resources/ibrd-articlesofagreement.pdf.

151. Bradlow, *supra* note 148, at 63.

152. Stiglitz, *supra* note 138, at 16.

153. Human rights barely merited a mention in the Bank's review of conditionality. *See* World Bank, Review of Conditionality (2005), available at http://siteresources.worldbank.org/PROJECTS/Resources/40940-1114615847489/webConditionalitysept05.pdf.

154. Like the IMF, the World Bank is prohibited by its charter from interfering in domestic politics. *See* Bradlow, *supra* note 148, at 54–62.

155. Nouriel Roubini and Stephen Mihm, Crisis Economics 247 (2010).

156. *See* Agreement Establishing the WTO, *supra* note 131, at art. XII, 1 (allowing new members to accede to WTO membership "on terms to be agreed between it and the WTO").

157. Stiglitz & Charleton, *supra* note 124, at 57–163.

158. Charles Derber, People Before Profit 148–51 (2002).

159. Stiglitz & Charleton, *supra* note 124, at 46–47.

160. Lant Pritchett, *The Cliff at the Border, in* Globalization and Growth 276 (M. Spence and D. Leipziger, eds. 2010).

161. Jennifer Gordon, *People Are Not Bananas: How Immigration Differs from Trade*, 104 Nw. L. Rev. 1109, 1145 (2010).

162. The World Bank, World Development Report 2006: Equity and Development (2005).

163. *Id.* at 17.

164. Philippe Aghion et al., *Inequality and Economic Growth: The Perspective of the New Growth Theories*, 37 J. Econ. Lit. 1615, 1615 (1999).

165. The World Bank, *supra* note 162, at 1–2.

166. *Id.*

167. William Easterly, *Inequality Does Cause Underdevelopment: Insights from a New Instrument*, 84 J. Dev. Econ. 755 (2007).

168. *Id.* at 773.

169. Era Dabla-Norris & Mark Gradstein, The Distributional Bias of Public Education: Causes and Consequences, IMF Working Paper, Nov. 2004, at 14 http://papers.ssrn.com/sol3/papers.cfm?abstract_id=879039.

170. *See* Glenn C. Loury, The Anatomy of Racial Inequality 70–71 (2002).

171. *Id.*

172. *See* Inaamul Haque & Ruxandra Burdescu, *Monterrey Consensus on Financing for Development: Response Sought from International Economic Law*, 27 B.C. Int'l & Comp. L. Rev. 219, 226 (2004) ("Poverty involves multiple deprivations and is indeed a denial of the most basic human rights: the right to freedom from hunger and malnutrition, the right to healthcare and education, the right to make one's own choices, and the right to development").

173. Ramirez, *supra* note 127, at 371.

174. *See* Jeff Faux, The Global Class War 1 (2006) ("Markets . . . inevitably produce . . . people who have more money and power than others. So, it would be odd if global markets were *not* creating an international upper class . . . whose economic interests have more in common with each other than with the majority of people who share their nationality").

175. *Id.* at 1, 3.

176. *Id.*

177. Eric C. Chaffee, *The Internationalization of Securities Regulation: The United States Government's Role in Regulating the Global Capital Markets*, 5 J. Bus. & Tech. L. 187, 190–93 (2010).

178. Joseph E. Stiglitz, Globalization and Its Discontents 74, 81, 139, 220, 233, 226–40, 249 (2002).

179. United Nations, Report of the Commission of Experts of the President of the United Nations General Assembly on Reforms of the International Monetary and Financial System 8, 16, 47–87, 103 (2010), *available at* http://www.un.org/ga/econcrisissummit/docs/FinalReport_CoE.pdf.

180. *Id.* at 135.

181. *Id.* at 87, 88, 91, 93, 97, and 135.

182. *Id.* at 96.

183. *Id.* at 18, 43, 100, 105, 132, and 133–34.

184. *Id.* at 47–87.

185. *Id.*

186. Stiglitz, *supra* note 178, at 81, 139, 220, 233, 226–40.

187. Eric C. Chafee, *Finishing the Race to the Bottom: An Argument for Harmonization and Centralization of International Securities Law*, 40 Seton Hall L. Rev. 1581, 1618 (2010) ("despite the promise of a new foundation for financial supervision and regulation, the United States and the world's other securities regulators have left in place the cracked and fragmented foundation that was in place prior to the financial crisis that began in 2008").

188. Stiglitz, *supra* note 178, at xii.

189. Steven A. Ramirez, *Market Fundamentalism's New Fiasco: Globalization as Exhibit B in the Case for a New Law and Economics,* 24 Mich. J. Int'l L. 831, 853 (2004) (review of Joseph E. Stiglitz, Globalization and Its Discontents (2002)).

190. Steven A. Ramirez, *The Dodd-Frank Act as Maginot Line*, 14 Chapman L. Rev.109 (2010).

CHAPTER 5

1. Dr. Martin Luther King, Speech at Western Michigan University, Dec. 18, 1963, http://www.wmich.edu/library/archives/mlk/transcription.html.

2. Paul M. Romer, *Economic Growth, in* The Concise Encyclopedia of Economics 183 (D. Henderson, ed. 1993), *available at* http://www.econlib.org/library/Enc/EconomicGrowth.html.

3. World Bank, World Development Report 2006 1–18 (2005).

4. Financial Crisis Inquiry Commssion, Financial Crisis Inquiry Report 111 (2011).

5. *Id.* at 8.

6. Stephen J. McNamee and Robert K. Miller, The Meritocracy Myth 189 (2009).

7. Daniel Golden, The Price of Admission 1, 1–21 (2006).

8. Jerome Karabel, The Chosen: The Hidden History of Admission and Exclusion at Harvard, Yale and Princeton 135 (2006).

9. Jonathan Gayles, *Steroids and Standardised Tests: Meritocracy and the Myth of Fair Play in the United States*, 35 Educ. Stud. 1 (2009).

10. Jonathan Kozol, The Shame of a Nation: The Restoration of Apartheid Schooling in America 7, 280–83 (2005).

11. *Id.* at 321–24.

12. Michael Paris, Framing Equal Opportunity 41 (2010).

13. Geraldine Fabrikant, *At Elite Prep Schools, College-Size Endowments*, N.Y. Times, 2008, Jan. 28, 2008, http://www.nytimes.com/2008/01/26/business/26prep.html.

14. Marianne Bertrand and Sendhil Mullainathan, *Are Emily and Greg More Employable Than Lakisha and Jamal? A Field Experiment on Labor Market Discrimination*, 94 Am. Econ. Rev. 991, 1006 (2004).

15. Bentley Coffey and Patrick A. McLaughlin, *Do Masculine Names Help Female Lawyers Become Judges? Evidence from South Carolina*, 11 Am. L. & Econ. Rev. 112 (2009).

16. Shelley J. Correll et al., *Getting a Job: Is There a Motherhood Penalty?*, 112 Am. J. Soc. 1297 (2007).

17. Ian Ayers et al., *To Insure Prejudice: Racial Disparities in Taxicab Tipping*, 114 Yale L.J. 1613 (2005).

18. David R. Hekman et al., *An Examination of Whether and How Racial and Gender Biases Influence Customer Satisfaction*, 53 Acad. Mgmt. J. 238 (2010).

19. Kerwin Kofi Charles and Jonathan Guryan, *Prejudice and Wages: An Empirical Assessment of Becker's "The Economics of Discrimination*," 118 J. Poli. Econ. 773 (2008).

20. Catalyst, 2005 Catalyst Census of Women Corporate Officers and Top Earners of the Fortune 500 10, 22 (2006), *available at* http://www.catalyst.org/file/207/2005%20cote.pdf.

21. Scott Pelley, *Homeless Children: The Hard Times Generation*, CBSNews.com, Mar. 6, 2011, http://www.cbsnews.com/stories/2011/03/06/60minutes/main20038927.shtml?tag=conten tMain;cbsCarousel.

22. *One in 4 Young Children Live in Poverty*, UPI.com, Sept. 23, 2011, www.upi. com/Health_News/2011/09/23/One-in-4-young-children-live-in-poverty/ UPI-43941316835582/#ixzz1ZemYVA8N.

23. Carol Morello and Ted Mellnik, *Hispanic Kids the Largest Group of Children Living in Poverty*, Wash. Post, Sept. 28, 2011, http://www.washingtonpost.com/local/hispanic-kids-the-largest-group-of-children-living-in-poverty/2011/09/28/gIQArfC54K_story.html.

24. UNICEF, Child Poverty in Rich Countries 2005 04 (2005), *available at* http://www.unicef-irc.org/publications/pdf/repcard6e.pdf.

25. Joseph E. Stiglitz, Freefall xix (2010).

26. Financial Crisis Inquiry Commission, *supra* note 4, at 12, 18–19.

27. McKinsey & Co., The Economic Impact of the Achievement Gap in America's Schools 5–6 (2009).

28. Paul Krugman, *Banks Gone Wild*, N.Y. Times, Nov. 23, 2007, http://www.nytimes. com/2007/11/23/opinion/23krugman.html.

29. Peggy Noonan, *There's No Pill for This Kind of Depression*, Wall St. J., Mar. 12, 2009, *available at* http://www.peggynoonan.com/article.php?article=460.

30. Financial Crisis Inquiry Commission, *supra* note 4, at 19.

31. Shaohua Chen and Martin Ravallion, *The Developing World Is Poorer Than We Thought, But No Less Successful in the Fight against Poverty* (table 5) (World Bank Policy Research Paper, Working Paper No. 4703, Aug. 2008), *available at* http://www-wds.worldbank.org/ servlet/WDSContentServer/WDSP/IB/2010/01/21/000158349_20100121133109/Rendered/ PDF/WPS4703.pdf.

32. World Bank, *supra* note 3, at xii (Foreword by World Bank President Paul D. Wolfowitz).

33. World Bank, *supra* note 3, at 6.

34. *Id.* at 2.

35. Steven A. Ramirez, *Bearing the Costs of Racial Inequality:* Brown *and the Myth of the Equality/Efficiency Trade-Off*, 44 Washburn L.J. 87 (2004).

36. *Id.*

37. Steven A. Ramirez, *Endogenous Growth Theory, Status Quo Efficiency and Globalization*, 17 Berkeley La Raza L.J. 1, 4 (2006).

38. World Bank, *supra* note 3, at 5–6.

39. *Id.* at 6.

40. *Id.* at 8 (citing Karla Hoff and Priyanka Pandey, *Economic Consequences of Social Identity: Discrimination, Social Identity, and Durable Inequalities,* 96 Am. Econ. Rev. 206 (2008)).

41. John Ogbu, *Immigrant and Involuntary Minorities in Comparative Perspective,* in Minority Status & Schooling 3, 13–27 (1991).

42. Joel L. Kincheloe & Shirley R. Steinberg, *Who Said It Can't Happen Here?, in* Measured Lies: The Bell Curve Examined 3, 7, 23 (Kincheloe et al. eds., 1996).

43. Sally M. Grantham-McGregor et al., *Effects of Early Childhood Supplementation with and Without Stimulation on Later Development in Stunted Jamaican Children,* 66 Am. J. Clin. Nutr. 247 (1997).

44. World Bank, *supra* note 3, at 11.

45. *Id.*

46. *Id.*

47. *Id. See also* Emanuele Baldacci et al., *Social Spending, Human Capital, and Growth in Developing Countries,* 36 World Dev. 1317 (2008) ("Both education and health spending have a positive and significant direct impact on the accumulation of human capital, and a positive and significant impact on growth").

48. Peter Lindert, Growing Public: Social Spending and Economic Growth Since the Eighteenth Century (2004).

49. Human Genome Project, Genetic Anthropology, Ancestry, and Ancient Human Migration, http://www.ornl.gov/sci/techresources/Human_Genome/elsi/humanmigration.shtml (last visited Mar. 11, 2011).

50. Luigi Luca Cavalli-Sforza, Genes, Peoples, and Languages 9–13 (2000).

51. Steven A. Ramirez, *A General Theory of Cultural Diversity,* 7 Mich. J. Race L. 33, 40–52 (2001).

52. *See* Rachel Moran, *Loving and the Legacy of Unintended Consequences,* 2007 Wisc. L. Rev. 239, 243–50.

53. Ian Haney Lopez, White by Law 38, 43 (1996).

54. Steven A. Ramirez, *A General Theory of Cultural Diversity,* 7 Mich. J. Race & L. 33 (2001).

55. Ian F. Haney Lopez, *The Social Construction of Race: Some Observations on Illusion, Fabrication, and Choice,* 29 Harv. C.R.-C.L. L. Rev. 1, 7 (1994).

56. Lani Guinier and Gerald Torres, The Miner's Canary 31 (2002).

57. Kwame Anthony Appiah and Henry Louis Gates Jr., Civil Rights: An A–Z Reference of the Movement That Changed America 71–72, 222–23, 397–98 (2004).

58. Brown v. Board of Education, 347 U.S.483, 495 (1954).

59. Ruqaiijah Yearby, *Does Twenty-Five Years Make a Difference in Unequal Treatment? The Persistence of Racial Disparities in Healthcare Then and Now,* 19 Annals Health L. 57 (2010).

60. *Id.*

61. Robert S. Levine et al., *Black–White Inequalities in Mortality and Life Expectancy, 1933–1999: Implications for Healthy People 2010,* 116 Pub. Health Rep. 474, 475, 480–82 (2001).

62. Jim Blascovich et al., *African Americans and High Blood Pressure: The Role of Stereotype Threat,* 12 Psycho. Sci. 225 (2001).

63. Michelle Alexander, The New Jim Crow 6–7 (2010).

64. U.S. Dept. of Justice, Prevalence of Imprisonment in the U.S. Population, 1974–2001 1 (2003), *available at* http://www.ojp.usdoj.gov/bjs/pub/ascii/piuspo1.txt.

65. Alexander, *supra* note 63, at 1–2, 95–136.

66. Claude Steele & Joshua Aronson, *Stereotype Threat and the Intellectual Test Performance of African Americans,* 69 J. Pers. Soc. Psychol. 797 (1995). *See also* Steven J. Spencer, Claude

M. Steele, & Diane M. Quinn, *Stereotype Threat and Women's Math Performance*, 35 J. of Experimental and Soc. Psych. 4 (1999) (showing operation of stereotype threat regarding women and math).

67. World Bank, *supra* note 3, at 11.

68. Dedrick Muhammad et al., The State of the Dream 2004: Enduring Disparities in Black and White 11 (2004), *available at* http://www.faireconomy.org/files/pdf/Stateofthe-Dream2004.pdf.

69. Amparo Castelló-Climent and Rafael Doménech, *Human Capital Inequality, Life Expectancy and Economic Growth*, 118 Econ. J. 653 (2008).

70. Muhammad et al., *supra* note 68, at 12, 13.

71. Kenneth J. Arrow, *What Has Economics to Say About Racial Discrimination?*, 12 J. Econ. Persp. 91, 92–96 (1998) (citing William A. Darity Jr. & Patrick L. Mason, *Evidence on Discrimination in Employment: Codes of Color, Codes of Gender*, 12 J. Econ. Persp. 63, 87 (1998) ("the strong evidence of persistent discrimination in labor markets calls into question any theoretical apparatus that implies that the discrimination must inevitably diminish or disappear"); John Yinger, *Evidence of Discrimination in Consumer Markets* 12 J. Econ. Persp. 23, 38 (1998) ("ongoing discrimination violates principles that are central to our democracy and imposes high costs both on black and African American households, whose choices are restricted, and on all Americans, who must deal with the hostility and lost opportunities that are its offspring").

72. Kerwin Kofi Charles and Jonathan Guryan, *Prejudice and Wages: An Empirical Assessment of Becker's "The Economics of Discrimination,"* 118 J. Poli. Econ. 773, 775 (2008).

73. Andrew F. Brimmer, *The Economic Cost of Discrimination Against Black Americans*, in Economic Perspectives on Affirmative Action 11, 12, 13 (M. Simms, ed. 1995).

74. *Id. See also* Leonard M. Baynes, *Falling Through the Cracks: Race and Corporate Law Firms*, 77 St. John's L. Rev. 785, 791 (2003) (showing impaired opportunities for lawyers of color in law firms).

75. Brimmer, *supra* note 73, at 20.

76. *Id.* at 12 and 29.

77. United States Census Bureau, Income, Poverty, and Health Insurance Coverage in the United States: 2009 6 (2010), *available at* http://www.census.gov/prod/2010pubs/p60-238.pdf.

78. Population Research Bureau, *In the News: U.S. Population Is Now One-Third Minority*, PRB.org, May 2006, http://www.prb.org/Articles/2006/IntheNewsUSPopulationIsNowOneThirdMinority.aspx?p=1U.S.

79. McKinsey & Co., The Economic Impact of the Achievement Gap in America's Schools 5–6 (2009), *available at* http://www.mckinsey.com/clientservice/Social_Sector/our_practices/Education/Knowledge_Highlights/Economic_impact.aspx.

80. United States Census Bureau, *supra* note 77, at 11.

81. Irving L. Janis, Groupthink: Psychological Studies of Policy Decisions and Fiascoes 250 (2d ed. 1982). *See also* Irving L. Janis, Victims of Groupthink: A Psychological Study of Foreign-policy Decisions and Fiascoes (1972).

82. *See generally* Henri Tajfel, *Experiments in Intergroup Discrimination*, 223 Sci. Am. 96 (1970).

83. Jacob M. Rabbie and Murray Horwitz, *Arousal of Ingroup-Outgroup Bias by a Chance Win or Loss*, 13 J. Personality & Soc. Psychol. 269 (1969).

84. Nilanjana Dasgupta, *Implicit Ingroup Favoritism, Outgroup Favoritism, and Their Behavior Manifestations*, 17 Soc. Justice Res. 143, 163 (2004).

85. Anthony G. Greenwald et al., *A Unified Theory of Implicit Attitudes, Stereotypes, Self-Esteem, and Self-Concept*, 109 Psychol. Rev. 3 (2002).

86. Mary Kreiner Ramirez, *Into the Twilight Zone: Informing Judicial Discretion in Federal Sentencing*, 57 Drake L. Rev. 591, 638–39 (2009); Michael E. Murphy, *The Nominating Process for Corporate Boards of Directors: A Decision-Making Analysis*, 5 Berkeley Bus. L.J. 131, 160 (2008).

87. Andrew Scott Baron and Mahzarin R. Banaji, *The Development of Implicit Attitudes: Evidence of Race Evaluations from Ages 6 and 10 and Adulthood*, 17 Psychol. Sci. 53 (2005).

88. James R. Elliott and Ryan A. Smith, *Race, Gender and Workplace Power*, 69 Am. Soc. Rev. 365 (2004).

89. James D. Westphal & Edward J. Zajac, *Who Shall Govern?: CEO/Board Power, Demographic Similarity, and New Director Selection*, 40 Admin. Sci. Q. 60, 77 (1995).

90. Ivan E. Brick et al., *CEO Compensation, Director Compensation, and Firm Performance: Evidence of Cronyism?*, 12 J. Corp. Fin. 402, 404, 421–22 (2006).

91. Poppy Lauretta McLeod et al., *Ethnic Diversity and Creativity in Small Groups*, 27 Small Group Res. 248, 252 (1996).

92. David A. Carter et al., *Corporate Governance, Board Diversity and Firm Value*, 38 Fin. Rev. 33, 36 (2003).

93. Maureen I. Muller-Kahle and Krista B. Lewellyn, *Did Board Configuration Matter? The Case of US Subprime Lenders*, 19 Corp. Gov.: An Int'l Rev. 405 (2011).

94. Gianmarco I.P. Ottaviano and Giovanni Peri, *The Economic Value of Cultural Diversity: Evidence from U.S. Cities*, 6 J. Econ. Geog. 9, 11 (2006).

95. Nicholas A. Bowman, *College Diversity Experiences and Cognitive Development: A Meta-Analysis*, 80 Rev. Educ. Res. 4, 22 (2010).

96. U.S. Department of Justice, *Annual Determination of Average Cost of Incarceration*, Fed. Reg., Feb. 3, 2011, http://www.federalregister.gov/articles/2011/02/03/2011-2363/annual-determination-of-average-cost-of-incarceration.

97. Predatory Lending Practices: Hearing Before the H. Comm. on Banking & Fin. Servs., 106th Cong. 25 (2000) (testimony of William Apgar, Assistant Secretary for Housing and Federal Housing Commissioner), *available at* http://financialservices.house.gov/banking/52400apg.htm.

98. Edward Gramlich, *Subprime Mortgage Lending*, Nat'l Mortgage News, May 31, 2004, at 4.

99. Greg Ip, *Did Greenspan Add to Subprime Woes?*, Wall St. J., June 7, 2010, at B1.

100. Steven L. Ross et al., *Mortgage Lending in Chicago and Los Angeles: A Paired Testing Study of the Pre-application Process*, 63 J. Urban Econ. 908 (2008).

101. Richard Williams et al., *The Changing Face of Inequality in Home Mortgage Lending*, 52 Soc. Problems 181 (2005).

102. Amaad Riveria et al., Foreclosed: State of the Dream 2008 14 (2008), *available at* http://www.faireconomy.org/files/pdf/StateOfDream_01_16_ 08_Web.pdf.

103. Elvin K. Wyly, *The Subprime State of Race*, in The Blackwell Companion to the Economics of Housing: The Housing Wealth of Nations 381, 387–405 (2010).

104. John A. Karikari, Neighborhood Patterns of Racial Steering of Subprime Mortgage Lending, Sept. 23, 2009, at 20, *available at* http://papers.ssrn.com/sol3/papers.cfm?abstract_id=1439854 (finding in 2005 that evidence suggested racial steering away from low-cost FHA loans in five major metropolitan cities that have been severely affected by subprime lending).

105. Debbie Gruenstein Bocian et al., *Race, Ethnicity and Subprime Home Loan Pricing*, 60 J. Econ. Bus. 110, 121 (2008) (depending on the loan product "all else being equal, the odds

of an African-American borrower receiving a higher-rate loan range from 1.17 to 1.84 times greater than for a non-Latino white borrower" and "the odds of a Latino borrower receiving a higher-rate loan range from 1.52 to 2.89 times greater than for a non-Latino white borrower").

106. Charlie Savage, *Justice Department Fights Bias in Lending*, N.Y. Times, Jan. 10, 2010, at A18.

107. John L. Ropiequet et al., *Fair Lending Developments: The End of Discretionary Pricing?*, 65 Bus. Law. 571 (2010); Katherine Skiba, *Settlement Announced over Countrywide Loans*, Chi. Trib., Dec. 11, 2011, http://articles.chicagotribune.com/2011-12-21/news/chi-settlement-announced-over-countrywide-loans-20111221_1_countrywide-loans-dan-frahm-full-spectrum-lending.

108. Austin Kilgore, *Former Employees Allege Reverse Redlining at Wells Fargo*, Housing Wire, Jan. 10, 2010, *available at* http://www.housingwire.com/2010/01/04/former-employees-allege-reverse-redlining-at-wells-fargo/; Michael Powell, *Bank Accused of Pushing Mortgage Deals on Blacks*, N.Y. Times, June 7, 2009, at A16 (quoting former Wells Fargo employees in Maryland who attest that Wells Fargo targeted African American borrowers for subprime loans, referred to such borrowers as "mud people," and the "company put 'bounties' on minority borrowers"). See also Ruth Simon, *Court Hits Wells Over Mortgages*, Wall St. J., Nov. 11, 2011, http://online.wsj.com/article/SB10001424052970204621904577014301671480044.html (reporting on lawsuit brought by the state of Illinois which "alleges that Wells Fargo Home Mortgage provided financial incentives for employees to steer borrowers eligible for prime mortgages into more costly and riskier mortgage loans").

109. Williams et al., *supra* note 101, at 198.

110. Elvin Wyly et al., *Cartographies of Race and Class: Mapping the Class-Monopoly Rents of American Subprime Mortgage Capital*, 33 Int'l J. Urban Reg. Res. 332, 339 (2009).

111. *Id.* at 33–34.

112. Kristopher Gerardi, Financial Literacy and Subprime Mortgage Delinquency: Evidence from a Survey Matched to Administrative Data, FRB Atlanta Working Paper 2010-10, Apr. 2010, http://www.frbatlanta.org/documents/pubs/wp/wp1010.pdf.

113. *Id.* Wyly, *supra* note 110, at 10, 21.

114. *Id.* at 3, 24, and 46.

115. Written Testimony of Benjamin Clark of the National Fair Housing Alliance, Submitted to Raquel Rolnik, United Nations Special Rapporteur on Adequate Housing, October 26, 2009, *available at* http://www.nationalfairhousing.org/Portals/33/B%20%20%20Clark%20Testimony%20for%20UN%20Special%20Rapporteur.pdf.

116. Simon Johnson and James Kwak, 13 Bankers 6, 115, 203 (2010).

117. Paul Krugman, *Bigger Than Bush*, N.Y. Times, Jan. 1, 2009, http://www.nytimes.com/2009/01/02/opinion/02krugman.html.

118. Paul Krugman, *Reagan Did It*, N.Y. Times, May 31, 2009, http://www.nytimes.com/2009/06/01/opinion/01krugman.html.

119. Lee Hockstader, Michael Steele says Something . . . Sensible?!, Wash. Post., Apr. 23, 2010, http://voices.washingtonpost.com/postpartisan/2010/04/michael_steele_says_somethings.html.

120. Mike Allen, *RNC Chief to Say It Was "Wrong" to Exploit Racial Conflict for Votes*, Wash. Post, July 14, 2005, http://www.washingtonpost.com/wp-dyn/content/article/2005/07/13/AR2005071302342.html.

121. David Brooks, *History and Calumny*, N.Y. Times, Nov. 9, 2007, http://www.nytimes.com/2007/11/09/opinion/09brooks.html.

122. Garn–St. Germain Depository Institutions Act of 1982, Pub L. No. 97-320, 96 Stat. 1469 (codified as amended at 12 U.S.C. § 3901-3806 (2006)).

123. Johnson and Kwak, *supra* note 116, at 72.

124. Pub. L. 98-440, § 101, 98 Stat. 1689 (1984) (codified as amended at 15 U.S.C. § 78c(a)(41) (1988)).

125. Joseph C. Shenker & Anthony J. Colletta, *Asset Securitization: Evolution, Current Issues and New Frontiers,* 69 Tex. L. Rev. 1369, 1386 (1991).

126. Paul Frymer, *Race, Representation and Elections: The Politics of Parties and Courts, in* American Politics and Society Today 56 (Robert Singh, ed. 2002) (quoting Stanley B. Greenberg, "Report on Democratic Defection," report to the Democratic Party, Apr. 15, 1985, p. 13); Stanley B. Greenberg, Middle Class Dreams: The Politics and Power of the New American Majority 39 (rev. ed. 1996).

127. Frymer, *supra* note 126, at 67.

128. Glenn C. Loury, The Anatomy of Racial Inequality 70–71, 201 (2002).

129. Democratic National Committee, The Democratic Platform for America: Strong at Home, Respected in the World 18 (2004).

130. Republican National Committee, 2004 Republican Party Platform: A Safer World and a More Hopeful America 74 (2004).

131. United States Department of the Treasury, Blueprint for a Modernized Financial Regulatory Structure 6, 81 (2008), *available at* http://www.treasury.gov/press-center/press-releases/Documents/Blueprint.pdf.

132. Johnson and Kwak, *supra* note 116, at 143.

133. *E.g.,* OCC, Preemption Determination and Order, 68 Fed. Reg. 46,264 (Aug. 5, 2003); Letter from Carolyn J. Buck, Chief Counsel, Office of Thrift Supervision, Department of the Treasury (Jan. 21, 2003) (concluding that federal law preempts application of various provisions of the Georgia Fair Lending Act to federal savings associations and their operating subsidiaries), *available at* http://www.ots.treas.gov/_files/56301.pdf (last visited May 10, 2010).

134. *E.g.,* Watters v. Wachovia Bank, 550 U.S. 1 (2007).

135. andré douglas pond cummings, *Racial Coding and the Financial Markets,* 2011 Utah L. Rev. 1, 8, 63–75 (2011).

136. *Id.* at 72 (citing Neil Bhutta & Glenn B. Canner, *Did the CRA Cause the Mortgage Market Meltdown?,* Fed. Res. Bank of Minneapolis, Mar. 2009, http://www.minneapolisfed.org/publications_papers/pub_display.cfm?id=4136).

137. Federal Housing Finance Agency, Conservator's Report on the Enterprises' Financial Performance Second Quarter 2011 14 (2011), http://www.fhfa.gov/webfiles/22615/ConservatorsReport2Q2011.pdf.

138. Financial Crisis Inquiry Commission, The Financial Crisis Inquiry Report xxvi, 414, 417–19, 437 (2011).

139. Charles R. Lawrence III & Mari J. Matsuda, We Won't Go Back: Making the Case for Affirmative Action 26 (1997).

140. Anne Lawton, The *Meritocracy Myth and the Illusion of Equal Employment Opportunity,* 85 Minn. L. Rev. 587, 599–602 (2000).

141. Sumi Cho, *Post-Racialism,* 94 Iowa L. Rev. 1589 (2009).

142. Steven A. Ramirez, *A General Theory of Cultural Diversity,* 7 Mich. J. Race L. 33 (2001).

143. Steven A. Ramirez, *The New Cultural Diversity and Title VII,* 6 Mich. J. Race L.127 (2000).

144. Steven A. Ramirez, *Games CEOs Play: Why Diversity Lags in the Boardroom and What to Do About It,* 61 Wash. & Lee L. Rev. 1583 (2004).

145. Lani Guinier and Gerald Torres, The Miner's Canary 30–31, 67–107, 294 (2002).

146. Richard Delgado, *Linking Arms: Recent Books on Interracial Coalition as an Avenue of Social Reform*, 88 Cornell L. Rev. 855, 885 (2003).

CHAPTER 6

1. Charles P. Kindleberger, Manias, Panics and Crashes: A History of Financial Crises 220–21 (4th ed. 2000).

2. *Id.* at 1–2.

3. Hyman P. Minsky, Stabilizing an Unstable Economy 324–29 (rev. ed. 2008).

4. Robert E. Lucas Jr., *Economic Priorities*, 93 Am. Econ. Rev. 1 (2003).

5. Richard C. Koo, The Holy Grail of Macroeconomics 11, 13, 16, 19, 26–27, 28–38 (2008).

6. *A Special Report on Debt: Repent at Leisure,* The Economist, June 24, 2010, http://www. economist.com/node/16397110?story_id=16397110.

7. Chairman Alan Greenspan, Understanding Today's International Financial System, Remarks Before the 34th Annual Conference on Bank Structure and Competition of the Federal Reserve Bank of Chicago (May 7, 1998), www.federalreserve.gov/boarddocs/ speeches/1998/19980507.htm.

8. Bill Barnhart, *Dow Drops 684 Points as Trading Resumes,* Chi. Trib., Sept. 17, 2001, http:// www.chicagotribune.com/business/chi-010917markets,0,5287650.story.

9. John Maynard Keynes, The General Theory of Employment, Interest and Money 161–62 (Great Minds ed. 1991) (1936).

10. Dimitri B. Papadimitriou, *Minsky's* Stabilizing an Unstable Economy: *Two Decades Later, in* Hyman P. Minsky, Stabilizing an Unstable Economy xvii–xviii (2008).

11. *Id.* at 324.

12. Steven A. Ramirez, *The Law and Macroeconomics of the New Deal at 70,* 62 Md. L. Rev. 515 (2003).

13. Dawn Kopecki and Catherine Dodge, *U.S. Rescue May Reach $23.7 Trillion, Barofsky Says,* Bloomberg, July 20, 2009, http://www.bloomberg.com/apps/news?pid=newsarchive&sid= aYotX8UysIaM.

14. United States General Accountability Office, Federal Reserve System: Opportunities Exist to Strengthen Policies and Processes for Managing Emergency Assistance 131 (2011), *available at* http://www.gao.gov/new.items/d11696.pdf.

15. *Id.* at 149.

16. Thomas Ferguson and Robert Johnson, *Too Big to Bail: The "Paulson Put," Presidential Politics, and the Global Financial Meltdown (Part I),* 38 Int'l J. Pol. Econ. 3, 25 (2009).

17. Thomas Ferguson and Robert Johnson, *Too Big to Bail: The "Paulson Put" Presidential Politics, and the Global Financial Meltdown (Part II),* 38 Int'l J. Pol. Econ. 5, 13 (2009).

18. *E.g.,* Christian A. Johnson, *Exigent and Unusual Circumstances: The Federal Reserve and the U.S. Financial Crisis,* __ Euro. Bus. Org. L. Rev. __ (2010).

19. Simon Johnson, *Silent Coup,* The Atlantic, May 2009, http://www.theatlantic.com/ magazine/archive/2009/05/the-quiet-coup/7364/.

20. Simon Johnson, *Tax Cutters Set Up Tomorrow's Fiscal Crisis: Simon Johnson,* Bloomberg, Dec. 22, 2010, http://www.bloomberg.com/news/2010-12-23/tax-cutters-set-up-tomorrow-s-fiscal-crisis-commentary-by-simon-johnson.html.

21. *See* Koo, *supra* note 5, at xiv.

22. *See* William H. Gross, PIMCO Investment Outlook, Six Pac(k)in', Oct. 2011, http://www. pimco.com/EN/Insights/Pages/SixPackin.aspx ("almost all remedies proposed by global

authorities to date have approached the problem from the standpoint of favoring capital as opposed to labor").

23. Alan Abel and Ben Bernanke, Macroeconomics 266–69, 522–32 (5th ed. 2005).

24. *See* Steven A. Ramirez, *Depoliticizing Financial Regulation,* 41 Wm. & Mary L. Rev. 503, 542 (2000).

25. *Id.* at 526–27.

26. *See* Koo, *supra* note 5, at 2–3.

27. *E.g.,* David C. Wheelock, *Monetary Policy in the Great Depression: What the Fed Did and Why,* Fed. Res. Bank St. Louis Rev., Mar./Apr. 1992, at 3.

28. Steven A. Ramirez, *The Law and Macroeconomic of the New Deal at 70,* 62 Md. L. Rev. 515, 540 (2003).

29. Ramirez, *supra* note 24, at 522–25 and 553.

30. Robert Schiller, Irrational Exuberance 224–30 (2nd ed. 2005).

31. Telis Demos, *Dudley Calls for Regulation to Combat Bubbles,* FT.com, Apr. 7, 2010, available at http://www.ft.com/cms/s/0/44e5da90-426f-11df-8c60-00144feabdco.html.

32. Steven A. Ramirez, *Fear and Social Capitalism: The Law and Macroeconomics of Investor Confidence,* 42 Washburn L.J. 31, 48, 68–70, 69 n. 236 (2002).

33. Timothy A. Canova, *Financial Market Failure as a Crisis in the Rule of Law: From Market Fundamentalism to a New Keynesian Regulatory Model,* 3 Harv. L. & Pol'y Rev. 369 (2009).

34. Federal Reserve Board of Governors, The Federal Reserve System Purposes & Functions 3–5 (9th ed. 2005).

35. Hyman P. Minsky, Stabilizing an Unstable Economy 362 (2nd ed. 2008).

36. Shahien Nasiripour, *Stiglitz, Nobel Prize–Winning Economist, Says Federal Reserve System "Corrupt,"* HuffingtonPost, Mar. 5, 2010, http://www.huffingtonpost.com/2010/03/03/stiglitz-nobel-prize-winn_n_484943.html.

37. Ramirez, *supra* note 24, at 542–43.

38. Federal Reserve Board, *supra* note 25, at 13.

39. Robert E. Hall and Susan Woodward, The Fed Needs to Make a Policy Statement, Apr. 9, 2009, available at http://www.voxeu.org/index.php?q=node/3444.

40. Scott Sumner, *Have We Misdiagnosed the Crisis?,* The American, Oct. 8, 2009, available at http://www.american.com/archive/2009/october/have-we-misdiagnosed-the-crisis.

41. Michael R. Crittenden and Marshall Eckblad, *Lending Falls at Epic Pace,* Wall St. J., Feb. 24, 2010 at A1.

42. Mark Whitehouse, *Number of the Week: Companies' Cash Hoard Grows,* WSJ.com, Mar. 11, 2011, http://blogs.wsj.com/economics/2011/03/12/number-of-the-week-companies-cash-hoard-grows/.

43. Thomas Palley, *The Politics of Paying Interest on Bank Reserves: A Criticism of Bernanke's Exit Strategy,* Challenge, May/June 2010, at 49.

44. Comstock Partners, *Total Private Market Debt's Decline Should Be a Glaring Warning Sign,* CreditWritedowns, Sept. 22, 2011, http://www.creditwritedowns.com/2011/09/total-private-market-debts-decline-should-be-a-glaring-warning-sign.html.

45. Financial Crisis Inquiry Commission, Financial Crisis Inquiry Report 103–40 (2011).

46. *Id.*

47. Sumner, *supra* note 40, at ix.

48. Minsky, *supra* note 35, at 327.

49. *A Special Report on Debt: Repent at Leisure,* The Economist, June 24, 2010.

50. Minsky, *supra* note 35, at 329.

51. Paul Krugman, *Liquidity Trap*, N.Y. Times, Sept. 17, 2008, http://krugman.blogs.nytimes. com/2008/09/17/liquidity-trap/.

52. Financial Crisis Inquiry Commission, *supra* note 45, at 356–57.

53. Paul Krugman, *Less Than Zero*, Sept. 18, 2008, N.Y. Times, http://krugman.blogs.nytimes. com/2008/09/18/less-than-zero/.

54. George Melloan, *We're All Keynesians Again*, WSJ.com, Jan. 13, 2009, http://online.wsj. com/article/SB123180502788675359.html.

55. Paul Krugman, *It's Baaack: Japan's Slump and the Return of the Liquidity Trap*, 2 Brookings Papers on Econ. Activity 137 (1998).

56. John Maynard Keynes, The General Theory of Employment, Interest, and Money 207–8 (Prometheus Books 1997) (1936).

57. Norman Gemmell et al., *The Timing and Persistence of Fiscal Policy Impacts on Growth: Evidence from OECD Countries*, 121 Econ. J. F33 (2011).

58. Keynes, *supra* note 45, at 378.

59. Hyman P. Minsky, Stabilizing an Unstable Economy 327–70 (2nd ed. 2008).

60. *Id.* at 336–39.

61. *Id.* at 343–49.

62. *Id.* at 333–34.

63. *Id.* at 327–33.

64. Richard C. Koo, The Holy Grail of Macroeconomics 118 (2008).

65. *Dr Keynes's Chinese Patient*, The Economist, Nov. 13, 2008, http://www.economist.com/ node/12601956.

66. Address by H.E. Wen Jiabao, Premier of the State Council of the People's Republic of China at the World Economic Forum Annual Meeting of the New Champions 2010, Sept. 13, 2010, http://bw.china-embassy.org/eng/xwdt/t753189.htm.

67. Michael S. Arnold, *China's Rebound Eases Slump Fears*, WSJ.com, Sept. 1, 2010, http:// online.wsj.com/article/SB10001424052748703882304575464842437541292.html.

68. Shawn Tully, *How Obama Got Keynes Wrong*, Fortune, Feb. 5, 2010, http://money.cnn. com/2010/02/04/news/economy/meltzer_keynes.fortune/ (interview of Allan Meltzer).

69. Peter H. Lindert, Growing Public 32–33 (2004).

70. Staff Report, Subcommittee on Education and Health, Joint Economic Committee, A Cost-Benefit Analysis of Government Investment in Post-Secondary Education Under the World War II GI Bill, at 1 (Dec. 14, 1988) (unpublished report, on file with author) (estimating enhanced tax revenues of 5–12 times outlays).

71. William Easterly and Sergio Rebelo, *Fiscal Policy and Economic Growth: An Empirical Investigation*, 32 J. Mon. Econ. 417 (1993).

72. Joseph E. Stiglitz, *The Mauritius Miracle*, Project Syndicate, Mar. 7, 2011, http://www. project-syndicate.org/commentary/stiglitz136/English.

73. Adam Smith, Wealth of Nations 473 (Prometheus Books 1991) (1776).

74. Koo, *supra* note 64, at 191–92. Koo also argues that innovation requires inculcating diverse worldviews. *Id.* at 192.

75. Steven A. Ramirez, *Fear and Social Capitalism: The Law and Macroeconomics of Investor Confidence,* 42 Washburn L.J. 31, 48, 68–70, 69 n. 236 (2002).

76. Shayne Henry and Samuel Sherraden, *Costs of the Infrastructure Deficit*, New America Foundation, Mar. 2, 2011, http://newamerica.net/publications/policy/ costs_of_the_infrastructure_deficit.

77. Mark C. Long, *Changes in the Returns to Education and College Quality*, 29 Econ. Educ. Rev. 338 (2010).

78. *Alternative Energy: Will U.S. Lead or Follow?*, CBS News.com, Aug. 15, 2010, http://www.cbsnews.com/stories/2010/08/15/sunday/main6774678.shtml.

79. *US Ranks 28th in Internet Connection Speed: Report*, AFP, Aug. 25, 2009, http://www.google.com/hostednews/afp/article/ALeqM5jPAHHWxwC93wUjFhB3ESs2f6Kkfw

80. Patrick Allen, *U.S. Will Be the World's Third Largest Economy, Citi Says*, USA Today, Feb. 2011, http://www.usatoday.com/money/economy/2011-02-26-cnbc-us-will-be-worlds-third-largest-economy_N.htm.

81. Koo, *supra* note 64, at 146.

82. *Id.* at 26–27.

83. OECD, Revenue Statistics 1965–2011: 2011 Edition 118 (2011).

84. *Military Ranking*, The Economist, Mar. 9, 2011, http://www.economist.com/blogs/dailychart/2011/03/defence_budgets.

85. OECD, *supra* note 83, at 19; Federal Reserve Bank of St. Louis, Economic Research, Graph: Civilian Employment–Population Ratio (EMRATIO), http://research.stlouisfed.org/fred2/graph/?s%5B1%5D%5Bid%5D=EMRATIO (last visited Apr. 22, 2012) (showing employment ratio, the broadest measure of employment of our population, peaking at approximately 64.5 percent in 2000).

86. Simon Johnson, *Tax Cutters Set Up Tomorrow's Fiscal Crisis: Simon Johnson*, Bloomberg, Dec. 23, 2010, http://www.bloomberg.com/news/2010-12-23/tax-cutters-set-up-tomorrow-s-fiscal-crisis-commentary-by-simon-johnson.html.

87. *See* Kate Stith, *Rewriting the Fiscal Constitution: The Case of Gramm-Rudd-Hollings*, 76 Cal. L. Rev. 595, 597 (1996).

88. Steven A. Ramirez, *Fear and Social Capitalism: The Law and Macroeconomics of Investor Confidence*, 42 Washburn L.J. 31, 70–74 (2002).

89. Congressional Budget Office, Estimated Impact of the American Recovery and Reinvestment Act on Employment and Economic Output from January 2010 Through March 2010, May 2010, http://www.cbo.gov/ftpdocs/115xx/doc11525/05-25-ARRA.pdf.

90. *E.g.*, J. Bradford De Long, *Stimulus Too Small*, WSJ.com, Jan. 25, 3010, http://online.wsj.com/article/SB10001424052748704055104574652314270243466.html.

91. Koo, *supra* note 64, at 238.

92. Congressional Budget Office, *supra* note 74, at 6.

93. Koo, *supra* note 64, at 145–46.

94. Paul Krugman, *Block Those Metaphors*, N.Y. Times, Dec. 12 2010, http://www.nytimes.com/2010/12/13/opinion/13krugman.html.

95. 12 U.S.C. § 18310 (2006).

96. Robert R. Bliss & George C. Kaufman, *U.S. Corporate and Bank Insolvency Regimes: A Comparison and Evaluation*, 2 Va. L. & Bus. Rev. 143, 145, 156–67 (2007).

97. *JPMorgan Buys Failed WaMu Assets for $1.9 Billion*, CNBC.com, Sept. 25, 2008, http://www.cnbc.com/id/26893741.

98. Bliss & Kaufman, *supra* note 96, at 157, 160–61.

99. Kenneth Ayotte & David A. Skeel Jr., *Bankruptcy or Bailouts?* 4, 8–9, 20 (Univ. of Pa. Law School, Inst. for Law & Econ., Working Paper 09-11, 2009), *available at* http://papers.ssrn.com/sol3/papers.cfj? abstract_id=1362639.

100. *Bailouts Are Common, But Results Are Mixed*, MSNBC.com, Sept. 21, 2008, http://www. msnbc.msn.com/id/26825453/ns/business-stocks_and_economy/.

101. Nick Timiraos, *Fannie, Freddie Overhaul Could Cost $685 Billion*, WSJ.com, Nov. 4, 2010, http://online.wsj.com/article/SB10001424052748703805704575594300330039336.html.

102. *See* Emergency Economic Stabilization Act of 2008, Pub. L. No. 110-343, §§ 101-136, 122 Stat. 3765 (codified at 12 U.S.C. § 5201).

103. Much of this discussion draws upon my prior work regarding the bailouts of 2008 and 2009. *See* Steven A. Ramirez, *Subprime Bailouts and the Predatory State*, 35 Dayton L. Rev. 81, 85–92 (2009).

104. Thomas Ferguson and Robert Johnson, *Too Big to Bail: The "Paulson Put," Presidential Politics, and the Global Financial Meltdown (Part II)*, 38 Int'l J. Pol. Econ. 3, 25–27 (2009).

105. Simon Johnson and James Kwak, 13 Bankers 164 (2010).

106. Alexandra Twin, *Stocks Crushed*, CNNMoney.com, Sept. 29, 2008, http://money.cnn. com/2008/09/29/markets/markets_newyork/index.htm.

107. Michael Dorsch, Bailouts for Sale? The Political Economy of the TARP Bill, May 11, 2010, http://laep.univ-paris1.fr/SEPIO/SEPIO100525Dorsch.pdf.

108. Simon Johnson, *The Quiet Coup*, Atlantic, May 2009, at 46, 49, 53.

109. Nouriel Roubini, *Public Losses for Private Gain*, Guardian.co.uk, Sept. 18, 2008, http:// www.guardian.co.uk/commentisfree/2008/sep/18/marketturmoil.creditcrunch.

110. Joseph E. Stiglitz, *Obama's Ersatz Capitalism*, N.Y. Times, Apr. 1, 2009, at A31.

111. Paul Krugman, *Banking on the Brink*, N.Y. Times, Feb. 23, 2009, at A27.

112. Paul Romer, *Let's Start Brand New Banks*, Wall St. J., Feb. 6, 2009, at A13.

113. Cong. Oversight Panel, April Oversight, Assessing Treasury's Strategy: Six Months of TARP 5 (2009), *available at* http://cop.senate.gov/documents/cop-040709-report.pdf.

114. Johnson and Kwak, *supra* note 105, at 173.

115. Michael R. Crittenden and Marshall Eckblad, *Lending Falls at Epic Pace*, Wall St. J., Feb. 10, 2010, available at http://online.wsj.com/article/SB10001424052748704188104575083332005 461558.html.

116. Ramirez, *supra* note 103, at 98–99.

117. Federal Reserve Bank of St. Louis, Economic Research, Graph: Excess Reserves of Depository Institutions (EXCRESNS), http://research.stlouisfed.org/fred2/graph/?s[1] [id]=EXCRESNS# (last visited Apr. 15, 2012). *See also* 2011 Annual Report of the Federal Reserve Bank of Dallas, Choosing the Road to Prosperity: Ending Too Big to Fail—Now 1 (2012) ("Many of the biggest banks have sputtered their balance sheets still clogged with toxic assets accumulated during the boom years").

118. *Id.* at 82.

119. Gary H. Stern and Ron J. Feldman, Too Big to Fail: The Hazards of Bank Bailouts 53 (2009).

120. *What If?*, The Economist, Sept. 10, 2009, http://www.economist.com/node/14401566.

121. Ramirez, *supra* note 103, at 86–87.

122. Spencer Weber Waller, *Corporate Governance and Competition Policy*, 18 Geo. Mason L. Rev. 833, 877 (2011) (citing a Federal Reserve report on 250 prior studies that bank mergers produced "no meaningful cost efficiencies"). *See also* Sheila Bair, *Why It's Time to Break up the "Too big to Fail" Banks*, CNNMoney, Jan. 18, 2012, http://finance.fortune.cnn. com/2012/01/18/big-banks-break-up-bair/ ("Comparing the valuation for the supersize banks . . . with their simpler, leaner competitors isn't pretty. Price/earnings per share for the supersizers averages 5.8, compared with 8.1 for smaller, more focused . . . regional

banks" and "the ratio of share price to tangible book value . . . is 72% of book [for super-sized banks] compared . . . 142% for the big regionals").

123. Johnson and Kwak, *supra* note 88, at 212.

124. Chris Arnold, *Zombie Banks Feed Off Bailout Money,* NPR, Feb. 9, 2009, http://www.npr.org/templates/story/story.php?storyId=100762999.

125. *Zombie Banks,* FT.Com, Dec. 28, 2010, http://www.ft.com/cms/s/0/5db725e4-11e8-11e0-92d0-00144feabdc0.html#axzz1GjfcQtcM.

126. *Pay Czar: 17 Bailed-Out Banks Overpaid Execs,* CBS News.com, July 23, 2010, http://www.cbsnews.com/stories/2010/07/23/politics/main6705793.shtml.

127. Steven A. Ramirez, *The Chaos of 12 U.S.C. Section 1821(k): Congressional Subsidizing of Negligent Bank Directors and Officers,* 65 Fordham L. Rev. 625 (1996).

128. Steven A. Ramirez, *Subprime Bailouts and the Predator State,* 35 Dayton L. Rev. 81, 106–11 (2009).

129. Frank Rich, *Obama's Make or Break Summer,* N.Y. Times, June 21, 2009, at WK8, http://www.nytimes.com/2009/06/21/opinion/21rich.html (quoting Senator Dick Durbin).

130. Gretchen Morgenson & Don Van Natta Jr., *Even in Crisis, Banks Dig in for Battle Against Regulations,* N.Y. Times, June 1, 2009, at A1.

131. Fredreka Schouten, *Exceptions to Ethics Rules Under Scrutiny,* USA Today, Jan. 29, 2009, at 4A.

132. Opensecrets.org, Top Contributors to John McCain, http://www.opensecrets.org/pres08/contrib.php?cycle=2008&cid=n00006424 (last visited Nov. 20, 2009).

133. Opensecrets.org, Top Contributors to Barack Obama, http://www.opensecrets.org/pres08/contrib.php?cycle=2008&cid=N00009638 (last visited Nov. 20, 2009).

134. Opensecrets.org, Washington Lobbying Grew to $3.2 Billion Last Year, Despite Economy, http://www.opensecrets.org/news/2009/01/washington-lobbying-grew-to-32.html (last visited Dec. 28, 2009).

135. Nathaniel Popper, *Banks Step up Spending on Lobbying to Fight Proposed Stiffer Regulations,* L.A. Times, Feb. 16, 2010, available at http://articles.latimes.com/2010/feb/16/business/la-fi-bank-lobbying16-2010feb16.

136. Johnson and Kwak, *supra* note 105, at 93–104.

137. Testimony of Professor Elizabeth Warren, Chair, Congressional Oversight Panel, Submitted to the Senate Finance Committee, March 31, 2009, http://cop.senate.gov/documents/testimony-033109-warren.pdf ("For each $100 Treasury invested in these financial institutions, it received on average stock and warrants worth only about $66").

138. Johnson and Kwak, *supra* note 105, at 168, 169, and 180.

139. Anna Jacobson Schwartz, *Man Without a Plan,* N.Y. Times, July 25, 2009, http://www.nytimes.com/2009/07/26/opinion/26schwartz.html.

140. Andrew Clark, *How Close Are Goldman Sachs's Connections with the US Treasury?,* The Guardian, Aug. 10, 2009, http://www.guardian.co.uk/business/andrew-clark-on-america.

141. Gretchen Morgenson and Don Van Natta Jr., *Paulson's Calls to Goldman Tested Ethics,* N.Y. Times, Aug. 8, 2009, http://www.nytimes.com/2009/08/09/business/09paulson.html?pagewanted=all.

142. Mary Williams Walsh, *A.I.G. Lists Banks It Paid with U.S. Bailout Funds,* N.Y. Times, Mar. 2009, http://www.nytimes.com/2009/03/16/business/16rescue.html.

143. Glenn Somerville, *U.S. Posts 19th Straight Monthly Deficit,* Reuters, May 10, 2010, http://www.reuters.com/article/2010/05/12/us-usa-budget-idUSTRE64B53W20100512.

144. Steven A. Ramirez, *Dodd-Frank as Maginot Line,* 14 Chapman L. Rev. 109 (2011).

145. Dodd-Frank Wall Street Reform and Consumer Protection Act, Pub. L. No. 111-203, 124 Stat. 1376, §§ 201-210 (2010).

146. Dodd-Frank Act § 204.

147. Ron Suskind, Confidence Men 215–20, 246–49, 457–58 (2011).

148. Dodd-Frank Act § 1105. *See also* 2011 Annual Report of the Federal Reserve Bank of Dallas, Choosing the Road to Prosperity: Ending Too Big to Fail—Now 1 (2012) (statement of Dallas Fed President Richard W. Fisher that "Dodd-Frank does not eradicate too big to fail" and instead "may actually perpetuate an already dangerous trend of increasing banking industry consolidation").

149. Dodd-Frank Act § 1101.

150. Thomas M. Hoenig, President, Federal Reserve Bank of Kansas City, Speech at Women in Housing and Finance, Washington, D.C., Feb. 23, 2011, http://www.kansascityfed.org/publicat/speeches/hoenig-DC-Women-Housing-Finance-2-23-11.pdf.

CHAPTER 7

1. John Stuart Mill, *The Negro Question (1850)*, in XXII The Collected Works of John Stuart Mill, Essays on Equality, Law, and Education (John M. Robson, ed. 1984), available at http://oll.libertyfund.org/?option=com_staticxt&staticfile=show.php%3Ftitle=255&chapter=21657&layout=html&Itemid=27.

2. *See* George Akerloff and Paul Romer, *Looting: The Economic Underworld of Bankruptcy for Profit*, 2 Brookings Papers Econ. Activity 1 (1993) ["Our theoretical analysis shows that an economic underground can come to life if firms have an incentive to go broke for profit at society's expense (to loot)" and "[b]ankruptcy for profit will occur if poor accounting, lax regulation, or low penalties for abuse give [those in control] an incentive to pay themselves more than their firms are worth and then default on their debt obligations"].

3. Daniel Inviglio, *Is Wall Street Wrong to Avoid Higher Taxes Through Early Bonuses?*, Atlantic, Dec. 6, 2010 (finding that Bush tax cuts saved Wall Street bankers $414 million attributable to their 2010 bonuses alone).

4. *See* Calvert Investments, Examining the Cracks in the Ceiling: A Survey of Corporate Diversity Practices of the S&P 100 3–4 (2010).

5. 130 S. Ct. 876 (2010) (holding that a provision of the Bipartisan Campaign Reform Act prohibiting corporations and other organizations from broadcasting electioneering communications within sixty days of a general election or thirty days of a primary violates the First Amendment to the United States Constitution).

6. Mancur Olson, The Rise and Decline of Nations 41, 226 (1982) (stating that "small groups organize first" and "small groups of businesses" enjoy the greatest success seeking government indulgences).

7. *See* Henry M. Paulson Jr., On the Brink 259 (2010) (quoting Fed Chair Ben Bernanke as stating to congressional leaders on September 18, 2008, that "[i]t is a matter of days before there is a meltdown in the global financial system").

8. Jon R. Bond et al., The Promise and Performance of American Democracy 46 (2005).

9. Ron Chernow, The House of Morgan xii (2010).

10. Suzanne Mettler, Soldiers to Citizens 156 (2005).

11. *See* Christina Romer, *Changes in Business Cycles: Evidence and Explanations*, J. Econ. Persp., Spring 1999, at 23, 33 ("In the post–World War II period, macroeconomic policy and related reforms have eliminated or dampened many of the shocks that caused recessions in the past, and thus brought about longer expansions and fewer severe recessions").

12. Paul Krugman, The Conscience of a Liberal 102, 108, 182 (2007).

13. Jacob S. Hacker and Paul Pierson, Winner-Take-All Politics 134 (2011).

14. Special Inspector General, Troubled Asset Relief Program, Quarterly Report to Congress 7 (2011), available at http://www.sigtarp.gov/reports/congress/2011/January2011_Quarterly_Report_to_Congress.pdf.

15. Peter Boone and Simon Johnson, The Doomsday Cycle, Centerpiece, Winter 2009/10, at 2, 6, available at http://cep.lse.ac.uk/pubs/download/cp300.pdf .

16. Jeffrey Rosen, The Supreme Court: The Personalities and Rivalries That Defined America 89–90 (2007).

17. Oliver Wendell Holmes, Justice Oliver Wendell Holmes: His Book Notices and Uncollected Letters and Papers 104–10 (H. C. Shriver ed. 1936). While Holmes emphasized legislation as a power contest, there is no coherent basis for limiting his power-based approach to just the legislative branch. Albert W. Alschuler, Law Without Values: The Life, Work, and Legacy of Justice Holmes 61 (2000).

18. See Office of the Curator, Supreme Court of the United States, The West Pediment: Information Sheet (2003), http://www.supremecourt.gov/about/westpediment.pdf (describing pediment carvings).

19. 1 Thucydides, The History of the Pelopennesian War 258 (S. Bloomfield trans. Longman, Brown, Green & Longmans ed. 1842).

20. Marbury v. Madison, 5 U.S. 137, 163 (1803).

21. Daron Acemoglu, Deep Roots, Fin. & Dev., June 2003, at 27.

22. James Q. Wilson, American Government (Brief Version) 19 (9th ed. 2009).

23. David M. Kennedy, Freedom from Fear 373, 376 (1999).

24. Id. at 373.

25. Brian Z. Tamanaha, On the Rule of Law: History, Politics, Theory 3, 92, 65–66 (2004).

26. Id. at 65–66.

27. Id. at 3.

28. Brian Tamanaha, A Concise Guide to the Rule of Law, in Relocating the Rule of Law 3–16 (Neil Walker and Gianluigi Palombella, eds. 2009).

29. International Comm'n of Jurists, The Rule of Law in a Free Society 3 (1959).

30. Frank B. Cross, The Error of Positive Rights, 48 UCLA L. Rev. 857, 923–24 (2001).

31. See Daron Acemoglu, A Microfoundation for Social Increasing Returns in Human Capital Accumulation, 111 Q. J. Econ. 779 (1996) (creating model to explain empirical evidence of increasing rather than diminishing returns to human capital formation).

32. Steven A. Ramirez, Taking Economic Human Rights Seriously After the Debt Crisis, 42 Loy. U. Chi. L.J. 713 (2010).

33. Order in the Jungle, Economist, Mar. 13, 2008, http://www.economist.com/node/10849115 (quoting the Harvard economist Dani Rodrik).

34. See Kristopher Gerardi et al., Financial Literacy and Subprime Mortgage Delinquency: Evidence from a Survey Matched to Administrative Data, Federal Reserve Bank of Atlanta Working Paper no. 2010-10, Apr. 2010, at 4, http://www.frbatlanta.org/documents/pubs/wp/wp1010.pdf ("We explicitly test for the role of financial literacy and cognitive limitations in the rise of subprime mortgage delinquencies and defaults, and present robust evidence of a correlation between a specific aspect of financial literacy, numerical ability, and mortgage delinquency").

35. Daniel Kruger and Liz Capo McCormick, Geithner Tells Obama Debt Expense to Rise to Record, Bloomberg, Feb. 14, 2011, http://www.bloomberg.com/news/2011-02-14/geithner-quietly-tells-obama-debt-to-gnp-cost-poised-to-increase-to-record.html.

36. Mark Whitehouse, *Q&A: Ken Rogoff Says Crises Are Like Heart Attacks, Predicting Timing Is Tough,* WSJ.com, Feb. 10, 2011, http://blogs.wsj.com/economics/2011/02/10/qa-ken-rogoff-says-crises-are-like-heart-attacks-predicting-timing-is-tough/.

37. Gretchen Morgenson, *Case on Mortgage Official Is Said to Be Dropped,* N.Y. Times, Feb. 20, 2011, at A20.

38. *BofA in $8.6 bln Settlement over Countrywide Loans,* Reuters, Oct. 6, 2008, http://www.reuters.com/article/2008/10/06/sppage012-bng287494-oisbn-idUSBNG28749420081006.

39. William K. Black, *Countrywide Control Fraud, but Inch Deep Prosecutions,* Benzinga, Feb. 28, 2011, http://www.benzinga.com/news/11/02/890766/countrywide-control-fraud-but-inch-deep-prosecutions.

40. Michael Beckel, *Ex–Countrywide Chairman Angelo Mozilo, Namesake of Controversial VIP Mortgage Program, Once Aided Pols,* OpenSecrets.org, Feb. 25, 2011, http://www.opensecrets.org/news/2011/02/ex-countrywide-chairman-angelo-mozilo.html.

41. Amir Efreti, *AIG Executives Won't Face Criminal Charges,* WSJ.com, May 22, 2010, http://online.wsj.com/article/SB10001424052748704852004575259240428335282.html.

42. Christian Plumb, *U.S. Drops Criminal Probe of AIG Executives,* Reuters, May 22, 2010, http://www.reuters.com/article/2010/05/23/us-aig-doj-idUSTRE64L09W20100523.

43. Andrew Frye and Sarah Frier, *Cassano, Goldman Sachs's Cohn to Testify to Crisis Commission,* Bloomberg, June 26, 2010, http://www.businessweek.com/news/2010-06-26/cassano-goldman-sachs-s-cohn-to-testify-to-crisis-commission.html.

44. *In a State,* Economist, Mar. 9, 2009, http://www.economist.com/node/13213322.

45. Financial Crisis Inquiry Commission, The Financial Crisis Inquiry Report 272 (2011).

46. *No Ordinary Joe,* Economist, July 1, 2010, http://www.economist.com/node/16485620.

47. Michael Beckel, *Looking Back at the Political Past of Former AIG Executive Joseph Cassano, Financial Crisis' "Patient Zero,"* OpenSecrets.org, Feb. 28, 2011, http://www.opensecrets.org/news/2011/02/political-past-of-former-aig-executive-joseph-cassano.html.

48. Gretchen Morgenson, *Attorney General of N.Y. Is Said to Face Pressure on Bank Foreclosure Deal,* N.Y. Times, Aug. 21, 2011, at B1; Gretchen Morgenson & Louise Story, *In Financial Crisis, No Prosecutions of Top Figures,* N.Y. Times, Apr. 14, 2011, at A1.

49. Ron Suskind, Confidence Men 27–28, 31, 104–5, 117–19, 242, 447–48 (2011).

50. William K. Black, *2011 Will Bring More de Facto Decriminalization of Elite Financial Fraud,* Huffington Post, Dec. 28, 2010, http://www.huffingtonpost.com/william-k-black/the-role-of-the-criminal_b_802115.html.

51. William D. Cohan, *Will Wall Street Go Free?,* N.Y. Times, May 27, 2010, http://opinionator.blogs.nytimes.com/2010/05/27/will-wall-street-go-free/.

52. James K. Galbraith, *Tremble, Banks, Tremble,* The New Republic, July 9, 2010, http://www.tnr.com/article/economy/76146/tremble-banks-tremble?page=0,1.

53. *See* Mary K. Ramirez, *Prioritizing Justice: Combating Corporate Crime from Task Force to Top Priority,* 93 Marq. L. Rev. 971, 1018 (2010) (arguing that "[c]reating a Corporate Crimes Division to focus national policy and to pursue fraudulent activity . . . will undermine the temptation of big business to pursue profits at any cost, and protect individual investors and the public fisc from the fallout of corporate crimes. Benefits gained from a cohesive national pursuit of corporate criminality well outweigh any risks associated with such a pursuit").

54. Joseph E. Stigliz, *Ersatz Capitalism,* N.Y. Times, Apr. 1, 2009, at A31.

55. Simon Johnson, *The Quiet Coup,* The Atlantic, May 2009, at 46.

56. Steven A. Ramirez, *Subprime Bailouts and the Predator State,* 35 Dayton L. Rev. 81 (2009).

57. U.S. Bank, N.A. v. Ibanez, 458 Mass. 637 (2011) (Cordy, J., concurring).

58. Vicki Needham, *Banks Could Face Billions in Fines over Foreclosures,* The Hill, Feb. 27, 2011, http://thehill.com/blogs/on-the-money/banking-financial-institutions/146319-banks-could-face-billions-in-fines-over-foreclosures.

59. Christopher Peterson, *Foreclosure, Subprime Mortgage Lending, and the Mortgage Electronic Registration System,* 78 U. Cin. L. Rev. 1359 (2010).

60. Katherine Porter, *Mistake and Misbehavior in Bankruptcy Mortgage Claims,* 98 Tex. L. Rev. 121 (2008).

61. Peter Coy, *Mortgages Lost in the Cloud,* BusinessWeek.com, Oct. 14, 2010, http://www.businessweek.com/magazine/content/10_43/b4200009860564.htm (quoting property rights expert Hernando de Soto: "Your recession is going to last. And it's going to last, and it's going to last, because essentially the trust has broken down").

62. *See* Joseph E. Stiglitz, *Justice for Some,* Project Syndicate, Nov. 10, 2010, http://www.project-syndicate.org/commentary/stiglitz131/English ("In today's America, the proud claim of 'justice for all' is being replaced by the more modest claim of 'justice for those who can afford it.' And the number of people who can afford it is rapidly diminishing"); Paul Krugman, *The Mortgage Morass,* N.Y. Times, Oct. 14, 2010, at A33 ("the mortgage mess is making nonsense of claims that we have effective contract enforcement—in fact, the question is whether our economy is governed by any kind of rule of law").

63. James Podgers, *US Lags Well Behind Other Wealthy Nations on Rule of Law, Report Says,* ABA J., Oct. 14, 2010, http://www.abajournal.com/news/article/us_lags_well_behind_other_wealthy_nations_on_rule_of_law_report_says (citing The World Justice Project, Rule of Law Index (2010)).

64. Roderick B. Mathews and Juan Carlos Botero, *Access to Justice in the United States,* Va. Law., Dec. 2010, at 24, 25.

65. The World Justice Project, Rule of Law Index 92, 96 (2010).

66. The Fund for Peace, Failed State Index 2010, http://www.fundforpeace.org (last visited Feb. 19, 2011).

67. Dan Froomkin, *Access to Justice in U.S. at Third-World Levels, Says Survey,* Huffington Post, Oct. 14, 2010, http://www.huffingtonpost.com/2010/10/14/access-to-justice-in-us-a_n_762355.html.

68. Daniel Kaufmann, *Governance Matters 2010: Worldwide Governance Indicators Highlight Governance Successes, Reversals, and Failures,* Brookings.com, Sept. 24, 2010, available at http://www.brookings.edu/opinions/2010/0924_wgi_kaufmann.

69. *Id.*

70. Nicholas D. Kristof, *Our Banana Republic,* N.Y. Times, Nov. 7, 2010, at WK10.

71. World Economic Forum, Global Competitiveness Report 2010–2011 18, 23 (2010).

72. Korematsu v. United States, 323 U.S. 214 (1944).

73. Swann v. Charlotte-Mecklenburg Board of Education, 402 U.S. 1 (1971).

74. *Ex parte* Merryman, 17 F. Cas. 144 (1861).

75. Steven A. Ramirez, *Bearing the Costs of Racial Inequality:* Brown *and the Myth of the Equality/Efficiency Trade-Off,* 44 Washburn L.J. 87, 87–88, 100–4 (2004).

76. *See, e.g.,* Gary Orfield & Chungmei Lee, Historic Reversals, Accelerating Resegregation and the Need for New Integration Strategies 22 (2007), http://civilrightsproject.ucla.edu/research/k-12-education/integration-and-diversity/historic-reversals-accelerating-resegregation-and-the-need-for-new-integration-strategies-1/orfield-historic-reversals-accelerating.pdf.

77. Citizens United v. Fed. Election Comm'n, 130 S. Ct. 876 (2010).

78. Montoy v. State, 138 P.3d 755, 764 (Kan. 2006).

79. Laurie Reynolds, *Full State Funding of Education as a State Constitutional Imperative*, 60 Hastings L.J. 749, 749–50 (2009).

80. San Antonio Indep. Sch. Dist. v. Rodriguez, 411 U.S. 1, 11–16 (1973).

81. *See* Steven A. Ramirez, *Taking Economic Human Rights Seriously After the Debt Crisis*, 42 Loy. U. Chi. L.J. 713 (2011).

82. Cass R. Sunstein, The Second Bill of Rights 202–29 (2004).

83. Cass R. Sunstein, *Why Does the American Constitution Lack Social and Economic Guarantees?*, in American Exceptionalism and Human Rights 90, 95 (Michael Ignatieff, ed. 2005).

84. Harry Markopolos, No One Would Listen 267 (2011).

85. John W. Cioffi, *The Global Financial Crisis: Conflicts of Interest, Regulatory Failures, and Politics,* Policy Matters, Spring 2010, at 1, available at http://www.policymatters.ucr.edu/archives/vol4/v4-issue1-cioffi.html.

86. Steven A. Ramirez, *Depoliticizing Financial Regulation*, 42 Wm. & Mary L. Rev. 503, 522–32 (2000).

87. Financial Crisis Inquiry Commission, The Financial Crisis Inquiry Report xvii–xxviii, 418 (2011). Historically, the extent to which the economy suffers recessions and depressions has diminished greatly since the creation of the Fed. 2011 Annual Report of the Federal Reserve Bank of Dallas, Choosing the Road to Prosperity: Ending Too Big to Fail—Now 4 (2012) ("Before the Federal Reserve's founding in 1913, recession held the economy in its grip 48 percent of the time. In the nearly 100 years since the Fed's creation, the economy has been in recession about 21 percent of the time").

88. Christian Johnson, *Exigent and Unusual Circumstances: The Federal Reserve and the U.S. Financial Crisis*, __Euro. Bus. Org. L. Rev. __ (2010).

89. Financial Crisis Inquiry Commission, *supra* note 84, at 52–56.

90. Damian Paletta and Jon Hilsenrath, *Senate Democrats Seek Sweeping Curbs on Fed*, WSJ. com, Nov. 11, 2009, http://online.wsj.com/article/SB125786789140341325.html.

91. Financial Crisis Inquiry Commission, *supra* note 86, at 22.

92. *Did the Fed Cause the Housing Bubble?*, WSJ.com, Mar. 27, 2009, http://online.wsj.com/article/SB123811225716453243.html.

93. Irvin B. Tucker, Macroeconomics for Today 362 (6th ed. 2010).

94. Timothy Canova, *The Federal Reserve We Need*, Am. Prospect, Oct. 11, 2010, http://www.prospect.org/cs/articles?article=the_federal_reserve_we_need ("Today's new normal is a central bank captured by private financial interests that is pursuing an elite agenda of deregulation, fiscal austerity, and bailouts and bonuses for bankers").

95. Shahien Nasiripour, *Stiglitz, Nobel Prize–Winning Economist, Says Federal Reserve System "Corrupt,"* Huffington Post, Mar. 5, 2010, http://www.huffingtonpost.com/2010/03/03/stiglitz-nobel-prize-winn_n_484943.html.

96. Timothy A. Canova, *Lincoln's Populist Sovereignty: Public Finance of, by, and for the People*, 12 Chap. L. Rev. 561, 582–83 (2009).

97. Kara Scannell and Jenny Strasburg, *Madoff Report Reveals Extent of Bungling*, Wall St. J., Sept. 9, 2009, http://online.wsj.com/article/SB125210039740087421.html.

98. Financial Crisis Inquiry Commission, The Financial Crisis Inquiry Report 169–70 (2011).

99. *Id. See also* Jake Bernstein and Jesse Eisinger, *SEC Just Now Seeking Key Information on Meltdown*, NPR, Dec. 16, 2009, http://www.npr.org/templates/story/story.

php?storyId=121520292 ("To date, the agency has little to show for its probes into the causes of the crisis that engulfed global financial markets just over a year ago").

100. H. David Kotz, SEC's Oversight of Bear Stearns and Related Entities: The Consolidated Supervised Entity Program, Report No. 446-A at viii–xi (Sept. 25, 2008), available at http://www.sec-oig.gov/Reports/AuditsInspections/2008/446-a.pdf.

101. Richard Painter, *Standing up to Wall Street,* 101 Mich. L. Rev. 1512 (2003) (book review of Arthur Levitt, Take on the Street: What Wall Street and Corporate America Don't Want You to Know (2002)) ("The most powerful theme in Levitt's book is his struggle with a political system that gave regulated industries extraordinary influence in Congress").

102. *See* Arthur Levitt, Take on the Street: What Wall Street and Corporate America Don't Want You to Know 106–15 (2002) (recounting how "the business lobby" and "CEOs" successfully used Congress to thwart reform efforts in securities regulation).

103. *See id.* at 299–300 (letter dated September 20, 2000, from Kenneth L. Lay, Chairman and Chief Executive Officer, Enron Corporation, to Arthur Levitt, Chairman, Securities Exchange Commission, stating that "for the past several years, Enron has successfully utilized its independent audit firm's expertise and professional skepticism to help improve the overall control environment within the company").

104. *See* Scot J. Paltrow, *SEC Chief Shift on Investor Bill Is Linked to Senate Pressure,* L.A. Times, Nov. 22, 1995, at D1 (quoting Andrew R. Vermilye, legislative director to Senator Richard H. Bryan, that senators "threatened to turn off the lights" at the SEC if it opposed the PSLRA).

105. *See* Joel Seligman, *Self-Funding for the Securities and Exchange Commission,* 28 Nova L. Rev. 233, 233, 246–49, 253–56 (2004).

106. Levitt, *supra* note 102, at 237.

107. *E.g.,* John C. Coffee Jr., *A Course of Inaction: Where Was the SEC When the Mutual Fund Scandal Happened?,* Legal Aff., Apr. 2004, at 46.

108. Financial Crisis Inquiry Report, *supra* note 98, at 173–74.

109. Rachel Barkow, *Insulating Agencies: Avoiding Capture Through Institutional Design,* 89 Texas L. Rev. 15, 79 (2010).

110. *Id. See also* Ramirez, *supra* note 86, at 592 ("The degree of political insulation to be accorded an agency seems to turn upon many factors, but the most important are the funding of the agency and the extent of the political commitment to an agency's independence").

111. Steven A. Ramirez, *The End of Corporate Governance Law: Optimizing Regulatory Structure for a Race to the Top,* 24 Yale J. Reg. 313 (2007).

112. Roscoe Pound, The Lawyer from Antiquity to Modern Times 5 (1953).

113. Michael J. Polelle, *Who's on First, and What's a Professional?,* 33 U.S.F. L. Rev. 205, 226 (1999).

114. Steven A. Ramirez, *The Professional Obligations of Securities Under Federal Law: An Antidote for Bubbles,* 70 Cin. L. Rev. 527, 540–48, 567–68 (2002).

115. Polelle, *supra* note 113, at 206–7.

116. Mike Hudson and E. Scott Reckard, *Workers Say Lender Ran "Boiler Rooms,"* L.A. Times, Feb. 4, 2005, http://www.latimes.com/business/la-fi-ameriquest4feb0405,1,7774916,full. story.

117. Financial Crisis Inquiry Commission, *supra* note 98, at xix ("Our examination revealed stunning instances of governance breakdowns and irresponsibility").

118. *Id.* at xxv, 147–50.

119. *Id.* at xxii.

120. Jean Edward Smith, FDR 352 (2010).

121. The Presidents: A Reference History xxxiv (Graff, H., ed., 3rd ed. 2002).

122. *See Ever Higher Society, Ever Harder to Ascend,* The Economist, Dec. 29, 2004, http://www.economist.com/node/3518560?Story_ID=3518560 ("A growing body of evidence suggests that the meritocratic ideal is in trouble in America").

123. David Gergen, *The National Deficit—of Leadership,* U.S. News & World Report, Oct. 23, 2009, http://www.usnews.com/news/best-leaders/articles/2009/10/23/david-gergen-the-national-deficitof-leadership_print.html.

124. Staff Report, Subcommittee on Education and Health, Joint Economic Committee, A Cost-Benefit Analysis of Government Investment in Post-Secondary Education Under the World War II GI Bill, at 1 (Dec. 14, 1988) (unpublished report, on file with author).

125. Scott Pelley, *Homeless Children: The Hard Times Generation,* CBSNews.com, Mar. 6, 2011, http://www.cbsnews.com/stories/2011/03/06/60minutes/main20038927.shtml.

126. H.R. Rep. No. 73-85, at 1–2 (1933) ("[w]hat we seek is a return to a clearer understanding of the ancient truth that those who manage banks, corporations and other agencies handling or using other people's money are trustees acting for others").

127. John Maynard Keynes, The General Theory of Employment, Interest, and Money 159 (1936).

128. Steven A. Ramirez, *Arbitration and Reform in Private Securities Litigation: Dealing with the Meritorious as Well as the Frivolous,* 40 Wm. & Mary L. Rev. 1055 (1999).

129. 511 U.S. 164 (1994).

130. 552 U.S. 148 (2008).

131. 511 U.S. at 193 (citing Brennan v. Midwestern United Life Ins. Co., 259 F.Supp. 673, 680 (N.D. Ind. 1966)).

132. Restatement of Torts § 876(b) (1939).

133. 511 U.S. at 189.

134. 552 U.S. at 175. *See* Douglas M. Branson, *Running the Gauntlet: A Description of the Arduous, and Now Often Fatal Journey for Plaintiffs in Federal Securities Law Actions,* 65 U. Cin. L. Rev. 3, 6 (1997) ("In forty federal securities law decisions, the Court decided thirty-two cases for defendants and, in almost every one, significantly narrowed the reach of federal securities laws").

135. Susan Antilla, *Investors Lose Again,* Bloomberg, Jan. 8, 2008, http://www.bloomberg.com/apps/news?pid=newsarchive&refer=columnist_antilla&sid=aPf3HyyGWduw.

136. 552 U.S. at 164.

137. Rafael La Porta et al., *What Works in Securities Laws?,* 61 J. Fin. 1, 28 (2006).

138. Robert Prentice, Stoneridge, *Securities Fraud Litigation, and the Supreme Court,* 45 Am. Bus. L.J. 611, 612, 682–83 (2008).

139. Blue Chip Stamps v. Manor Drug Stores, 421 U.S. 723, 739 (1975).

140. Merrill Lynch, Pierce, Fenner & Smith Inc. v. Dabit, 547 U.S. 71, 80 (2006); Central Bank, N.A. v. First Interstate Bank of Denver, N.A., 511 U.S. 164, 189 (1994); *see also* Tellabs, Inc. v. Makor Issues & Rights, Ltd., 551 U.S. 308, 320 (2007).

141. 377 U.S. 426 (1964).

142. Financial Crisis Inquiry Commission, The Financial Crisis Inquiry Report 192 (2011).

143. Felix Salmon, *The Magnetar Trade,* Reuters, Apr. 9, 2010, http://blogs.reuters.com/felix-salmon/2010/04/09/the-magnetar-trade/.

144. Financial Crisis Inquiry Report, *supra* note 142, at 193.

145. *Id.* at 192–93.

146. John Gapper, *A Short Story of a Star Hedge Fund*, FT.com, Apr. 14, 2010, http://www.ft.com/cms/s/0/8a79c6f6-47f7-11df-b998-00144feab49a.html?dbk#axzz1FWZHO8YG.

147. Financial Crisis Inquiry Report, *supra* note 142, at 193.

148. *Id.* at 192–93.

149. Yves Smith, Econned 260 (2010).

150. Financial Crisis Inquiry Report, *supra* note 142, at 192.

151. Yves Smith, *Rahm Emanuel and Magnetar Capital: The Definition of Compromised,* Naked Capitalism, Apr. 13, 2010, http://www.nakedcapitalism.com/2010/04/rahm-emanuel-and-magnetar-capital-the-definition-of-compromised.html.

152. Securities and Exchange Commission, SEC Charges Goldman Sachs with Fraud in Structuring and Marketing of CDO Tied to Subprime Mortgages, Rel. 2010-59, Apr. 16, 2010, http://www.sec.gov/news/press/2010/2010-59.htm (last visited Mar. 2, 2011).

153. Financial Crisis Inquiry Report, *supra* note 142, at 193.

154. Harry Markopolos, No One Would Listen 267 (2011) ("The SEC . . . has suffered through decades of sloth, abysmal leadership, underfunding and benign neglect").

155. *See* Carl Bogus, Why Lawsuits Are Good for America 3 (2001) (arguing that common law liability plays a regulatory role in setting appropriate incentives).

156. Ayn Rand, The Virtue of Sefishness 110–12 (1961).

157. Charles Murdock, *Corporate Corruption and the Complicity of Congress and the Supreme Court—the Tortuous Path from* Central Bank *to* Stoneridge Investment Partners, LLC. v. Scientific-Atlanta, Inc., 6 Berkeley Bus. L.J. 131 (2009).

158. Financial Crisis Inquiry Commission, *supra* note 142, at xii.

159. *Id.*

160. Steven A. Ramirez, *The Law and Macroeconomics of the New Deal at 70*, 62 Md. L. Rev. 515, 522–32 (2003).

161. Ferdinand Pecora, Wall Street Under Oath ix–x (1939).

162. Janet Hook and John McKinnon, *Congress Passes Tax Deal*, WSJ.com, Dec. 17, 2010, http://online.wsj.com/article/SB10001424052748703395204576023772342189318.html.

163. Derrick A. Bell Jr., *Brown v. Board of Education and the Interest-Convergence Dilemma*, 93 Harv. L. Rev. 518 (1980).

164. *See* Steven A. Ramirez, *Games CEOs Play and Interest Convergence Theory: Why Diversity Lags In Corporate Boardrooms and What to Do About It*, 61 Wash. & Lee L. Rev.1583, 1602–7 (2004).

165. Richard Delgado, *Crossroads and Blind Alleys: A Critical Examination of Recent Writing About Race*, 82 Tex. L. Rev. 121, 137 (2003).

166. Mary L. Dudziak, *Desegregation as a Cold War Imperative*, 41 Stan. L. Rev. 61, 66 (1988) (marshaling evidence that "demonstrates Derrick Bell's interest-convergence thesis").

167. Suzanne Mettler, Soldiers to Citizens 152, 156 (2005).

168. Matthew Brzezinski, Red Moon Rising 165–87, 274 (2007).

169. J. Bradford De Long and Barry J. Eichengreen, The Marshall Plan: History's Most Successful Structural Adjustment Program 3–6, 12–13 (1991), available at http://www.j-bradford-delong.net/pdf_files/marshall_large.pdf.

170. Steven A. Ramirez, *Market Fundamentalism's New Fiasco: Globalization as Exhibit B in the Case for a New Law and Economics*, 24 Mich. J. Int'l L. 831 (2003) (review of Joseph E. Stiglitz, Globalization and Its Discontents (2002)).

171. Michael S. Arnold, *China's Rebound Eases Slump Fears*, WSJ.com, Sept. 1, 2010, http://online.wsj.com/article/SB10001424052748703882304575464842437541292.html.

172. Martin Wolf, *Wen Is Right to Worry About China's Growth*, FT.com, Sept. 21, 2010 http://www.ft.com/cms/s/0/a1df57c0-c5b5-11df-ab48-00144feab49a.html#axzz1G30Yyf9T.

173. Andrew Batson, *OECD: Inequality in China Leveling Off*, WSJ.com, Feb. 3, 2010, http://online.wsj.com/article/SB10001424052748704022804575040814244036390.html.

174. Bob Davis and Jeremy Page, *China's Focus Turns to Its Poor*, WSJ.com, 2011, Mar. 7, 2011, http://online.wsj.com/article/SB10001424052748703362804576184364247082474.html.

175. *See* James J. Heckman, *China's Human Capital Investment*, 6 China Econ. Rev. 50, 53 (2005) (showing massive private and public investments in human capital and even more in physical infrastructure).

176. *See* Fareed Zakaria, *Are America's Best Days Behind Us?*, Time, Mar. 7, 2011, at 28, 30 (comparing U.S. with China and other rapidly growing nations and concluding that U.S. must invest more in education, infrastructure, and science despite the efforts of "influential interest groups").

177. *See* Eric A. Hanushek and Ludger Woessmann, *The Role of Cognitive Skills in Economic Development*, 46 J. Econ. Lit. 607, 609 (2008) ("[C]ognitive skills have a strong impact on individual earnings. More than that, however, cognitive skills have a strong and robust influence on economic growth").

178. Bin Gu and Laura Hitt, Transaction Costs and Market Efficiency, ICIS 2001 Proceeding, Paper 11, http://grace.wharton.upenn.edu/~lhitt/tcme.pdf.

179. J. Bradford DeLong et al., *Noise Trader Risk in Financial Markets*, 98 J. Poli. Econ. 703 (1990).

180. *See* James A. Fanto, *We're All Capitalists Now: The Importance, Nature, Provision and Regulation of Investor Education*, 49 Case W. Res. L. Rev. 105, 156–64 (1998).

181. Richard A. Posner, A Failure of Capitalism xii (2009) ("We need a more active and intelligent government to keep our model of a capitalist economy from running off the rails").

182. John J. Curran and Jesse Hamilton, *Schapiro SEC Seen as Ineffectual Amid Dodd-Frank Funding Curbs*, Bloomberg, Mar. 30, 2011, http://www.bloomberg.com/news/2011-03-31/schapiro-sec-seen-ineffectual-amid-dodd-frank-funding-curbs.html.

183. Mary L. Schapiro, Chairman, SEC, News Conference Call: Statement Concerning Agency Self-Funding (Apr. 15, 2010) (transcript available at http://www.sec.gov/news/speech/2010/spch041510mls.htm) ("[S]elf funding ensures independence, facilitates long-term planning, and closes the resource gap between the agency and the entities we regulate. . . . [I]t allows the SEC to better protect millions of investors whose savings are at stake").

184. Steven A. Ramirez, *Dodd-Frank as Maginot Line*, 14 Chapman L. Rev. 213 (2011).

185. *Id.* at 111–17.

186. *Id.* at 123–27.

187. Simon Johnson, *Tax Cutters Set Up Tomorrow's Fiscal Crisis*, Bloomberg, Dec. 22, 2010, http://www.bloomberg.com/news/2010-12-23/tax-cutters-set-up-tomorrow-s-fiscal-crisis-commentary-by-simon-johnson.html.

188. See Joe Klein, *Who's Afraid of Reforming Wall Street*, Time, Mar. 14, 2011, at 27.

189. 130 S. Ct. 876 (2010).

190. Richard L. Hasen, *Money Grubbers: The Supreme Court Kills Campaign Finance Reform*, Slate, Jan. 21, 2010, http://www.slate.com/id/2242209/ (discussing *Citizens United* and the "activist" court).

191. Reuven S. Avi-Yonah, Citizens United *and the Corporate Form*, 2010 Wis. L. Rev. 999.

192. Alexander Polikoff, *So How Did We Get into This Mess? Observations on the Legitimacy of Citizens United*, 105 Nw. U. L. Rev. Colloquy 203, 225 (2011).

193. Public Citizen, 12 Months After: The Effects of Citizens United on Elections and the Integrity of the Legislative Process 9, 12 (2011).

194. *Id.* at 16.

195. Nina Totenberg, *Justice O'Connor Criticizes Campaign Finance Ruling*, Nat'l Pub. Radio (Jan. 26, 2010), http://www.npr.org/templates/story/story.php?storyId=122993740&ft=1&f=1003.

196. Michael H. LeRoy, *Do Partisan Elections of Judges Produce Unequal Justice When Courts Review Employment Arbitrations?*, 95 Iowa L. Rev. 1569, 1602 (2010).

197. Thomas Stratmann, *How Prices Matter in Politics: The Returns to Campaign Advertising*, 140 Public Choice 357 (2009); Gary C. Jacobson, *The Effects of Campaign Spending in Congressional Elections*, 72 Am. Pol. Sci. Rev. 469, 482–85 (1978).

198. *See, e.g.*, Thomas Stratmann, *Can Special Interests Buy Congressional Votes? Evidence from Financial Services Legislation*, 45 J.L. & Econ. 345, 368 (2002).

199. Michael Dorsch, Bailouts for Sale? The Political Economy of the TARP Bill, working paper, May 11, 2010, http://laep.univ-paris1.fr/SEPIO/SEPIO100525Dorsch.pdf ("the financial bailout bill was passed by a legislative body that was . . . influenced by the campaign contributions of financial special interests" and because "the TARP bill may not have passed with less money in the system, this paper can only conclude that the bailout was 'for sale'").

200. andré douglas pond cummings, *Procuring "Justice"?: Citizens United, Caperton, and Partisan Judicial Elections*, 95 Iowa L. Rev. Bull. 89 (2010), http://www.uiowa.edu/~ilr/bulletin/ILRB_95_cummings.pdf.

201. Richard L. Hasen, Citizens United *and the Illusion of Coherence*, 109 Mich. L. Rev. 581, 623 (2011).

202. Morris B. Hoffman, *Book Review*, 54 Stan. L. Rev. 597, 614 (reviewing Albert W. Alschuler, Law Without Values: The Life, Work and Legacy of Justice Holmes (2002)).

EPILOGUE

1. Paul M. Romer, *Economic Growth*, in The Concise Encyclopedia of Economics 183 (D. Henderson, ed. 1993), available at http://www.econlib.org/library/Enc/EconomicGrowth.html.

2. Ronald Bailey, *Post-Scarcity Prophet*, Reason, Dec. 2001, http://reason.com/archives/2001/12/01/post-scarcity-prophet/singlepage (interview of Paul Romer).

3. Paul Romer, *Economic Growth and Investment in Children*, Daedlus, Fall 1994, at 141 (1994).

4. John Maynard Keynes, *Economic Possibilities for Our Grandchildren, in* Essays in Persuasion 358 (1963).

5. *Id.*

6. *Print Me a Stradivarius*, The Economist, Feb. 12, 2011, at 11.

7. Lant Pritchett, *The Cliff at the Border* in Equity and Growth in a Globalizing World 263, 277 (Ravi Kanbur and Michael Spence, eds. 2010).

8. McKinsey & Co., The Economic Impact of the Achievement Gap in America's Schools 5 (2009), available at http://www.mckinsey.com/app_media/images/page_images/offices/socialsector/pdf/achievement_gap_report.pdf.

9. Paul Gompers et al., *Corporate Governance and Equity Prices*, 118 Q.J. Econ. 107, 145 (2003) (finding that potential gains from improvements in corporate governance "would be enormous").

10. David Reilly, *Fed's Weapons of Mass Distraction*, Wall St. J., Sept. 14, 2011, http://online.wsj.com/article/SB10001424053111904265504576568761509430644.html.

11. Ben Casselman and Justin Lahart, *Companies Shun Investment, Hoard Cash*, Wall St. J., Sept. 17, 2011, http://online.wsj.com/article/SB10001424053111903927204576574720017009568.html.

12. Ming Zen, *"Dollar Trap" Ties Reluctant Foreign Central Banks To U.S. Treasurys*, Wall St. J., July 28, 2011, http://online.wsj.com/article/SB10001424053111904800304576474340028810266.html.

13. *See Debt, Deficits and Markets*, The Economist, Sept. 21, 2011, http://www.economist.com/blogs/dailychart/2011/09/government-debt ("As the euro area's sovereign-debt crisis has gone from bad to worse, financial tensions now pose a grave threat not just to the European economy but beyond").

INDEX

ABOUT THE AUTHOR

Steven A. Ramirez is Professor of Law at Loyola University Chicago, where he also directs the Business and Corporate Governance Law Center. He has spent the past thirty years studying the intersection of the law and the economy. During that time he has written extensively on issues related to law and macroeconomics, race and diversity, globalization, law and monetary policy, law and fiscal policy, corporate governance law and regulation, securities law, and the rule of law.